ASP.NET 4.0 Programming

"Joydip Kanjilal's *ASP.NET 4.0 Programming* is more than a feature tour of "What's New." It is a high-voltage jump-start for learning how to build production web sites with ASP.NET 4.0 and Visual Studio 2010 from start to finish, with solid coverage of the new technologies like LINQ and integrating jQuery, as well as detail on often overlooked topics like scale and performance. A ton of information in a concise package!"

—Joe Stagner, Senior Program Manager,
Developer Tools & Platform, Microsoft Corporation

"This is the right book to shorten your learning curve and become a cutting-edge ASP.NET developer. Explanations are clear and convincing, and the examples will help you master the fundamentals and core and advanced techniques. I found Chapter 9, which is dedicated to client-side scripting using jQuery, and Chapter 20, which shows how to improve the performance of ASP.NET applications, to be the most informative."

—Alessandro Gallo, .NET Consultant/Developer,
NeoSystem IT, Italy

"With *ASP.NET 4.0 Programming*, Joydip Kanjilal has produced a book that touches on everything you need to know to become an effective ASP.NET C# developer. From simple HTML sites and data-intensive business applications to highly interactive AJAX-driven sites, you will find examples in this book that will help you through the stickiest points in your ASP.NET development."

—Russell Jones, Executive Editor,
Internet.com

"If you are looking for information on Web Forms, Dynamic Data, MVC, Silverlight, WCF, or jQuery, then *ASP.NET 4.0 Programming* has you covered. Joydip has put the knowledge you need to leverage all of these tools at your finger tips. All you have to do is start reading."

—Brendan Enrick, ASP.NET MVP; Senior Consultant,
Nimble Software Professionals

This book is dedicated to my parents, Mr. Amal Kanti Kanjilal
and Mrs. Rama Kanjilal, for their blessings, love, inspiration, and support.

About the Author

Joydip Kanjilal is a Microsoft Most Valuable Professional in ASP.NET since 2007. He has over 12 years of industry experience in IT with more than 6 years in Microsoft .NET and its related technologies. He was selected as MSDN Featured Developer of the Fortnight (MSDN) a number of times and was also selected as Community Credit Winner at www.community-credit.com several times. Joydip has authored several ASP.NET and programming books. He has also authored more than 200 articles for some of the most reputable sites, such as www.asptoday.com, www.devx.com, www.aspalliance.com, www.aspnetpro.com, www.sql-server-performance.com, www.sswug.com, and others. Many of these articles have been selected at www.asp.net—Microsoft's official site for ASP.NET.

Joydip is currently working as a freelance software developer and author. He has years of experience in designing and architecting solutions for various domains. His technical strengths include, C, C++, VC++, Java, C#, ASP.NET, Ajax, design patterns, SQL Server, operating systems, and computer architecture. Joydip blogs at http://aspadvice.com/blogs/joydip.

About the Technical Editor

Anand Narayanaswamy, a Microsoft Most Valuable Professional works as technical editor for ASPAlliance.com based in Trivandrum, India, and runs www.learnxpress.com and www.dotnetalbum.com. He graduated from the University of Kerala and is the author of *Community Server Quickly* (Packt Publishing). Anand has contributed several articles and reviews for various web sites and print magazines. He also worked as a technical editor for various books published by Sams, Addison-Wesley, Packt, and Manning. He has been recognized with the prestigious Hall of Fame award by community-credit.com and he blogs at www.visualanand.net.

ASP.NET 4.0 Programming

Joydip Kanjilal

New York   Chicago   San Francisco
Lisbon   London   Madrid   Mexico City
Milan   New Delhi   San Juan
Seoul   Singapore   Sydney   Toronto

The McGraw·Hill Companies

Library of Congress Cataloging-in-Publication Data

Kanjilal, Joydip.
 ASP.NET 4.0 programming / Joydip Kanjilal.
   p. cm.
 ISBN 978-0-07-160410-9 (alk. paper)
 1. Active server pages. 2. Ajax (Web site development technology) 3.
Application software—Development. 4. Microsoft .NET. I. Title.
 TK5105.8885.A26K364 2010
 006.7'882—dc22

 2009045076

McGraw-Hill books are available at special quantity discounts to use as premiums and sales promotions, or for use in corporate training programs. To contact a representative, please e-mail us at bulksales@mcgraw-hill.com.

ASP.NET 4.0 Programming

1 2 3 4 5 6 7 8 9 0   WFR WFR   0 1 9

ISBN   978-0-07-160410-9
MHID   0-07-160410-3

Sponsoring Editor Jane K. Brownlow	**Technical Editor** Anand Narayanaswamy	**Production Supervisor** George Anderson
Editorial Supervisor Jody McKenzie	**Copy Editor** Andy Carroll	**Composition** Glyph International
Project Manager Vipra Fauzdar, Glyph International	**Proofreader** Bev Weiler	**Illustration** Glyph International
Acquisitions Coordinator Joya Anthony	**Indexer** Steve Ingle	**Art Director, Cover** Jeff Weeks

Contents

Foreword

One of the things that makes Software Development a unique profession is that both the nature of the problems we solve, and the tools we use to solve them, are constantly changing. When I first saw a prototype of ASP.NET (then called ASP+) in 1999, I knew that Mark Anders and Scott Guthrie had discovered an idea that would revolutionize the way professional web applications would be developed. It was the motivator for my coming to work at Microsoft in 2001. The really exciting part was not just what ASP.NET 1.0 looked like, but rather the kind of evolution that I anticipated Microsoft would be able to accomplish based on that amazing foundation.

Here we are, a full decade after that first glimpse of ASP.NET, and now it is time for ASP.NET 4. One of the fundamental goals of ASP.NET version 1 was to make web development easily possible for the hoards of client/server developers that were suddenly being called on to deliver functionality for their business applications to the World Wide Web. Over the years, those developers have learned about the plumbing of the web, and the needs and desires of Web Developers have evolved. ASP.NET has evolved to meet those needs and desires.

There is a great deal new in ASP.NET 4 and, even though backward compatibility has remained a priority for the ASP.NET team, it is a good time to "reset" how one approaches building ASP.NET applications. Many developers have come to prefer LINQ and the Entity Framework for Data Access and now use it by default instead of ADO.NET. Windows Communication Foundation is quickly becoming the preferred technology for implementing REST and SOAP Services, Ajax, jQuery, Silverlight, ADO.NET Data Services, and more! All provide great new opportunities to build truly great web applications that bring great value to their owners and users and that can evolve over time to enjoy a long functional lifespan.

Keeping up with the rapidly changing landscape of technology is a hard thing, and we all fall behind more than we would like. Joydip's book is not just a "what's new" in ASP.NET 4 book, but rather a "How to develop web applications with ASP.NET and Microsoft technologies from a version 4 perspective." For new developers, it is just a no-brainer to start with the latest, richest set of tools available. For experienced developers, it is super valuable to do more than just learn new features but also consider those new features and technologies in the context of design, best practices, etc. That way, the "new stuff" becomes part of our thought process.

Welcome to ASP.NET 4!

Joe Stagner, Senior Program Manager,
Developer Tools & Platform, Microsoft Corporation

Acknowledgments

Writing a book is always a rewarding and challenging experience. My special thanks to Jane Brownlow for providing me with the opportunity to author this book—turning this idea into a reality. I am also thankful to Joya Anthony and the entire McGraw-Hill team for their support. My heartiest thanks to Joe Stagner, Russell Jones, Alessandro Gallo, and Brendan Enrick for reviewing this book and providing valuable comments. My thanks to Anand Narayanaswamy in particular for spending his valuable time reviewing this book and providing his valuable feedback.

I am also thankful to Abhishek Kant (Microsoft), Steve Smith (AspAlliance), Steve Jones (SSWUG), Jude Kelly (SQL Server Performance), and Douglas Paterson (Packt Publishing) for their inspiration and support. I am also thankful to all my friends—Tilak, Vinod, and Taj—for their continued inspiration and support.

My deepest respect and gratitude to my parents for their love, blessings, and encouragement throughout my life. My thanks to my other family members too, for their support, and to little Jini in particular, for her continued inspiration and love. Thank you all so much!

Introduction

ASP.NET, one of the most successful web technologies ever, has been around for over a decade now. It is Microsoft's web application development framework, which programmers can use to build dynamic web sites, web applications, and XML web services. Since its inception, ASP.NET has been growing at an exponential rate. There have been a lot of changes in ASP.NET over the years—from ASP.NET 1.x to ASP.NET 4.0.

ASP.NET 4.0 Programming is part of a new series of programming books consisting of cutting-edge programming and development topics geared to experienced programmers and web developers. It presents the new and existing features of ASP.NET 4.0 in lucid language, and it's packed with plenty of ready-to-use code examples.

The book is targeted at web application developers working on ASP.NET who would like to use ASP.NET 4.0 to design and implement applications that are scalable, responsive, and high performant. Even readers with a basic knowledge of ASP.NET and C#, and who are willing to master the features of ASP.NET 4.0, can benefit from this book.

The book is based on Visual Studio 2010 and ASP.NET 4.0, and it takes you from the fundamentals of ASP.NET through to advanced techniques. The advanced topics discussed in this book include LINQ, PLINQ, ADO.NET Entity Framework, ADO.NET Data Services, ASP.NET Ajax 4.0, WCF 4.0, and the ASP.NET MVC Framework. You will learn how to build REST-based applications to support the increasingly demanding world of web application development. This book also discusses tips and tricks to improve ASP.NET application performance.

To work with the concepts and code examples discussed in this book, you should have the following installed on your system:

- Visual Studio 2010
- SQL Server 2005 or 2008

You should also have a good knowledge of C# and how to work with SQL Server to create databases, stored procedures, and the like.

In a nutshell, here is what you can learn from this book:

- Master the core concepts of ASP.NET
- Learn how to work with the standard ASP.NET server controls for displaying and managing data efficiently

- Understand how to leverage the features of ASP.NET Ajax framework to build fast and responsive applications
- Explore web services
- Explore the features of the ADO.NET Entity Framework and LINQ
- Explore ADO.NET Data Services and learn how to use it
- Explore Web Services and WCF
- Learn how to make the best use of jQuery in ASP.NET applications
- Master the best practices in designing scalable and high performant ASP.NET applications

Here's a quick glance at what's discussed in each of the chapters of the book.

Chapter 1 introduces the core concepts of ASP.NET and the new concepts in ASP.NET 4.0.

Chapter 2 discusses state management techniques in ASP.NET with plenty of code examples where applicable. It discusses both server-side and client-side state management techniques.

Chapter 3 discusses how to work with ADO.NET to perform CRUD operations. The chapter highlights the major components of ADO.NET—an object-oriented data-access technology from Microsoft that supports both connected and disconnected modes of operation. It also discusses the ADO.NET Entity Framework—an extended ORM from Microsoft—and how to leverage its features to build robust data-driven applications.

Chapter 4 discusses how to bind data to the data controls in ASP.NET. It discusses these controls in detail:

- List controls (ListBox, DropDownList, CheckBoxList, RadioButtonList, BulletedList)
- Repeater control
- DataList control
- DataGrid control
- GridView control
- DetailsView control
- FormView control
- TreeView control
- ListView control
- DataPager control

It also discusses the following data-source controls in ASP.NET 4.0:

- ObjectDataSource control
- XmlDataSource control

- LinqDataSource control
- SqlDataSource control
- AccessDataSource control
- EntityDataSource control

This chapter concludes with a discussion of the GeneratedImage and Chart controls in ASP.NET 4.0

Chapter 5 discusses the techniques of building and deploying web sites in ASP.NET. It also discusses the differences between the web site and the web application model in ASP.NET.

Chapter 6 discusses how to internationalize applications created using ASP.NET 4.0.

Chapter 7 covers the security model of ASP.NET. It also presents the provider model in ASP.NET and the new features available in the ASP.NET 4.0 security model.

Chapter 8 discusses debugging and tracing—two of the best techniques for efficiently detecting and tracking bugs in an ASP.NET application at execution time.

Chapter 9 looks at the Dynamic Data framework—a framework that allows you to quickly build data-driven applications that can leverage the powerful features of LINQ to SQL or the ADO.NET Entity Framework.

Chapter 10 discusses how one can use Silverlight in ASP.NET applications to create rich, secure, scalable web applications that can run on any platform.

Chapter 11 covers web parts and how they can be implemented in ASP.NET 4.0 applications.

Chapter 12 discusses LINQ—a query translation pipeline integrated right into Microsoft's .NET Framework to provide querying capabilities using languages that run on top of the managed environment. It also presents tips and techniques to improve the data-access performance of applications that use LINQ to SQL in the data-access layer. Finally, it looks at how LINQ to Entities and LINQ to SQL differ.

Chapter 13 discusses the features of the ASP.NET Ajax framework and its architectural components. It also discusses the other Ajax frameworks available.

Chapter 14 discusses how to write programs that can leverage the features of ASP.NET Ajax to design and implement applications that are fast and responsive.

Chapter 15 covers web services—how to implement them and consume them from client-side code. It also discusses the differences between .NET Remoting and Web Services, and when to use one over the other in applications.

Chapter 16 discusses how to leverage the features of Windows Communication Foundation (WCF) for designing and developing REST-based applications that can intercommunicate. It also discusses service-oriented architecture (SOA) and the components that make it. It then discusses the architectural components of WCF in detail.

Chapter 17 discusses the ASP.NET MVC Framework—a framework from Microsoft that facilitates a clean separation of concerns and promotes testability, plugability, and maintainability. It starts with the Model-View-Controller (MVC) architecture and its components and then covers the architectural components of the ASP.NET MVC Framework.

Chapter 18 discusses how to program the ASP.NET MVC Framework and perform CRUD operations.

Chapter 19 presents the jQuery library—an extensible open source JavaScript library that's fast, lightweight, and CSS3 and cross-browser compliant. jQuery can simplify event handling and animations and facilitate the design and development of responsive web applications. The chapter also discusses how to consume a web service from the client side using jQuery in ASP.NET 4.0 applications.

Chapter 20 presents the best practices and techniques for designing applications that are high performant, scalable, and responsive. It also discusses the best practices in deploying ASP.NET applications.

CHAPTER 1

Introduction to ASP.NET 4.0

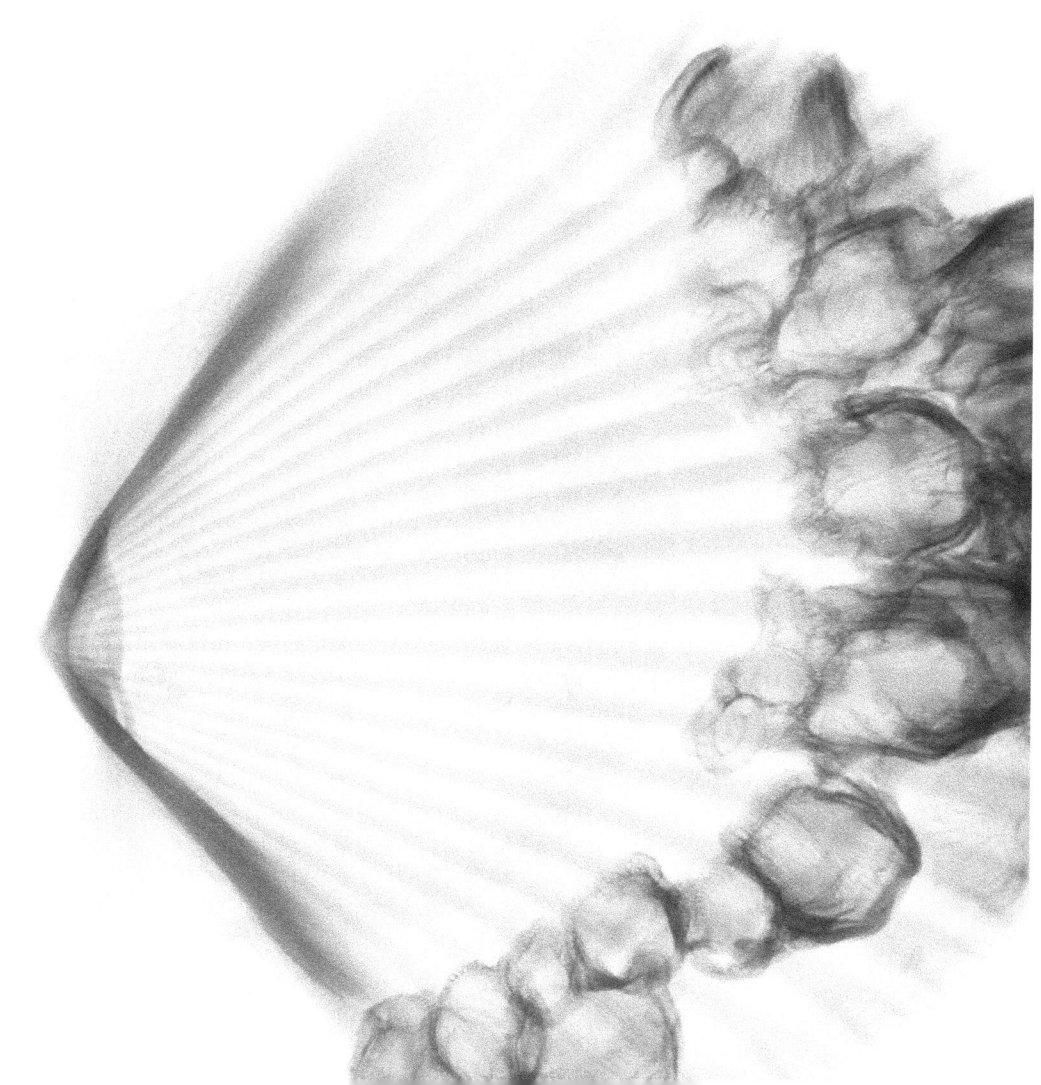

Web application development has seen a sea change over the past decade. ASP .NET is one of the most popular web technologies in recent times, and it marks the beginning of a new era—a departure from the way traditional web applications were developed using ASP. ASP.NET is a powerful server-side technology—a web application development framework that you can use to build and deploy web applications and dynamic web sites on a managed platform. It is built on top of the Common Language Runtime (CLR) and can be programmed in any language that targets the CLR. ASP.NET promises to be the technology of choice for building robust and scalable web applications for a long time to come. Our journey towards mastering ASP.NET 4.0 has just begun!

Prerequisites

To implement the code samples discussed in this book, you should have the following software installed on your system:

- Visual Studio 2010
- SQL Server 2005 or 2008
- AdventureWorks Database

You should have a basic understanding of the C# programming language and of how to work with SQL Server to create databases, tables, stored procedures, etc. AdventureWorks is a sample database for SQL Server.

The Microsoft .NET Framework

Microsoft .NET provides a framework that facilitates designing and developing applications that are portable, scalable, and robust, and that can be executed in a distributed environment. It presents a platform- and device-independent computing model in a managed environment.

The Microsoft .NET Framework provides a lot of features, the most notable of them being the support for cross-language integration, the Common Type System, the Base Class Library, Common Language Runtime (CLR), the just-in-time (JIT) compiler, and support for implicit or automated garbage collection. There have also been a lot of improvements in Microsoft .NET Framework 4.0 compared to its earlier versions. The most important is the introduction of support for parallel computing using PLINQ and the Dynamic Language Runtime.

Cross-Language Integration

You can use Microsoft .NET to develop applications that are interoperable. This means that you can use C# to call the methods and properties of a library written in VB.NET, or access C# libraries from VB.NET. The trick to achieving this is writing programs that use CLR-compliant types, which are types that are not specific to any language.

The Common Type System

The Common Type System (CTS) defines a set of types and rules that are common to all languages targeted at the CLR. It supports both value and reference types. *Value types* are created in the stack and include all primitive types, structs, and enums. In contrast, *reference types* are created in the managed heap and include objects, arrays, collections, etc.

The Base Class Library

The .NET Framework Class Library (FCL) is a set of managed classes that provide a lot of services to the CLR, such as file handling, remoting, sockets, web services, and data access. Some of the most important namespaces in the .NET Base Class Library include: System, System.Collections, System.Diagnostics, System.Globalization, System.IO, System.Reflection, System.Security, System.Threading, System.Net, System .Runtime, System.IO, System.Text, System.Resources, System.Data, System.Management, System.Configuration, and System.Linq.

The Common Language Runtime

The Common Language Runtime (CLR) is the managed runtime environment of Microsoft .NET. It is the runtime engine that provides support for memory management, type safety, exception handling, just-in-time (JIT) compilation, automated garbage collection, etc.

The Dynamic Language Runtime

The support for the Dynamic Language Runtime environment has been included in .NET Framework 4.0. The Dynamic Language Runtime (DLR) is a runtime environment that runs on top of the Common Language Runtime (CLR) and includes a .NET language integration layer, a set of runtime code components, and language binders. It adds a set of services to CLR that enables you to execute dynamic languages and also add dynamic features to statically typed languages inside the managed environment of the CLR. These services include support for a dynamic type system, a standard hosting model, expression trees, and fast and dynamic code generation. Typical examples of dynamically typed languages include: Python, Ruby, and JavaScript. The DLR enables these languages to reside side-by-side with statically typed languages like C#, Managed C++, and Visual Basic. Microsoft .NET Framework 4.0 provides support for the DLR through the new System.Dynamic namespace.

Portability

When the source code of a program written in a CLR-compliant language (a language that is targeted at the managed environment of the CLR) is compiled, it generates a machine-independent and intermediate code. This was originally called the Microsoft Intermediate Language (MSIL) and has now been renamed as the Common Intermediate Language (CIL). CIL is the key to portability in .NET. Note that the CIL code that is generated contains the same op-codes as any language that is CLR-compliant.

The Just-in-Time (JIT) Compiler

The just-in-time (JIT) compiler is the component that converts the intermediate machine-independent CIL code to machine-dependent code. The CIL code and its metadata are loaded into memory by the CLR. The JIT compiler then compiles this CIL code to machine code at runtime.

Garbage Collection

Garbage collection is a mechanism employed by Microsoft .NET to clean up unused objects in order to reclaim memory used by them. The garbage collector is the component responsible for reclaiming memory occupied by managed objects once they are no longer needed. Managed objects are those that are created in the managed heap. Objects that are no longer in use are identified as "garbage" objects.

Code Verification

Code verification is a feature of Microsoft .NET that enforces security by verifying the code before it is executed. Code verification enforces type safety and prevents the code executing within the CLR from performing any illegal operations, like accessing memory occupied by the host operating system, accessing the system's hardware, etc.

Assemblies

Assemblies are the building blocks of the .NET Framework—they are the fundamental unit of versioning, security, deployment, version control, and reusability of code. An assembly consists of the metadata (information about the assembly), the compiled CIL code, and resources. Assembly metadata typically consists of the assembly's identity information (name, version, etc.), culture information, type, dependencies, and security information.

Private and Shared Assemblies

Depending on their accessibility, assemblies are of two types: private and shared. A *private assembly* is one that can be used by a single application. *Shared assemblies* are those that are stored in a central location called the Global Assembly Cache (GAC) and can be accessed by multiple applications.

The Global Assembly Cache (GAC)

The Global Assembly Cache (GAC) is the central storage location for shared assemblies. Such assemblies are identified by having globally unique identifiers called *strong names*. Strong names consist of the assembly's identity information, a public key, and a digital signature. Assemblies that have strong names are also called strong named assemblies.

Static and Dynamic Assemblies

Assemblies can be static or dynamic. *Static assemblies* are stored on the disk as physical files, whereas *dynamic assemblies* are not saved to disk before execution and are executed directly from memory.

Assembly Version

An assembly consists of a 128-bit version number that is divided into four distinct parts: the major version, the minor version, build, and revision. So, if the version of an assembly is 1.0.1.1, it implies that the assembly has 1 as the major version, 0 as the minor version, 1 as the build, and 1 as the release.

From ASP to ASP.NET—A Paradigm Shift

Active Server Pages (ASP), a server-side scripting engine, was Microsoft's first development framework for implementing web applications with dynamic and interactive web pages. ASP 1.0 was released in December 1996, and was followed by ASP 2.0 in 1997, and ASP 3.0 in the fall of 2000. The default scripting language used in ASP was VBScript.

However, traditional ASP had some limitations. It had no support for object orientation and ASP pages were interpreted and not compiled, resulting in poor performance. ASP.NET, first released in 2002, is a much improved technology, with support for writing "clean" code using .NET's code-behind model, support for object orientation, better scalability support, faster development, a simplified deployment model, support for XML, and a robust security model.

ASP.NET Versions

ASP.NET is a language-neutral, interoperable server-side technology that allows the creation, execution, and deployment of scalable web applications and services.

From ASP.NET 1.0 to ASP.NET 4.0

ASP.NET 1.0 was released in January 2002 as part of Microsoft .NET Framework version 1.0 and was included in Visual Studio .NET 2002. ASP.NET 1.1 was released in April 2003 as part of Microsoft .NET Framework 1.1 and was included in Visual Studio 2003. ASP.NET 2.0 was released in November 2005 as part of Microsoft .NET Framework 2.0 and was packed inside Visual Studio 2005. ASP.NET 3.5 was introduced as part of Visual Studio 2008. ASP.NET 4.0 will be shipped as part of Visual Studio 2010, which is due to be released in the fall of 2009. ASP.NET 4.0 is based on .NET Framework 4.0.

New Features in ASP.NET 4.0

ASP.NET 4.0 is included as part of Visual Studio 2010. It includes both better support for Ajax and a lot of enhanced features. ASP.NET 4.0 also includes built-in support for dynamic data thorough the use of its Dynamic Data controls. In this section we will take a look at the new features/enhancements in ASP.NET 4.0.

New Data Controls

ASP.NET 4.0 includes two relatively new data controls: the ListView and the DataPager. These controls were first introduced in the ASP.NET 3.5 release, and there have been a few enhancements to them in ASP.NET 4.0.

ListView Control   ListView is an ASP.NET data control that allows you to have complete control over the generated HTML markup code. Apart from performing CRUD (create, update, read, and delete) operations, you can also implement data paging when you use the DataPager control. In ASP.NET 4.0, the LayoutTemplate of the ListView control is optional, and you can only use the ItemTemplate to display data. Here is an example:

Listing 1-1
```
<asp:ListView ID="ListView1" runat="server"
 DataSourceID="SqlDataSource1">
         <ItemTemplate>
             Employee ID:
             <asp:Label ID="lblEmployeeID"
runat="server" Text='<%# Eval("EmployeeID") %>' />
             <br />
             First Name:
             <asp:Label ID="lblFirstName"
runat="server" Text='<%# Eval("FirstName") %>' />
             <br />
             Last Name:
             <asp:Label ID="lblLastName"
runat="server"
 Text='<%# Eval("LastName") %>' />
             <br />
             Address:
             <asp:Label ID="lblAddress"
 runat="server"
 Text='<%# Eval("Address") %>' />
             <br />
             Phone:
             <asp:Label ID="lblPhone"
runat="server"
Text='<%# Eval("Phone") %>' />
             <br />
         </ItemTemplate>
     </asp:ListView>
     <asp:SqlDataSource ID="SqlDataSource1"
 runat="server"
         ConnectionString="<%$ ConnectionStrings:ConnectionString %>"
         SelectCommand="SELECT * FROM [Employees]">
</asp:SqlDataSource>
```

DataPager Control   The DataPager control can be used to provide paging support to the ListView control. As of this writing, the DataPager control supports data paging with the ListView control only.

Integrated Ajax Support

Asynchronous JavaScript and XML (Ajax) is a technology that can be used to implement fast and responsive web applications with intuitive user interfaces. You can use Ajax to reduce the hits to the server and hence design applications with improved performance. In the earlier versions of ASP.NET, Ajax had to be installed as a separate installation, but ASP.NET 4.0 provides integrated support for Ajax.

Another great new feature of ASP.NET 4.0 is that application services like authentication, membership, role management, profiles, etc., have been exposed as web services—they can be called from client-side scripts much as you call other web services.

Support for LINQ

Language Integrated Query (LINQ) is a query language that is integrated into the .NET Framework. You can use LINQ with ASP.NET 4.0 to query objects, databases, and XML seamlessly, and also to bind data to the data controls.

New Assemblies

The new assemblies introduced in ASP.NET 4.0 include System.Core.dll, System.Data .Linq.dll, System.Web.dll, System.Xml.Linq.dll, System.Web.Extensions.dll, and System .Data.DataSetExtensions.dll.

New Merge Tool

ASP.NET 4.0 includes a new merge utility called Aspnet_merge.exe. You can use it to merge precompiled assemblies created using the ASP.NET precompilation tool, called Aspnet_Compiler.exe. Precompilation is a feature that minimizes the initial load time of your ASP.NET web pages and boosts the application's performance. Deployment becomes easy when using precompilation—you need not deploy your source code to the server.

New ClientID Property

There have been quite a few enhancements to Web Forms. ASP.NET 4.0 includes a new property called ClientID that you can use to access a server control from a client script. Note that each server control in ASP.NET contains this read-only property. You can also set how the ClientID for a control should behave using the ClientIDMode property. This property can accept one of the following values:

- **Legacy**   If this is set, the ClientID property for the control would behave the same as in the previous versions of ASP.NET.
- **Static**   If this is set, then the ClientID for the control would have the same value as set in code.
- **Inherit**   If the ClientIDMode is set to this value, the control's ClientID will inherit the value of its parent.
- **Predictable**   This is set when you are using repeating templates.

You can also achieve the same results programmatically, as shown in the following code:

Listing 1-7

```
public partial class WebForm1 : System.Web.UI.Page
{
    protected void Page_Load(object sender, EventArgs e)
    {
        Page.Keywords = "Mc-Graw Hill";
        Page.Description = "This is a test page";
    }
}
```

New and Improved Features in Visual Studio 2010

Visual Studio 2010 includes a lot of additional features compared to earlier releases. It provides better code formatting and IntelliSense support for JavaScript. It adds much improved support for the popular JavaScript libraries, like jQuery, Prototype, Ext JS, etc. It also provides enhanced support for Windows Communication Foundation (WCF) services, as well as IntelliSense and debugging support for classic ASP. Visual Studio 2010 now also includes the built-in designer for creating ADO.NET Entity Data Models.

The Visual Studio 2010 IDE provides some new interesting features, like multitargeting support, JavaScript IntelliSense and debugging support, and improved design-time support for designing and implementing applications.

Improved Support for CSS Compatibility

Visual Studio 2010 includes improved support for CSS 2.1 standards. It is more robust than earlier versions of Visual Studio, with improved support for rendering, layout, etc.

Improved Packaging and Deployment Support

Visual Studio 2010 now includes support for the following:

- Web packaging
- Web configuration file transformation
- Database deployment
- ClickOnce publishing

Debugging Enhancements

Visual Studio 2010 provides the following debugging enhancements:

- **Breakpoint enhancements**   This enables you to add search and label breakpoints in the Breakpoints window.
- **WPF debugging enhancements**   This enables you to view events in your WPF application.

Historical debugging is another great new feature in Visual Studio Team System 2010. This feature enables you to record all events, like method calls, method parameters, and so on, even if there is no breakpoint set.

Multitargeting Support

You can use Visual Studio 2010 to build applications that are targeted at multiple versions of the .NET Framework. The term "multitargeting" in this context implies Visual Studio 2010's support for multiple versions of Microsoft .NET Framework, as shown in Figure 1-1. It allows you to develop applications that are targeted at .NET Framework versions 2.0, 3.0, or 3.5. Thus, you can use Visual Studio 2010 to develop ASP.NET 2.0, 3.0, 4.0 applications.

JavaScript Debugging and IntelliSense Support

JavaScript IntelliSense was a much-awaited feature that was absent in earlier versions of Visual Studio. It supports both inline JavaScript and externally referenced JavaScript files.

Another new feature in Visual Studio 2010 is built-in support for JavaScript debugging. You can now set breakpoints in your JavaScript code.

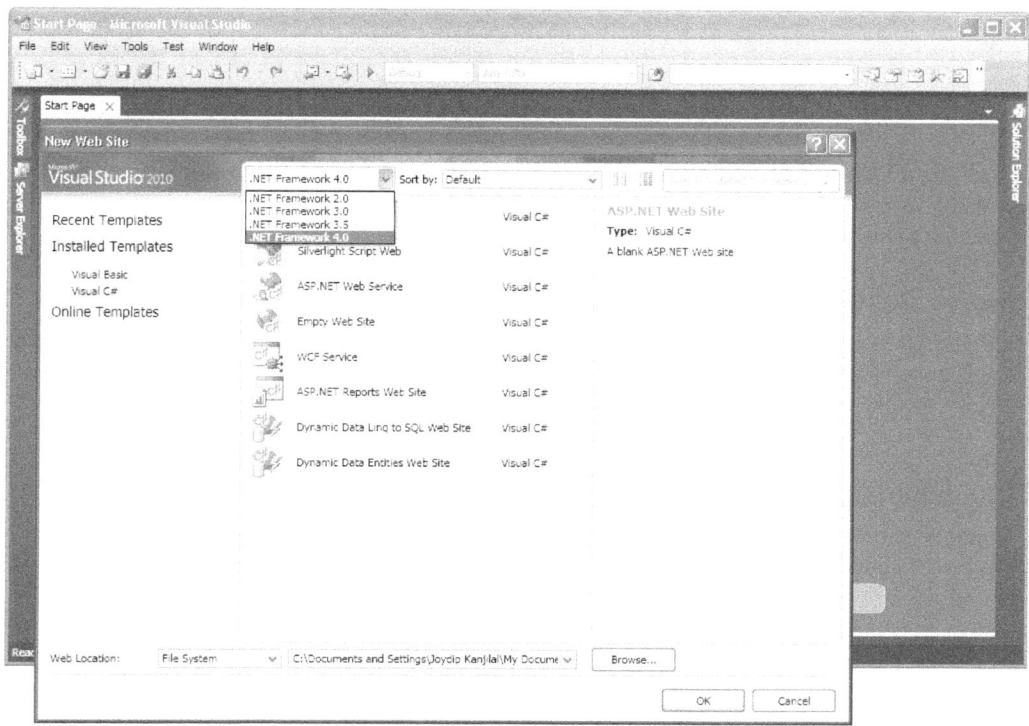

FIGURE 1-1   Multitargeting support in Visual Studio 2010

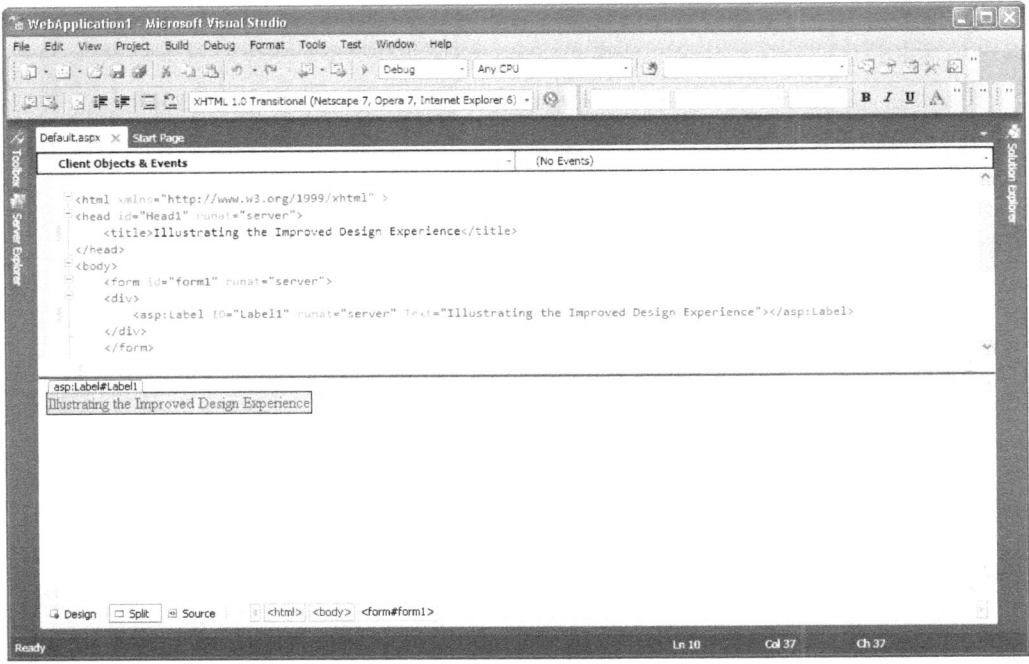

FIGURE 1-2 Better design-time support in Visual Studio 2010

Visual Studio 2010 also includes improved support for JScript IntelliSense. In addition, it provides over 200 HTML and JScript snippets, and you can download and use additional snippets.

Better Design-Time Support

Visual Studio 2010 offers an improved web designer interface. In Figure 1-2, you can see the vertical split view—an excellent feature that enables you to view the design of your web page while you are designing it with markup code.

Getting Started with ASP.NET 4.0

To get started using ASP.NET 4.0, you first need to install Visual Studio 2010 on your system. The installation process is similar to that of previous versions of Visual Studio. If you are new to Visual Studio 2010, insert the installation disc into your system and follow the instructions displayed on the screen.

The ASP.NET Folder Structure

With a view to organizing content efficiently, ASP.NET 4.0 comes with a lot of predefined folders. Figure 1-3 illustrates how these folders are organized.

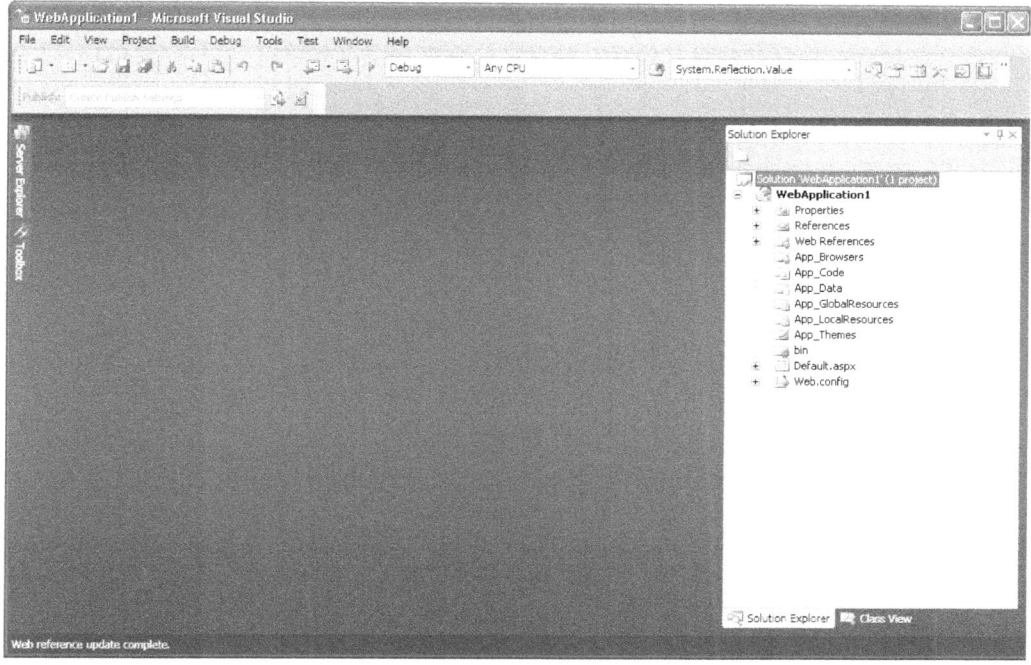

FIGURE 1-3   The ASP.NET 4.0 folder structure

App_Code
This folder contains all the code files—including classes, interfaces, typed datasets, and others that are globally accessible to the entire application. However, this folder doesn't contain the code-behind files for the web pages in the application. The contents of this folder are compiled at runtime, and the resulting compiled assemblies are placed in the Bin folder.

App_Themes
This folder contains the application's themes, which are used to apply a consistent look and feel to your application.

App_Data
This folder contains the application's data in the form of XML, MDF, text, etc.

Bin
This folder contains the compiled assemblies and components that are globally accessible to the entire application.

App_LocalResources
This folder contains the local resources, which are resources that belong to a particular web page.

App_GlobalResources

This folder contains the application's globally accessible resources in the form of .resx or .resources files. These resources can be used to provide support for globalization.

App_WebReferences

This folder contains the files associated with a web service, such as web references, proxy classes, schemas, discovery document files, etc.

App_Browsers

This folder contains specific browser definition files, which have .browser extensions.

The ASP.NET Application Life Cycle

A sequence of events takes place when a request is sent from the client to the web server. Here is the sequence of events at a glance:

1. The web server (IIS in our case) picks up the request and searches for server extensions. Server extensions are mapped in IIS, so if the server extension of this request is .aspx, IIS maps the request to the aspnet_isapi.dll file. The ASP.NET worker process is loaded as part of this .dll file, and it initializes the HttpPipeline

2. The HttpPipeline contains a set of objects, including HttpRuntime, HttpWorkerRequest, HttpApplicationFactory, etc. If an HttpApplication object doesn't exist, it either creates a new one or picks up one from the HttpApplicationFactory's pool of HttpApplication objects and passes the incoming request to the object to handle.

3. The ASP.NET worker process calls the HttpRuntime.ProcessRequest() method

4. The HttpRuntime creates the HttpContext and calls the HttpApplicationFactory to create an instance of the web page object select the appropriate HttpApplication object to handle the incoming request.

5. The HttpApplication object determines the type of incoming request and invokes the appropriate PageHandlerFactory for that requesting page. To select the appropriate handler for the requesting page, it searches the <httpHandlers> section of the machine.config file.

NOTE *The web page class extends the System.Web.UI.Page class and implements the IHttpHandler interface.*

6. The PageHandlerFactory creates an instance of the page using the page handler for that page.

7. The page instance is returned to the HttpRuntime with the help of the HttpApplicationFactory.

8. The HttpRuntime makes use of the page instance and invokes the ProcessRequest() method for the page, which calls the FrameworkInitialize() method and then calls the page life-cycle methods.

We will discuss the page life-cycle methods of ASP.NET next.

The ASP.NET Page Life Cycle

HttpModules are .NET components that are responsible for filtering, editing requests and responses in the HttpPipeLine. On the contrary, HttpHandlers are .NET components that implement the System.Web.IHttpHandler interface and are responsible for processing requests at the endpoint of the ASP.NET engine and initiating the rendering process. Incidentally, our web page classes extend the System.Web.UI.Page class and implement the IHttpHandler interface. Web pages in ASP.NET are known as Web Forms. All web pages in ASP.NET inherit the System.UI.Page class; they have an .aspx extension; and they usually contain HTML markup code, server controls, user controls, and even dynamic server-side code.

Between the time a request is sent to the web server and the time the response is sent back to the web browser, a lot of events are executed one after the other. These events are associated with their respective event handlers (methods that are fired when an event occurs). Event handlers can be overridden so you can customize these events and incorporate your own custom code. Note that it is the ProcessRequest() method that actually fires the page events in the life cycle of a web page in ASP.NET.

This is the sequence of events that are fired in the life cycle of an ASP.NET web page:

1. Page_Init
2. LoadViewState
3. LoadPostData
4. Page_Load
5. RaisePostDataChangedEvent
6. RaisePostBackEvent
7. Page_PreRender
8. SaveViewState
9. Page_Render
10. Page_UnLoad

Page_Init

The first stage in the life cycle of an ASP.NET page is initialization, and the Page_Init event is the first to be triggered. This event typically contains initialization code; for example, the server controls of your web page are initialized to their default values here. You can override this event to create or re-create the controls dynamically.

The OnInit() event handler is called when this event is triggered. Listing 1-8 shows what the OnInit() event handler looks like.

Listing 1-8
```
protected override void OnInit(EventArgs e)
{
 //Write your code here to create your controls dynamically
 //or perform any initialization code
base.OnInit(e); //Call the base method
}
```

LoadViewState

This event restores the page's ViewState information from its last saved state. ViewState maintains the state of web pages between postbacks to the web server. It is a hidden field named __ViewState, and it holds the IDs and values of the controls in your web page.

The following code snippet illustrates what the LoadViewState () method looks like:

Listing 1-9
```
protected override void LoadViewState(Object viewState)
{
    if (viewState == null)
    {
        base.LoadViewState(viewState);
    }
}
```

LoadPostBackData

This event populates the server controls in your web page with the posted data.

Page_Load

The Page_Load event restores the control values of the web page. In the event handler associated with this event, you can write code to bind data to the data controls, or code that needs to be executed for each postback of the web page.

There is an important property of the Page class called IsPostBack. You can use this property to check whether the event handler associated with the Page_Load event has been called as a result of a postback to the web server or not. The Page_Load() event handler is shown in listing 1-9.

Listing 1-10
```
protected void Page_Load(object sender,
EventArgs e){if (!IsPostBack)
{
//Code written here would be called
// the first time the page has been loaded
}
}
```

Pre_Render

The Pre_Render event, as the name suggests, is called prior to the rendering of the page content. This is where you can add code to make changes to the rendered output if you need to.

SaveViewState

The SaveViewState event is responsible for saving the ViewState information of a web page into __Viewstate—the hidden field associated with every web page for which ViewState is enabled.

Page_Render

This event renders the content of the web page in the web browser using the OutputStream of the Response property of your web page. You can make changes to the rendered output here. The rendering event is the next stage in the web page's life cycle.

Page_UnLoad

This is the last event in the life cycle of an ASP.NET page. It is called after the page has been rendered in its entirety and is responsible for releasing resources and discarding the web page from memory. Once this event has been executed, the response is displayed in the web browser.

Application Domains and Runtime Hosts

An application domain is a lightweight process. It is a logical and physical unit of isolation built around every .NET application by the CLR, and contains its own set of code, data, and configuration settings. This isolation ensures that the failure of one application domain will not affect other application domains. It should be noted that an application domain can belong to one process only, but a process can have multiple application domains.

NOTE *A* process *is the running instance of a program. Each and every process can have one or more threads; a* thread *is the path of execution within a process.*

A default application domain is first created when the CLR is loaded. This unit of isolation enables you to load multiple .NET applications in a single process but in separate application domains. Note that each ASP.NET application runs in its own application domain, but under the same worker process, named aspnet_wp.exe in IIS 5.0 and w3wp.exe in IIS 6.0.

Every application in .NET (console applications, Windows applications, Web services, etc.) is hosted by a Win32 process. This is the *runtime host*. The runtime hosts that ship with the .NET Framework by default are ASP.NET, IE, and Shell.

ASP.NET Configuration Files

The ASP.NET configuration files include web.config and machine.config. Both of these are based on XML. The former is used to specify the application-wide settings for the ASP.NET application, and the latter is used to apply configuration settings for all applications in the entire system.

The Web.Config File

The web.config file is an XML-based configuration file that contains application-wide settings. It is typically present in the application's root directory. You can have one or more web.config files for your application (one for each subdirectory of your application).

However, you can have only one machine.config file for your system. Here is how the web.config file is organized:

Listing 1-11
```
<configuration>
 <system.web>
 <!— Specify your Compilation, Custom Error,
 Authentication, Authorization, etc sections here -->
 </system.web>
 <appSettings>
 <!— Specify the Database connection string,
File path, Server Name and other Custom Settings here -->
 </appSettings >
</configuration>
```

You can use the <pages> section of the <system.web> section group to specify whether session or view state will be enabled or disabled. Here is an example:

Listing 1-12
```
<configuration>
    <system.web>
        <pages enableSessionState="true" />
    </system.web>
</configuration>
```

You can also set the authentication mode for your application in your application's web.config file. Here is how you can do this:

Listing 1-13
```
<authentication mode="Windows" />
<authorization>
  <allow roles="Users" />
  <deny users="*" />
</authorization>
```

Similarly, you can specify the trace and globalization information.

Listing 1-14
```
<trace enabled="true" localOnly="true"
 pageOutput="false" />
<globalization requestEncoding="utf-8"
 responseEncoding="utf-8" culture="en-GB" />
```

You can also use the <customErrors> section to specify the application-wide error information. Here is an example:

Listing 1-15
```
<customErrors mode="On">
<error statusCode="404"
redirect="FileUnavailable.aspx"/>
</customErrors>
```

You can use the <identity impersonate> section of the web.config file to impersonate a user:

Listing 1-16
```
<identity impersonate="true"
userName="joydip" password="joydip1@3"/>
```

And the following code snippet illustrates how you can specify session state storage mode in your application's web.config file:

Listing 1-17
```
<sessionState mode="InProc" />
```

NOTE *Session state storage modes in ASP.NET can be one of the following: InProc, OutProc, SQLServer.*

The <appSettings> section is typically used to store key-value pairs of data. You can also store database connection settings, server names, and file paths in this section. The following example illustrates how you can store key-value pairs:

Listing 1-18
```
<appSettings>
    <add key="key" value ="value"/>
</appSettings >
```

Here is how you can store connection string information in your application's web .config file:

Listing 1-19
```
<add key="ConnectionString"
value="server=(localhost);
database=AdventureWorks;
uid=joydip;pwd=joydip1@3"/>
```

You can also specify an external configuration file in the web.config file. Here is an example:

Listing 1-20
```
<appSettings file="MGHExternalSettings.config"/>
<connectionStrings>
    <add name ="Test"
        connectionString="server=(localhost);
database=AdventureWorks;
        uid=adWorks;pwd=adWorks1@3"/>
</connectionStrings>
```

To create a new configuration section, you need to add the name of the configuration section using the <configSections> attribute. Here is an example:

Listing 1-21
```
<configuration>
    <configSections>
        <section name="DBSettings"
 type="MGH.Settings" />
    </configSections>
</configuration>
```

The Machine.Config File

The machine.config file is located in the C:\WINDOWS\Microsoft.NET\Framework\ vx.x.xxxx\CONFIG directory and is used to specify system-wide configuration settings. The most important sections in the machine.config file include:

- processModel
- sessionState
- appSettings

The <processModel> section of the machine.config file can be used to recycle or shut down the ASP.NET worker process. To shut down the worker process, you can use the shutDownTimeout attributes in the <processModel> section.

You can also specify trust levels in the machine.config file to indicate whether or not a particular piece of code is trusted. By default, any ASP.NET web application has full trust and unrestricted permissions, but you can change this using the <trust level> attribute. The trust levels in the machine.config file can have any of these values:

- Full
- High
- Medium
- Low
- Minimal

The following piece of code illustrates how you can specify trust levels in the machine.config file:

Listing 1-22
```
<system.web>
   <trust level="Medium" originUrl=""/>
</system.web>
```

Implementing Your First ASP.NET 4.0 Application

Once you have installed Visual Studio 2010 on your system, you can use it to develop your ASP.NET 4.0 applications. To write your first application using ASP.NET, follow these steps:

1. Open Visual Studio 2010 and select File | New Project.

2. Select ASP.NET Web Application from the list of projects displayed in the New Project dialog box (shown in Figure 1-4), provide a name for the project, select .NET Framework 4.0 from the list of the framework versions displayed, and click OK.

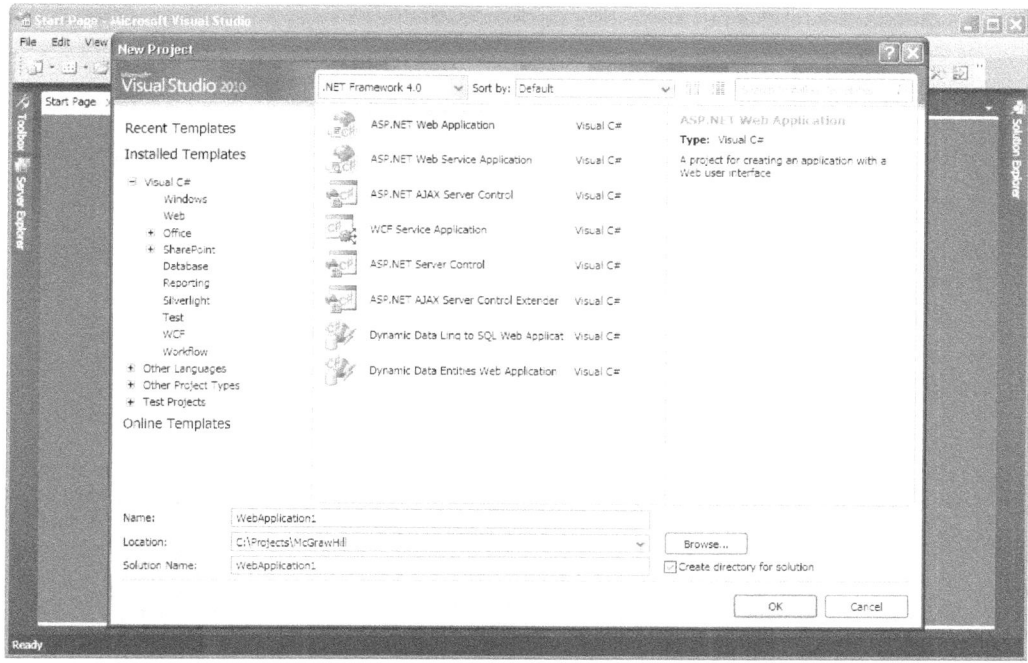

FIGURE 1-4   Visual Studio 2010 project templates

The project will be created and the default web page for the project will be a file named Default.aspx.

3. Switch to the Design view of the Default.aspx web form, and drag a Label control onto it from the toolbox.

4. Specify a title for the web form and the text for the Label control. The resulting markup code in the Default.aspx file should look something like this:

Listing 1-23

```
<head runat="server">
    <title>Welcome to the World of ASP.NET</title>
</head>
<body>
    <form id="form1" runat="server">
    <div>
        <asp:Label ID="Label1" runat="server"
```

```
       Text="Our First ASP.NET Application">
   </asp:Label>
       </div>
       </form>
   </body>
   </html>
```

5. Press F5 to execute your application.

You're done! You have implemented your first ASP.NET application. The output will look something like what you can see in Figure 1-5.

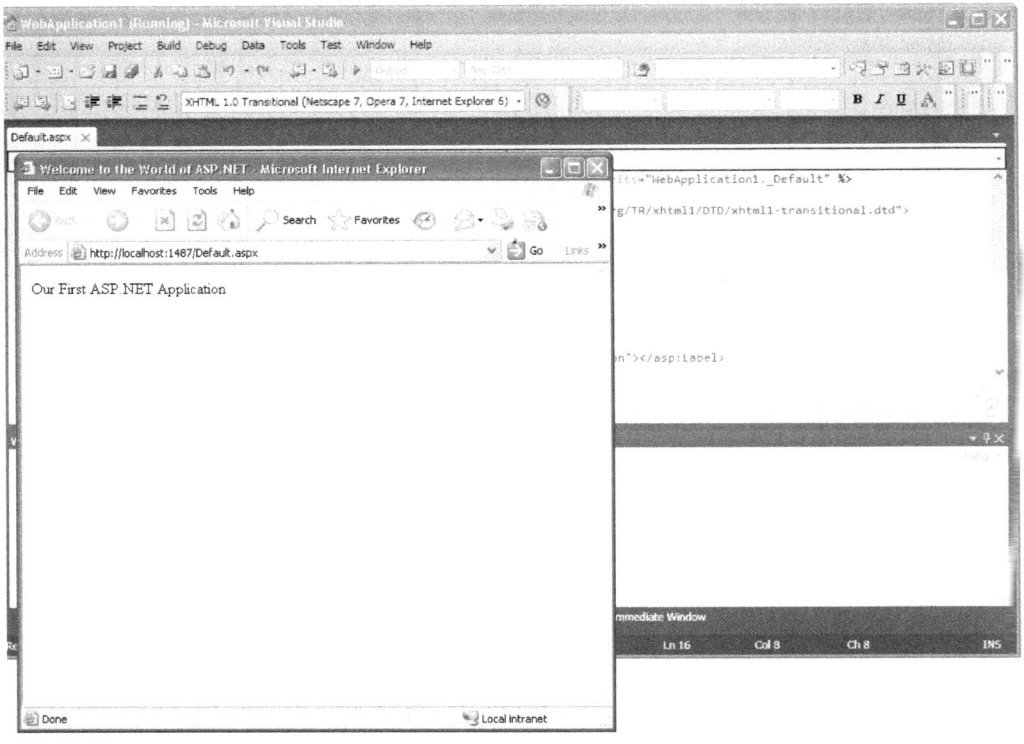

FIGURE 1-5   Your first ASP.NET 4.0 application at work!

CHAPTER 2

ASP.NET State Management

A SP.NET is based on the stateless HTTP protocol, so each request from the client browser to the web server is understood as an independent request. State management is one of the most important concepts in ASP.NET. It is a technique used to maintain state information for ASP.NET web pages across multiple requests. ASP.NET comes with built-in support for state management, both at the server and client ends. This chapter takes a look at the various state management options available and how they can be implemented in your ASP.NET applications. It also looks at the new state management options and enhancements available in ASP.NET 4.0.

Server-Side State Management

Server-side state management is the technique used to store state information on the server side. You can manage state information on the server using the Application, Session, or Cache objects. In this section, we will look at the various strategies for doing this.

Application Object

The Application object in ASP.NET is used to store data that is accessible to all users across the application. Objects stored in the Application state are made globally accessible to all modules of the application, and they are available as long as the application is running. Note that you need to apply proper synchronization techniques to ensure thread safety and to handle concurrency conflicts. Data stored in the Application state will persist until the application is terminated.

The Cache object in ASP.NET provides similar capabilities, though you don't have to use lock and unlock mechanisms while storing data to or accessing it and from the Cache. That's because the Cache provides a thread-safe way of storing your application's data.

Here is an example that illustrates how you can store a site counter in the Application object and then display it:

Listing 2-1

```
using System;
using System.Web;
using System.Web.UI;
using System.Web.UI.WebControls;
namespace ApplicationObject
{
    public partial class _Default : System.Web.UI.Page
    {
        static int siteCounter = 0;
        private static readonly Object lockObj = new Object();
        protected void Page_Load(object sender, EventArgs e)
        {
            ++siteCounter;
            lock (lockObj)
            {
                Application["SiteCounter"] = siteCounter;
            }
            Response.Write("This site has been visited "+
                siteCounter.ToString() + " times");
        }
    }
}
```

The site counter in Listing 2-1 would be updated with each refresh of the web page. Note how the lock keyword has been used to synchronize access to data.

Session Object

The Session object is used to store user-specific data as long as the user's session is active. A *session* is defined as the duration of connectivity between a client and a server application. The Session object is created and maintained on the web server and is unique to a user's session of communication with the web server. Any object that needs to be persisted in the Session object should be serializable.

When a session starts, the web browser sends a cookie with a session identifier along with every request. The IIS web server uses this session ID to determine to which SessionID a particular request belongs. If none is found, a session ID (120-bit string) is generated along with the request. You can specify the session timeout in the application's web.config file. When storing session state in SQL Server, session expiration is carried out by the SQL Agent using a registered job.

The SessionID persists as long as the browser instance is unchanged, even though the session object expires after the specified timeout. As a result, the same SessionID can represent multiple sessions over time. Note that if the application has never stored anything in the session state, a new session state with a new SessionID is created with every request.

If your session is using cookies, SessionIDs are stored inside them. If you are using a cookieless session, the SessionID is embedded in the URL itself. You can specify whether or not you want a cookieless session in your application's web.config file, as shown here:

Listing 2-2
```
<configuration>
  <system.web>
    <sessionState cookieless="false" />
  </system.web>
</configuration>
```

You may want to use a cookieless session for your application, especially if you want to ensure that your application can be supported in all browsers, regardless of whether cookies have been enabled in them. In such cases, you need to disable cookie support for session state in your application's web.config file, as shown here:

Listing 2-3
```
<configuration>
  <system.web>
    <sessionState cookieless="true" />
  </system.web>
</configuration>
```

Session State Storage Modes

Session state in ASP.NET can be stored in the InProc, State Server, or SQL Server storage modes. In InProc mode, the session data is stored in the ASP.NET worker process. In State Server mode, it is stored inside a separate process that is managed by the aspnet_state.exe file. In SQL Server mode, the session data is persisted in the database.

Here is the complete syntax for specifying session state in the web.config file using the mode attribute:

Listing 2-4
```
<sessionState mode = <"inproc" |
  "sqlserver" | "stateserver">
        cookieless = <"true" | "false">
timeout = <positive integer indicating
the session timeout in minutes>
   sqlconnectionstring =
<SQL connection string that is only
used in the SQLServer mode>
        server = <The server name
that is only required
when the mode is State Server>
        port = <The port number
that is only required
when the mode is State Server>
```

Storing Session State in the InProc Mode

The InProc mode of session state storage is the fastest of the modes and it stores the session data in the ASP.NET worker process. If the amount of data stored in the session is large, performance will be drastically affected.

However, the session state will be lost if the ASP.NET worker process named aspnet_wp.exe recycles or if the application domain restarts. The session state here entirely depends on the lifetime of the application domain in which it is stored.

Storing Session State in a State Server

The State Server mode uses a stand-alone Microsoft Windows service that is independent of IIS and can run on a separate server. In the State Server mode, the session state is serialized and stored in memory in a separate process that is managed by the aspnet_state.exe file. Note that State Server can be on a different system.

This storage mode has some performance drawbacks due to the overhead involved in serializing and deserializing objects. Note that the ASP.NET state service is like any other Windows NT/2000 service and runs as its own process and has its own memory space. If you want the session data to be stored in State Server mode, this service has to be started.

This is the required setting in the web.config file to store the session state in State Server mode:

Listing 2-5
```
<sessionState mode="StateServer"
  stateConnectionString="tcpip=127.0.0.1:42424"
sqlConnectionString="data source=127.0.0.1;

user id=joydip;password=joydip"
  cookieless="false" timeout="20"/>
```

The primary advantage of storing the session state in a State Server mode is that it is not in the same process as ASP.NET, and a crash of ASP.NET would in no way destroy the session data. Secondly, this mode of storing session state enables you to share the information across a web garden or a web farm. The main disadvantage, however, is that this mode is slow compared to the InProc mode, because it is stored in an external process.

Storing Session State Using SQL Server

The SQL Server mode of storing session state offers reliable, secure, and centralized storage of session state with transactional facilities. In this storage mode, the session data is serialized and stored in a database table in the SQL Server database. It can typically be used in web farms.

However, it has performance bottlenecks like State Server mode because of the overhead involved in serializing and deserializing the objects that are being stored and retrieved. SQL Server mode is more secure than the InProc or the State Server modes because you can configure SQL Server security.

To use the SQL Server mode for storing session data, you need to execute the InstallSqlState.sql file. When you execute this file, the necessary database and tables in the tempdb database will be created to store the session data. To remove all the databases and the tables created by the InstallSqlState.sql file, use the UninstallSQLState.sql file. The following is the required setting in the web.config file for storing session state in SQL Server mode.

Listing 2-6
```
<sessionState mode="SQLServer"
   sqlConnectionString=
"data source=server;
user id=joydip;

password=joydip1@3"
   cookieless="false" timeout="20" />
```

Note that the InstallSqlState.sql file is located at System drive\Windows Directory\Microsoft.NET\Framework\Version\.

If the connection you are using to connect to SQL Server is a trusted one, you should change the ownership of the state database to "sa" after creation. To do this, execute the following statement:

Listing 2-7
```
exec sp_changedbowner 'sa','true'
```

Choosing the Right Session Storage Mode

When choosing the session state storage mode for your application, you need to consider speed, reliability, security, and scalability.

For sites that run on a single server, the InProc storage mode is the best. It is the fastest of the three modes, but it has its own limitations. The major problem is that it is volatile; the durability of the session state data is dependent on the lifetime of the Application domain that the application runs in. Once the Application domain restarts or shuts down, the session is lost. In a production environment (that is, an environment where the application has been successfully deployed), the InProc mode is not feasible.

When you are using web farms, the OutProc mode (meaning either the State Server mode or the SQL Server mode) is the best option, especially when traffic is heavy on the site. The SQL Server mode is best suited for when you need to secure the session data or when you require scalability and reliability, but it takes more time to store data to and retrieve it from the database table.

Configuring Session Timeout

The session timeout value is specified in the web.config file. It is a sliding expiration value and indicates the time (in minutes) that the session can be idle before it is abandoned. You can configure the session timeout value using the <sessionState> attribute in the application's web.config file. For example, you can increase the default session timeout value to your desired value using the following statement in the web.config file:

Listing 2-8
```
<sessionState timeout="40" />
```

The preceding statement doubles the session timeout value from the default value of 20 minutes to 40 minutes.

The session timeout information can be included with the mode and cookieless statements in the <sessionState> attribute of the application's web.config file:

```
<configuration>
 <sessionState  mode="Inproc" cookieless="false"  timeout="20"/>
</configuration>
```

The preceding statement indicates that the session storage mode is Inproc, indicating that the session state would be stored inside the ASP.NET worker process.

Another way to increase timeout time is to set a refresh in the meta tag as follows:

Listing 2-9
```
<meta http-equiv="refresh"
 content="600">
```

Storing, Retrieving, and Deleting Objects in the Session

In order to add objects to the session, use the HttpSessionState.Session.Add(name,value) method. The name and value of the item to be added are passed to the method as parameters. Note that the HttpSessionState class is located in the System.Web namespace in the System.Web.dll file.

Alternatively, you can add objects to the session as follows:

Listing 2-10
```
HttpSessionState.Session["UserName"] = "Joydip";
```

This automatically creates a new item called "UserName" in the session state collection (if none exists) and sets its value to "Joydip".

The following method is used to retrieve a previously stored object from the session state.

Listing 2-11
```
string userName = HttpSessionState.Session
["UserName"].ToString();
```

The ToString() method is called because data is stored in the session state as objects. Therefore, conversion or casting to the appropriate type is necessary to retrieve the current user's name as a string.

The following method removes an object from the session state.

Listing 2-12
```
HttpSessionState.Remove(objectName);
```

This method deletes the object specified in the parameter from the session state collection, provided it exists. In this case, if the session state collection does not contain the element specified, the collection remains unchanged, but no exception is thrown.

To clear the session, use one or the other of the following methods:

Listing 2-13
```
Session.Abandon();

data.Session.Clear();
```

Both methods clear session data, but there is a subtle difference between the two.

If you call Session.Abandon(), the Session_End event will be fired (for InProc mode) and in the next request, Session_Start will be fired. The Session_OnEnd event is invoked by the runtime environment when you make a call to the Session.Abandon() method or when the user's session times out.

NOTE *The Session_End event is supported only in the InProc mode and is fired internally by the web server, based on an internal timer. Thus, there is no HttpRequest when that happens. This is why the methods Response.Redirect or Server.Transfer do not work in the Session_End event.*

The Session.Clear() method just clears the session data without killing the session. Further, any change made to the settings in the web.config file unloads both the application domain and the session state. You can use the IsNewSession property of the HttpSessionState class to detect whether a session has timed out or was abandoned.

You can use the Session_End event to write log information when the session ends. Here is an example:

Listing 2-14
```
public void Session_End(object sender, EventArgs e)
{
    String userName = Session("userName");
    Logger logger = new Logger(Server.MapPath("logfile"), "SessionLog");
    logger.Write("Some data");
    if (userName != null) {
        MembershipUser user = Membership.GetUser(userName);
        user.LastActivityDate = DateTime.Now;
        Membership.Provider.UpdateUser(user);
    }
}
```

Enabling and Disabling Session State in ASP.NET

Session state in ASP.NET can be enabled and disabled both at the page and application levels.

Page-Level Session State You can disable session state for pages that do not require access to session data by using the EnableSessionState statement in the Page directive of a page, as follows:

Listing 2-15
```
<%@ Page EnableSessionState="False" %>
```

Session state for a page can also be set to read-only for pages that require access to the session data but do not need to modify it:

Listing 2-16
```
<%@ Page EnableSessionState="ReadOnly" %>
```

Application-Level Session State Session state can also be disabled for all the pages of an application by using the EnableSessionState attribute at the application level in the configuration section of the web.config file. Here's an example:

Listing 2-17
```
<configuration>
  <system.web>
   <pages enableSessionState="false" />
  </system.web>
</configuration>
```

It is also possible to set the session state to read-only for all pages in the application:

Listing 2-18
```
<configuration>
  <system.web>
    <pages enableSessionState=
"ReadOnly" />
  </system.web>
</configuration>
```

Performance and Security Considerations for the Session

In a distributed web server environment, the use of session variables can degrade performance. Storing basic types in session state is much faster than storing object types due to the serialization and deserialization overhead involved.

Never use a Response.Redirect or Server.Transfer method call after you set the session in the login page of your application. Both of these methods call the Response .End method internally, which stops execution of the page; the session ID would be lost. Use the FormsAuthentication.RedirectFromLoginPage method instead, or the following overloaded version of the Response.Redirect method:

Listing 2-19
```
Response.Redirect("~/menu.aspx", false);
```

This will not abort the current thread and will prevent the session ID from being lost.

Cache Object

Caching is a state management technique that can dramatically improve the performance of your application by storing frequently used but relatively stale data in main memory. This cached data can then be used to serve incoming requests, reducing network traffic, minimizing the use of server resources, and boosting the overall performance of the application. Serving cached data from memory is much faster than recreating or retrieving it from a database or other storage device.

Types of Caching

There are three types of caching in ASP.NET: page output caching, page fragment caching (also known as partial page caching), and data caching.

Page Output Caching   In page output caching, the entire page is cached in memory so subsequent requests for the same page are addressed from the cache itself. When a new request arrives, the runtime checks to see if the page being requested exists in the cache. If so, it is rendered from the cache directly; otherwise the page is rendered dynamically. Page output caching is particularly useful for pages that are static and thus do not change for a considerable period of time.

Note that in page output caching, a copy of the HTML response is saved in memory. All subsequent requests are served from the cache until the cache expires. This results in a considerable improvement in performance—the page is rendered much more quickly.

You can implement page output caching at design time using the OutputCache directive, or at runtime using the HttpPolicy class. The following code snippet illustrates the complete syntax of the page output caching directive:

Listing 2-20
```
<%@ OutputCache
Duration="no of seconds"
Location="Any | Client | Downstream | Server | None"
VaryByControl="control'
VaryByCustom="browser customstring"
VaryByHeader="headers"
VaryByParam="parameter" %>
```

The following statement implements output caching in an ASPX page at design time. The directive is placed at the top of the ASPX page.

Listing 2-21
```
<%@OutputCache Duration="30"
VaryByParam="none" %>
```

The duration parameter specifies how long the page will be cached. In listing 2-21, the cache duration is 30 seconds. Cache duration is a required field, and it must be set to an integer greater than 0.

The VaryByParam parameter, which is also required, specifies whether to cache different views of the page. It is particularly useful in situations where you need to cache a page based on certain criteria. A value of * in this parameter indicates that the page will be cached based on all the Get/Post parameters. You can also specify one or more Get/Post parameters, so the statement in listing 2-21 could have several variations.

For example, you might need to cache a specific page based on the EmployeeID:

Listing 2-22
```
<%@OutputCache Duration="30"
VaryByParam="*" Location = "Any"%>
<%@OutputCache Duration="30"
VaryByParam="EmployeeID"
Location = "Client" %>
<%@OutputCache Duration="30"
VaryByParam="EmployeeID;Basic" %>
```

The VaryByParam parameter can have multiple variations, as shown in the preceding listing. The location parameter is used to specify the cache location, either on the server or the client.

To set a page's cacheability programmatically, you have to use the Response.Cache .SetCacheability method. This method accepts a value of NoCache, Private, Public, or Server for its parameter. The following code snippet shows how to set a page's cacheability programmatically:

Listing 2-23
```
Response.Cache.SetCacheability
(HttpCacheability.Server);
```

Additionally you can set other properties that map to the same fields that are available when using the OutputCache directive on the page:

Listing 2-24
```
Response.Cache.SetExpires
(DateTime.Now.AddSeconds(30));
Response.Cache.SetValidUntilExpires(true);
Response.Cache.VaryByParams["EmployeeID"]= true;
```

Page Fragment or Partial Page Caching   Page fragment caching allows specific portions of the page to be cached rather than the whole page. This is useful when you have a page that contains both static and dynamic content. The following code depicts how this can be accomplished:

Listing 2-25
```
<%@ OutputCache Duration="15"
VaryByControl="EmpID;DeptID" VaryByParam="*"%>
```

This directive is placed at the top of any user control (.axcx file).

Data Caching   Data caching enables you to store relatively stale data in the cache for retrieval later so as to reduce the load on the server's resources. Here is an example of how to implement data caching:

Listing 2-26
```
public DataSet GetDataFromCache
(String cacheKey)
{
  String cacheKey = "EmployeeDetails";
  DataSet dataSet =
```

```
Cache[cacheKey] as DataSet;
  if (dataSet == null)
 {
   dataSet = GetEmployeeDetailsFromDatabase();
   Cache.Insert(cacheKey, dataSet,
null, NoAbsoluteExpiration,
   TimeSpan.FromHours(15),
CacheItemPriority.High, null);
}
return dataSet;
}
private DataSet
GetUserDetailsFromDatabase()
{
// Code that would retrieve
//employee records from the database,
//populate a DataSet instance with these
//records and then return the instance.
}
```

Once this is done, you can call the GetDataFromCache method, as follows:

Listing 2-27
```
DataSet employeeDataSet =
GetDataFromCache("Employees");
```

Cache Expirations

Cache expiration policies can be set to refresh the cache to keep it in sync with the data store (a database or an XML file). Cache expirations can be time-based, file-based, or key-based.

Time-Based Expiration   A time-based expiration specifies a specific period of time for which the page will remain in the cache. When the time elapses, the item is removed from the cache and subsequent requests to retrieve the item returns a null.

The following statement specifies a time-based expiration for a page in the code-behind of a file using C#:

Listing 2-28
```
Response.Cache.SetExpires
(DateTime.Now.AddSeconds(120));
```

This can also be accomplished in the output cache directive, as shown here:

Listing 2-29
```
<%@OutputCache Duration="60"
VaryByParam="None" %>
```

Time-based expiration strategies can be either absolute or sliding. The following code snippet illustrates how you can implement absolute expiration:

Listing 2-30
```
Cache.Insert("UserInfo", dsUserInfo, null,
DateTime.Now.AddMinutes(1), NoSlidingExpiration);
```

This next snippet illustrates how you can implement sliding expiration:

Listing 2-31
```
Cache.Insert("UserInfo",
dsUserInfo, null,
NoAbsoluteExpiration,
TimeSpan.FromSeconds(60));
```

Note that you cannot use both absolute and sliding expirations at the same time.

File-Based Expiration   File-based expiration is implemented by using a file as a dependency. Whenever the contents of the dependency file are changed, the cached information is invalidated. The following code snippet shows an example:

Listing 2-32
```
CacheDependency cacheDependency =
new CacheDependency
("EmployeeData.xml");
Cache.Insert("UserInfo",
xmldocumentObject,cacheDependency);
```

Key-Based Expiration   Cache dependency is a logical dependency between an item in the cache and a file or folder. When this dependency is broken, the cached item is removed from the cache.

Here's the syntax you would use to implement cache dependency in your application:

Listing 2-33
```
CacheDependency
cacheDependency = new CacheDependency(fileName, dateTime);
cache.Insert(key, value, cacheDependency);
```

With key-based expiration, you can use a key as a dependency. When the depended-upon entry changes or expires, the dependent entry will also expire. An array of keys can be specified as a single CacheDependency, as shown in the following listing:

Listing 2-34
```
string[] keys = new string[] {"E0001","E0002"};
CacheDependency cacheDependency = new CacheDependency(null,keys);
Cache.Insert("EmployeeData ", xmldocumentObject,cacheDependency);
```

You might want to cache only particular pages. To achieve this, you can hook up a callback that will be called when the time has come to return a cached version of your web page. To do this, you would use Response.Cache.AddValidationCallback as shown in the following code snippet:

Listing 2-35
```
public void Page_Load()
{
  Response.Cache.AddValidationCallback
(new HttpCacheValidateHandler
(CheckStatus), "Test");
}
```

```
public void CheckStatus(HttpContext context,
 Object data, ref HttpValidationStatus
 httpValidationStatus)
{
    if (context.Request.QueryString
["PageID"].Equals("UI001"))
        httpValidationStatus =
 HttpValidationStatus.IgnoreThisRequest;
    else
        httpValidationStatus =
HttpValidationStatus.Valid;
}
```

NOTE *The CacheDependency class was sealed in earlier versions of ASP.NET to prevent further inheritance. However, the ASP.NET Cache API provides the ability to create custom cache dependency classes that are inherited from the CacheDependency class.*

Client-Side State Management

In this section, we will take a look at the client-side state management techniques in ASP.NET. To manage state information on the client side, you can use ViewState, hidden fields, query strings, or cookies.

ViewState

ViewState is a state management technique that is used to maintain the state of an ASP.NET page as it moves back and forth. Note that ViewState does not hold the page's controls; rather, it holds the control IDs and their corresponding values that would otherwise have been lost due to a postback to the web server. In essence, ViewState represents the state of a page when it was last processed on the web server.

ViewState is a property of all server controls, and it is stored as a key-value pair using the System.Web.UI.StateBag object. ViewState works with primitive types, arrays of primitive types, array lists, hash tables, and any serializable objects. You can store any serializable object in the ViewState or any object for which a type converter is defined.

When the page is first created, all controls are serialized to the ViewState, which is rendered as a hidden form field named __ViewState. This hidden field corresponds to the server-side object known as the ViewState. When a postback occurs, the page deserializes the ViewState and recreates all controls. The ViewState for the controls in a page is stored as base-64 encoded hashed strings in name-value pairs. When a page is reloaded, two methods pertaining to ViewState are called: the LoadViewState method and the SaveViewState method.

Enabling and Disabling ViewState

ViewState is enabled for all server controls by default, but you can enable and disable it at the page, control, application, and machine levels.

To enable or disable ViewState at the page level, include one of the following lines in the Page directive of the ASP.NET page:

Listing 2-36
```
<%@ Page EnableViewState ="False" %>
<%@ Page EnableViewState ="True" %>
```

To enable or disable ViewState at the control level, use one or the other of the following statements:

Listing 2-37
```
<asp:TextBox id="txtEmployeeName"
 runat="server" EnableViewState="false" />
<asp:TextBox id="txtEmployeeName"
runat="server" EnableViewState="true" />
```

To enable or disable ViewState at the application level, use one or the other of the following lines:

Listing 2-38
```
<pages enableViewState="false" />
<pages enableViewState="true" />
```

To enable or disable ViewState at the machine level, use one or the other of the following lines:

Listing 2-39
```
<pages enableViewState="true" enableViewStateMac="true" ... />
<pages enableViewState="false" ... />
```

Storing Values to and Retrieving Them from the ViewState

The following code snippet illustrates how you can store an ArrayList instance to the ViewState:

Listing 2-40
```
ArrayList arrList = new ArrayList();
arrList.Add("Kolkata");
arrList.Add("Delhi");
arrList.Add("Chennai");
arrList.Add("Mumbai");
ViewState["Cities"] = arrList;
```

To retrieve this ArrayList instance of cities, you could use the following code:

Listing 2-41
```
ArrayList arrList = (ArrayList)ViewState["Cities"];
```

Performance and Security Considerations for ViewState

Using ViewState is a good choice if you want to store a small amount of data for a page that will postback to itself. However, using ViewState, you should be aware of the performance impact of its usage—if your ViewState data is large, the application will be slow. Remember that the ViewState data makes a round trip and incurs more network bandwidth usage. You should optimize the ViewState size prior to deploying your application to yield better response times and improved performance.

To start, you should disable ViewState for the page that doesn't require it. To do this, you need to set the EnableViewState property for the page or for a particular control on the page to false. As we have already discussed, you can also disable ViewState at the application and machine levels.

Note that controls contained inside the <form runat=server> tag in the ASPX page can use ViewState. Consider a page that has a size of 10KB with ViewState enabled for some or all of its controls. If you disable ViewState for the entire page, the rendered page size will not be reduced by 10KB. Even if you disable ViewState for a page, the page still stores 20 bytes of information in ViewState. If the page doesn't need a postback at all, you can get rid of this by removing the runat="server" tag completely from the <form> tag. In doing so, the size of your page will be reduced by 20 bytes, which can be substantial if the application has a number of such pages running over the network.

To ensure that the ViewState remains secure and is not tampered with, you can adopt one of the following measures:

- Use the EnableViewStateMac property
- Encrypt the ViewState content

The EnableViewStateMac property ensures a machine authentication check is performed. This property should be set at the page level or in the application's web.config file. When set, it appends a hash code to the ViewState before rendering it. Whenever a postback occurs, this hash code is recalculated and checked against the one that is stored in the __ViewState hidden field of the form. If they do not match, the page is rejected, thus ensuring that the ViewState is not tampered with.

TIP *There is a ViewState error that is often encountered when transferring the control from one ASPX page to another. Suppose there are two ASPX pages: first.aspx, which has a text box and a submit button, and second.aspx. If you use Server.Transfer in the handler for the submit button click event in the first.aspx page to transfer control to the second .aspx page, a ViewState error will occur. This is because the EnableViewStateMac property of the second.aspx page is set to true by default, just as it is in all ASPX pages. This problem can be overcome by setting the EnableViewStateMac property to false in the second.aspx page.*

To encrypt the contents of the ViewState, use the following line in the machine. config file:

Listing 2-42 `<machineKey validation="3Des" /> or <machineKey validation="SHA1"/>`

You can also store the ViewState data in a persistent medium like a database or file for better security. To do this, use the virtual methods provided by the Page class in ASP.NET:

Listing 2-43
```
protected virtual void
SavePageStateToPersistenceMedium
(object viewState);
protected virtual object
LoadPageStateFromPersistenceMedium();
```

You can override these methods and write your own custom code to persist and depersist your ViewState data. Here is how you can override the SavePageStateToPersistenceMedium method to save your ViewState data into a persistent storage location:

Listing 2-44
```
protected override
SavePageStateToPersistenceMedium (object ViewState)
{
  StringBuilder stringBuilder
 = new StringBuilder ();
  StringWriter stringWriter =
 new StringWriter (stringBuilder);
  LosFormatter formatter =
 new LosFormatter ();
  formatter.Serialize
 (stringWriter, viewState);
  stringWriter.Close ();
  //Write code here to
  //persist the ViewState data
}
```

To depersist your ViewState data, you can override the LoadPageStateFromPersistenceMedium method, as follows:

Listing 2-45
```
protected override object
LoadPageStateFromPersistenceMedium()
{
  Object viewStateObject;
  //Write code here to read the
  //ViewState data previously saved in a
  //database or any other persistent medium
  LosFormatter formatter =
 new LosFormatter();
  try
  {
    viewStateObject = formatter.Deserialize (strViewState);
  }
  catch
```

```
    {
       throw new HttpException
    ("Error in retrieving ViewState data");
    }
    return viewStateObject;
}
```

Hidden Fields

You can maintain state information using hidden fields in ASP.NET. The HtmlInputHidden control in ASP.NET is used to create hidden fields and store values in them.

Here is how you can use this control declaratively:

Listing 2-46
```
<asp:hiddenfield id="hiddenControl"
  value="Joydip" runat="server"/>
```

And here is how you can use this control programmatically:

Listing 2-47
```
System.Web.UI.HtmlControls.HtmlInputHidden
  hiddenControl;
hiddenControl.Value="Joydip";
//Store a string value in the hidden control
String strControlValue=hiddenControl.Value;
// Retrieve the stored string value
```

Query Strings

A query string is string data that is appended at the end of a URL. You can use query strings to pass data from one ASP.NET page to another, so you can use query strings to store state information too. However, most browsers impose a 255-character limit, which means the length of the query string cannot exceed 255 characters. Further, data passed through query strings is not secure. But when you want to transfer a small amount of data from one ASP.NET page to another, and security is not an issue, a query string is a good choice.

Query strings are typically used to store nonsensitive and nonconfidential data like page numbers, search data, and the like. A query string is composed of a series of field-value pairs, like these:

Listing 2-48
```
id=1&firstname=Joydip&lastname=Kanjilal&address=Hyderabad
```

Suppose you have the following query string: "http://localhost/employee.aspx?id=12&name=joydip". You could retrieve data from this query string as follows:

Listing 2-49
```
String employeeID=Request.Params["id"];
String employeeName=Request.Params["name"];
```

You should check whether the query string is null or it contains data in order to avoid runtime exceptions. Here is an example:

Listing 2-50

```
if (!String.IsNullOrEmpty
(Request.QueryString["id"]))
{
  //Some code
}
if (!String.IsNullOrEmpty
(Request.QueryString["name"]))
{
  //Some code
}
```

Cookies

Cookies are used as a client-side state management technique. A cookie is a text file stored on the client side that the browser uses to store textual messages. These files store data as name-value pairs separated by the equals sign (=). They are stored in the Cookies directory on your system with names like user@domain.

There are two types of cookies in ASP.NET: temporary cookies and permanent cookies.

A temporary (or transient or session) cookie is alive in main memory for as long as the user's session is alive. It expires as soon as the user's session terminates or the web browser is closed.

A permanent cookie is stored in a physical location on the client system, and its durability depends on the expiration date and time set. A permanent cookie is deleted automatically when its expiration date is reached or when it is deleted by the user from its physical location. Note that you don't set the expiration policy for a cookie; it is created in the memory of the user's system and remains alive for as long as the user's session is alive.

Programming Cookies Using the System.Web Namespace

For working with cookies, the System.Web namespace provides the HttpCookie, HttpResponse, and HttpRequest classes.

The HttpCookie class provides a type-safe way to work with the HTTP cookies. It provides overloaded constructors for creating cookies. Here is an example that illustrates how you can work with cookies in ASP.NET:

Listing 2-51

```
HttpCookie objectName =
new HttpCookie("EmployeeName");
HttpCookie objectName =
new HttpCookie("EmployeeName",
 "Joydip Kanjilal");
```

You can use the HttpCookieCollection class in the System.Web namespace to manipulate a collection of cookies. Here is an example:

Listing 2-52
```
HttpCookieCollection httpCookieCollection;
HttpCookie httpCookie;
httpCookie = Request.Cookies;
string[] cookieCollection =
httpCookieCollection.AllKeys;
for (int i=0, j =
cookieCollection.Length;
 i < j; i++)
{
httpCookie = httpCookieCollection
[cookieCcllection[i]];
Response.Write("Name: "+
httpCookie.Name +
 " , " + " Value: "+
httpCookie.Value);
}
```

Creating, Reading, and Deleting Cookies Using the Request and Response Objects   To create a cookie, you can use the Response object, as follows:

Listing 2-53
```
Response.Cookies["Name"].Value = "Joydip";
```

You can specify the duration for which the cookie will be alive like this:

Listing 2-54
```
Response.Cookies["Name"].Expires = DateTime.Now.AddDays(1);
```

You can also add multiple key-value pairs in a single cookie with the following code:

Listing 2-55
```
Response.Cookies["Employee"]["FirstName"] = "Joydip";
Response.Cookies["Employee"]["LastName"] = "Kanjilal";
```

To read a cookie, you can use the following code:

Listing 2-56
```
String employeeName;
if(Request.Cookies["Name"] != null)
    employeeName = Request.Cookies["Name"].Value;
```

To delete a cookie, you can just set the expiration time to a value that precedes the current date and time. Here is an example:

Listing 2-57
```
if (Request.Cookies["Name"] != null)
{
    Response.Cookies["Name"].Expires =
        DateTime.Now.AddDays(-1);
}
```

Cookies and Scope By default, all pages of the site get access to the cookies for that site. You can also specify the scope for a cookie in two ways: limiting the scope of a cookie to a particular folder in the web server, and limiting the scope of the cookie to a particular domain.

To limit the cookies to a particular folder on the server, you can use the following code:

Listing 2-58
```
HttpCookie httpCookie =
new HttpCookie("MyCookie");
httpCookie.Value = DateTime.Now.ToString();
httpCookie.Expires = DateTime.Now.AddDays(5);
httpCookie.Path = "/MyApplicationFolder";
Response.Cookies.Add(httpCookie);
```

By default, any cookie is associated with a particular domain. To scope a cookie to a particular subdomain, just set the domain property of the cookie as shown in this example:

Listing 2-59
```
Response.Cookies("myAppDomain").Value =
  DateTime.Now.ToString();
Response.Cookies("MyAppDomain").Expires =
  DateTime.Now.AddDays(1);
Response.Cookies("MyAppDomain").Domain =
  "support.www.mc-grawhill.com";
```

If you want your cookie to be shared across all subdomains, you can use the following code instead:

Listing 2-60
```
Response.Cookies("myAppDomain").Value =
  DateTime.Now.ToString();
Response.Cookies("MyAppDomain").Expires =
  DateTime.Now.AddDays(1);
Response.Cookies("MyAppDomain").Domain =
  "www.mc-grawhill.com";
```

Performance and Security Considerations for Cookies

Most browsers have a 4KB limitation on the size of cookies. There are also some browsers that allow only 20 cookies per site, and delete older ones once you pass this limit.

Because cookies are stored as text files on the client system, they are not reliable for storing sensitive data. Nonpersistent cookies are useful when working on a public computer where you would not want cookie information to be persisted for security reasons. But for storing sensitive data, it is always preferable to use databases or Secure Socket Layer (SSL) to pass the cookie data. Moreover, cookie files can be easily viewed, edited, or deleted by the user.

You should also be aware that cookies can be disabled in the web browser. To determine whether cookies have been disabled at the browser, you can use the following piece of code:

Listing 2-61
```
if(Request.Browser.Cookies == true)
{
  //Cookies are enabled at the browser level
}
else
{
  //Cookies have been disabled at the browser level
}
```

So what should you use cookies for? Typically they are best used to store a small amount of user data where security is not an issue.

New State-Management Techniques in ASP.NET 4.0

The most important state-management features added to ASP.NET 4.0 include support for a diverse type of cache storage, and support for extensible output caching and output cache substitution. Output caching is a feature that enables pages and controls to reside in memory so that all subsequent requests for those pages and controls can be fetched from the cache rather than from disk. This boosts the performance of the application as a whole.

Cache Storage

The new, extensible, flexible Object Cache API supports both client and server applications—you don't need to include System.Web.dll in your Winforms projects. The new API provides a consistent programming model to use the following types of cache storages:

- Disk-based output caches
- Custom object caches
- Distributed object caches
- Cloud-based object caches

Extensible Output Caching

ASP.NET 4.0 provides support for extensible output caching. You can now configure one or more custom output-cache providers, which are APIs that can persist pages and controls using any storage mechanism, including local or remote disks, or even distributed cache engines. Moreover, you can use this new output caching strategy to implement distributed caching efficiently.

To create a custom output cache provider, you need to create a class that extends the System.Web.Caching.OutputCacheProvider class. Next, you need to specify the configuration details in your application's web.config file, as shown in the following code snippet:

Listing 2-62
```
<caching>
  <outputCache defaultProvider=
"AspNetInternalProvider">
    <providers>
      <add name="MyCustomDiskCache"
          type="McGrawHill.OutputCacheEx.
          MyCustomCacheProvider,
          MyCustomCacheProvider"/>
    </providers>
  </outputCache>
</caching>
```

Then, you can specify the output cache providers declaratively in your ASP.NET web page, like this:

Listing 2-63
```
<%@ OutputCache Duration="30"
VaryByParam="None"
providerName="MyCustomDiskCache" %>
```

Note that in ASP.NET 4.0, all HTTP responses, rendered pages, and controls use the in-memory output cache. The default provider is set to AspNetInternalProvider, but you can change this to the output cache provider you want use for the application by specifying a different provider in the defaultProvider attribute.

You can programmatically retrieve the custom provider name by overriding the GetOutputCacheProviderName method as follows:

Listing 2-64
```
public override string
GetOutputCacheProviderName
(HttpContext context)
{
    if (context.Request.Path.EndsWith
("Welcome.aspx"))
        return " MyCustomDiskCache ";
    else
        return
base.GetOutputCacheProviderName
(context);
}
```

There is also a new compression technique for out-of-process session state providers in ASP.NET 4.0—a great feature indeed! Here is how you can use it in your application's web.config file:

Listing 2-65
```
<sessionState
    mode="SqlServer"
    sqlConnectionString="data source=
localhost;

Initial Catalog=aspnetstate"
    allowCustomSqlDatabase="true"
    compressionEnabled="true"
/>
```

Cache Invalidation and Output Cache Substitution

With the newly introduced automatic database server cache invalidation technique, you can ensure that the data in the cache is in sync with the database automatically. Unlike previous versions of ASP.NET, where you had to invalidate an item in the cache based on a certain set of dependencies, this new feature enables you to invalidate an item in the cache automatically when the data in the database changes.

Output cache substitution is another great new feature that has been added in the newer versions of ASP.NET. You no longer need to split your pages into multiple .ascx user control files to implement page fragment caching or partial page caching. You can use output cache substitution to cache the output of a web page that contains dynamic portions.

The following code snippet illustrates how you can implement output cache substitution using the <asp:Substitution> control:

Listing 2-66
```
<asp:Substitution ID=
"mySubstitutionBlock"
 runat="server"
MethodName="myMethod" />
```

CHAPTER 3

Working with ADO.NET

Microsoft introduced ADO (ActiveX Data Objects), a data-access technology for connecting to databases, in 1996. ADO.NET is an extension of ADO, and it enables you to connect to and work with databases from within the managed environment of .NET.

ADO is an object-oriented data-access technology that supports both connected and disconnected modes of operation. You can use ADO.NET to perform CRUD (create, read, update, and delete) operations in your application. ADO.NET also provides support for XML data access and it has a rich object model.

ADO.NET Architecture Components

In this section we will take a look at the major components of the ADO.NET architecture.

DataSet

ADO.NET can work both in connected and disconnected modes. The DataSet is the core component of the disconnected architecture of ADO.NET. It is an in-memory representation of a database, providing a consistent relational programming model irrespective of the source of the data, which has been read into it. The DataSet contains one or more tables, in addition to their relationship and constraints information. DataSets can be either typed or untyped. You can use a DataSet to cache data locally, and track changes to your data.

The following code snippet shows how you can create an instance of a DataSet.

Listing 3-1
```
DataSet customers = new DataSet("Customers");
```

DataTable

A DataTable is used to represent a table in the database. It consists of a collection of rows and columns. You can add the required columns to the DataTable by using the Columns collection.

The following code snippet shows how you can work with a DataTable:

Listing 3-2
```
DataSet customerDataSet = new DataSet("Test");
DataTable customerDataTable =
customerDataSet.Tables.Add("Customer");
customerDataTable.Columns.Add("CustomerID",
typeof(System.Guid));
customerDataTable.Columns.Add("Name", typeof(string));
customerDataTable.Columns.Add("Address", typeof(string));
customerDataTable.Columns.Add("City", typeof(string));
customerDataTable.Columns.Add("PostalCode", typeof(string));
DataRow customerRow = customerDataTable.NewRow();
customerRow["CustomerID"] = System.Guid.NewGuid();
customerRow["Name"] = "Peter Smith";
customerRow["Address"] = "56 Stafford Road";
customerRow["City"] = "London";
customerRow["PostalCode"] = "76809";
customerDataTable.Rows.Add(customerRow);
```

DataView

A DataView provides a customized view of a DataTable. You can use it to sort or filter the rows of a DataSet.

Here is a code snippet that illustrates how you can use a DataView:

Listing 3-3
```
DataView dataView = dataSet.Tables["employee"].DefaultView;
dataView.RowFilter = "city like 'Hyderabad%'";
dataView.Sort = "basic ASC";
```

Data Provider

A data provider provides access to the database. Note that there are different data providers for specific databases. ADO.NET supports Oracle, SQL Server, OLE DB, and ODBC data providers. In essence, a data provider encapsulates the protocols that are needed to make connection, and perform CRUD operations with various databases.

The ADO.NET data provider classes include Connection, Command, DataReader, and DataAdapter.

Connection Object

The Connection object is used to establish a connection to the database. You can use the OleDbConnection, OdbcConnection, OracleConnection, and SqlConnection connection objects in ADO.NET, depending on the underlying database in use.

Command Object

The Command object is used to send SQL statements to the database in order to execute CRUD operations. Commands are used to insert data, retrieve data, and execute stored procedures and other database objects. Depending on the underlying database in use, you can use the OracleCommand, SqlCommand, OleDbCommand, and OdbcCommand objects in ADO.NET.

The Command object makes use of the ExecuteScalar, ExecuteReader, ExecuteNonQuery, and ExecuteXmlReader methods to send and execute the SQL statements.

- ExecuteScalar returns a single value from a query.
- ExecuteReader returns a collection of rows and columns as a resultset.
- ExecuteNonQuery performs inserts, updates, and deletes of data, and returns an integer representing the number of rows affected by the operation.
- ExecuteXmlReader returns an XmlReader object as a resultset of a query.

DataReader

A DataReader is a connected, forward-only, read-only stream of data that is used to read a sequential collection of records from a database. It is much faster than a DataSet but requires an open connection. Based on the type of underlying database in use, you can use the OracleDataReader, SqlDataReader, OleDbDataReader, and OdbcDataReader classes in ADO.NET.

DataAdapter

The DataAdapter is used in the disconnected mode of data access. It acts as a bridge between the database and a DataSet and is used to populate a DataSet with data from the underlying database.

The DataAdapter provides two methods: Fill and Update. The Fill method populates a DataSet instance with data from the database. The Update method is used to update the database with data contained in a DataSet. You can use the Update method of the DataAdapter class to commit changes back to the database.

The DataAdapter provides the SelectCommand, InsertCommand, UpdateCommand, and DeleteCommand command objects to perform CRUD operations.

Connected and Disconnected Modes in ADO.NET

You can work with ADO.NET in either the connected or disconnected mode. What connected or disconnected modes? What is the connection to? Well, a connected mode implies that the connection to the database is open. A typical example of a connected mode of operation in ADO.NET is using the DataReader—when you use a DataReader to read data from the database, the connection remains open unless you explicitly close the connection to the underlying database. In contrast to this, when you work with DataSets and DataAdapters, you're actually working in a disconnected mode—the DataAdapter populates the DataSet using its Fill() method and then closes the connection to the database. In other words, in the disconnected mode, the connection to the database is closed once the data has been retrieved or a specific operation has been performed.

NOTE *To compile and execute the examples given in this chapter, you will need to include the System.Data.SqlClient namespace in the examples.*

Working in the Connected Mode

When you work with ADO.NET in the connected mode, you follow these steps:

1. Create a connection.
2. Open the connection.
3. Create a Command object.
4. Execute SQL statements.
5. Close the connection.

Creating the Connection

To create a connection to the database, you need to use the connection class appropriate for the underlying database. You also need a connection string that contains the database credentials of the database you are connecting to.

Here's an example of how to create a connection to a SQL Server database:

Listing 3-4
```
SqlConnection sqlConnection = new SqlConnection();
sqlConnection.ConnectionString = "Data Source=.;
Initial Catalog=Employee;User ID=sa;Password=sa;
providerName=System.Data.SqlClient";
```

> **NOTE** *You need to use the appropriate provider based on the database you are using. If the database is SQLServer, you should use SqlConnection. Similarly, you need to use OracleConnection to connect to Oracle databases, OdbcConnection to connect to databases via the Odbc protocol, etc.*

Opening the Connection

To open the connection created in the preceding section, you need to call the Open method on the connection instance, as follows:

Listing 3-5
```
sqlConnection.Open();
```

Creating the Command

To create the Command object, use the class that corresponds to the database you are using. Hence, if you are using SQL Server as the database, you should use the SqlCommand class:

Listing 3-6
```
SqlCommand sqlCommand = new SqlCommand();
```

Executing Queries

To execute queries using the Command object, call the appropriate Command object method. Here is an example:

Listing 3-7
```
sqlCommand.CommandText =
"Select EmployeeID, EmployeeName from Employee";
sqlCommand.Connection = sqlConnection;
sqlCommand.ExecuteQuery();
```

Note that the ExecuteQuery method returns a DataReader instance.

Closing the Connection

Once you're done, you should close the connection to the database using the Close method on the connection instance, like this:

Listing 3-8
```
sqlConnection.Close();
```

Inserting, Updating, and Deleting Data

In the connected mode of operation, the connection to the database remains open. To perform create, update, or delete operations, you need to use the ExecuteQuery method on the Command object.

The following example shows how you can insert a record into the Employee table.

Listing 3-9
```
using System;
using System.Data.SqlClient;
using System.Data;
class Program
{
    static void Main(string[] args)
    {
      SqlConnection sqlConnection = new SqlConnection();
      SqlCommand sqlCommand = new SqlCommand();
      sqlConnection.ConnectionString =
      "Data Source=.;Initial Catalog=Employee;
      UserID=sa;Password=sa;
      providerName=System.Data.SqlClient";

      try
      {
          sqlConnection.Open();
          sqlCommand.CommandText = "Insert into Employee
              (EmployeeID, EmpName, EmpAddress, EmpPhone) values
              (1, 'Joydip Kanjilal', 'Hyderabad','1234567890')";
          sqlCommand.Connection = sqlConnection;
          sqlCommand.ExecuteQuery();
      }
      catch (Exception ex)
      {
      //Write your exception handling code here
      }
      finally
      {
          sqlConnection.Close();
      }
    }
}
```

To update an employee record, you would use the Update statement, as follows:

Listing 3-10
```
sqlCommand.CommandText =
"Update Employee Set EmpName =
'Joydip', EmpAddress = 'Kolkata'
Where EmployeeID = 1";
```

Similarly, you would use the SQL Delete statement to delete an employee record.

Listing 3-11
```
sqlCommand.CommandText = "Delete From Employee
Where EmployeeID = 1";
```

Working in the Disconnected Mode

To work in disconnected mode, you need a DataAdapter and DataSets.

The following code listing shows how you can use a DataAdapter to connect to the database and fetch data into a DataSet:

Listing 3-12

```
using System;
using System.Data.SqlClient;
using System.Data;
class Program
{
    static void Main(string[] args)
    {
      SqlConnection sqlConnection = new SqlConnection();
      SqlDataAdapter sqlDataAdapter = null;

       try
       {
       sqlConnection.ConnectionString =
       "Data Source=.;Initial Catalog=Employee;
       UserID=sa;Password=sa;
       providerName=System.Data.SqlClient";
       sqlConnection.Open();
       sqlDataAdapter = new SqlDataAdapter
        ("Select EmployeeID, EmployeeName from Employee", sqlConnection);
        DataSet dataSet = new DataSet();
        sqlDataAdapter.Fill(dataSet);
       }
        catch (Exception ex)
        {
         //Write your error handling code here
        }
        finally
        {
         sqlConnection.Close();
        }
    }
}
```

Using Stored Procedures in ADO.NET

A stored procedure is a set of T-SQL statements stored in a database with a specified name. They are typically used to group and store reusable T-SQL statements for later use.

Here is how you can create a stored procedure:

Listing 3-13

```
Create Procedure ListAllEmployees
as
Select * from Employee
Go
```

You can later execute this stored procedure as follows:

Listing 3-14
```
exec ListAllEmployees
```

The following code snippet illustrates how you can use stored procedures with ADO.NET programmatically:

Listing 3-15
```
using System;
using System.Data.SqlClient;
using System.Data;
class Program
{
    static void Main(string[] args)
    {
      SqlConnection sqlConnection = new SqlConnection();
      try
      {
      sqlConnection.ConnectionString =
      "Data Source=.;Initial Catalog=Employee;
      UserID=sa;Password=sa; providerName=System.Data.SqlClient";
      sqlConnection.Open();
      SqlCommand sqlCommand = new SqlCommand();
      sqlCommand.Connection = sqlConnection;
      sqlCommand.CommandText = "Employee_Insert";
      sqlCommand.CommandType = CommandType.StoredProcedure;
      sqlCommand.Parameters.Add("@EmpName","Joydip Kanjilal");
      sqlCommand.Parameters.Add("@EmpAddesss","Hyderabad");
      int NumOfRecordsinsertedUpdated=
      sqlCommand.ExecuteNonQuery();
      }
      catch (Exception ex)
      {
        //Usual code
      }
      finally
      {
        sqlConnection.Close();
      }
    }
}
```

Refer to the code listing above. Note that you need to specify the stored procedure name using the CommandText property of the command object. Also, you should specify the command type using the CommandType property of the command object and, in this case, set it to CommandType.StoredProcedure. To pass parameters to your stored procedure, you need to use the Add() method of the Parameters collection. The ExecuteNonQuery() method that is called on the command object to execute the stored procedure returns the number of rows that have been affected. If the call to the stored procedure fails, it would return -1.

Transaction Handling in ADO.NET

A transaction is a block of statements that will either be executed as a whole or not executed at all. In essence, it guarantees that all or none of the statements in the block are executed.

To work with transactions in ADO.NET, follow these simple steps:

1. Create a connection.
2. Open the connection.
3. Create a transaction instance.
4. Start the transaction.
5. Execute the SQL statements.
6. Commit the transaction or roll back the transaction.
7. Close the connection.

To start a transaction, you need to call the BeginTransaction() method on the active connection instance. This method returns a transaction instance. You can commit the transaction using the Commit() method, or roll back your changes using the Rollback() method on the transaction instance. In short, to work with transactions, you need to invoke the BeginTransaction() method of the appropriate database connection instance, execute your T-SQL statements, and then call either the Commit() or Rollback() method on the returned transaction object reference, depending on the circumstances.

Here is a code listing that illustrates how you can perform a transactional insert into two database tables simultaneously:

Listing 3-16

```
using System;
using System.Data.SqlClient;
using System.Data;
class Program
{
    static void Main(string[] args)
    {
        SqlConnection sqlConnection = new SqlConnection();
        sqlConnection.ConnectionString =
        sqlConnection.ConnectionString =
"Data Source=.;Initial Catalog=Employee;
    User ID=sa;Password=sa; providerName=System.Data.SqlClient";
        SqlCommand sqlCommand = new SqlCommand();
        try
          {
            sqlConnection.Open();
            SqlTransaction sqlTransaction = null;
             sqlTransaction = sqlConnection.BeginTransaction();
            sqlCommand.Transaction = sqlTransaction;
            sqlCommand.CommandText = "Insert into Sales
```

```
    (SalesID, ItemCode, Quantity, Amount)
     values (12,100, 15000.00)";
  sqlCommand.Connection = sqlConnection;
  sqlCommand.ExecuteNonQuery();
  sqlCommand.CommandText =
  "Update Stock Set Quantity =
  Quantity - 100";
  sqlCommand.CommandText += " where ItemCode = 12";
  sqlCommand.Connection = sqlConnection;
  sqlCommand.ExecuteNonQuery();
  sqlTransaction.Commit();
  }
catch (Exception e)
{
  sqlTransaction.Rollback();
}
finally
{
  sqlConnection.Close();
}
    }
}
```

You can also use the Using statement to manage your resources efficiently. The Using statement defines a scope. Objects that fall inside this scope are disposed once the control comes out of this scope, or throw an exception. Here is an updated version of the previous listing that uses the Using statement.

Listing 3-17

```
using System;
using System.Data.SqlClient;
using System.Data;
class Program
{
    static void Main(string[] args)
    {
      String connectionString = "Data Source=.;Initial
Catalog=Employee;
      User ID=sa;Password=sa; providerName=System.Data.SqlClient";
      using (SqlConnection sqlConnection =
      new SqlConnection(connectionString))
  {
          SqlCommand sqlCommand = connection.CreateCommand();
          SqlTransaction sqlTransaction = null;
          try
          {
          sqlConnection.Open();
          sqlTransaction = sqlConnection.BeginTransaction();
          sqlCommand.Transaction = transaction;
          sqlCommand.CommandText = "Insert into Sales ";
          sqlCommand.CommandText +=
```

```
                " (SalesID, ItemCode, Quantity, Amount) ";
                sqlCommand.CommandText += " values (12,100, 15000.00)";
                sqlCommand.Connection = sqlConnection;
                sqlCommand.ExecuteNonQuery();
                sqlCommand.CommandText =
                "Update Stock Set Quantity
= Quantity - 100";
            sqlCommand.CommandText += " where ItemCode = 12";
            sqlCommand.Connection = sqlConnection;
                sqlCommand.ExecuteNonQuery();
                sqlTransaction.Commit();
              }
              catch(Exception ex)
              {
                sqlTransaction.Rollback();
              }
          }
      }
}
```

NOTE *The Using statement would degenerate into a "try-finally" combination. In other words, the Using statement is a short form of "try-finally" blocks. Also, the Using statement can only be used on disposable resources, i.e., on objects of classes that implement the IDisposable interface.*

Note that you should assign the SqlTransaction object returned by the BeginTransaction() method to the Transaction property of the Command object. Otherwise, an InvalidOperationException will be thrown when executing the transaction.

Concurrency Handling in ADO.NET

The ability of ADO.NET to work in both connected and disconnected modes is truly remarkable, but it poses a serious threat for data concurrency. Concurrency handling is a technique that enables you to resolve conflicts that can arise out of concurrent access to the same resource. Note that there are two main approaches to handling concurrency conflicts in ADO.NET, namely, optimistic and pessimistic.

In the pessimistic model, it is assumed that a conflict can occur when a read operation is about to be performed, so locks are imposed on the data or table being read to ensure that other users cannot access the data while an operation is being performed. In the optimistic mode, it is assumed that a request can modify the data that is being read by another request. You can use row-level versioning to avoid any concurrency conflicts that can arise here.

NOTE *SQL Server follows the pessimistic model, and the ADO.NET architecture follows the optimistic concurrency model.*

You can check for concurrency violations by using a TimeStamp column in your database table. When there are concurrent accesses to the same record, you can then check whether the value in the TimeStamp column in your database has changed from the time it was last read in the memory.

Here is an example that illustrates how you can check for concurrency violations in an Update statement:

Listing 3-18
```
UPDATE Employee SET FirstName=?, LastName=?
WHERE ((EmployeeID=?) AND
(ConcurrencyCheck = ?));
```

The ConcurrencyCheck column in this example is of type TimeStamp.

Advanced Features in ADO.NET

There have been a lot of advancements in ADO.NET over the years. These include the following:

- TransactionScope class
- DataTable class enhancements
- Optimized DataSet serialization
- Conversion of a DataReader to a DataSet or DataTable, and vice versa
- Data paging
- Batch updates
- Asynchronous data access
- The Common provider model
- Bulk copying
- Entity Framework

TransactionScope

The TransactionScope class in the System.Transactions namespace can be used to execute a batch of SQL statements. You can also create and manage distributed transactions using the TransactionScope class.

Note that if you use TransactionScope, you need not commit or roll back the transaction instance manually—this makes your transaction-handling code much simpler.

The following piece of code illustrates how you can use the TransactionScope class to perform transactional operations using ADO.NET:

Listing 3-19
```
bool IsConsistent = false;
String connectionString =
"Data Source=.;Initial Catalog=Employee;
```

```
User ID=sa;Password=sa;
providerName=System.Data.SqlClient";
using (System.Transactions.TransactionScope
transactionScope =
new System.Transactions.TransactionScope())
{
    SqlConnection sqlConnection = new SqlConnection(connectionString);
    SqlCommand sqlCommand;
    sqlConnection.Open();
    try
    {
        sqlCommand = new SqlCommand
("Delete from Department where
DeptCode = 1", sqlConnection);
        sqlCommand.ExecuteNonQuery();
        sqlCommand = new SqlCommand
("Delete from Employee where DeptCode = 1",
 sqlConnection);
        sqlCommand.ExecuteNonQuery();
        IsConsistent = true;
    }
    catch (SqlException ex)
    {
        //Write your error handling code here
    }
    sqlConnection.Close();
}
```

Note the use of the Using statement in the preceding code for automatically disposing of objects when they are not in use. You can use the Using statement only for objects that implement the IDisposable interface.

Optimized DataSet Serialization

Dataset serialization is a feature that enables you to serialize an instance of DataSet to pass it across the wire. Serialization may be defined as the process of converting an in-memory object into a serial stream of bytes to enable the stream to be passed or transported. Serialized objects can be persisted in a persistent storage media (such as a file or database). In ADO.NET 1.x, the support for serialization was restricted to XML only. This had performance drawbacks due to an overhead of large serialized data. However, in ADO.NET 2.0 and later, support for serialization has been improved to a great extent. Now, you can use the RemotingFormat property of the DataSet class to support binary serialization. You can use this property to specify that the data to be serialized is to be stored directly in a binary format.

This is shown in the following code example.

Listing 3-20
```
BinaryFormatter binaryFormatter = new BinaryFormatter();
FileStream fileStream = new FileStream
("c:\\employee.dat", FileMode.CreateNew);
DataSet empDataSet = GetEmployeeDataSet();
 //This is a custom method that creates,
//populates, and then returns a DataSet instance.
empDataSet.RemotingFormat = SerializationFormat.Binary;
//Serialize the employee Data Set
//instance as binary. In order to serialize the
//same instance as XML, specify the Serialization format as
//SerializationFormat.XML
binaryFormatter.Serialize(fileStream,empDataSet);
fileStream.Close();
```

Conversion of a DataReader to a DataSet or DataTable, and vice versa

You can load a DataReader object into a DataSet or a DataTable and vice versa. It should be noted that both DataSet and DataTable classes in ADO.NET have the Load() method, which in turn can be used to load a DataReader instance into a DataSet or a DataTable seamlessly.

The following code shows how a DataTable can be loaded in a DataReader instance:

Listing 3-21
```
string connectionString = ....; //Some connection string
SqlConnection sqlConnection = new SqlConnection(connectionString);
sqlConnection.Open();
SqlCommand sqlCommand = new SqlCommand
("Select * from Employee", sqlConnection);
SqlDataReader sqlDataReader =
sqlCommand.ExecuteReader
(CommandBehavior.CloseConnection);
DataTable dataTable = new DataTable("Employee");
dataTable.Load(sqlDataReader);
```

You can use the GetDataReader() method of both the DataSet and DataTable classes to retrieve a DataReader instance from either a DataSet or a DataTable seamlessly. Note that if this method is executed on a DataSet object that contains multiple DataTable instances, the resultant DataReader instance will also have multiple resultsets with each resultset corresponding to a DataTable instance.

Data Paging

Data paging is a very powerful feature in ADO.NET that can be used to implement paging functionality for your application's data. In ADO.NET 1.x you needed to use stored procedures to incorporate data paging in your applications, but the ExecutePageReader method in the SqlDataReader class provides a much simpler way of paging data. The following code snippet illustrates how this feature can be used:

Listing 3-22
```
string connectionString = ....; //some connection string
SqlConnection sqlConnection = new SqlConnection(connectionString);
sqlConnection.Open();
SqlCommand sqlCommand = new SqlCommand
("Select * from Employee", sqlConnection);
SqlDataReader sqlDataReader = sqlCommand.ExecutePageReader
(CommandBehavior.CloseConnection, 1, 25);
```

Batch Updates

In ADO.NET 1.x, a call to the Update() method on the DataAdapter would result in round trips to the database for each modified row in the DataSet. Batch Update is a feature that enables you to reduce database round trips and hence improve the application's performance. Note that database roundtrips degrade the performance of application on a whole on account of increased network traffic. Hence, if you had 10 rows to be updated, the DataAdapter would perform 10 separate update operations— one for each row. This was a major performance hindrance.

The UpdateBatchSize property of the DataAdapter introduced in ADO.NET 2.0 and later, can be used to specify the size of a batch—that is, the number of statements to be executed in a batch. In other words, the UpdateBatchSize property of the DataAdapter class determines the number of changed rows that are sent to the database server in a single operation. Executing the Update statements in batches improves performance.

As an example, if the UpdateBatchSize is 10 and you have two batches to update, the RowUpdating event will be called 10 times per batch, so it will be executed 20 times in all. In contrast, the RowUpdated event will be fired only twice—the number of times batches are submitted. Here is a code snippet that illustrates this:

Listing 3-23
```
using System;
using System.Collections.Generic;
using System.Text;
using System.Data.SqlClient;
using System.Data;
namespace BatchUpdate
{
    class Program
    {
        static String connectionString =
"Data Source=.;Initial Catalog=Employee;
User ID=McGrawHill;Password=joydip;
providerName=System.Data.SqlClient";
        private static int recordsUpdated = 0;
        private static int batchCount = 0;
```

```
        private const int BatchSize = 0;
          static void Main(string[] args)
        {
            SqlConnection sqlConnection = new SqlConnection();
            sqlConnection.ConnectionString = connectionString;
            try
            {
                sqlConnection.Open();
                SqlDataAdapter sqlDataAdapter = new
                SqlDataAdapter("Select * from Employee", sqlConnection);
                //Binding event handlers
                sqlDataAdapter.RowUpdating += new
                SqlRowUpdatingEventHandler(sqlDataAdapter_RowUpdating);
                sqlDataAdapter.RowUpdated += new
                SqlRowUpdatedEventHandler(sqlDataAdapter_RowUpdated);
                //Populating a DataSet instance
// with data from the database
                DataSet dataSet = new DataSet();
                sqlDataAdapter.Fill(dataSet, "Employee");
                //Updating data in the DataSet
                foreach (DataRow row in dataSet.Tables[0].Rows)
                {
                    String name = row["EmpName"].ToString();
                    row["EmpName "] = name;
                    String address = row["EmpAddress"].ToString();
                    row["EmpAddress"] = address;
                    String phone = row["EmpPhone"].ToString();
                    row["EmpPhone"] = phone;
                }
                //Creating Command instance
                SqlCommand sqlCommand = new SqlCommand();
                sqlCommand.Connection = sqlConnection;
                sqlCommand.CommandType = CommandType.Text;
                sqlCommand.CommandText = "Update Employee
Set EmpName=@EmpName,
            EmpAddress = @EmpAddress, EmpPhone =
@EmpPhone where EmployeeID=@EmployeeID";
                                //Creating parameters
                SqlParameter sqlParamName =
                   new SqlParameter("@EmpName", SqlDbType.VarChar);
                sqlParamName.SourceColumn = "EmpName";
                            SqlParameter sqlParamAddress =
                   new SqlParameter("@EmpAddress", SqlDbType.VarChar);
                sqlParamAddress.SourceColumn = "EmpAddress";
                            SqlParameter sqlParamPhone =
                   new SqlParameter("@EmpPhone", SqlDbType.VarChar);
                sqlParamPhone.SourceColumn = "EmpPhone";
                            SqlParameter sqlParamEmployeeID =
```

```
            new SqlParameter("@EmployeeID", SqlDbType.VarChar);
            sqlParamEmployeeID.SourceColumn = "EmployeeID";
            sqlCommand.Parameters.Insert(0, sqlParamName);
            sqlCommand.Parameters.Insert(1, sqlParamAddress);
            sqlCommand.Parameters.Insert(2, sqlParamPhone);
            sqlCommand.Parameters.Insert(3, sqlParamEmployeeID);
            sqlCommand.UpdatedRowSource = UpdateRowSource.None;
            sqlDataAdapter.UpdateCommand = sqlCommand;
            sqlDataAdapter.UpdateBatchSize = BatchSize;
            sqlDataAdapter.Update(dataSet, "Employee");
            Console.WriteLine("Records updated :" + recordsUpdated);
            Console.WriteLine("Batch count :" + batchCount);
        }
        catch (Exception ex)
        {
            //Write your exception handling code here
        }
        finally
        {
            sqlConnection.Close();
        }
    }
    private static void sqlDataAdapter_RowUpdating
    (object sender, SqlRowUpdatingEventArgs e)
    {
        //This event will be fired for each record.
        recordsUpdated++;
    }
    private static void sqlDataAdapter_RowUpdated
    (object sender, SqlRowUpdatedEventArgs e)
    {
        //This event will be fired for each batch
        batchCount++;
    }
    }
}
```

Asynchronous Data Access

The asynchronous mode (also called the *non-blocking mode*) of data access can execute multiple threads at the same time. The new versions of ADO.NET provide support for asynchronous execution or asynchronous data access.

In ADO.NET 1.x, the synchronous ExecuteReader, ExecuteScalar, and ExecuteNonQuery methods blocked the currently executing thread. In ADO.NET 2.0 and later, there are asynchronous Begin and End versions of these methods that provide support for asynchronous execution: BeginExecuteReader, EndExecuteReader,

BeginExecuteNonQuery, EndExecuteNonQuery, BeginExecuteXmlReader, and EndExecuteXmlReader. As you can see, you have methods with the same names prefixed with "Begin" and "End" to start and end asynchronous non-blocking calls.

The Common Provider Model

The System.Data.Common namespace in ADO.NET helps you implement a provider-independent data-access code without referencing the provider-specific classes. You have a class called DbProviderFactory that contains two methods namely, GetFactoryClasses() and GetFactory(). While the former is used to get all the providers supported, and the latter is used to retrieve a specific provider. The following code snippet demonstrates how you can make use of this class to create a SQL connection:

Listing 3-24
```
DbProviderFactory dbProviderFactory =
DbProviderFactories.GetFactory
("System.Data.SqlClient");
DbConnection dbConnection = dbProviderFactory.CreateConnection();
```

Bulk Copying

The SqlBulkCopy feature in the ADO.NET 2.0 and later enables you to copy large volumes of source data to a destination easily. Most importantly, there aren't any major performance drawbacks in using this feature. You just need to specify the source and the target locations to copy the data.

The following code snippet illustrates how this feature can be used:

Listing 3-25
```
SqlConnection connectionObjSource =
new SqlConnection(sourceConnectionString);
connectionObjSource.Open();
SqlConnection connectionObjTarget = new
SqlConnection(destinationConnectionString);
connectionObjTarget.Open();
SqlCommand sqlCommand = new SqlCommand
("Select * from SourceTable", connectionObjSource);
SqlDataReader sqlDataReader = sqlCommand.ExecuteReader
(CommandBehavior.CloseConnection);
DataTable dt = new DataTable("SourceTable");
SqlBulkCopy sqlBulkcopy =
new SqlBulkCopy(connectionObjTarget);
bulkcopy.DestinationTableName = "DestinationTable";
bulkcopy.WriteToServer(sqlDataReader);
```

DataTable Enhancements

ADO.NET supports serialization of DataSet and DataTable instances. You can easily expose such serialized instances and pass them through web services or other technologies that need serialized data. In ADO.NET, a DataTable instance can be serialized by itself without having to wrap a DataTable instance within a DataSet instance.

The RemotingFormat property of the DataTable class can be used to specify one of the two available serialization formats: binary or XML. Here is an example:

Listing 3-26
```
DataTable dataTable = new DataTable();
//Some code
datatable.RemotingFormat =
SerializationFormat.Binary;
//Some code
```

The DataTable class supports two methods: Load and Save. The Load method can load data from XML into the DataTable instance, and the Save method can persist the DataTable instance to a persistant storage media. Also, the DataTable class in ADO .NET contains a method called CreateTableReader that returns a DataTableReader instance, which can be used not only to read forward only data, but also in a disconnected mode of operation. The next section discusses how you can work with a DataTableReader.

The DataTableReader

Although DataReaders are much faster compared to DataSets and consume less memory resources, the major drawback in using DataReaders are that they require an open and active connection to operate. This meant you needed to explicitly close the database connection when you were done using it. With ADO.NET 2.0 and later, you have the DataTableReader class that is similar to other data readers with an added feature—its ability to work in a disconnected mode as well.

The CreateDataReader method of the DataTableReader class can be used to create a DataTableReader. The following listing shows how this is done:

Listing 3-27
```
public DataTableReader GetDataTableReader (string connectionString)
{
SqlConnection sqlConnection  = new SqlConnection(connectionString);
sqlConnection .Open()
SqlDataAdapter sqlDataAdapter =
new SqlDataAdapter("Select * from Employee",
sqlConnection);
DataTable dataTable = new DataTable ("Employee");
sqlDataAdapter.Fill(dataTable);
DataTableReader datatableReader =
dataTable.CreateDataReader();
sqlConnection.Close();
return datatableReader;
}
```

The DataTableReader is a lightweight, forward-only set of data that maintains the same structure as a DataTable, so it exposes the same rows and columns as the DataTable. The following code listing illustrates how you can read data using a DataTableReader instance:

Listing 3-28
```
String connectionString = "Data Source=.;
Initial Catalog=Employee;User ID=sa;Password=sa;
providerName=System.Data.SqlClient";
DataTableReader dataTableReader = GetDataTableReader(connectionString);
Console.WriteLine("Displaying the names of all the Employees:--");
while (dataTableReader.Read())
{
   Console.WriteLine(DataTableReader["EmpName"].ToString());
}
```

Working with Multiple Tables Seamlessly

Note that when you create a DataTableReader from a DataSet that contains multiple tables, the DataTableReader instance will also contain multiple resultsets. Actually you will have one resultset for each DataTable you had in the DataSet instance. You can also iterate through those resultsets using the NextResult() method. This is shown in the following code listing.

Listing 3-29
```
String connectionString = "Data Source=.;
Initial Catalog=Employee;User ID=sa;Password=sa;
providerName=System.Data.SqlClient";
DataTableReader dataTableReader =
GetDataTableReader(connectionString);
while(dataTableReader.NextResult())
  // Iterate through all the result sets
{
        while(dataTableReader.Read())
//Iterate through all the records in a resultset
        {
             //Some code
        }
}
```

Loading Data to a DataTable from a DataReader

The Load() method of the DataTable class can be used to load an instance of a DataReader directly into a DataTable instance seamlessly. The following listing shows how this can be done:

Listing 3-30
```
SqlConnection sqlConnection = new SqlConnection(sqlConnectionString);
sqlConnection.Open();
SqlCommand command = new SqlCommand("Select EmpName, Address,
 Phone from Employee", sqlConnection);
SqlDataReader sqlDataReader = command.ExecuteReader();
DataTable dataTable = new DataTable ();
dataTable.Load(sqlDataReader, LoadOption.OverwriteChanges);
```

Copying One DataTable into Another

The DataTable class's Copy() method can be used to make an exact copy of one DataTable into another DataTable, and that too, by retaining the entire schema and data. In essence, the entire schema and data of the source DataTable would be intact. This is illustrated in the following code snippet:

Listing 3-31
```
string connectionString = "Data Source=.;
Initial Catalog=Employee;User ID=sa;Password=sa;
providerName=System.Data.SqlClient";
DataTable dataTable = new DataTable("Employee");
SqlConnection sqlConnection =
new SqlConnection(connectionString));

SqlCommand sqlCommand = sqlConnection.CreateCommand();
sqlCommand.CommandText =
"SELECT empCode, empName from employee";
sqlConnection.Open();
dataTable.Load(sqlCommand.ExecuteReader(
CommandBehavior.CloseConnection));
DataTable cloneTable = dataTable.Copy();
```

Merging Multiple DataTables

In ADO.NET 1.x, you had to use the Merge() method of the DataSet class to merge a DataTable with another DataTable as there wasn't any Merge() method available in the DataTable class. Things have however changed with ADO.NET 2.0 and later. The Merge() method of the DataTable class in ADO.NET in its recent versions allow you to merge the contents of one DataTable with another easily.

As an example, suppose we have two DataTable instances, dt1 and dt2. We can merge the contents of dt2 with that of dt1 as shown in the following code snippet:

Listing 3-32
```
dt1.Merge(dt2);
```

In ADO.NET 1.1, the two DataTable instances would have had to be wrapped inside a DataSet instance to merge them this way.

Seamless Support for XML

The DataTable class in ADO.NET 2.0 and later contains four important methods, namely, ReadXml(), WriteXml(), ReadXmlSchema(), and WriteXmlSchema() methods for performing basic XML operations. These methods weren't provided in the DataTable class in ADO.NET 1.x.

The ADO.NET Entity Framework

ADO.NET vNext, also called ADO.NET Entity Framework, is a new component in ADO.NET 4.0 that you can use to decouple your applications from the relational or logical model by providing a layer of abstraction on top of the relational model. You can use ADO.NET Entity Framework to isolate the logical model of data from the application's object model, and, in doing so, raise the level of abstraction.

The Entity Framework is an extended object-relational mapping (ORM) framework. Its features include the following:

- Support for the Entity SQL query language to query the Entity Data Model
- Support for querying data using LINQ
- Support for the object services layer
- Support for entity inheritance, identity resolution, and change tracking

The most important component in the ADO.NET Entity Framework is the Entity Data Model (EDM).

The Entity Data Model

The Entity Data Model (EDM) is the core of the Entity Framework and is responsible for providing a level of abstraction between the relational or logical model and the object model. It makes use of mapping files to isolate your application's code from any changes in the relational schema. In essence, the logical model is abstracted from the object model. When you write programs to query data, you only query the conceptual model of data—the EDM. To query data against the EDM, you can use one of the following:

- **LINQ to entities**   Used to query entity objects through the EDM in a strongly typed manner
- **Entity SQL**   A derivative of T-SQL used to query data retrieved through the EDM
- **Object services**   Provides services such as state management, change tracking, identity resolution, and lazy loading

The EDM is mainly composed of three layers:

- **CSDL (Conceptual Data Language)**   Defined using .CSDL files
- **SSDL (Store-Specific Data Language)**   Defined using .SSDL files
- **MSL (Mapping Schema Language)**   Defined using .MSL files

---

NOTE *If you generate your EDM using the EDMGen command-line tool, the CSDL, SSDL, and MSL sections of the EDM will be stored in separate files with the .CSDL, .SSDL, and .MSL extensions. If your EDM is generated using the ADO.NET Entity Data Model Wizard, it will be stored in a single file with a .edmx extension.*

Getting Started with the ADO.NET Entity Framework

There are two ways to create an EDM: using the EDMGen.exe command-line tool, or using the Entity Data Model Wizard. We will use the Wizard because it is more convenient and easier to use.

To create an EDM using the Entity Data Model Wizard, follow these steps:

1. Create a new Web Application project in Visual Studio 2010.
2. Right-click on the Solution Explorer and select Add New Item.

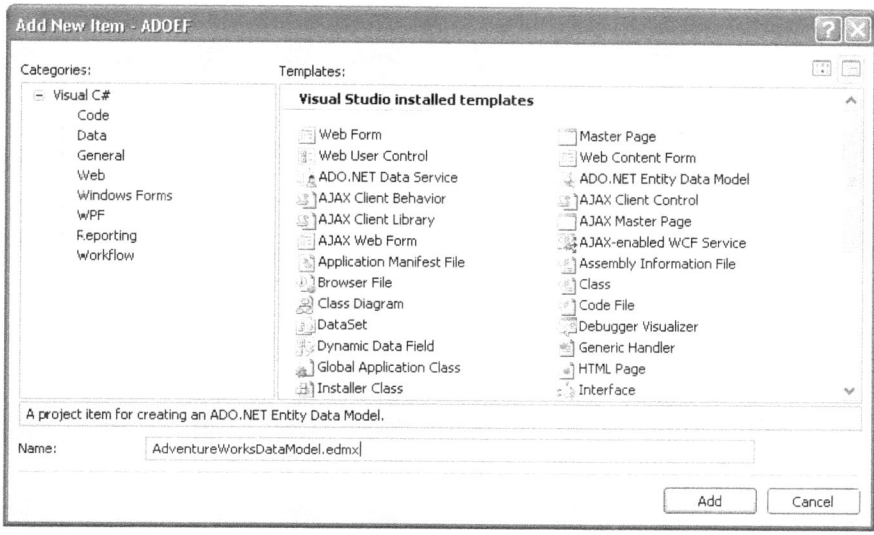

FIGURE 3-1   The ADO.NET EDM architectural components

3. From the list of the templates displayed, select ADO.NET Entity Data Model (see Figure 3-1).

4. Name the EDM **AdventureWorksDataModel** and click Add.

5. Select Generate from Database to generate your EDM from the AdventureWorks database, and click Next.

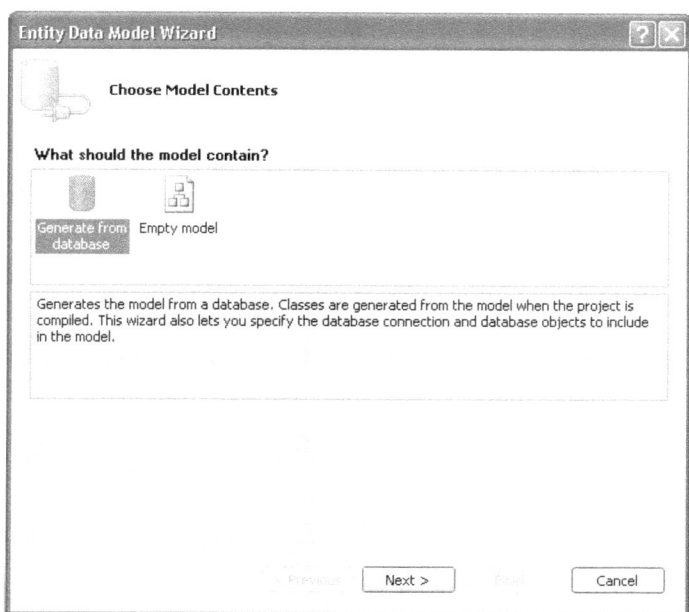

6. Specify the connection details and test your connection before you proceed.

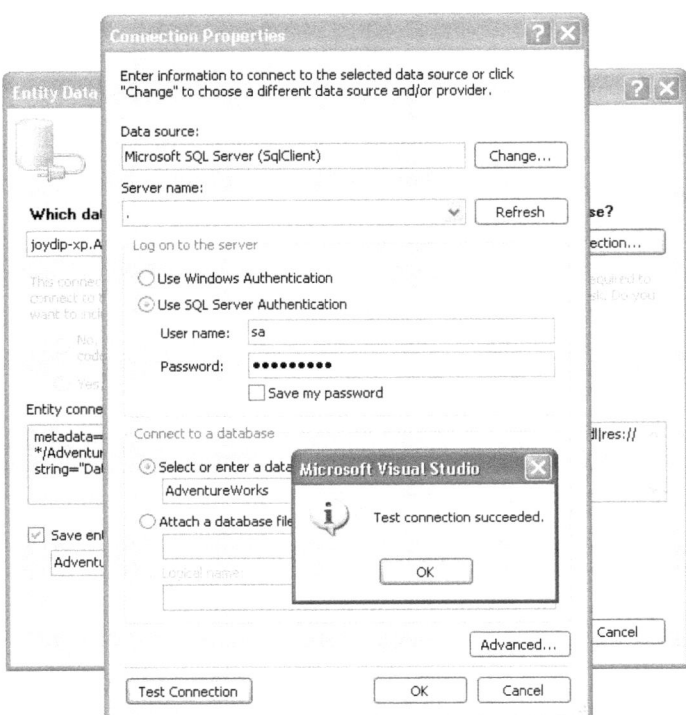

The entity connection string used to connect to the EDM is generated automatically by the wizard. This string will be saved in the ConnectionStrings section of your application's web.config file. This is what it will look like:

Listing 3-33

```
<connectionStrings>
<add name="AdventureWorksEntities"
connectionString="metadata=
res://*/AdventureWorksDataModel.csdl|
res://*/AdventureWorksDataModel.ssdl|
res://*/AdventureWorksDataModel.msl;provider=
System.Data.SqlClient;provider
connection string=&quot;Data Source=.;
Initial Catalog=AdventureWorks;User ID=sa;
Password=joydip1@3;
MultipleActiveResultSets=True&quot;"
providerName="System.Data.EntityClient"/>
</connectionStrings>
```

7. Specify the list of the tables you would like to use in the EDM. In this case, select the Contact, Employee, and EmployeeAddress tables from the list of tables displayed.

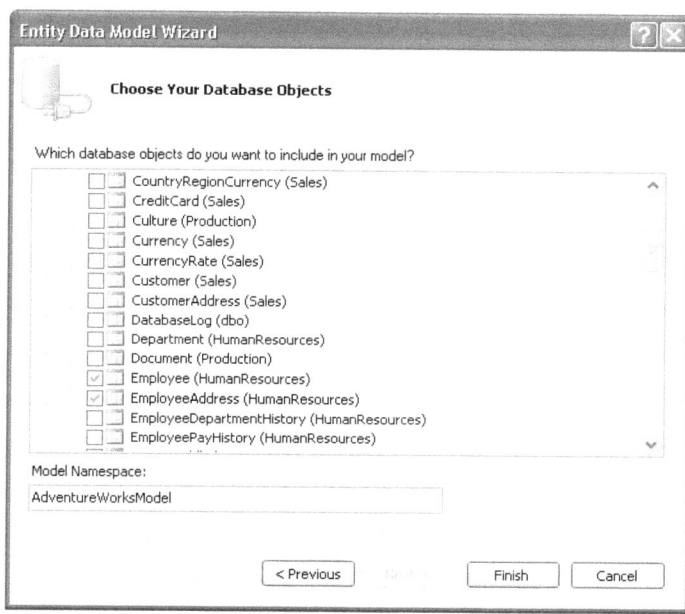

8. Click Finish to generate the EDM.

The EDM will be generated and saved in an .edmx file. Figure 3-2 shows what the EDM looks like in the ADO.NET Entity Data Model Designer.

Understanding the AdventureWorks EDM

An EDM (represented by a .edmx file) is divided into three sections, SSDL, MSL, and CSDL, as you can see here:

Listing 3-34
```
<edmx:Runtime>
  <!-- SSDL content -->
  <edmx:StorageModels>
   </edmx:StorageModels>
  <!-- CSDL content -->
  <edmx:ConceptualModels>
   </edmx:ConceptualModels>
  <!-- C-S mapping content -->
  <edmx:Mappings>
   </edmx:Mappings>
</edmx:Runtime>
```

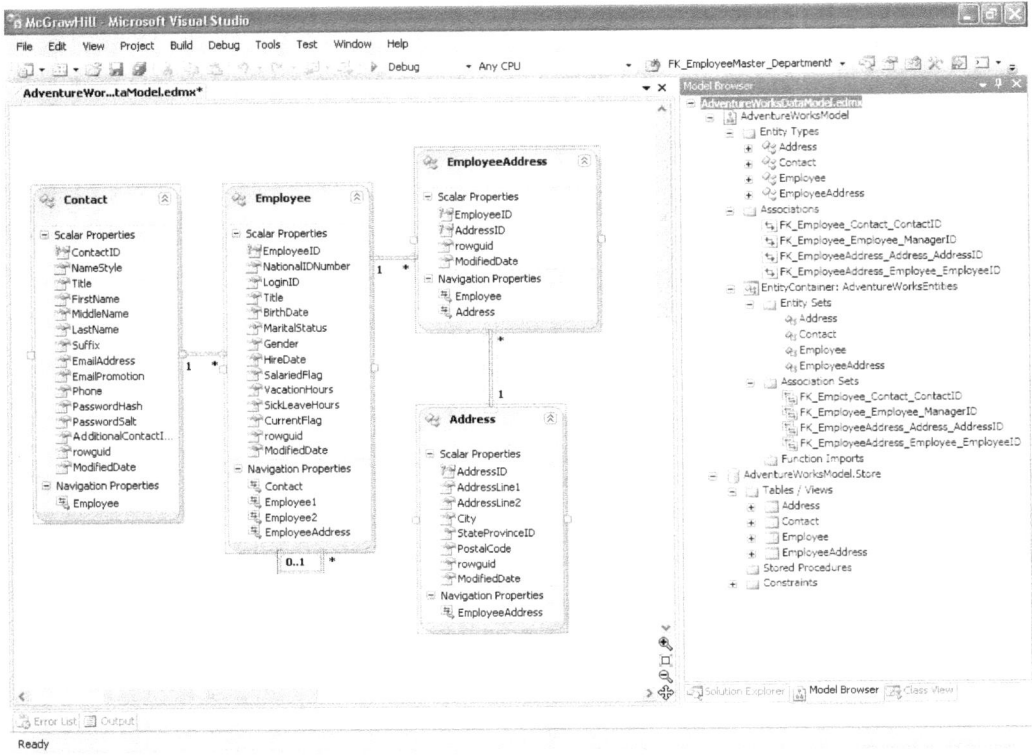

FIGURE 3-2 The AdventureWorks EDM

The CSDL and SSDL sections in the EDM are organized as a collection of EntitySets, AssociationSets, EntityTypes, and AssociationTypes as in the following listing.

Listing 3-35

```
<EntityContainer>
<EntitySet>
<EntitySet/>
<EntitySet>
<EntitySet/>
<EntitySet>
<EntitySet/>
<EntitySet>
<EntitySet/>
<AssociationSet>
</AssociationSet>
<AssociationSet>
</AssociationSet>
</EntityContainer>
```

```
<EntityType>
</EntityType>
<EntityType>
</EntityType>
<Association>
</Association>
<Association>
</Association>
```

The MSL section consists of one or more EntitySetMapping and AssociationSetMapping attributes that map the SSDL and CSDL sections of the EDM.

Listing 3-36
```
<EntityContainerMapping>
<EntitySetMapping>
<EntitySetMapping>
<EntitySetMapping>
<AssociationSetMapping>
<AssociationSetMapping>
<AssociationSetMapping>
</EntityContainerMapping>
```

The EDM consists of a collection of entities, entity types, entity sets, and their relationships. An *entity* is used to model real-world objects, and it is an instance of an *entity type*, such as employee, product, or customer. An *entity set* is a logical grouping of entities of similar types.

The EDM we just created will contain three EntitySets, as follows:

Listing 3-37
```
<EntitySet Name="Employee" EntityType=
"AdventureWorksModel.Store.Employee"
store:Type="Tables" Schema="HumanResources" />
        <EntitySet Name="EmployeeAddress"
EntityType="AdventureWorksModel.Store.EmployeeAddress"
 store:Type="Tables" Schema="HumanResources" />
        <EntitySet Name="Contact"
EntityType="AdventureWorksModel.Store.Contact"
store:Type="Tables" Schema="Person" />
```

An EntityContainer is a logical grouping of EntitySets and RelationshipSets. While entities are instances of entity types and are grouped in EntitySets, relationships amongst these entities are logically grouped in RelationshipSets. Here is an example:

Listing 3-38
```
<EntityContainer Name="AdventureWorksModelStoreContainer">
        <EntitySet Name="Employee" EntityType="AdventureWorksModel
.Store.Employee"
 store:Type="Tables" Schema="HumanResources" />
        <EntitySet Name="EmployeeAddress"
EntityType="AdventureWorksModel.Store.EmployeeAddress"
 store:Type="Tables" Schema="HumanResources" />
        <EntitySet Name="Contact"
```

```
EntityType="AdventureWorksModel.Store.Contact"
 store:Type="Tables" Schema="Person" />
         <AssociationSet Name=
"FK_Employee_Contact_ContactID"
Association="AdventureWorksModel.Store.
FK_Employee_Contact_ContactID">
             <End Role="Contact" EntitySet="Contact" />
             <End Role="Employee" EntitySet="Employee" />
         </AssociationSet>
         <AssociationSet Name=
"FK_Employee_Employee_ManagerID"
Association="AdventureWorksModel.Store.
FK_Employee_Employee_ManagerID">
             <End Role="Employee" EntitySet="Employee" />
             <End Role="Employee1" EntitySet="Employee" />
         </AssociationSet>
         <AssociationSet Name=
"FK_EmployeeAddress_Employee_EmployeeID"
Association="AdventureWorksModel.Store.
FK_EmployeeAddress_Employee_EmployeeID">
             <End Role="Employee" EntitySet="Employee" />
             <End Role="EmployeeAddress" EntitySet="EmployeeAddress" />
         </AssociationSet>
       </EntityContainer>
```

An EntityType would typically contain the properties pertaining to that entity. Here is an example of the Employee EntityType for the EDM we created earlier:

Listing 3-39

```
<EntityType Name="Employee">
       <Key>
         <PropertyRef Name="EmployeeID" />
       </Key>
       <Property Name="EmployeeID"
Type="int" Nullable="false"
StoreGeneratedPattern="Identity" />
       <Property Name="NationalIDNumber"
 Type="nvarchar" Nullable="false" MaxLength="15" />
       <Property Name="ContactID" Type="int" Nullable="false" />
       <Property Name="LoginID"
Type="nvarchar" Nullable="false"
MaxLength="256" />
       <Property Name="ManagerID" Type="int" />
       <Property Name="Title"
Type="nvarchar" Nullable="false"
MaxLength="50" />
       <Property Name="BirthDate"
```

```
Type="datetime" Nullable="false" />
          <Property Name="MaritalStatus"
Type="nchar" Nullable="false" MaxLength="1" />
          <Property Name="Gender" Type="nchar"
 Nullable="false" MaxLength="1" />
          <Property Name="HireDate" Type="datetime" Nullable="false" />
          <Property Name="SalariedFlag" Type="bit" Nullable="false" />
          <Property Name="VacationHours"
Type="smallint" Nullable="false" />
          <Property Name="SickLeaveHours"
 Type="smallint" Nullable="false" />
          <Property Name="CurrentFlag" Type="bit" Nullable="false" />
          <Property Name="rowguid"
Type="uniqueidentifier" Nullable="false" />
          <Property Name="ModifiedDate"
Type="datetime" Nullable="false" />
        </EntityType>
```

An AssociationSet represents a set of associations. Note that associations and entities represent the types, but AssociationSets and EntitySets represent the storage locations for those types.

The following code snippet illustrates how an AssociationSet is defined in the EDM:

Listing 3-40
```
<AssociationSet Name="FK_Employee_Contact_ContactID"
Association="AdventureWorksModel.Store.
FK_Employee_Contact_ContactID">
          <End Role="Contact" EntitySet="Contact" />
          <End Role="Employee" EntitySet="Employee" />
        </AssociationSet>
        <AssociationSet Name=
"FK_Employee_Employee_ManagerID"
Association="AdventureWorksModel.Store.
FK_Employee_Employee_ManagerID">
          <End Role="Employee" EntitySet="Employee" />
          <End Role="Employee1" EntitySet="Employee" />
        </AssociationSet>
        <AssociationSet Name=
"FK_EmployeeAddress_Employee_EmployeeID"
Association="AdventureWorksModel.Store.
FK_EmployeeAddress_Employee_EmployeeID">
          <End Role="Employee" EntitySet="Employee" />
          <End Role="EmployeeAddress" EntitySet="EmployeeAddress" />
        </AssociationSet>
```

EntitySets are mapped using EntitySetMapping attributes in the MSL layer. Here is an example:

Listing 3-41
```
<EntitySetMapping Name="Contacts">
<EntityTypeMapping TypeName=
"AdventureWorksModel.Contact">
<MappingFragment StoreEntitySet="Contact">
          <ScalarProperty Name="ContactID" ColumnName="ContactID" />
          <ScalarProperty Name="NameStyle" ColumnName="NameStyle" />
          <ScalarProperty Name="Title" ColumnName="Title" />
          <ScalarProperty Name="FirstName" ColumnName="FirstName" />
          <ScalarProperty Name="MiddleName"
 ColumnName="MiddleName" />
          <ScalarProperty Name="LastName" ColumnName="LastName" />
          <ScalarProperty Name="Suffix" ColumnName="Suffix" />
          <ScalarProperty Name="EmailAddress"
 ColumnName="EmailAddress" />
          <ScalarProperty Name="EmailPromotion"
ColumnName="EmailPromotion" />
          <ScalarProperty Name="Phone" ColumnName="Phone" />
          <ScalarProperty Name="PasswordHash"
 ColumnName="PasswordHash" />
          <ScalarProperty Name="PasswordSalt"
 ColumnName="PasswordSalt" />
          <ScalarProperty Name="AdditionalContactInfo"
ColumnName="AdditionalContactInfo" />
          <ScalarProperty Name="rowguid" ColumnName="rowguid" />
          <ScalarProperty Name="ModifiedDate"
 ColumnName="ModifiedDate" />
        </MappingFragment>
</EntityTypeMapping>
</EntitySetMapping>
```

The ScalarProperty attribute is mapped to the respective ColumnName attribute in the storage layer. Similarly, AssociationSets are also mapped in the MSL layer using the <EndProperty> mapping attributes:

Listing 3-42
```
    <AssociationSetMapping Name="FK_Employee_Contact_ContactID"
    TypeName="AdventureWorksModel.FK_Employee_Contact_ContactID"
    StoreEntitySet="Employee">
            <EndProperty Name="Contact">
              <ScalarProperty Name="ContactID"
ColumnName="ContactID" />
            </EndProperty>
            <EndProperty Name="Employee">
              <ScalarProperty Name="EmployeeID"
ColumnName="EmployeeID" />
            </EndProperty>
          </AssociationSetMapping>
          <AssociationSetMapping Name=
```

```
"FK_Employee_Employee_ManagerID"
TypeName="AdventureWorksModel.FK_Employee_Employee_ManagerID"
StoreEntitySet="Employee">
            <EndProperty Name="Employee">
              <ScalarProperty Name="EmployeeID"
ColumnName="ManagerID" />
            </EndProperty>
            <EndProperty Name="Employee1">
              <ScalarProperty Name="EmployeeID"
ColumnName="EmployeeID" />
            </EndProperty>
            <Condition ColumnName="ManagerID" IsNull="false" />
          </AssociationSetMapping>
          <AssociationSetMapping Name=
"FK_EmployeeAddress_Employee_EmployeeID"
TypeName="AdventureWorksModel.
FK_EmployeeAddress_Employee_EmployeeID"
StoreEntitySet="EmployeeAddress">
            <EndProperty Name="Employee">
              <ScalarProperty Name="EmployeeID"
 ColumnName="EmployeeID" />
            </EndProperty>
            <EndProperty Name="EmployeeAddress">
              <ScalarProperty Name="EmployeeID"
 ColumnName="EmployeeID" />
              <ScalarProperty Name="AddressID"
 ColumnName="AddressID" />
            </EndProperty>
          </AssociationSetMapping>
```

The Complete AdventureWorks EDM

Here is the complete source of the AdventureWorks EDM for your reference:

Listing 3-43
```
<edmx:Runtime>
    <!-- SSDL content -->
    <edmx:StorageModels>
      <Schema Namespace="AdventureWorksModel.Store"
 Alias="Self" Provider="System.Data.SqlClient"
 ProviderManifestToken="2008"
xmlns:store="http://schemas.microsoft.com/
ado/2007/12/edm/EntityStoreSchemaGenerator"
xmlns="http://schemas.microsoft.com/ado/2009/02/edm/ssdl">
        <EntityContainer Name="AdventureWorksModelStoreContainer">
        <EntitySet Name="Employee"
EntityType="AdventureWorksModel.Store.Employee"
 store:Type="Tables" Schema="HumanResources" />
        <EntitySet Name="EmployeeAddress"
EntityType="AdventureWorksModel.Store.EmployeeAddress"
 store:Type="Tables" Schema="HumanResources" />
```

```
        <EntitySet Name="Contact"
EntityType="AdventureWorksModel.Store.Contact"
store:Type="Tables" Schema="Person" />
        <AssociationSet Name=
"FK_Employee_Contact_ContactID" Association=
"AdventureWorksModel.Store.FK_Employee_Contact_ContactID">
            <End Role="Contact" EntitySet="Contact" />
            <End Role="Employee" EntitySet="Employee" />
        </AssociationSet>
        <AssociationSet Name=
"FK_Employee_Employee_ManagerID"
Association="AdventureWorksModel.Store.
FK_Employee_Employee_ManagerID">
            <End Role="Employee" EntitySet="Employee" />
            <End Role="Employee1" EntitySet="Employee" />
        </AssociationSet>
        <AssociationSet Name=
"FK_EmployeeAddress_Employee_EmployeeID"
Association="AdventureWorksModel.Store.
FK_EmployeeAddress_Employee_EmployeeID">
            <End Role="Employee" EntitySet="Employee" />
            <End Role="EmployeeAddress" EntitySet="EmployeeAddress" />
        </AssociationSet>
      </EntityContainer>
      <EntityType Name="Employee">
        <Key>
          <PropertyRef Name="EmployeeID" />
        </Key>
        <Property Name="EmployeeID"
Type="int" Nullable="false"
StoreGeneratedPattern="Identity" />
        <Property Name="NationalIDNumber"
 Type="nvarchar" Nullable="false" MaxLength="15" />
        <Property Name="ContactID"
Type="int" Nullable="false" />
        <Property Name="LoginID"
Type="nvarchar" Nullable="false"
MaxLength="256" />
        <Property Name="ManagerID" Type="int" />
        <Property Name="Title"
Type="nvarchar" Nullable="false"
MaxLength="50" />
        <Property Name="BirthDate"
Type="datetime" Nullable="false" />
        <Property Name="MaritalStatus"
Type="nchar" Nullable="false" MaxLength="1" />
        <Property Name="Gender"
```

```
Type="nchar" Nullable="false" MaxLength="1" />
          <Property Name="HireDate" Type="datetime" Nullable="false" />
          <Property Name="SalariedFlag" Type="bit" Nullable="false" />
          <Property Name="VacationHours"
Type="smallint" Nullable="false" />
          <Property Name="SickLeaveHours"
Type="smallint" Nullable="false" />
          <Property Name="CurrentFlag" Type="bit" Nullable="false" />
          <Property Name="rowguid"
Type="uniqueidentifier" Nullable="false" />
          <Property Name="ModifiedDate"
Type="datetime" Nullable="false" />
        </EntityType>
        <EntityType Name="EmployeeAddress">
          <Key>
            <PropertyRef Name="EmployeeID" />
            <PropertyRef Name="AddressID" />
          </Key>
          <Property Name="EmployeeID" Type="int" Nullable="false" />
          <Property Name="AddressID" Type="int" Nullable="false" />
          <Property Name="rowguid"
Type="uniqueidentifier" Nullable="false" />
          <Property Name="ModifiedDate"
Type="datetime" Nullable="false" />
        </EntityType>
        <EntityType Name="Contact">
          <Key>
            <PropertyRef Name="ContactID" />
          </Key>
          <Property Name="ContactID"
Type="int" Nullable="false"
StoreGeneratedPattern="Identity" />
          <Property Name="NameStyle" Type="bit" Nullable="false" />
          <Property Name="Title" Type="nvarchar" MaxLength="8" />
          <Property Name="FirstName"
Type="nvarchar" Nullable="false"
MaxLength="50" />
          <Property Name="MiddleName" Type="nvarchar" MaxLength="50" />
          <Property Name="LastName"
Type="nvarchar" Nullable="false"
MaxLength="50" />
          <Property Name="Suffix" Type="nvarchar" MaxLength="10" />
          <Property Name="EmailAddress"
Type="nvarchar" MaxLength="50" />
          <Property Name="EmailPromotion"
Type="int" Nullable="false" />
          <Property Name="Phone" Type="nvarchar" MaxLength="25" />
          <Property Name="PasswordHash"
```

```
Type="varchar" Nullable="false"
 MaxLength="128" />
          <Property Name="PasswordSalt"
Type="varchar" Nullable="false"
MaxLength="10" />
          <Property Name="AdditionalContactInfo" Type="xml" />
          <Property Name="rowguid"
Type="uniqueidentifier" Nullable="false" />
          <Property Name="ModifiedDate"
Type="datetime" Nullable="false" />
        </EntityType>
        <Association Name="FK_Employee_Contact_ContactID">
          <End Role="Contact" Type=
"AdventureWorksModel.Store.Contact"
Multiplicity="1" />
          <End Role="Employee"
Type="AdventureWorksModel.Store.Employee"
Multiplicity="*" />
          <ReferentialConstraint>
            <Principal Role="Contact">
              <PropertyRef Name="ContactID" />
            </Principal>
            <Dependent Role="Employee">
              <PropertyRef Name="ContactID" />
            </Dependent>
          </ReferentialConstraint>
        </Association>
        <Association Name="FK_Employee_Employee_ManagerID">
          <End Role="Employee"
Type="AdventureWorksModel.Store.Employee"
 Multiplicity="0..1" />
          <End Role="Employee1"
Type="AdventureWorksModel.Store.Employee"
 Multiplicity="*" />
          <ReferentialConstraint>
            <Principal Role="Employee">
              <PropertyRef Name="EmployeeID" />
            </Principal>
            <Dependent Role="Employee1">
              <PropertyRef Name="ManagerID" />
            </Dependent>
          </ReferentialConstraint>
        </Association>
        <Association Name="FK_EmployeeAddress_Employee_EmployeeID">
          <End Role="Employee"
Type="AdventureWorksModel.Store.Employee"
 Multiplicity="1" />
```

```
            <End Role="EmployeeAddress"
Type="AdventureWorksModel.Store.EmployeeAddress"
 Multiplicity="*" />
          <ReferentialConstraint>
            <Principal Role="Employee">
              <PropertyRef Name="EmployeeID" />
            </Principal>
            <Dependent Role="EmployeeAddress">
              <PropertyRef Name="EmployeeID" />
            </Dependent>
          </ReferentialConstraint>
        </Association>
      </Schema>
    </edmx:StorageModels>
    <!-- CSDL content -->
    <edmx:ConceptualModels>
      <Schema Namespace="AdventureWorksModel"
Alias="Self" xmlns:store=
"http://schemas.microsoft.com/ado/2007/12/edm/
EntityStoreSchemaGenerator"
xmlns="http://schemas.microsoft.com/ado/2008/09/edm">
        <EntityContainer Name="AdventureWorksEntities">
          <EntitySet Name="Employees"
EntityType="AdventureWorksModel.Employee" />
          <EntitySet Name="EmployeeAddresses"
EntityType="AdventureWorksModel.EmployeeAddress" />
          <EntitySet Name="Contacts"
EntityType="AdventureWorksModel.Contact" />
          <AssociationSet Name=
"FK_Employee_Contact_ContactID" Association=
"AdventureWorksModel.FK_Employee_Contact_ContactID">
            <End Role="Contact" EntitySet="Contacts" />
            <End Role="Employee" EntitySet="Employees" />
          </AssociationSet>
          <AssociationSet Name="FK_Employee_Employee_ManagerID"
Association="AdventureWorksModel.FK_Employee_Employee_ManagerID">
            <End Role="Employee" EntitySet="Employees" />
            <End Role="Employee1" EntitySet="Employees" />
          </AssociationSet>
          <AssociationSet Name=
"FK_EmployeeAddress_Employee_EmployeeID" Association=
"AdventureWorksModel.FK_EmployeeAddress_Employee_EmployeeID">
            <End Role="Employee" EntitySet="Employees" />
            <End Role="EmployeeAddress"
EntitySet="EmployeeAddresses" />
          </AssociationSet>
        </EntityContainer>
```

```
        <EntityType Name="Employee">
          <Key>
            <PropertyRef Name="EmployeeID" />
          </Key>
          <Property Name="EmployeeID"
Type="Int32" Nullable="false"
store:StoreGeneratedPattern="Identity" />
          <Property Name="NationalIDNumber"
 Type="String" Nullable="false"
MaxLength="15" Unicode="true"
 FixedLength="false" />
          <Property Name="LoginID"
Type="String" Nullable="false"
 MaxLength="256" Unicode="true"
FixedLength="false" />
          <Property Name="Title"
Type="String" Nullable="false"
MaxLength="50" Unicode="true"
FixedLength="false" />
          <Property Name="BirthDate"
Type="DateTime" Nullable="false" />
          <Property Name="MaritalStatus"
 Type="String" Nullable="false" MaxLength="1"
 Unicode="true" FixedLength="true" />
          <Property Name="Gender"
Type="String" Nullable="false"
MaxLength="1" Unicode="true"
FixedLength="true" />
          <Property Name="HireDate" Type="DateTime" Nullable="false" />
          <Property Name="SalariedFlag"
Type="Boolean" Nullable="false" />
          <Property Name="VacationHours"
 Type="Int16" Nullable="false" />
          <Property Name="SickLeaveHours"
 Type="Int16" Nullable="false" />
          <Property Name="CurrentFlag"
 Type="Boolean" Nullable="false" />
          <Property Name="rowguid" Type="Guid" Nullable="false" />
          <Property Name="ModifiedDate"
Type="DateTime" Nullable="false" />
          <NavigationProperty Name="Contact"
Relationship="AdventureWorksModel.
FK_Employee_Contact_ContactID"
FromRole="Employee" ToRole="Contact" />
          <NavigationProperty Name="Employee1"
Relationship="AdventureWorksModel.
FK_Employee_Employee_ManagerID"
```

```
FromRole="Employee" ToRole="Employee1" />
          <NavigationProperty Name="Employee2"
Relationship="AdventureWorksModel.
FK_Employee_Employee_ManagerID" FromRole="Employee1"
ToRole="Employee" />
          <NavigationProperty Name="EmployeeAddresses"
Relationship="AdventureWorksModel.
FK_EmployeeAddress_Employee_EmployeeID"
 FromRole="Employee" ToRole="EmployeeAddress" />
        </EntityType>
        <EntityType Name="EmployeeAddress">
          <Key>
            <PropertyRef Name="EmployeeID" />
            <PropertyRef Name="AddressID" />
          </Key>
          <Property Name="EmployeeID" Type="Int32" Nullable="false" />
          <Property Name="AddressID" Type="Int32" Nullable="false" />
          <Property Name="rowguid" Type="Guid" Nullable="false" />
          <Property Name="ModifiedDate"
Type="DateTime" Nullable="false" />
          <NavigationProperty Name="Employee"
Relationship="AdventureWorksModel.
FK_EmployeeAddress_Employee_EmployeeID"
FromRole="EmployeeAddress" ToRole="Employee" />
        </EntityType>
        <EntityType Name="Contact">
          <Key>
            <PropertyRef Name="ContactID" />
          </Key>
          <Property Name="ContactID"
Type="Int32" Nullable="false"
store:StoreGeneratedPattern="Identity" />
          <Property Name="NameStyle" Type="Boolean" Nullable="false" />
          <Property Name="Title" Type="String"
 MaxLength="8" Unicode="true"
FixedLength="false" />
          <Property Name="FirstName"
Type="String" Nullable="false"
MaxLength="50" Unicode="true"
FixedLength="false" />
          <Property Name="MiddleName"
Type="String" MaxLength="50"
Unicode="true" FixedLength="false" />
          <Property Name="LastName"
Type="String" Nullable="false"
MaxLength="50" Unicode="true"
FixedLength="false" />
          <Property Name="Suffix"
```

```xml
Type="String" MaxLength="10" Unicode="true"
FixedLength="false" />
          <Property Name="EmailAddress"
Type="String" MaxLength="50"
Unicode="true" FixedLength="false" />
          <Property Name="EmailPromotion"
 Type="Int32" Nullable="false" />
          <Property Name="Phone"
Type="String" MaxLength="25"
Unicode="true" FixedLength="false" />
          <Property Name="PasswordHash"
 Type="String" Nullable="false"
 MaxLength="128" Unicode="false"
FixedLength="false" />
          <Property Name="PasswordSalt"
 Type="String" Nullable="false"
MaxLength="10" Unicode="false"
FixedLength="false" />
          <Property Name="AdditionalContactInfo"
 Type="String" MaxLength="Max"
Unicode="true" FixedLength="false" />
          <Property Name="rowguid" Type="Guid" Nullable="false" />
          <Property Name="ModifiedDate"
Type="DateTime" Nullable="false" />
          <NavigationProperty Name="Employees"
Relationship="AdventureWorksModel.
FK_Employee_Contact_ContactID"
FromRole="Contact" ToRole="Employee" />
        </EntityType>
        <Association Name="FK_Employee_Contact_ContactID">
          <End Role="Contact"
Type="AdventureWorksModel.Contact"
Multiplicity="1" />
          <End Role="Employee"
Type="AdventureWorksModel.Employee"
 Multiplicity="*" />
        </Association>
        <Association Name="FK_Employee_Employee_ManagerID">
          <End Role="Employee"
Type="AdventureWorksModel.Employee"
 Multiplicity="0..1" />
          <End Role="Employee1"
Type="AdventureWorksModel.Employee"
Multiplicity="*" />
        </Association>
        <Association Name="FK_EmployeeAddress_Employee_EmployeeID">
          <End Role="Employee"
```

```xml
Type="AdventureWorksModel.Employee"
Multiplicity="1" />
          <End Role="EmployeeAddress"
Type="AdventureWorksModel.EmployeeAddress"
Multiplicity="*" />
          <ReferentialConstraint>
            <Principal Role="Employee">
              <PropertyRef Name="EmployeeID" />
            </Principal>
            <Dependent Role="EmployeeAddress">
              <PropertyRef Name="EmployeeID" />
            </Dependent>
          </ReferentialConstraint>
        </Association>
      </Schema>
    </edmx:ConceptualModels>
    <!-- C-S mapping content -->
    <edmx:Mappings>
<Mapping Space="C-S"
xmlns="http://schemas.microsoft.com/ado/2008/09/mapping/cs">
        <EntityContainerMapping StorageEntityContainer=
"AdventureWorksModelStoreContainer"
CdmEntityContainer="AdventureWorksEntities">
          <EntitySetMapping Name="Employees">
<EntityTypeMapping TypeName=
"AdventureWorksModel.Employee">
<MappingFragment StoreEntitySet="Employee">
            <ScalarProperty Name="EmployeeID"
 ColumnName="EmployeeID" />
            <ScalarProperty Name="NationalIDNumber"
 ColumnName="NationalIDNumber" />
            <ScalarProperty Name="LoginID" ColumnName="LoginID" />
            <ScalarProperty Name="Title" ColumnName="Title" />
            <ScalarProperty Name="BirthDate" ColumnName="BirthDate" />
            <ScalarProperty Name="MaritalStatus"
ColumnName="MaritalStatus" />
            <ScalarProperty Name="Gender" ColumnName="Gender" />
            <ScalarProperty Name="HireDate" ColumnName="HireDate" />
            <ScalarProperty Name="SalariedFlag"
 ColumnName="SalariedFlag" />
            <ScalarProperty Name="VacationHours"
ColumnName="VacationHours" />
            <ScalarProperty Name="SickLeaveHours"
 ColumnName="SickLeaveHours" />
            <ScalarProperty Name="CurrentFlag"
 ColumnName="CurrentFlag" />
            <ScalarProperty Name="rowguid" ColumnName="rowguid" />
            <ScalarProperty Name="ModifiedDate"
```

```
ColumnName="ModifiedDate" />
          </MappingFragment></EntityTypeMapping></EntitySetMapping>
          <EntitySetMapping Name="EmployeeAddresses">
<EntityTypeMapping TypeName=
"AdventureWorksModel.EmployeeAddress">
<MappingFragment StoreEntitySet="EmployeeAddress">
          <ScalarProperty Name="EmployeeID"
 ColumnName="EmployeeID" />
          <ScalarProperty Name="AddressID" ColumnName="AddressID" />
          <ScalarProperty Name="rowguid" ColumnName="rowguid" />
          <ScalarProperty Name="ModifiedDate"
ColumnName="ModifiedDate" />
          </MappingFragment></EntityTypeMapping></EntitySetMapping>
          <EntitySetMapping Name="Contacts">
<EntityTypeMapping TypeName=
"AdventureWorksModel.Contact">
<MappingFragment StoreEntitySet="Contact">
          <ScalarProperty Name="ContactID" ColumnName="ContactID" />
          <ScalarProperty Name="NameStyle" ColumnName="NameStyle" />
          <ScalarProperty Name="Title" ColumnName="Title" />
          <ScalarProperty Name="FirstName" ColumnName="FirstName" />
          <ScalarProperty Name="MiddleName"
 ColumnName="MiddleName" />
          <ScalarProperty Name="LastName" ColumnName="LastName" />
          <ScalarProperty Name="Suffix" ColumnName="Suffix" />
          <ScalarProperty Name="EmailAddress"
 ColumnName="EmailAddress" />
          <ScalarProperty Name="EmailPromotion"
 ColumnName="EmailPromotion" />
          <ScalarProperty Name="Phone" ColumnName="Phone" />
          <ScalarProperty Name="PasswordHash"
 ColumnName="PasswordHash" />
          <ScalarProperty Name="PasswordSalt"
 ColumnName="PasswordSalt" />
          <ScalarProperty Name=
"AdditionalContactInfo" ColumnName=
"AdditionalContactInfo" />
          <ScalarProperty Name="rowguid" ColumnName="rowguid" />
          <ScalarProperty Name="ModifiedDate"
ColumnName="ModifiedDate" />
          </MappingFragment></EntityTypeMapping></EntitySetMapping>
          <AssociationSetMapping Name=
"FK_Employee_Contact_ContactID"
TypeName="AdventureWorksModel.
FK_Employee_Contact_ContactID"
StoreEntitySet="Employee">
          <EndProperty Name="Contact">
            <ScalarProperty Name="ContactID"
```

```
ColumnName="ContactID" />
            </EndProperty>
            <EndProperty Name="Employee">
              <ScalarProperty Name="EmployeeID"
ColumnName="EmployeeID" />
            </EndProperty>
        </AssociationSetMapping>
        <AssociationSetMapping Name=
"FK_Employee_Employee_ManagerID"
TypeName="AdventureWorksModel.
FK_Employee_Employee_ManagerID"
StoreEntitySet="Employee">
            <EndProperty Name="Employee">
              <ScalarProperty Name="EmployeeID"
ColumnName="ManagerID" />
            </EndProperty>
            <EndProperty Name="Employee1">
              <ScalarProperty Name="EmployeeID"
ColumnName="EmployeeID" />
            </EndProperty>
            <Condition ColumnName="ManagerID" IsNull="false" />
        </AssociationSetMapping>
        <AssociationSetMapping Name=
"FK_EmployeeAddress_Employee_EmployeeID"
TypeName="AdventureWorksModel.
FK_EmployeeAddress_Employee_EmployeeID"
StoreEntitySet="EmployeeAddress">
            <EndProperty Name="Employee">
              <ScalarProperty Name="EmployeeID"
 ColumnName="EmployeeID" />
            </EndProperty>
            <EndProperty Name="EmployeeAddress">
              <ScalarProperty Name="EmployeeID"
 ColumnName="EmployeeID" />
              <ScalarProperty Name="AddressID"
ColumnName="AddressID" />
            </EndProperty>
        </AssociationSetMapping>
      </EntityContainerMapping>
    </Mapping>
  </edmx:Mappings>
 </edmx:Runtime>
```

Using the AdventureWorks EDM

Let's look at an example of how to use the EDM. We will use an EntityDataSource
control to retrieve data from the EDM, and then bind this data to a GridView control.
The EntityDataSource control is a new data source control included as part of Visual

Studio 2008 Service Pack 1. Note that Visual Studio 2008 SP1 is included as part of Visual Studio 2010. You needn't install this service pack separately if you have Visual Studio 2010 installed in your system. It can be used to bind data retrieved from an EDM to the ASP.NET data-bound controls.

Follow these steps:

1. Open the Default.aspx file in Design view, and drag and drop an EntityDataSource control from the toolbox.

   If you cannot locate the EntityDataSource control in the toolbox, you will have to add it manually. Right-click on the toolbox and click the Browse button in the Choose Toolbox Items window that is displayed. Locate the System.Web.Entity. dll file in the folder where Microsoft .NET Framework 3.5 was installed. Then click OK.

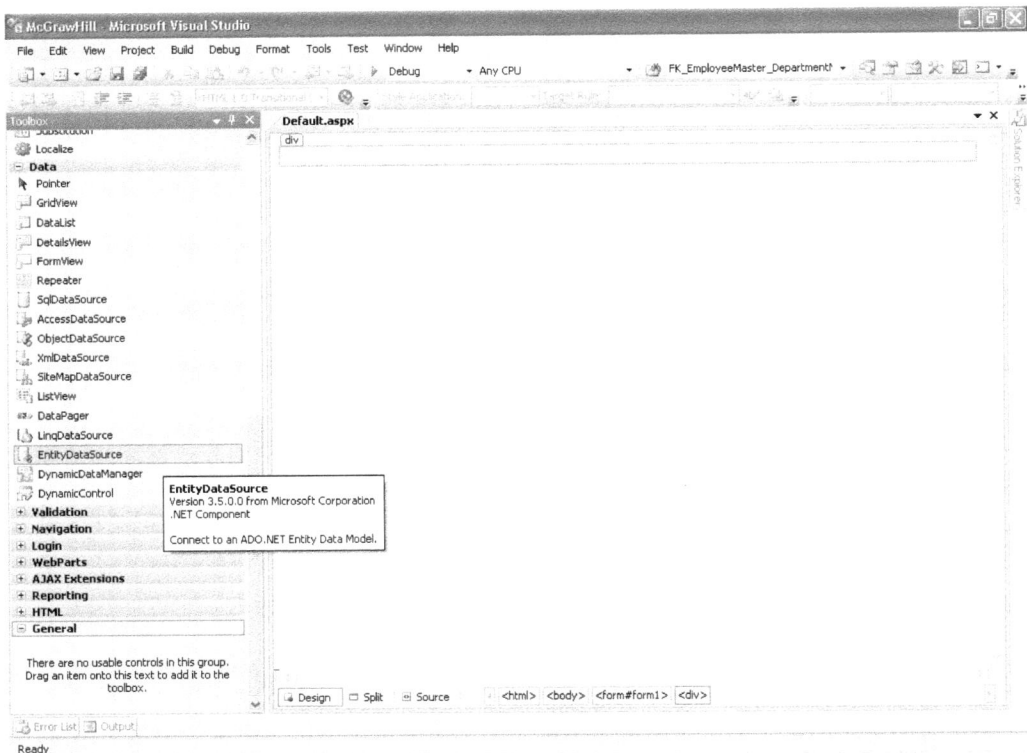

2. Configure the ObjectContext by specifying the Named Connection as AdventureWorksEntities. Then click Next.

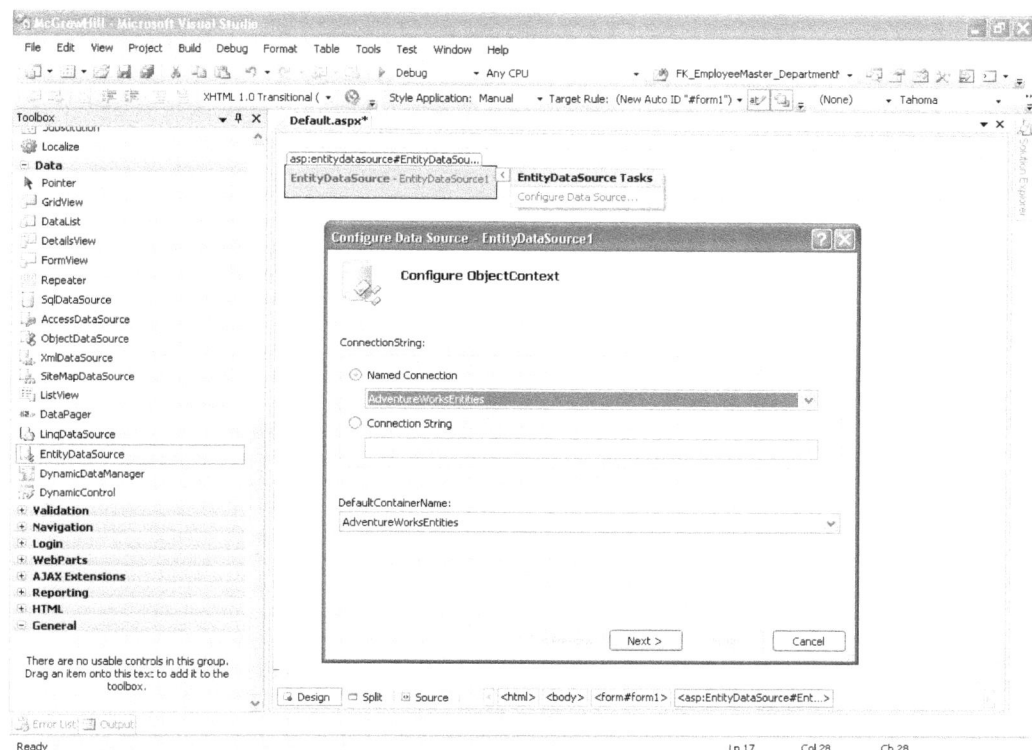

3. Select the EntitySetName and the fields you would like, as shown in the following illustration. When you're done, click Finish.

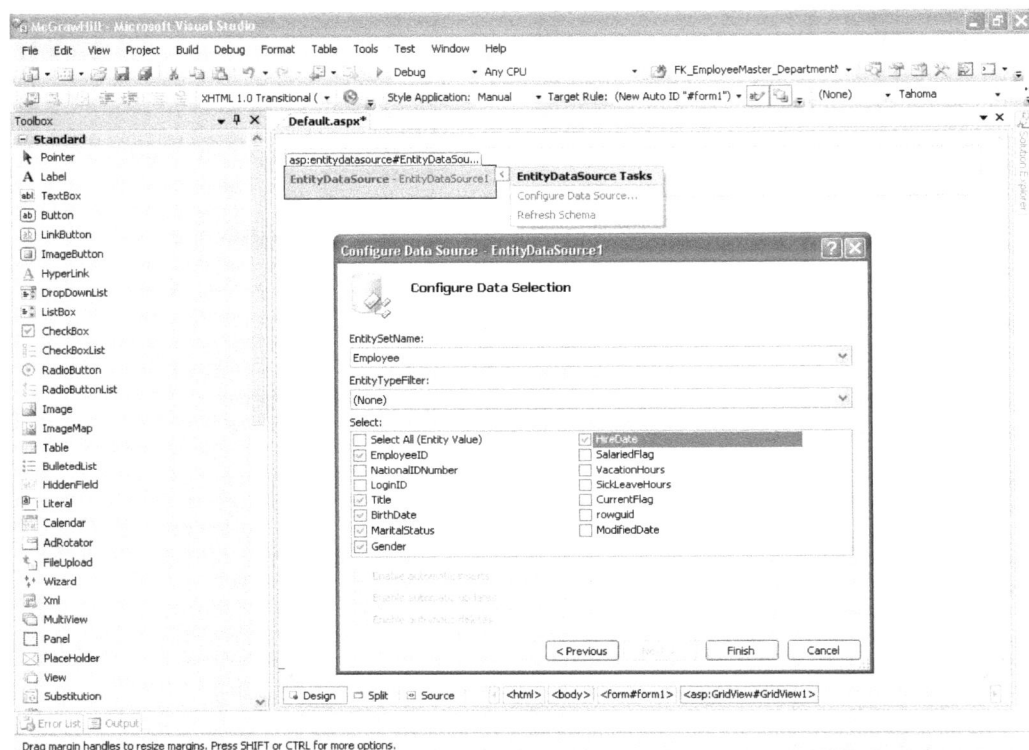

Once your EntityDataSourceControl has been configured, you can use it like other data source controls to bind data to any ASP.NET data control. In Design view, drag and drop a GridView control, and set its data source to the EntityDataSourceControl you just configured. Here is what the markup code will look like now:

Listing 3-44

```
<html xmlns="http://www.w3.org/1999/xhtml" >
<head runat="server">
    <title>Displaying Employee Records</title>
</head>
<body>
    <form id="form1" runat="server">
    <asp:EntityDataSource ID="EntityDataSource1" runat="server"
        ConnectionString="name=AdventureWorksEntities"
        DefaultContainerName=
```

```
"AdventureWorksEntities"
 EntitySetName="Employee"
        Select="it.[EmployeeID],
it.[MaritalStatus],
 it.[BirthDate], it.[Gender],
it.[Title], it.[HireDate]">
    </asp:EntityDataSource>
    <asp:GridView ID="GridView1"
runat="server"
 AutoGenerateColumns="False"
        DataSourceID="EntityDataSource1">
        <Columns>
            <asp:BoundField DataField=
"EmployeeID"
 HeaderText="Employee ID"
                SortExpression="EmployeeID" />
            <asp:BoundField DataField="Gender"
HeaderText="Gender"
                SortExpression="Gender" />
            <asp:BoundField DataField="Title"
 HeaderText="Title" SortExpression="Title" />
            <asp:BoundField DataField="BirthDate"
 DataFormatString="{0:d}"
                HeaderText="Birth Date"
SortExpression="BirthDate" />
            <asp:BoundField DataField="HireDate"
 DataFormatString="{0:d}"
                HeaderText="Hire Date"
SortExpression="HireDate" />
            <asp:BoundField DataField=
"MaritalStatus"
 HeaderText="Marital Status"
                SortExpression="MaritalStatus" />
        </Columns>
    </asp:GridView>
    </form>
</body>
</html>
```

When you execute the application, the output will look something like what you see in Figure 3-3.

Employee ID	Gender	Title	Birth Date	Hire Date	Marital Status
1	M	Production Technician - WC60	5/15/1972	7/31/1996	M
2	M	Marketing Assistant	6/3/1977	2/26/1997	S
3	M	Engineering Manager	12/13/1964	12/12/1997	M
4	M	Senior Tool Designer	1/23/1965	1/5/1998	S
5	M	Tool Designer	8/29/1949	1/11/1998	M
6	M	Marketing Manager	4/19/1965	1/20/1998	S
7	F	Production Supervisor - WC60	2/16/1946	1/26/1998	S
8	F	Production Technician - WC10	7/6/1946	2/6/1998	M
9	F	Design Engineer	10/29/1942	2/6/1998	M
10	M	Production Technician - WC10	4/27/1946	2/7/1998	S
11	M	Design Engineer	4/11/1949	2/24/1998	M
12	F	Vice President of Engineering	9/1/1961	3/3/1998	S
13	M	Production Technician - WC10	10/1/1946	3/5/1998	M
14	M	Production Supervisor - WC50	5/3/1946	3/11/1998	M
15	M	Production Technician - WC10	8/12/1946	3/23/1998	S
16	F	Production Supervisor - WC60	11/9/1946	3/30/1998	S
17	F	Production Technician - WC10	5/6/1946	4/11/1998	M
18	M	Production Supervisor - WC60	9/8/1946	4/18/1998	M
19	F	Production Technician - WC10	4/30/1946	4/29/1998	M
20	M	Production Technician - WC30	6/15/1967	1/2/1999	M
21	M	Production Control Manager	12/4/1972	1/2/1999	M
22	M	Production Technician - WC45	10/14/1952	1/3/1999	S
23	M	Production Technician - WC45	11/18/1960	1/3/1999	S
24	M	Production Technician - WC30	12/3/1969	1/3/1999	S
25	M	Production Supervisor - WC10	11/26/1973	1/4/1999	S
26	M	Production Technician - WC20	2/4/1972	1/5/1999	M
27	M	Production Technician - WC40	12/15/1970	1/5/1999	S

FIGURE 3-3   The employee records displayed in the web browser

CHAPTER 4

Binding Data in ASP.NET

Controls that can be bound to data are known as data controls in ASP.NET. There are plenty of such data controls in ASP.NET and they offer powerful features. The term *data binding* in ASP.NET refers to the ability of data controls to be bound to data retrieved from data sources. These data sources can be databases, XML files, or even flat files. A data source is one that exposes data to be used by the application, i.e., it is the name given to the source of the data that the application uses. Apart from the ability to be bound to data retrieved from external data sources, data controls can be used to perform CRUD (create, read, update, and delete) operations, sort data, filter data, and so on. However, not all data controls provide support for these features.

In this chapter we will discuss the most popular data controls in ASP.NET. We will also discuss how we can work with the ImageGenerator and Chart controls in ASP.NET applications.

The ASP.NET Data Controls

Data controls are controls that can be bound to data retrieved from data sources (databases, XML documents, etc.). There are plenty of data controls in ASP.NET. The following ones are widely used in applications:

- List controls (ListBox, DropDownList, CheckBoxList, RadioButtonList, BulletedList)
- Repeater control
- DataList control
- DataGrid control
- GridView control
- DetailsView control
- FormView control
- TreeView control
- ListView control
- DataPager control

In the sections that follow, we will take a look at each of these controls and how we can use them in our ASP.NET applications.

The List Controls

The list controls in ASP.NET can be used to display lists to enable users to select one or more data items. All list controls in ASP.NET are derived from the ListControl base class, so these controls share a common set of methods and properties. You can use the DataSource property of these controls to bind data. As with other data controls, data in a list control can be bound both declaratively and programmatically.

The following list controls are available in ASP.NET:

- ListBox control
- DropDownList control
- CheckBoxList control
- BulletedList control
- RadioButtonList control

Declarative Data Binding

Here is an example that shows how you can declaratively bind data to a ListBox control:

Listing 4-1
```
<asp:ListBox ID="ListBox1" runat="server" Height="150px" Width="350px">
    <asp:ListItem Value="1">Joydip Kanjilal</asp:ListItem>
    <asp:ListItem Value="2">Oindrilla Roy Chowdhury</asp:ListItem>
    <asp:ListItem Value="3">Soma Roy Chowdhury</asp:ListItem>
    <asp:ListItem Value="4">Tilak Tarafder</asp:ListItem>
    <asp:ListItem Value="5">Amal Kanjilal</asp:ListItem>
    <asp:ListItem Value="6">Rama Kanjilal</asp:ListItem>
    <asp:ListItem Value="7">Indronil Roy Chowdhury</asp:ListItem>
    <asp:ListItem Value="8">Debanjan Banerjee</asp:ListItem>
</asp:ListBox>
```

Programmatic Data Binding

To bind data to any of the list controls programmatically, you need to add list items to the Items collection of the control. Here is an example:

Listing 4-2
```
protected void Page_Load(object sender, EventArgs e)
{
    if (!IsPostBack)
    {
        CheckBoxList1.AutoPostBack = true;
        CheckBoxList1.RepeatColumns = 1;
        CheckBoxList1.RepeatDirection = RepeatDirection.Vertical;
        CheckBoxList1.RepeatLayout = RepeatLayout.Flow;
        CheckBoxList1.TextAlign = TextAlign.Right;
        CheckBoxList1.Items.Add(new ListItem("HR"));
        CheckBoxList1.Items.Add(new ListItem("Finance"));
        CheckBoxList1.Items.Add(new ListItem("Marketing"));
        CheckBoxList1.Items.Add(new ListItem("Software"));
        CheckBoxList1.Items.Add(new ListItem("Hardware"));
        CheckBoxList1.Items.Add(new ListItem("Personnel"));
        CheckBoxList1.Items.Add(new ListItem("Sales"));
    }
}
```

You can also retrieve data from the database and bind it to these controls. Here is an example:

Listing 4-3
```
protected void Page_Load(Object sender, EventArgs e)
{
  if (!IsPostBack)
  {
    radioButtonList1.DataSource = GetDataFromDatabase();
    radioButtonList1.DataTextField="Name";
    radioButtonList1.DataValueField="Code";
    radioButtonList1.DataBind();
  }
}
```

The GetDataFromDatabase() is a custom method. Here is the source code for the GetDataFromDatabase() method, which retrieves data from the database and returns this data as a collection of Employee records:

Listing 4-4
```
private List<Employee> GetDataFromDatabase()
{
 //Code to retrieve data from the
 //database and return it as a collection
}
```

As you can see in the above code listing, the GetDataFromDatabase() method returns a generic List of type Employee. The Employee class contains a list of properties that pertain to the entity called Employee. Here is the code for this class:

Listing 4-5
```
public class Employee
{
 public String Code{get;set;}
public String FirstName{get;set;}
public String LastName{get;set;}
public String Address{get;set;}
}
```

The Repeater Control

The Repeater control in ASP.NET is a data-bound container control that can be used to bind data. In a Repeater control, data is rendered as a collection of DataItems, which are in turn defined using one or more templates. You can use the DataSource property of this control to bind data of type ICollection, IEnumerable, or IListSource. You then need to call the DataBind() method on this control to bind the data.

There are quite a few templates that you can use in Repeater controls to display data and customize the display:

- **HeaderTemplate**   Creates the header rows for the table of data being displayed.
- **FooterTemplate**   Creates the footer rows for the table of data being displayed.
- **ItemTemplate**   Formats the items to be displayed. Typically, this template is used to specify elements that are displayed once in each row of data.
- **AlternatingItemTemplate**   Formats alternate rows being displayed by the control.
- **SeparatorTemplat**e   Specifies styles for separating rows and columns.

Here is the complete syntax for using the Repeater control:

Listing 4-6
```
<asp:Repeater id="repEmployee" runat="server">
<HeaderTemplate>
...
</HeaderTemplate>
<ItemTemplate>
...
</ItemTemplate>
<FooterTemplate>
...
</FooterTemplate>
<AlternatingItemTemplate>
...
</AlternatingItemTemplate>
</asp:Repeater>
```

The following simple example illustrates how you can use a Repeater control and bind its data source to a data-source control.

Listing 4-7
```
<asp:Repeater ID="Repeater1"
DataSourceID="SqlDataSource1"
 runat="server" </asp:Repeater>
```

And here is the markup code for the SqlDataSource control used in the preceding code line:

Listing 4-8
```
<asp:SqlDataSource ID="SqlDataSource1" runat="server"
ConnectionString=
"<%$ ConnectionStrings:
TestConnectionString %>
" SelectCommand="SELECT [EmployeeID],
 [FirstName], [LastName], [Address]
 FROM [Employee]">
</asp:SqlDataSource>
```

The DataList Control

The DataList control, like the Repeater control, is a template-driven lightweight data control that can be used as a container for repeated data items. Here is how the templates of this control are organized:

Listing 4-9
```
<asp:DataList id="EmployeeList" runat="server">
<HeaderTemplate>
...
</HeaderTemplate>
<ItemTemplate>
...
</ItemTemplate>
<AlternatingItemTemplate>
...
</AlternatingItemTemplate>
<FooterTemplate>
...
</FooterTemplate>
</asp:DataList>
```

The DataGrid Control

The DataGrid is a very powerful control in ASP.NET, but it has been deprecated in ASP.NET 2.0 and later versions. The GridView is now the preferred control.

Here is an example of what the markup code for the DataGrid control looks like:

Listing 4-10
```
<asp:DataGrid id="PatientGrid" HeaderStyle-CssClass="Header"
 runat="server" Width="100%"
 AutoGenerateColumns="False"
 CellPadding="3">
<ItemStyle CssClass="GridRow"></ItemStyle>
<HeaderStyle CssClass="GridHeader"></HeaderStyle>
  <Columns>
      <asp:BoundColumn DataField="Code"
      HeaderText="Patient Code">
      </asp:BoundColumn>
      <asp:BoundColumn
      DataField="FirstName"
      HeaderText="First Name">
      </asp:BoundColumn>
      <asp:BoundColumn
      DataField="LastName"
      HeaderText="Last Name">
      </asp:BoundColumn>
      <asp:BoundColumn
      DataField="Address"
      HeaderText="Address">
      </asp:BoundColumn>
      <asp:BoundColumn
```

```
        DataField="Phone"
       HeaderText="Phone">
         </asp:BoundColumn>
    </Columns>
</asp:DataGrid>
```

To bind data programmatically to this control, you can use a method in the code-behind file that returns a collection of items, as shown here:

Listing 4-11
```
protected void Page_Load(object sender, EventArgs e)
     {
         if (!IsPostBack)
         {
             PatientGrid.DataSource = GetPatientData();
             PatientGrid.DataBind();
         }
     }
private void GetPatientData()
{
  //Write code here to retrieve data
  //from the Patient table in the database
  //and return this data as a collection
}
```

The GridView Control

The GridView is an improved form of the DataGrid control that can be used to display views of data. Here is the complete syntax of this control:

Listing 4-12
```
<asp:GridView id="value" Runat="Server"
   AllowPaging="True|False"
   AllowSorting="True|False"
   AutoGenerateColumns="True|False"
   Caption="string"
   CaptionAlign="Left|NotSet|Right|Justify"
   CellPadding="n"
   CellSpacing="n"
   DataSourceID="datasourceid"
   EmptyDataText="string"
   GridLines="Both|Horizontal|Vertical|None"
   PageSize="n"
   ShowHeader="True|False"
   ShowFooter="True|False"
     property="value"
     Style="style"
     HeaderStyle-property="value"
     RowStyle-property="value"
     AlternatingRowStyle-property="value"
     FooterStyle-property="value"
 />
```

The following is typical markup code for a GridView control bound to data retrieved from SQL Server:

Listing 4-13
```
<asp:GridView ID="GridView1" runat="server"
  AutoGenerateColumns="False" DataKeyNames="PatientID"
        DataSourceID="SqlDataSource1">
        <Columns>
              <asp:BoundField
      DataField="PatientID"
      HeaderText="Patient ID"
      InsertVisible="False"
                  ReadOnly="True"
       SortExpression="PatientID" />
              <asp:BoundField DataField="FirstName"
      HeaderText="First Name" SortExpression="FirstName" />
              <asp:BoundField
      DataField="LastName"
      HeaderText="Last Name"
      SortExpression="LastName" />
<asp:BoundField DataField="Address" HeaderText="Address"
      SortExpression="Address" />
        </Columns>
</asp:GridView>
```

Here is how you need to configure the SqlDataSource control used in the preceding listing:

Listing 4-14
```
<asp:SqlDataSource ID="SqlDataSource1"
    runat="server" ConnectionString=
    "Data Source=.;Initial Catalog=Test;
     User ID=sa;Password=joydip1@3"
     ProviderName="System.Data.SqlClient"
     SelectCommand="SELECT [PatientID],
     [FirstName], [LastName],
     [Address] FROM [Patient]">
</asp:SqlDataSource>
```

You can enable paging in a GridView control by setting the AllowPaging property of the control to true. Here's an example:

Listing 4-15
```
<asp:GridView ID="GridView1" runat="server" AllowPaging ="true"
PageSize = "10" RowStyle-BackColor = "Blue"
AutoGenerateColumns= "False" DataKeyNames="StoreID"
DataSourceID="SqlDataSource1">
```

The DetailsView Control

The DetailsView control is similar to the GridView control with one major difference—it displays one record at a time. However, you can bind data to this control much the same way you do with the GridView control. The DetailsView control can be used with the GridView control to display a master details view of the data.

Here is a typical example of how this control can be used:

Listing 4-13

```
<asp:DetailsView ID="DetailsView1"
 runat="server" Height="150px"
 Width="750px" BorderStyle="None"
 BorderColor="Blue" BorderWidth="1px"
 AutoGenerateRows="False"
DataSourceID="SqlDataSource1"
 AllowPaging="True">
            <FooterStyle ForeColor="Red"
              BackColor="White">
            </FooterStyle>
        <RowStyle ForeColor="Teal"></RowStyle>
        <PagerStyle ForeColor="Blue"
        HorizontalAlign="Left"
        BackColor="White">
        </PagerStyle>
            <Fields>
<asp:BoundField DataField="PatientID"
HeaderText="Patient ID"
SortExpression="PatientID" />
<asp:BoundField DataField="FirstName"
 HeaderText="First Name"
SortExpression="FirstName" />
<asp:BoundField DataField="LastName"
 HeaderText="Last Name"
SortExpression="LastName" />
<asp:BoundField DataField="AdmissionDate"
 HeaderText="Date of Admission"
SortExpression="AdmissionDate"
HtmlEncode="False" DataFormatString="{0:d}"/>
<asp:BoundField DataField="BilledAmount"
 HeaderText="Total Billed Amount"
SortExpression="BilledAmount" HtmlEncode="False"
 DataFormatString="{0:C}"/>
<asp:BoundField DataField="DoctorID"
 HeaderText="Doctor ID"
SortExpression="DoctorID" />
<asp:BoundField DataField="PatientAddress"
 HeaderText="Patient Address"
 SortExpression="PatientAddress" />
            </Fields>
        <HeaderStyle ForeColor="White"
Font-Bold="True" BackColor="#336699">
</HeaderStyle>
</asp:DetailsView>
```

The markup code for the SqlDataSource control follows:

Listing 4-17
```
<asp:SqlDataSource ID="SqlDataSource1"
runat="server" ConnectionString=
"<%$ ConnectionStrings:TestConnectionString %>
" SelectCommand="SELECT [PatientID], [FirstName],
 [LastName], [PatientAddress], [AdmissionDate],
 [DoctorID] FROM [Patient]">
</asp:SqlDataSource>
```

The FormView Control

The FormView is another data-bound control that renders one record at a time. It is similar to the DetailsView control with one major difference—while FormView renders data in a tabular format, DetailsView requires user-defined templates to render data.

The following example shows how you can use this control:

Listing 4-18
```
<asp:FormView ID="FormView1"
runat="server"
 AllowPaging="True" BackColor="White"
     BorderColor="Red" BorderStyle="None"
 BorderWidth="1px" CellPadding="3"
CellSpacing="2"
             DataKeyNames="PatientID"
DataSourceID="SqlDataSource1"
GridLines="Both">
             <FooterStyle BackColor="#F7DFB5" ForeColor="#8C4510" />
             <EditRowStyle BackColor="#738A9C"
Font-Bold="True"
ForeColor="White" />
             <RowStyle BackColor="White" ForeColor="Black" />
             <PagerStyle ForeColor="Blue" HorizontalAlign="Center" />
             <ItemTemplate>
                 Patient ID:
                 <asp:Label ID="lblPatientID"
runat="server" Text=
'<%# Eval("PatientID") %>'>
                 </asp:Label><br />
                 First Name:
                 <asp:Label ID="lblFirstName"
 runat="server" Text=
'<%# Bind("FirstName") %>'>
                 </asp:Label><br />
                 Last Name:
                 <asp:Label ID="lblLastName"
 runat="server" Text='<%# Bind("LastName") %>'>
</asp:Label><br />
         Address:
```

```
                    <asp:Label ID="lblAddress"
runat="server"
 Text='<%# Bind("Address") %>'>
</asp:Label><br />
                    Billed Amount:
                    <asp:Label ID="lblBilledAmount"
 runat="server" Text='<%# Bind("BilledAmount") %>'>
</asp:Label><br />
                    Doctor ID:
                    <asp:Label ID="lblDoctorID" runat="server"
 Text='<%# Bind("DoctorID") %>'>
                    </asp:Label><br />
                </ItemTemplate>
                <HeaderStyle BackColor="Blue"
 Font-Bold="True"
 ForeColor="White" />
        </asp:FormView>
```

And here is the markup code for the SqlDataSource control used to bind data to the FormView control:

Listing 4-19
```
<asp:SqlDataSource ID="SqlDataSource1"
runat="server" ConnectionString=
"Data Source=.;Initial Catalog=Test;
User ID=sa;Password=joydip1@3"
SelectCommand="SELECT [EmployeeID],
 [EmployeeName], [JoiningDate], [Salary],
 [DepartmentID] FROM [Employee]">
</asp:SqlDataSource>
```

The TreeView Control

The TreeView control in ASP.NET can be used to display hierarchical data from a data source. Once you drag and drop a TreeView control from the toolbox onto your web form, the markup code of the control will look like this:

Listing 4-20   `<asp:TreeView ID="TreeView1" runat="server"></asp:TreeView>`

Here is a typical example of a TreeView control that is bound to an XmlDataSource:

Listing 4-21
```
<asp:TreeView ID="PatientTreeView"
runat="server"
 DataSourceID="XmlDataSource1"
BackColor="White"
 Font-Bold="True" ForeColor="Blue">
    <ParentNodeStyle Font-Bold="True"
ForeColor="Black" BackColor="Yellow" />
            <SelectedNodeStyle
```

```
Font-Underline="True"
 HorizontalPadding="0px" VerticalPadding="0px"
BackColor="#C04000" />
            <NodeStyle Font-Names="Verdana"
Font-Size="8pt" ForeColor="Black"
HorizontalPadding="5px"
            NodeSpacing="0px"
VerticalPadding="0px"
 BackColor="#00C0C0" />
        <DataBindings>
          <asp:TreeNodeBinding
DataMember="Address"
 ValueField="PatientAddress" />
          <asp:TreeNodeBinding
DataMember="FirstName"
 ValueField="FirstName" />
          <asp:TreeNodeBinding
DataMember="LastName"
 ValueField="LastName" />
        </DataBindings>
        <LeafNodeStyle BackColor="#FFE0C0" />
</asp:TreeView>
```

The ListView Control

The ListView control is a new data control introduced in ASP.NET 3.5. It provides you with complete control over the generated HTML markup code and also supports CRUD operations. Figure 4-1 illustrates the two new data controls added to ASP.NET 3.5: the ListView and the DataPager.

After you drag and drop a ListView control from the toolbox onto your web page, the markup code will look like this:

Listing 4-22 `<asp:ListView ID="ListView1" runat="server"/>`

The ListView control contains the following templates for customizing its look and feel:

- **ItemTemplate**   This template is used to place the content that needs to be rendered.
- **LayoutTemplate**   This template is used to specify the layout of the data display.
- **EmptyItemTemplate**   This template is used to render the content for an empty item.
- **EmptyDataTemplate**   This template is used to render the content when there is no data returned from the source of the data.

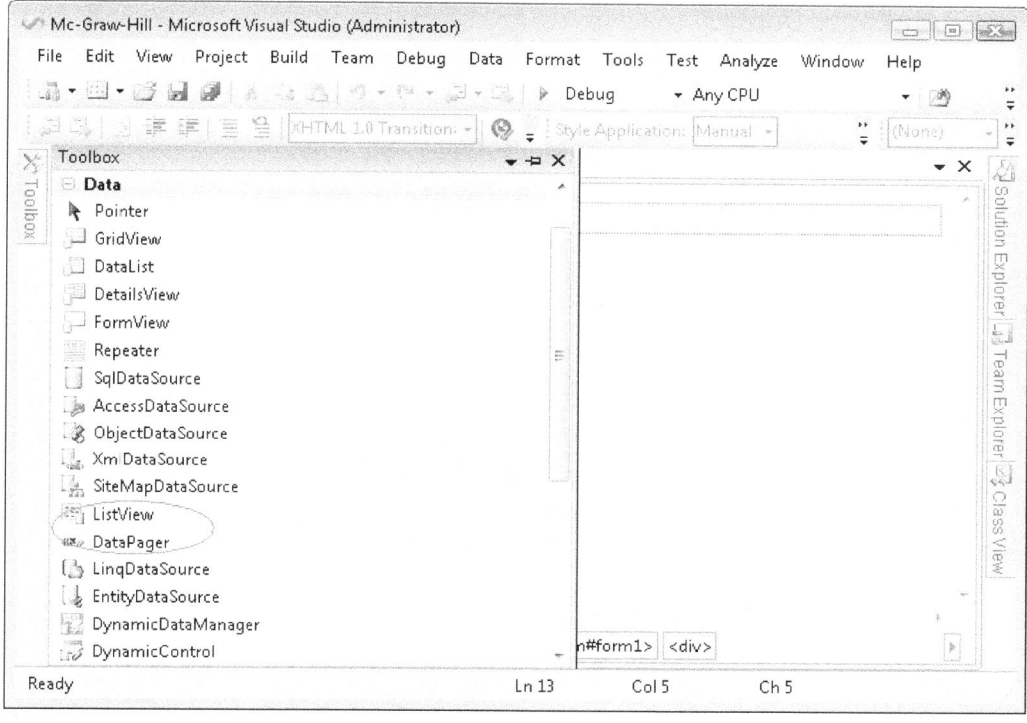

FIGURE 4-1   The ListView and DataPager controls

- **SelectedItemTemplate**   This template is used to render the content of the selected data item.

- **EditItemTemplate**   This template is used to render the content of the data item to be edited.

- **AlternatingItemTemplate**   This template is used to render the content of the alternating data item.

- **InsertItemTemplate**   This template is used to render the content of the data item to be inserted.

- **ItemSeparatorTemplate**   This template is used to render the content of the seperator for the data items.

- **GroupTemplate**   This template is used to render the content defined in ItemTemplate and EmptyItemTemplate for data items those are grouped.

- **GroupSeparatorTemplate**   This template is used to render the content between the group templates to act as a seperator amongst different groups of data.

The DataPager Control

The DataPager control is great for implementing custom paging of data bound to data controls in ASP.NET. For example, you can use the DataPager control to implement paging in the ListView control.

Here is some typical markup code for the DataPager control:

Listing 4-23
```
<asp:DataPager ID="DataPager1"
runat="server"
 PagedControlID="GridView1"
 PageSize="4">
    <Fields>
    <asp:NumericPagerField NextPageText=
"Next Page" PreviousPageText=
"Previous Page"/>
    </Fields>
</asp:DataPager>
```

The following complete example illustrates how you can use the ListView and DataPager controls together to display a page of records:

Listing 4-24
```
<html xmlns="http://www.w3.org/1999/xhtml" >
<head runat="server">
    <title>Using a ListView and Pager Control</title>
</head>
<body>
    <form id="form1" runat="server">
    <div>
    <asp:ListView ID="ListView1"  runat="server"
  DataSourceID="SqlDataSource1"
        DataKeyNames="CustomerID" ItemPlaceholderID="SqlDataSource1">
        <layouttemplate>
            <table>
                <tr>
                  <th>Customer ID</th>
                  <th>Customer Name</th>
                  <th>SalesPerson ID</th>
                </tr>
                        <tbody id="SqlDataSource1"
                            runat="server">
                        </tbody>
            </table>
<asp:Panel ID="itemContainer" runat="server">
                    <asp:DataPager ID="dataPager" runat="server"
                      PageSize="10" PagedControlID="ListView1">
                      <Fields>
                          <asp:NumericPagerField />
                      </Fields>
                    </asp:DataPager>
```

```
    </asp:Panel>
        </layouttemplate>
    <ItemTemplate>
        <tr>
            <td>
                <asp:Label ID="lblCustomerID" runat="server"
                    Text='<%# Eval("CustomerID") %>'/>
            </td>
            <td>
                <asp:Label ID="lblName" runat="server"
                    Text='<%# Eval("Name") %>'/>
            </td>
            <td>
                <asp:Label ID="lblSalesPersonID" runat="server"
                    Text='<%# Eval("SalesPersonID") %>'/>
            </td>
        </tr>
    </ItemTemplate>
</asp:ListView>
<asp:SqlDataSource ID="SqlDataSource1" runat="server"
        ConnectionString=
"<%$ ConnectionStrings:AdventureWorksConnectionString %>"
        SelectCommand="SELECT [CustomerID], [Name],
        [SalesPersonID] FROM [Sales].[Store]">
</asp:SqlDataSource>
    </div>
    </form>
</body>
</html>
```

Data Source Controls in ASP.NET

The data source controls in ASP.NET facilitate a simplified, powerful, consistent, and extensible approach to data binding. With ASP.NET 2.0 and later versions, you have a bunch of new data source controls, such as LinqDataSource, ObjectDataSource, XmlDataSource, and SqlDataSource. These data source controls are great because they allow you to implement CRUD operations in your applications without having to write much code. All of these controls support paging, sorting, caching, editing, inserting, selecting, and deleting data. You can use these controls to declaratively bind data to your ASP.NET controls (GridView, Repeater, ListView, etc.), without writing even a single line of code.

The following data source controls are available in ASP.NET:

- ObjectDataSource control
- XmlDataSource control
- LinqDataSource control

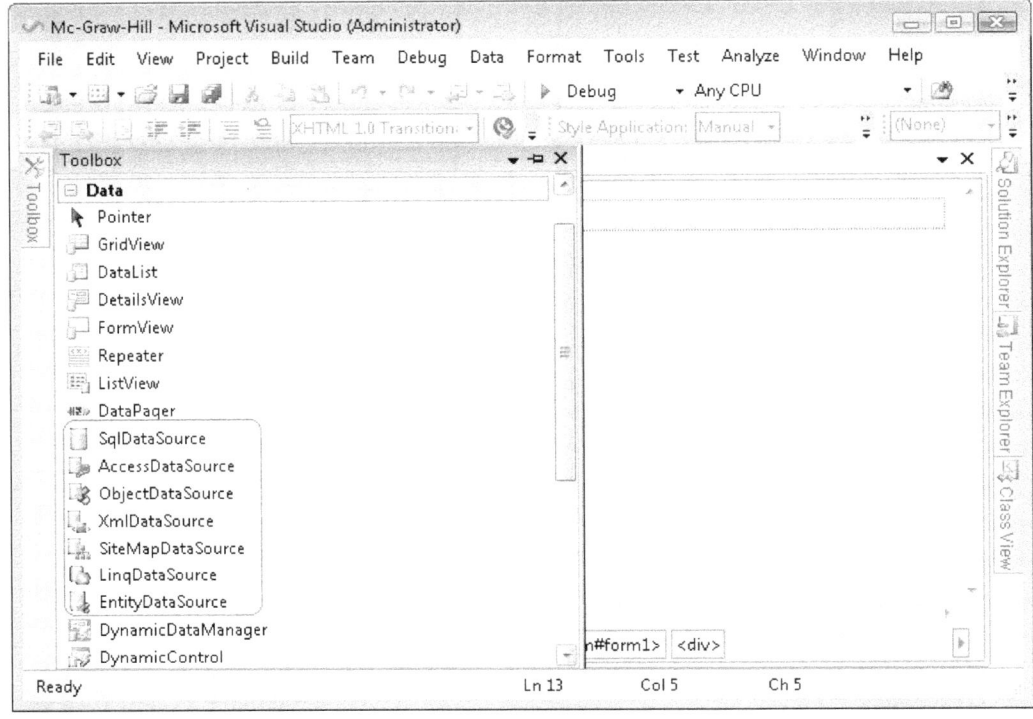

Figure 4-2   The ASP.NET data source controls

- SqlDataSource control
- AccessDataSource control
- EntityDataSource control
- SiteMapDataSource control

In addition to these controls, there is also a SiteMapDataSource control, which can be used to load a site map file and expose it to controls such as TreeView and SiteMapPath. Using these controls is easy: in the Design view of Visual Studio, simply drag and drop a control from the toolbox into your web form.

Figure 4-2 illustrates the data source controls in ASP.NET.

The ObjectDataSource Control

The AccessDataSource, SQLDataSource, and XMLDataSource controls are used to bind data to the ASP.NET data controls from Access, a SQL Server database, or XML data sources. You use the ObjectDataSource control to bind data from generic business objects to data controls. The ObjectDataSource control can be used to display, edit, and sort data on a web page with little or no code—you can use it declaratively as well as programmatically.

Here is how you can associate an ASP.NET ObjectDataSource control to an ASP.NET data source control:

Listing 4-25
```
<asp:GridView ID="GridView1"
 runat="server"
 DataSourceID="ObjectDataSource1" />
<asp:ObjectDataSource id="ObjectDataSource1" runat="server" />
```

The ObjectDataSource control's TypeName property can be used to instantiate a specific type that will be used for CRUD operations. The ObjectDataSource control supports properties such as SelectMethod, UpdateMethod, InsertMethod, and DeleteMethod that correspond to CRUD operations. Here is an example that illustrates how you can use these properties:

Listing 4-26
```
<asp:ObjectDataSource ID="ObjectDataSource1" TypeName="Employee"
SelectMethod="GetEmployees" UpdateMethod="UpdateEmployees"
DeleteMethod="DeleteEmployees"
 InsertMethod=
"InsertEmployees"
 runat="server"/>
```

The XmlDataSource Control

The XmlDataSource control is used to declaratively connect to an XML data source and perform CRUD operations against it. You can use the XmlDataSource control to support declarative data binding to XML data sources. The XmlDataSource control also supports hierarchical data-bound controls like Tree view and Menu controls, as well as binding data to the ASP.NET tabular data-bound controls like Repeater, GridView, and Data List.

Here is how you can use the XmlDataSource control with a Repeater control:

Listing 4-27
```
<asp:Repeater ID="Repeater"
 runat="server"
 DataSourceID="XmlDataSource1">
 <ItemTemplate>
    <%# XPath("@fname") %><br />
    <%#XPath("@lname")%><br />
    <%#XPath("@basic")%><br />
 </ItemTemplate>
</asp:Repeater>
<asp:XmlDataSource ID="XmlDataSource"
 runat="server"
 DataFile="~/Employee.xml"
 XPath="EmployeeRecords/Employee">
</asp:XmlDataSource>And, here is the content of the Employee.xml file:
<?xml version="1.0" encoding="utf-8" ?>
```

```
<EmployeeRecord>
 <Employee FName="Joydip">
 <LName>Kanjilal</LName>
 <Basic>2000</Basic>
 </Employee>
 <Employee FName="Manashi">
 <LName>Kanjilal</LName>
 <Basic>1000</Basic>
 </Employee>
 <Employee FName="Jini">
 <LName>Oindrilla</LName>
 <Basic>3000</Basic>
 </Employee>
</EmployeeRecord>
```

The LinqDataSource Control

You can use the LinqDataSource control both programmatically and declaratively in your code. Like the other data source controls, the LinqDataSource control can be used to declaratively bind data to your ASP.NET data controls in your web page. Using the LinqDataSource control, you can eliminate data-store-specific coding in your applications, because this control can be used to bind data to your ASP.NET data controls from any LINQ-enabled data model. You can even execute stored procedures and complex queries using this control. The LinqDataSource control is a good fit in applications where you need to perform CRUD operations by leveraging the advantage of the unified programming model that LINQ provides.

To get started with this control, simply drag and drop it from the toolbox onto your web form. The LinqDataSource control is very flexible in the sense that you can use it to bind data to a data control from a wide variety of data sources. Note that the LinqDataSource control will not connect to your database directly. Instead, it will interact with entity classes you need to generate using the Object Relational Designer or the SqlMetal.exe tools. The ContextTypeName property of the LinqDataSource control is used to map it to the entity class that represents the database, and the TableName property is used to map the control to the class that represents the database table in use.

Here's what the markup code of a typical LinqDataSource control looks like:

Listing 4-28
```
<asp:LinqDataSource
    runat="server"
    ContextTypeName="CustomerDataContext"
    TableName="Customer"
    ID=" myLinqDataSource">
</asp:LinqDataSource>
```

You can then create a data source control in your application and associate its DataSourceID property to the LinqDataSource control, as shown here:

Listing 4-29
```
<asp:GridView ID="GridView1" runat="server"
    DataSourceID=" LinqDataSource1" >
</asp:GridView>
```

You can also use bound fields of the GridView control to show data for just the columns of the Customer table you want. To do this, disable the AutoGenerateColumns attribute of the GridView control. Here's the complete markup code for both controls:

Listing 4-30
```
<asp:LinqDataSource ContextTypeName="CustomerDataContext"
    TableName="Customer" ID="myLinqDataSource"
    runat="server">
</asp:LinqDataSource>
<asp:GridView
    DataSourceID="LinqDataSource1"
    AutoGenerateColumns="false"
    ID="GridView1"
    runat="server">
    <Columns>
       <asp:BoundField DataField="Customer_Code" />
       <asp:BoundField DataField="Customer_Name" />
        <asp:BoundField DataField="Customer_Address" />
        <asp:BoundField DataField="Customer_Zip" />
 <asp:BoundField DataField="Customer_Phone" />
   </Columns>
</asp:GridView>
```

The SqlDataSource Control

The SqlDataSource control can be used to bind data to data controls retrieved from SQL Server databases. The following is typical markup code for the SqlDataSource control:

Listing 4-31
```
<asp:SqlDataSource ID="SqlDataSource1" runat="server"
     SelectCommand="SELECT [ProductID],
 [ProductName], [SupplierID],
 [CategoryID] FROM [Products]"
     ConnectionString=
"<%$ ConnectionStrings:NorthWindConnectionString %>"
     UpdateCommand="UPDATE Products SET ProductName = @ProductName,
     SupplierID= @SupplierID, CategoryID =
@CategoryID WHERE ProductID=@ProductID"
     DeleteCommand="DELETE FROM Products WHERE ProductID=@ProductID">
</asp:SqlDataSource>
```

The AccessDataSource Control

The AccessDataSource control, as the name implies, is used to connect to any Access database and perform CRUD operations. Here is what the markup code of the AccessDataSource control looks like:

Listing 4-32
```
<asp:AccessDataSource ID="AccessDataSource1" runat="server"
DataSourceMode="DataSet" DataFile="~/App_Data/Employee.mdb"
SelectCommand="SELECT [ID], [FirstName],
[LastName], [Basic] FROM [Employee]">
</asp:AccessDataSource>
```

The EntityDataSource Control

The EntityDataSource control is a newly added data source control that can connect to an ADO.NET Entity Data Model (EDM) to perform CRUD operations against the EDM. The EntityDataSource control is new in ASP.NET 3.5 and later versions (included as part of the Visual Studio 2008 Service Pack 1), and supports data binding in web applications using an EDM as the source of the data.

The following markup code illustrates how you can bind data retrieved through an EntityDataSource control to a GridView:

Listing 4-33
```
<head runat="server">
    <title>Displaying Employee Records</title>
</head>
<body>
    <form id="form1" runat="server">
    <asp:EntityDataSource ID="EntityDataSource1"
 runat="server"
        ConnectionString="name=AdventureWorksEntities"
        DefaultContainerName="AdventureWorksEntities"
 EntitySetName="Employee"
        Select="it.[EmployeeID], it.[MaritalStatus],
 it.[BirthDate], it.[Gender],
 it.[Title], it.[HireDate]">
    </asp:EntityDataSource>
    <asp:GridView ID="GridView1"
runat="server" AutoGenerateColumns="False"
        DataSourceID="EntityDataSource1">
        <Columns>
            <asp:BoundField DataField=
"EmployeeID" HeaderText="Employee ID"
                SortExpression="EmployeeID" />
            <asp:BoundField DataField="Gender" HeaderText="Gender"
                SortExpression="Gender" />
            <asp:BoundField DataField=
```

```
"Title" HeaderText="Title" SortExpression="Title" />
            <asp:BoundField DataField=
"BirthDate" DataFormatString="{0:d}"
                HeaderText="Birth Date" SortExpression="BirthDate" />
            <asp:BoundField DataField=
"HireDate" DataFormatString="{0:d}"
                HeaderText="Hire Date" SortExpression="HireDate" />
            <asp:BoundField DataField=
"MaritalStatus" HeaderText="Marital Status"
                SortExpression="MaritalStatus" />
        </Columns>
    </asp:GridView>
    </form>
</body>
```

The SiteMapDataSource Control

The SiteMapDataSource control can be used to place a site map on your web site. Here's what the markup code for this control looks like:

Listing 4-34   `<asp:SiteMapDataSource ID="SiteMapDataSource1" runat="server" />`

These are the important properties of this control:

- **SiteMapProvider**   This is used to get or set the site map provider.
- **StartingUrlNode**   This is used to set the root node.
- **ShowStartingNode**   This is a Boolean property that denotes whether or not the start node is a root node.

Navigating Sites with the SiteMapPath Control

The SiteMapPath control in ASP.NET is used to get the navigation information for a web site. The control will use the web.sitemap file located in the root directory of your application by default. In essence, the SiteMapPath control can be used to inform the user about the site hierarchy.

Here's what the markup code for a typical SiteMapPath control looks like:

Listing 4-35   `<asp:sitemappath runat="server"></asp:sitemappath>`

The SiteMapPath control is actually a site navigation control that makes use of the data that is fetched to it by the SiteMap object, which represents the relationship between the web pages of an application. To use SiteMap features on your site, simply add the SiteMap control to your page. If you need SiteMap features across all pages in your application, you can instead add the SiteMap control in a master page. All child or content pages that inherit the master page will inherit the SiteMap feature.

When you create the web.sitemap file, here's what it looks like by default:

Listing 4-36
```xml
<?xml version="1.0" encoding="utf-8" ?>
<siteMap xmlns="http://schemas.microsoft.com/AspNet/SiteMap-File-1.0" >
<siteMapNode url="" title=""  description="">
<siteMapNode url="" title=""  description="" />
<siteMapNode url="" title=""  description="" />
</siteMapNode>
</siteMap>
```

Here's what a typical .SiteMap file looks like:

Listing 4-37
```xml
<siteMap>
<siteMapNode url="default.aspx"
title="Home Page" description="Test">
<siteMapNode title="Sales" url=
"Sales.aspx" description=
"Sales Department">
<siteMapNode title=
"Human Resources" url=
"HR.aspx" description=
"HR Department">
<siteMapNode title="Finance"
 url="Finance.aspx"
description="Finance Department">
<siteMapNode title=
"Accounts" url="Accounts.aspx"
 description="Accounts Department">
<siteMapNode title=
"Software" url="Software.aspx"
 description="Software Department">
</siteMapNode>
</siteMap>
```

You can then create a master page and use a SiteMapPath control as shown here:

Listing 4-38
```
<head runat="server">
    <title></title>
    <asp:ContentPlaceHolder ID="Header" runat="server">
    </asp:ContentPlaceHolder>
</head>
<body>
    <form id="form1" runat="server">
    <div>
        <asp:SiteMapPath ID="SiteMapPath1"
 runat="server" SkipLinkText=
"Skip Menu" PathSeparator=" - "
            CurrentNodeStyle-BackColor=
"AliceBlue" RootNodeStyle-Font-Names=
```

```
"Verdana" Font-Size="Medium"
              RootNodeStyle-ForeColor="Blue"
  RootNodeStyle-BorderWidth="1">
        </asp:SiteMapPath>
        <asp:ContentPlaceHolder ID="Content1" runat="server">
        </asp:ContentPlaceHolder>
    </div>
    </form>
</body>
```

The GeneratedImage Control

The GeneratedImage control in ASP.NET can be used to display static and dynamic images in web pages. This control provides a simple way of transforming and caching images in ASP.NET applications. To use this control, you need to download Microsoft .Web.GeneratedImage.dll from this link: http://www.codeplex.com/aspnet/Release/ ProjectReleases.aspx?ReleaseId=16449.

Once you drag and drop the control from the toolbox, this is what the markup code looks like:

Listing 4-39
```
<cc1:GeneratedImage ID="GeneratedImageControl1"
runat="server"
  ImageHandlerUrl="~/ImageHandler1.ashx">
</cc1:GeneratedImage>
```

The default code of the ImageHandler looks like this:

Listing 4-40
```
<%@ WebHandler Language="C#" Class="ImageHandler1" %>
using System;
using System.Collections.Specialized;
using System.Drawing;
using System.Web;
using Microsoft.Web;
public class ImageHandler1 : ImageHandler
{
  public ImageHandler1() {
    // Set caching settings and add image transformations here
    // EnableServerCache = true;
  }
  public override ImageInfo GenerateImage
(NameValueCollection parameters) {
    // Add image generation logic here
    // and return an instance of ImageInfo
    throw new NotImplementedException();
  }
}
```

You will need to override this handler and create your own image handler. You can write your own code to seamlessly display images read from the database.

The Chart Control

The Chart control in ASP.NET can be used to implement a variety of charts: bar, pie, range, point, Ajax interactive, etc. Like other data controls, you can bind data to this control both declaratively and programmatically.

When you drag and drop a Chart control onto your web page, the markup code will looks like this:

Listing 4-41
```
<asp:Chart ID="Chart1" runat="server">
    <series>
        <asp:Series Name="Series1">
        </asp:Series>
    </series>
    <chartareas>
        <asp:ChartArea Name="ChartArea1">
        </asp:ChartArea>
    </chartareas>
</asp:Chart>
```

The following code shows how you can display the annual sales figures for two products graphically using the Chart control.

Listing 4-42
```
<asp:Chart ID="Chart1" runat="server" BackColor="Aquamarine">
    <Titles>
        <asp:Title Text=
"Illustrating Annual Sales
for Two Products"
 Visible="true" />
    </Titles>
    <Legends>
        <asp:Legend Name="MyLegend" Docking="Top" />
    </Legends>
    <Series>
        <asp:Series Name="Product-A">
            <Points>
                <asp:DataPoint XValue="2005" YValues="15400" />
                <asp:DataPoint XValue="2006" YValues="11200" />
                <asp:DataPoint XValue="2007" YValues="51900" />
                <asp:DataPoint XValue="2008" YValues="11200" />
                <asp:DataPoint XValue="2009" YValues="29060" />
            </Points>
        </asp:Series>
        <asp:Series Name="Product-B">
            <Points>
```

```
                <asp:DataPoint XValue="2005" YValues="22500" />
                <asp:DataPoint XValue="2006" YValues="23000" />
                <asp:DataPoint XValue="2007" YValues="24900" />
                <asp:DataPoint XValue="2008" YValues="16300" />
                <asp:DataPoint XValue="2009" YValues="16300" />
            </Points>
        </asp:Series>
    </Series>
    <ChartAreas>
        <asp:ChartArea Name="ChartArea1">
        </asp:ChartArea>
    </ChartAreas>
</asp:Chart>
```

Figure 4-3 shows what the output of this code looks like in a web browser.

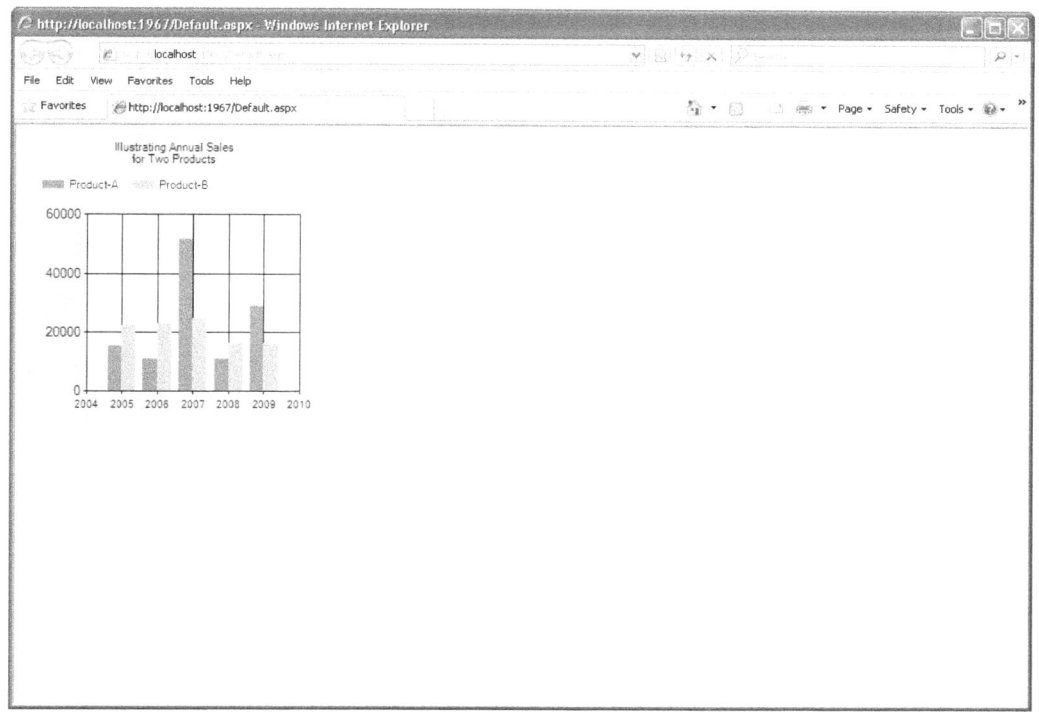

FIGURE 4-3   The Chart control in action

CHAPTER 5

Building and Deploying ASP.NET Web Sites

W hile creating ASP.NET applications in Visual Studio, you can choose from two different project types: Web Site and Web Application. ASP.NET provides you with a lot of features for designing professional web sites. You can use master pages, user controls, and themes to control the look and feel of your ASP.NET web sites.

Creating Web Sites in ASP.NET

To create a new web site in Visual Studio 2010, select File | New Web Site, and in the New Web Site dialog box choose ASP.NET Web Site and select C# as the language. Refer to Figure 5-1.

The Location drop-down control lets you choose where the web site will be stored. There are three options:

- File System
- HTTP
- FTP

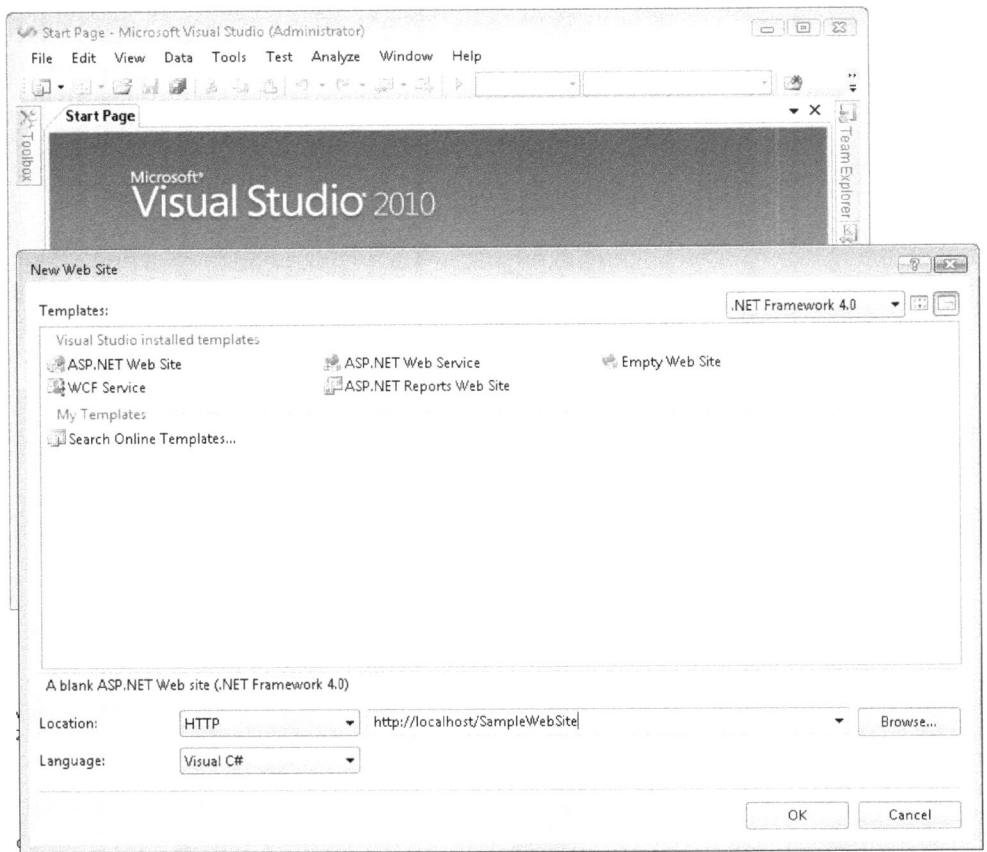

FIGURE 5-1   Creating a web site in Visual Studio 2010

If you select File System, you can store your web site in any directory on your hard drive or on any shared network drive. Note that you can run a web site from a filesystem by using the built-in ASP.NET Development Server—you need not have IIS installed on your system to run such web sites.

If you choose HTTP as the location, Visual Studio 2010 will create and store your web site inside an IIS virtual directory. In this case, you would need IIS installed on your system to run the web site.

The FTP option lets you store your web site on a remote server.

One of the major differences between the web site model and the web application model is that when you use the web site model, the settings are stored in the application's web.config file. When you use the web application model, the settings are stored in a project file.

Using ASP.NET Master Pages

Master pages in ASP.NET are files that have .master extensions. They allow you to create a consistent layout and look and feel for a group of pages (or all pages) in a web application. Each master page should have one or more content pages. A content page is just another page—it inherits a master page, and it contains the content you want to display.

The basic differences between a master page and a normal .aspx page are that master pages should have .master extensions and have the <%@ Master %> directive instead of the <%@ Page %> directive found in normal .aspx pages. Also, master pages can contain one or more ContentPlaceHolder controls, whereas normal .aspx pages cannot. A master page is actually a combination of itself and one or more content pages. A content page is just like a normal ASP.NET web page with the exception that it inherits a master page.

The following sequence of events occurs to combine the content of master and content pages before the combined content is rendered in the web browser on the client side:

1. Pre-initialize event of the content page

2. Initialize event of the child controls of the master page

3. Initialize event of the child controls of the content page

4. Initialize event of the master page

5. Initialize event of the content page

6. Preload event of the content page

7. Load event of the content page

8. Load event of the master page

9. Load event of the master page child controls

10. Load event of the child controls of the content page

User Controls versus Master Pages

The basic advantage of using master pages over user controls is that you can use the former to provide a consistent look and feel for all pages in your application that inherit the master page. If you use a user control to provide a consistent look and feel, you have to add it to all pages in your application.

Another disadvantage of using user controls is that you cannot visualize what the page looks like when you are creating it. You can only see the page once it is executed in the web browser.

You can, however, use a user control to create the login form for your application. You typically want the login form to appear only once the application is executed.

Creating a Master Page in Visual Studio

To create a master page in Visual Studio, follow these simple steps:

1. Open Visual Studio 2010 and create a new Web Application project.
2. Right-click on the web project in the Solution Explorer and select Add | New Item.
3. Select Master Page from the list of Visual Studio installed templates. (Alternatively, selecting Web Content Form from the list will create a content page.)

A master page will be created with the default name of Site1.master. The markup code in the file will look like this:

Listing 5-1
```
<!DOCTYPE html PUBLIC "-//W3C//DTD XHTML 1.0 Transitional//EN"
"http://www.w3.org/TR/xhtml1/DTD/xhtml1-transitional.dtd">
<html xmlns="http://www.w3.org/1999/xhtml" >
<head runat="server">
    <title>Untitled Page</title>
    <asp:ContentPlaceHolder ID="head" runat="server">
    </asp:ContentPlaceHolder>
</head>
<body>
    <form id="form1" runat="server">
    <div>
        <asp:ContentPlaceHolder
ID="ContentPlaceHolder1"
runat="server">
        </asp:ContentPlaceHolder>
    </div>
    </form>
</body>
</html>
```

The ContentPlaceHolder control named ContentPlaceHolder1 is where you place your content pages.

You can create a content page by following the steps outlined earlier in this section for creating a master page, and selecting Web Content Form from the list of Visual Studio installed templates. When prompted, you'll need to link the content page to its master page.

The markup code of the generated content page will look like this:

Listing 5-2
```
<%@ Page Language="C#"
MasterPageFile="~/Site1.Master"
AutoEventWireup="true"
CodeBehind="WebForm1.aspx.cs"
Inherits="WebApplication1.WebForm1"
 Title="Untitled Page" %>
<asp:Content ID="Content1" ContentPlaceHolderID="head" runat="server">
</asp:Content>
<asp:Content ID="Content2"
 ContentPlaceHolderID="ContentPlaceHolder1"
 runat="server">
</asp:Content>
```

What should your content page display to the end user? There should be some controls or text that shows some visual display, right? So, now let's add a few controls to the content page. Add two Label controls to the two Content controls, and add appropriate text in them, as shown here:

Listing 5-3
```
<%@ Page Language="C#"
 MasterPageFile="~/Site1.Master"
AutoEventWireup="true"
CodeBehind="WebForm1.aspx.cs"
 Inherits="WebApplication1.WebForm1"
 Title="Untitled Page" %>
<asp:Content ID="Content1" ContentPlaceHolderID="head" runat="server">
    <asp:Label ID="Label1" runat="server" Text="Content 1"></asp:Label>
</asp:Content>
<asp:Content ID="Content2"
 ContentPlaceHolderID=
"ContentPlaceHolder1"
 runat="server">
    <asp:Label ID="Label2" runat="server" Text="Content 2"></asp:Label>
</asp:Content>
```

Note the MasterPageFile attribute in the content page. This attribute provides a reference to the content page's master page. Further, there are no <form> or <html> tags in the content page, unlike a typical .aspx page.

Configuring a Master Page

Configuring a master page relates to defining it using directives, or, etc. You can configure a master page in three different ways:

- By using the MasterPageFile attribute in the page directive of your content page:

Listing 5-4
```
<%@ Page Language="C#"
 MasterPageFile="~/Site1.Master"
 AutoEventWireup="true"
CodeBehind="WebForm1.aspx.cs"
 Inherits="WebApplication1.WebForm1"
 Title="Untitled Page" %>
```

- By setting the master page programmatically in the pre-init event of the content page that uses the master page:

Listing 5-5
```
protected void Page_PreInit(object sender, EventArgs e)
        {
                Page.MasterPageFile = ="~/Site1.Master";
        }
```

- By setting the master page for all pages in the application via the application's web.config file:

Listing 5-6
```
<configuration>
  <system.Web>
    <pages master="Site1.Master" />
  </system.Web>
</configuration>
```

Accessing a Master Page from Within a Content Page

To access a master page from within a content page, you can use the FindControl() method, as shown here:

Listing 5-7
```
Label lblText=  Master.FindControl
("lblText") as Label;
lblText.Text = "This is a label";
```

Nesting Master Pages

A nested master page is one that references another master page as its master. A nested master page is ideal when you want to keep the main layout in the main master page and have this layout be inherited in another master page. Note that both the parent and child master pages will have .master extensions.

As an example, here is the markup code of a parent master page:

Listing 5-8
```
<%@ Master Language="C#"
 AutoEventWireup="true"
CodeBehind="Parent.master.cs"
 Inherits="WebApplication1.Parent" %>
<!DOCTYPE html PUBLIC "-//W3C//DTD XHTML 1.0 Transitional//EN"
"http://www.w3.org/TR/xhtml1/DTD/xhtml1-transitional.dtd">
<html xmlns="http://www.w3.org/1999/xhtml" >
<head runat="server">
    <title>Parent Master Page</title>
 </head>
<body>
<form id="form2" runat="server">
    <div>
        <asp:contentplaceholder id=
        "MasterContentPlaceHolder"          runat="server">
        </asp:contentplaceholder>
    </div>
    </form>
</body>
</html>
```

This is the base master page. Next, we will create the child master page. This is the markup code of the child master page:

Listing 5-9
```
<%@ Master Language="C#" AutoEventWireup="true"
MasterPageFile="~/Parent.Master" %>
<asp:Content ID="ChildMasterContent" runat="server"
ContentPlaceHolderID="MasterContentPlaceHolder">
<asp:ContentPlaceHolder ID="ChildContentPlaceHolder" runat="server">
</asp:ContentPlaceHolder>
</asp:Content>
```

Note the usage of the MasterPageFile statement in the above code snippet. This implies that this master page inherits the Parent.Master page.

This is the markup code of the content page:

Listing 5-10
```
<%@ Page Language="C#"
AutoEventWireup="true"
 CodeBehind="ContentPage.aspx.cs"
Inherits="WebApplication1.ContentPage"
MasterPageFile="~/Child.Master" %>
<asp:Content ID="Content1"
 ContentPlaceHolderID=
"ChildContentPlaceHolder"
 Runat="Server">
</asp:Content>
```

Using Themes in ASP.NET

Themes are a great feature in ASP.NET—they allow you to specify the appearance of the controls in your application, so you can ensure a consistent look and feel. You can either define a theme for a particular web page or define it in your application's configuration file.

To define a theme for a page, you can use code like the following in the @Page directive of your page:

Listing 5-11
```
<%@ Page Language="C#"
 AutoEventWireup="true"
 Theme="McGrawHillTheme"
CodeFile="Default.aspx.cs"
Inherits="_Default" %>
```

Alternatively, you could define the same theme in your application's configuration file by using the pages element as shown here:

Listing 5-12
```
<configuration>
    <appSettings/>
    <connectionStrings/>
    <system.web>
        <compilation debug="false" />
        <authentication mode="Windows" />
        <pages theme ="McGrawHillTheme" />
         </system.web>
</configuration>
```

You can also apply a theme to a particular page programmatically, like this:

Listing 5-13
```
protected void Page_PreInit(object sender, EventArgs e)
{
    Page.Theme = "McGrawHillTheme";
}
```

Best Strategies for Deploying ASP.NET Applications

There are various strategies available for efficiently deploying ASP.NET applications:

- Assembly versioning
- Strong naming of assemblies
- Obfuscation
- GAC deployment
- Other Deployment Options

These are some of the best practices for deploying your application to a production server.

Assembly Versioning

Make sure you have a solid versioning policy in place. Assembly Versioning is always a good practice. You can apply a version stamp using the AssemblyVersion attribute at compile time, for example:

Listing 5-14 `[assembly: AssemblyVersion("1.0.12.1234")]`

It's usually best to apply the same version number to all assemblies in an application during the build process.

Strong Naming of Assemblies

An assembly is the smallest unit of versioning, security, deployment, version control, and reusability of code in .NET. An assembly is composed of assembly identity information (name, version, etc.), manifest and metadata information, the MSIL code, type and security information of the assembly, and resources. An assembly with a strong name can be uniquely identified by a combination of its assembly version, culture information, and a digital signature.

You can create a strong name for your assembly by using the strong-name utility (sn.exe) provided by the .NET Framework. When you use the sn.exe command line tool at the command line, the resulting file created is called a *strong-named file*. Listing 5-15 shows how you can use this utility from the command line.

Listing 5-15 `sn -k McGrawHill.snk`

When you create a project in Visual Studio, you'll see a default file called AssemblyInfo.cs that you can use to specify the attributes for that project. Here is how you can specify the strong-name information in the AssemblyInfo.cs file:

Listing 5-16
```
[assembly: AssemblyCulture("")]
[assembly: AssemblyVersion("1.0.0.0")]
[assembly: AssemblyKeyFile("McGrawHill.snk")]
```

Obfuscation

It's good practice to obfuscate your assemblies before you deploy them. Obfuscation is a technique that protects your source code from potential security threats while keeping the application's functionality in place. It involves converting the code and data in your assemblies into an equivalent code or format such that it becomes difficult to reverse-engineer using decompiler tools. In essence, obfuscation is a process that reduces the size of your executable and protects your intellectual property while keeping the application's functionality intact. It also improves the application's performance as obfuscated assemblies optimized and are of reduced size.

Obfuscation is implemented at three levels: control flow, layout (objects, literals, variables, and method names), and data. The obfuscators scramble the symbols, code, and data of a program to a form that becomes almost impossible to reverse engineer using decompilers. Obfuscators also rename the namespaces, classes, methods, literals, etc, to names which are not meaningful and very difficult to interpret.

Obfuscators obfuscate your assemblies by using a specific encryption methodology to transform them into another assembly that is also obfuscated, but the source code or the application's functionality remains unchanged. Obfuscation removes some unnecessary information from the assembly metadata when it deems that it is safe to do so, thus making the assembly more difficult to understand or read after it is decompiled. Note that even if an application is compiled to native code at the time of execution, the Microsoft .NET runtime environment still requires the assembly metadata and IL code to be embedded in the assembly before it starts execution.

Although obfuscation is an excellent technology for protecting your intellectual property, there are a few downsides to obfuscation too. It is rather difficult to debug obfuscated code as the obfuscators remove debug information from the obfuscated assemblies and you don't have the exception stack trace information is not available in obfuscated code. Also, obfuscated code conflicts with the reflection APIs—reflecting on the types of an obfuscated assembly becomes difficult.

GAC Deployment

The Global Assembly Cache (GAC) is where you store public assemblies—those that can be shared by all applications running in the system. Deploying an assembly to the GAC improves its load performance; strong-named assemblies are verified at install time rather than at runtime, so the .NET framework skips verification at runtime for GAC-loaded assemblies. .NET refuses to load assemblies that are not trusted or that may have been tampered with.

Note that you must provide a strong name for assemblies you want to install in the GAC. A strong name is a unique identifier that identifies an assembly.

You place an assembly into the GAC using the GACUtil tool. The following command places MyProject.dll into the GAC, making it globally accessible:

Listing 5-17   `GacUtil /i McGrawHill.dll`

To uninstall the assembly from the GAC, you would use this command:

Listing 5-18   `GacUtil /u McGrawHill.dll`

You can also make your strong-named assembly globally accessible without placing it in the GAC. To do this, you need to deploy your assembly using the Xcopy command.

Other Deployment Options

You can deploy your ASP.NET application by copying it either with the Copy Web Site tool, or by using Xcopy.

Copy Web Site improves on Xcopy because you can use it to deploy your application to a filesystem, a local instance of IIS, an FTP site, or even to a remote site.

However, the Copy Web Site tool has one major disadvantage compared to Xcopy deployment—the initial load time of your web pages is slower because Copy Web Site copies all your source pages as source and performs no compilation. In addition, copying the source files allows people to see the source, a potential risk to your intellectual property.

Using the Copy Web Site Tool

Using the Copy Web Site tool in Visual Studio 2010 is easy. To copy an existing source web site (SampleWebSite, in this example) to a target web site (TestWebSite), follow these steps:

1. Create a target web site (TestWebSite) by selecting File | New | Web Site in Visual Studio and then choose the standard ASP.NET Web Site template from the New Web Site dialog box.

2. Right-click on the source web site (SampleWebSite) in Solution Explorer and choose Copy Web Site from the context menu.

3. Select the shared/remote web site and click Open. Note that this is actually the target web site.

   You'll see your source and target web sites listed in the left and right panes, as shown in Figure 5-2.

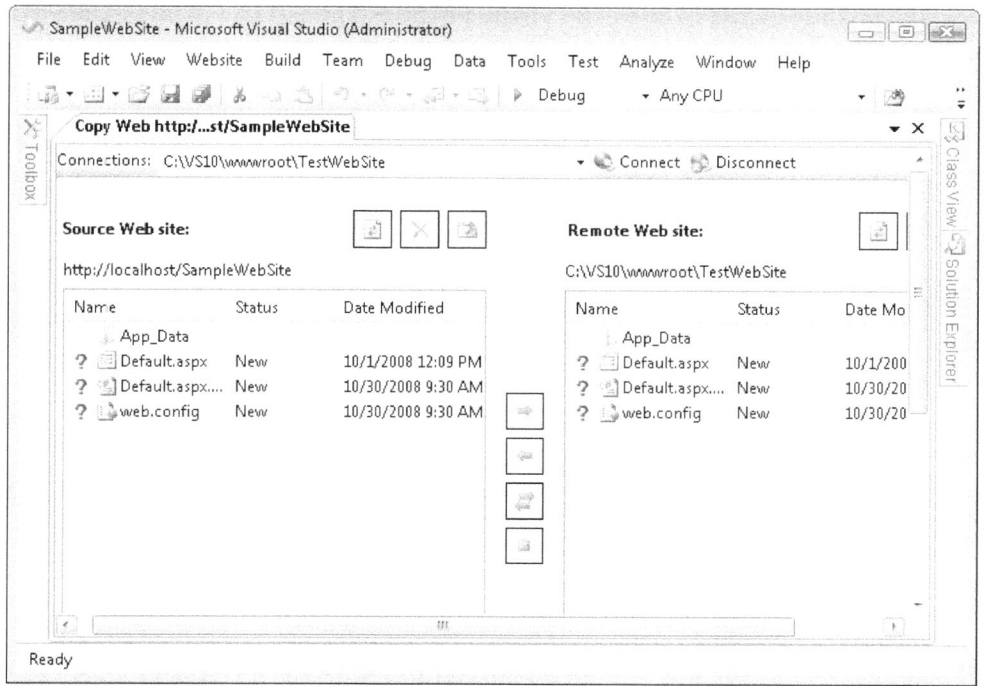

FIGURE 5-2 Using the Copy Web Site tool in Visual Studio 2010

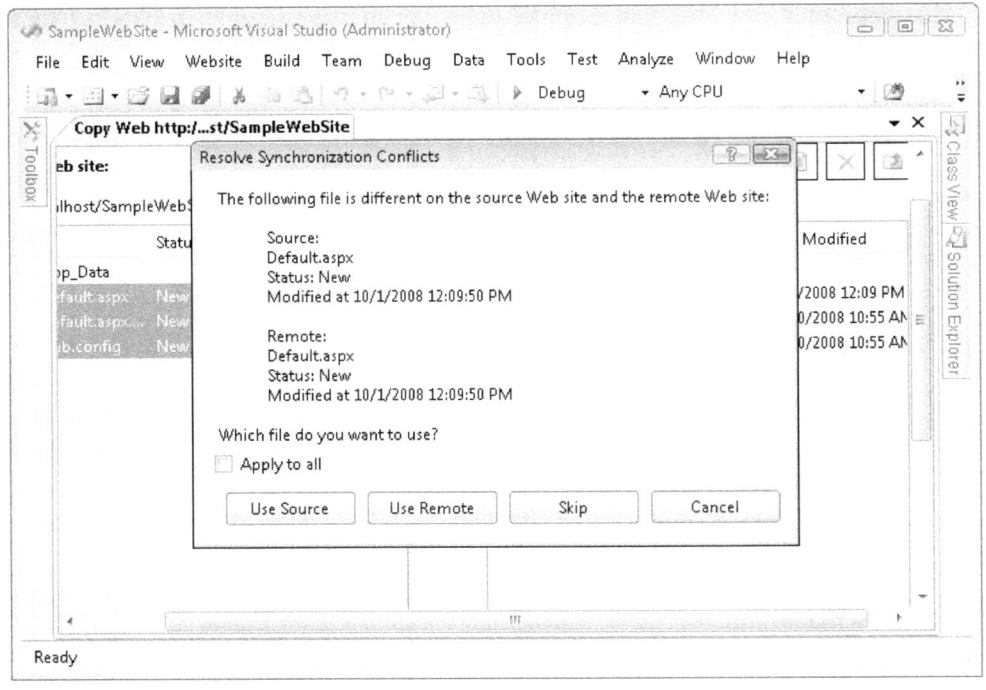

Figure 5-3 Resolving conflicts with the Copy Web Site Tool in Visual Studio 2010

If there are conflicts, you can easily resolve them before you copy the source web site. If the copy process finds file conflicts, it will prompt you to decide how the copy process should resolve the conflict, as shown in Figure 5-3.

If the sites have identically named subfolders, you can easily synchronize the source and remote web sites by selecting the Synchronize Files option. Clicking this button synchronizes selected files between the remote and local servers for files in matching paths.

4. Once any conflicts are resolved, you can click on the Copy Selected Files button to copy the files from the shared/remote web site to your local web site.

Deploying with Xcopy

Deploying an ASP.NET application to the production server is simple with Xcopy: just copy your application's entire folder structure to the production environment. Note that to use Xcopy, the folder structure at the source and target locations should match.

First, create the same folder structure at the target location. Then, use the Xcopy command to copy your site. The following command copies the TestWebSite folder and its subdirectories to the C:\ Projects\McGrawHill\SourceWebSite folder on the production system:

Listing 5-19   `XCOPY TestWebSite C:\Projects\McGrawHill\SourceWebSite /e /r /k /h /i /y`

Here's an explanation of the options:

Option	Description
/e	Copy all directories and subdirectories, including empty ones
/r	Overwrite existing read-only files
/k	Copy file and directory attributes
/h	Copy system and hidden files and directories
/y	Suppress "overwrite existing file" confirmation messages

You can easily deploy one or more files from the command prompt using the Xcopy command. To deploy a single file, use a command such as this:

Listing 5-20   `XCopy E:\McGrawHill\TestAssembly.dll C:\InetPub\wwwroot\bin`

To deploy all DLL files, you could use this command:

Listing 5-21   `Xcopy E:\McGrawHill\*.dll C:\InetPub\wwwroot\bin`

Precompiling

ASP.NET supports several new features that promise to enhance developer productivity, administration and management, extensibility, and performance. One of these features is precompilation, which developers or administrators can use to precompile ASP.NET applications before they are deployed. Moreover, the new precompilation feature can detect and provide warnings about any compilation failure issues, and lets you deploy applications without the need to store the source code on the deployment server. Precompilation can both reduce application response time and improve performance.

Why Precompile?

Dynamic compilation in ASP.NET compiles the application's code dynamically at runtime. Because the ASP.NET Framework senses changes to source pages, this capability means you can change your web page, and then reload it in a browser to see the page changes without having to recompile your entire web site. That feature is great during development, but not necessarily after deployment, when you're less likely to be changing pages regularly.

By default, ASP.NET still compiles pages the first time they are requested, even on the deployment server, and even if the pages haven't changed since the application was loaded. But what if you could precompile your entire web site before deployment? This is where ASP.NET's precompilation feature fits in.

You can use the ASP.NET precompilation feature to minimize the initial load time of your web pages and avoid having to deploy your source code to the server. Precompilation can detect and provide warnings about any compilation failure issues, and it can reduce application response time and improve performance.

Precompilation in ASP.NET is available in two modes: in-place precompilation and precompilation for deployment.

In-Place Precompilation

In-place precompilation enables you to precompile your entire project. In essence, it compiles each and every page of your application and displays any compilation errors that occur.

The tool you use to precompile applications is called aspnet_compiler, and it resides in the %WINDIR%\Microsoft.NET\Framework\vx.x.xxxx directory. The basic syntax for using this tool is as follows:

Listing 5-22
```
aspnet_compiler -v / -p
```

For example, you would use the following statement at the command line to precompile a TestWebSite virtual directory:

Listing 5-23
```
aspnet_compiler -v /TestWebSite
```

The -v option shown here specifies a virtual directory. By default, the precompiled library created by the preceding command is stored in the temporary ASP.NET files directory.

Precompilation for Deployment

Precompiling for deployment allows you to compile your project prior to its deployment. You can use this option to compile your projects into DLLs and copy those to the deployment server. In this case, you don't need to store your application's source code on the deployment server. With this option, you have to specify the path to your source code and the path to the target directory where you want the compiled library to be stored.

You can also precompile your web site using the Publish Web Site option in Visual Studio. However, if you check the "Allow this precompiled site to be updatable" option in the Publish Web Site dialog box, as shown in Figure 5-4, you'll find that the initial load time for web pages in the site will still be extensive. That's because when you specify this option, the ASP.NET runtime environment still has to compile the web page dynamically the first time it is requested. Unless you need to update your web pages frequently, precompile your web site with that option unchecked to minimize the initial load time.

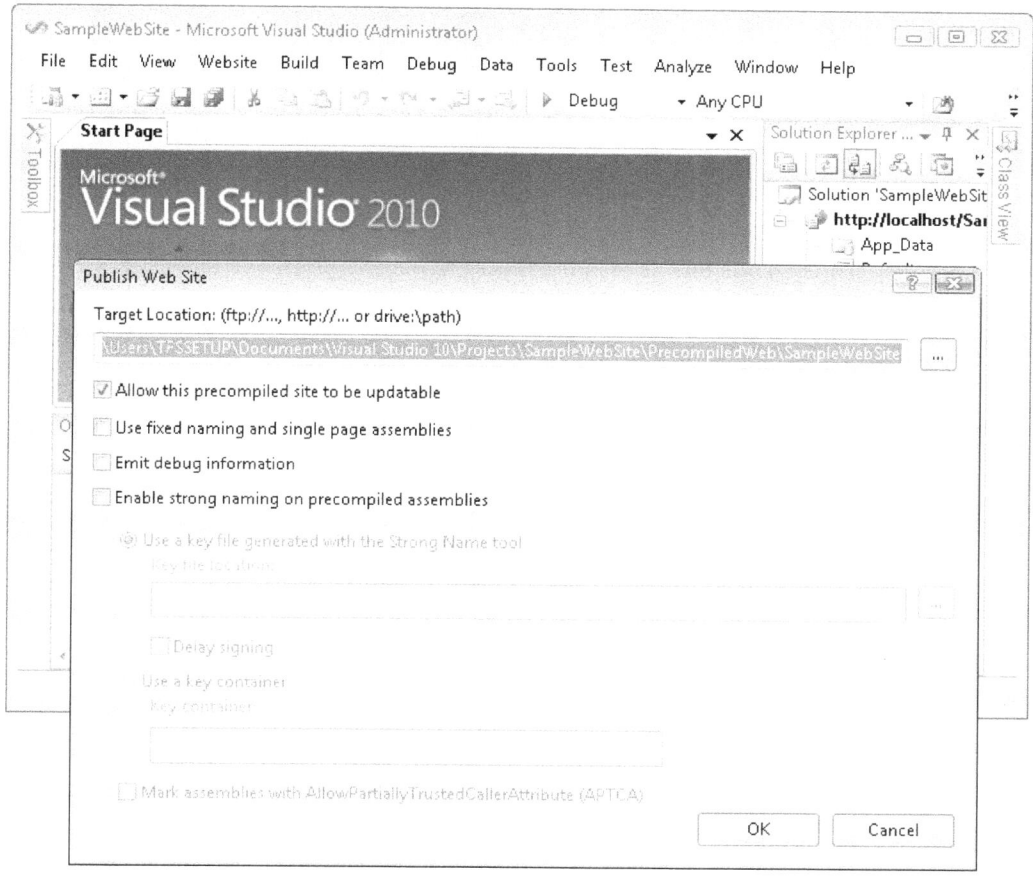

FIGURE 5-4   Using the Publish Web Site option in Visual Studio 2010

ClickOnce Deployment Strategy

ClickOnce deployment is a strategy you can use to deploy an application to a filesystem, local web server, remote web site, or FTP site. The essence of ClickOnce is that you have an application on the client that can detect when updates are available and download them, allowing you to configure your application to periodically get updates securely over the Internet. ClickOnce offers lower costs and automated updates with no version conflicts! You can use the ClickOnce deployment strategy to provide hot updates to the application, downloading and installing only the libraries that have changed.

However, there may be situations when ClickOnce does not work as expected. For example, if a browser's proxy server has already cached an older version of the deployment file, that client might not get the updates as expected. You can use HTTP content expiration to mitigate such issues.

New Deployment Options in Visual Studio 2010

Various new deployment strategies have been introduced in Visual Studio 2010. These include web packaging and database deployment. Here is the list of the deployment options in Visual Studio 2010:

- **MSDeploy**   This is a command line tool that is used for deploying and migrating web sites.
- **FTP**   You can use File Transfer Protocol to deploy your web sites.
- **File System**   You can use this if the development and deployment systems are on the same network. In this case, you use xcopy to copy the required content to the destination server.
- **FrontPage Server Extensions (FPSE)**   This provides a secure method of publishing content to the web server.

In Visual Studio 2010 you can use MSDeploy to create a .zip file (also known as a web package) for your application. You can just specify the connection string, and Visual Studio 2010 will automatically generate the schema, package it, and make it ready for deployment. This package includes the following:

- Metadata information
- IIS settings
- Web pages, controls, scripts, images
- SQL Server database
- Security certificates
- GAC components

You can also use XML Document Transform (XDT) to transform your application's web.config file and make it ready for deployment. Listing 5-24 shows an example of doing this.

Listing 5-24
```
<connectionStrings:xdt:Transform="Replace">
    <add name="MyDatabase" connectionString="..."/>
<connectionStrings/>
```

CHAPTER 6

Internationalization in ASP.NET

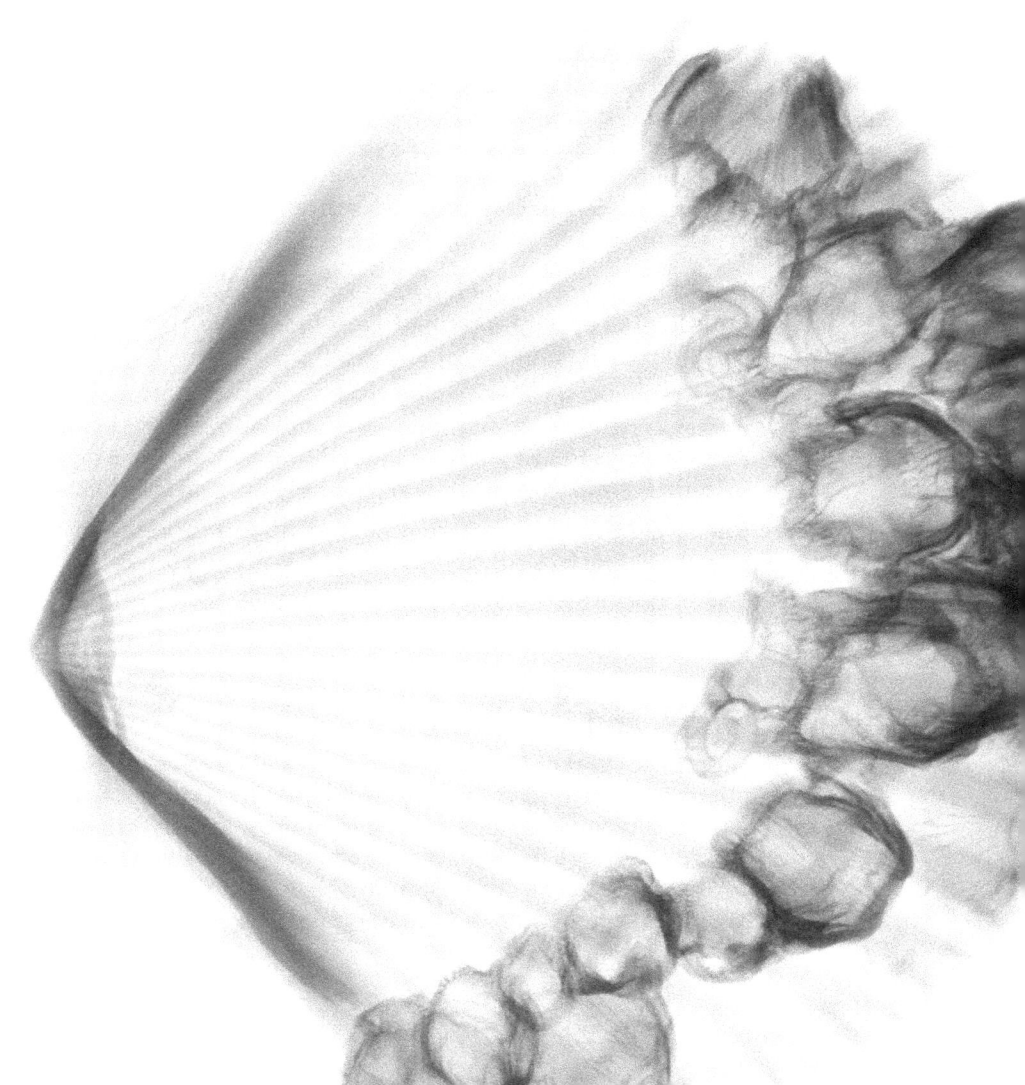

Microsoft's .NET Framework provides excellent support for globalization and localization through the System.Globalization, System.Resources, and System.Threading namespaces.

The System.Globalization namespace provides support in .NET for localized applications, which are applications that can support various locales. The System.Threading namespace contains classes and interfaces that are used to implement multithreaded programs. Such classes can also be used to access culture information. The System.Resources namespace contains classes and interfaces that are used for creating, storing, and managing culture-specific resources in an application. You can use these classes and interfaces to access, read, or write resources. The System.Text namespace contains classes that are used to represent ASCII, Unicode, UTF-7, and UTF-8 character encodings.

What Are Localization and Globalization?

Localization is the process of adapting a software application for a specific language or locale. *Globalization* is the process of identifying the specific portion of the application that needs to be different for different languages, and isolating them from the application's core. Therefore, it is the process of identifying the localizable resources of the application.

The Microsoft .NET library provides support for globalization and localization with four namespaces:

- The System.Globalization namespace provides support for developing multilingual applications in Microsoft .NET by allowing developers to define culture-specific information.

- The System.Resources namespace provides support for creating, storing, and managing the various culture-specific resources used in an application. This namespace contains a class named ResourceManager that allows access to resources either from the main assembly or from satellite assemblies.

- The System.Text namespace provides support for representing various character encodings, such as ASCII, Unicode, UTF-7, and UTF-8.

- The System.Threading namespace contains classes and interfaces that provide support for multithreaded programming.

Setting Culture and UICulture

Culture identifies a combination of a geographical location and the language spoken in that location. A culture is represented by a two-part code identifying the language and location: fr-FR (French language spoken in France), en-US (English language spoken in the US), or en-GB (English language spoken in Great Britain), for example.

There are two types of cultures in ASP.NET: culture and UICulture. The former is used to display formatted dates, numbers, and currencies based on a particular culture;

whereas the latter is used to determine the locale that the resources in the web page should load. Culture and UICulture can have separate values for a page.

You can set culture and UICulture at the page level, or at the application level for all pages in your application.

To set the culture and UICulture at the application level, in the application's web. config file, you can use code as shown in listing 6-1 next:

Listing 6-1
```
<configuration>
<system.web>
<globalization fileEncoding="utf-8"
requestEncoding="utf-8"
responseEncoding="utf-8"
 culture="en-GB"
uiCulture="fr-FR"/>
</system.web>
</configuration>
```

The specification in the preceding listing would ensure that the culture information is applicable throughout the application.

You can also set culture and UICulture at the page level; that is, in the .aspx markup as shown next:

Listing 6-2
```
<%@ Page UICulture="en" Culture="en-GB" %>
```

You can set it programmatically too, as follows:

Listing 6-3
```
Thread.CurrentThread.CurrentCulture =
CultureInfo.CreateSpecificCulture ("fr-FR");
Thread.CurrentThread.CurrentUICulture=new CultureInfo("en-GB");
```

Here is another example:

Listing 6-4
```
protected override void InitializeCulture()
{
    String culture = Session["Culture"].ToString();
    if (string.IsNullOrEmpty(culture))
        culture = "Auto";
    if (culture != "Auto")
    {
        System.Globalization.CultureInfo cultureInfo = new System
.Globalization.CultureInfo(culture);
        System.Threading.Thread.CurrentThread.CurrentCulture =
cultureInfo;
        System.Threading.Thread.CurrentThread.CurrentUICulture =
cultureInfo;
    }

    base.InitializeCulture();
}
```

Microsoft .NET provides the CultureInfo class in the System.Globalization namespace for working with culture-specific information. You can also use the System.Threading namespace to work with culture information.

You can also store and retrieve culture and UICulture information to and from a session. Here is an example:

Listing 6-5
```
Session["UICulture"] = Thread.CurrentThread.CurrentUICulture;
Session["Culture"] = Thread.CurrentThread.CurrentCulture;
```

To retrieve the culture and UICulture information from the session at a later time, you can use code like this:

Listing 6-6
```
if (Session["UICulture"] != null && Session["Culture"] != null)
    {
        Thread.CurrentThread.CurrentUICulture =
(CultureInfo)Session["UICulture"];
        Thread.CurrentThread.CurrentCulture =
(CultureInfo)Session["Culture"];
    }
```

You can also set the browser to display localized text. To do this, you'll need to specify the culture and UICulture properly. Here is an example:

Listing 6-7
```
<Globalization culture="auto" UIculture="auto"
 enableClientBasedCulture="true" />
```

You can also override the InitializeCulture method for a page to set the culture information. Here is an example:

Listing 6-8
```
public const string PostBackEventTarget = "__EVENTTARGET";
public const string DrpLanguageID = "ddlLanguage";
protected override void InitializeCulture()
{
    if (Request[PostBackEventTarget] != null)
        {
            string postbackControlID = Request[PostBackEventTarget];

            if (postbackControlID.Equals(DrpLanguageID))
                string culture = Request.Form[Request[PostBackEventTarget]]
    .ToString();
            Thread.CurrentThread.CurrentCulture =
                CultureInfo.CreateSpecificCulture(culture);
            Thread.CurrentThread.CurrentUICulture = new
                CultureInfo(culture);

        Session["UICulture"] = Thread.CurrentThread.CurrentUICulture;
        Session["Culture"] = Thread.CurrentThread.CurrentCulture;
    }
    base.InitializeCulture();
}
```

The markup code in the .aspx file for the preceding example would look like the following:

Listing 6-9

```
<form id="form1" runat="server">
    <div>
    <asp:DropDownList ID="ddlLanguage"
 AutoPostBack="true"
OnSelectedIndexChanged="ddlLanguage
_SelectedIndexChanged" runat="server">
        <asp:ListItem Value="en-US">English - US</asp:ListItem>
            <asp:ListItem Value="en-GB">English - GB</asp:ListItem>
        <asp:ListItem Value="zh-sg">Chinese</asp:ListItem>
        <asp:ListItem Value="ru">Russian</asp:ListItem>
        <asp:ListItem Value="en-GB">English - GB</asp:ListItem>
            <asp:ListItem Value="fr-FR">French</asp:ListItem>
                <asp:ListItem Value="es-MX">Español</asp:ListItem>
                <asp:ListItem Value="de-DE">Deutsch</asp:ListItem>
    </asp:DropDownList>
        </div>
    </form>
```

You can also use a cookie to specify globalization information in a MasterPage. Here is what you would need to do in the master page:

Listing 6-10

```
<asp:DropDownList ID="ddlLanguage"
AutoPostBack="true"
OnSelectedIndexChanged="ddlLanguage
_SelectedIndexChanged" runat="server">
        <asp:ListItem Value="en-US">English - US</asp:ListItem>
            <asp:ListItem Value="en-GB">English - GB</asp:ListItem>
        <asp:ListItem Value="zh-sg">Chinese</asp:ListItem>
        <asp:ListItem Value="ru">Russain</asp:ListItem>
        <asp:ListItem Value="en-GB">English - GB</asp:ListItem>
          <asp:ListItem Value="fr-FR">French</asp:ListItem>
            <asp:ListItem Value="es-MX">Español</asp:ListItem>
            <asp:ListItem Value="de-DE">Deutsch</asp:ListItem>
</asp:DropDownList>
```

You also would have to create the cookie in the SelectedIndexChanged event of the control, like this:

Listing 6-11

```
protected void ddlLanguage_SelectedIndexChanged
(object sender, EventArgs e){
    HttpCookie httpCookie = new HttpCookie("Culture");
    httpCookie.Value=ddlLanguage.UniqueID;
    Response.SetCookie(httpCookie);
}
```

In the Application_BeginRequest handler in the Global.asax.cs file, you'd need to set the culture information as shown here:

Listing 6-12
```
void Application_BeginRequest(Object sender, EventArgs e)
{
        String culture = String.Empty;
        HttpCookie httpCookie = Request.Cookies["Culture"];
        if (httpCookie != null && httpCookie.Value != null)
            culture = Request.Form[httpCookie.Value];
        Thread.CurrentThread.CurrentUICulture =
CultureInfo.GetCultureInfo(culture);
        Thread.CurrentThread.CurrentCulture = CultureInfo
.CreateSpecificCulture(culture);
}
```

You can ensure that only specific pages in your application display localized texts by storing the resource files in the App_LocalDirectory folder. This will restrict localization to specific pages rather than making it application wide.

Using Resource Files

Resource files are either text files or .resx files in .NET, and they contain non-executable resource data such as bitmaps, icons, cursors, and the like. Resource files are typically used to specify locale-specific settings, so you would have one resource file for each locale. If you need to support n cultures, you'll need to have n different resource files. The resource files are then compiled into satellite assemblies and accessed by the application.

Resource files provide excellent support for globalization by isolating the resource content from the application and promoting reusability. You can easily change resource content without changing the application's code at all.

Creating Resource Files

When creating resource files for specific locales, the following naming convention should be followed.

Listing 6-13
```
<base file name>.<locale>.txt
<base file name>.<locale>.resx
```

Therefore the resource file meant for the en-GB locale should be named TestResource.en-GB.txt or TestResource.en-GB.resx. Note that the TestResource.en-GB .resx filename contains the name of the resource.

The ResourceWriter class in the System.Resources namespace can be used to create a resource programmatically, or you can create a resource file using the Visual Studio 2008 IDE itself and save it with a .txt or a .resx extension. The resource file should be created using the intended culture if it is to be used for globalization or localization purposes.

The following code creates a resource file called Test.resources in the root directory of the C: drive.

Listing 6-14

```
using System;
using System.Resources;
class CreateResources
{
  public static void Main(string[]args)
  {
    ResourceWriter rw = new ResourceWriter("C:\\Test.resources");
    rw.AddResource("Copyright", "Copyright Message in English");
    rw.Close();
  }
}
```

The ResourceWriter class can also be used to store any other serializable object in the resource file.

Reading Resource Files

The content of the resource files can be read in the application by using the ResourceManager class defined in the System.Resources namespace. The ResourceManager class provides convenient access to culture-specific resources at runtime.

Listing 6-15

```
ResourceManager resourceManager = new
 ResourceManager("Internationalization.en-GB"+
culture, Assembly.GetExecutingAssembly());
CultureInfo cultureInfo = new CultureInfo(culture);
string message = resourceManager.GetString("ID",cultureInfo);
```

Compiling Resource Files

We created a resource file named TestResource.en-GB.resx in the previous section. Now let's compile it by using the ResGen utility that ships with the Microsoft .NET Framework

Listing 6-16

```
resgen Internationalization.en-GB.resx
   Internationalization.en-GB.resources
```

The preceding command will create a compiled resource for the en-GB locale with a .resources extension.

Working with Embedded Resource Files

An embedded resource is one that is embedded inside the application's code. Thus, when the application is compiled, this resource gets stored in the assembly that is generated.

For example, to create a text resource file called TextFile.txt and make it an embedded resource, you would select the properties of the same file and then set the Build Action in the item properties to "Embedded Resource." This will cause the resource to be embedded directly into the current assembly along with the code.

The following code snippet shows how you can retrieve the content of a resource as a string from the current executing assembly.

Listing 6-17
```
public string GetResourceFromAssembly(string resourceName)
{
  Assembly assembly = Assembly.GetExecutingAssembly();
  TextReader txtReader = new
  StreamReader(assembly.GetManifestResourceStream(resourceName));
  string str = txtReader.ReadToEnd();
  txtReader.Close();
  return str;
}
```

The preceding method accepts the fully qualified path to the resource as a parameter and returns the resource as a string from the current executing assembly. You can invoke the preceding method as follows:

Listing 6-18
```
Response.Write(GetResourceFromAssembly("Test.TextFile.txt"));
```

The GetResourceFromAssembly method will return the resource value from the specified resource file.

It is also possible to list all the embedded resources in the assembly, as shown here:

Listing 6-19
```
public string GetResourceNamesFromAssembly()
{
  Assembly assembly = Assembly.GetExecutingAssembly();
  string [] resourceNames = assembly.GetManifestResourceNames();
  StringBuilder stringBuilder = new StringBuilder();
  foreach(string str in resourceNames)
  {
   stringBuilder.Append(str);
   stringBuilder.Append("<BR>");
  }
 return stringBuilder.ToString();
}
```

The preceding method will return all the resource names from the current executing assembly.

You can invoke the preceding method like this:

Listing 6-20
```
Response.Write(GetResourceNamesFromAssembly());
```

Using Satellite Assemblies

An assembly is essentially a portable executable or library file containing partially compiled code for use in deployment, security, and versioning in Microsoft .NET's managed environment. The assembly is compiled into machine language instructions by the CLR. Note that a satellite assembly will be generated for each and every culture that your application supports.

Satellite assemblies are special assemblies associated with the main assembly. They are used to store compiled localized application resources and contain only resource data—no other code. Satellite assemblies are used to load the data dynamically, depending upon the culture of the application.

With satellite assemblies, resources are embedded in a binary format within a DLL. This makes the resources faster to access and keeps them from being very visible to the user. These assemblies can be deployed even after the application has been deployed.

Satellite assemblies can be created using the AL utility tool provided with Microsoft's .NET SDK. Here is how you could create a satellite assembly from a compiled resource file:

Listing 6-21
```
al /t:lib /culture:en-GB /embed: Internationalization.en-GB.resources
   /out: Internationalization.resources.dll
```

Note that Internationalization.en-GB.resources is a satellite assembly file that is created for the en-GB locale from the compiled resource file. It's a good practice to package the resources in your application with the application's main assembly, and then to create satellite assemblies for each language you want your application to support.

What Are Multilingual Applications?

A multilingual application is one that provides support for multiple languages. This section lists the steps you need to follow to implement a multilingual application in .NET using the concepts explained in previous sections.

These are the steps for implementing a multilingual application in .NET:

1. Create a resource file for each locale.

2. Save the resource files with a .resx extension.

3. Compile the resource files using the .NET SDK ResGen utility to create a compiled binary resource file.

4. Create a satellite assembly using the .NET SDK AL utility.

5. Create folders for the satellite assembly and store the satellite assembly there.

Creating Satellite Assemblies

Assume that the Internationalization.en-GB.resx file was created for the en-GB culture and compiled (as shown in Listing 6-5) to create the Internationalization.en-GB.resources file. This is the complied resources file, which can be used to create a satellite assembly.

The Internationalization.resources.dll file is the satellite assembly that can be used by the application. This satellite assembly should be placed in a subfolder inside the application's main folder and given the same name as the culture that the satellite assembly is targeted for. This satellite assembly can now be used to display locale-specific information in the application.

You can also use Microsoft .NET to retrieve resource information from satellite assemblies.

Using the CultureInfo Class

The CultureInfo class of the .NET Framework SDK provides access to the properties of a locale. An instance of the CultureInfo class can be created by passing the culture name as a string parameter.

The following code can be used to create a CultureInfo instance for English spoken in Great Britain:

Listing 6-22
```
CultureInfo c = new CultureInfo("en-GB");
```

The following code can be used to create a CultureInfo instance for the US English locale:

Listing 6-23
```
CultureInfo c = new CultureInfo("en-US");
```

Setting Culture Information for a Web Page Dynamically

Consider the markup code of the following DropDownList control:

Listing 6-24
```
<asp:DropDownList ID="dropDownList" runat="server" AutoPostBack="True">
        <asp:ListItem Value="auto">Auto</asp:ListItem>
        <asp:ListItem Value="en-US">English (US)</asp:ListItem>
        <asp:ListItem Value="en-GB">English (UK)</asp:ListItem>
        <asp:ListItem Value="fr-FR">French (France)</asp:ListItem>
</asp:DropDownList>
```

The InitializeCulture() method shown next can be used to set the culture for the web page appropriately based on the culture selected in the preceding DropDownList control.

```
Listing 6-5    protected override void InitializeCulture()
               {

                   if (Request[PostBackEventTarget] != null)
                   {
                       string controlID = Request[PostBackEventTarget];
                          if (controlID.Equals(dropDownList))
                       {
                          string selectedValue =
                                 Request.Form[Request[PostBackEventTarget]].ToString();
                             switch (selectedValue)
                          {
                              case "en-CA": SetCultureInformation("en-CA", "en-CA");
                                 break;
                              case "en-US": SetCultureInformation("en-US", "en-US");
                                 break;
                              case "en-GB": SetCultureInformation("en-AU", "en-GB");
                                 break;
                              case "fr": SetCultureInformation("fr-FR", "fr-FR");
                                 break;
                              default: SetCultureInformation("en-GB", "en-AU");
                                 break;
                          }
                       }
                   }
                   if (Session["UICulture"] != null && Session["Culture"] != null)
                   {
                       Thread.CurrentThread.CurrentUICulture = (CultureInfo)
               Session["UICulture"];
                       Thread.CurrentThread.CurrentCulture = (CultureInfo)
               Session["Culture"];
                   }
                   base.InitializeCulture();
               }
```

The SetCultureInformation() method sets the appropriate culture based on the culture name and locale passed to it as parameters.

```
Listing 6-26   protected void SetCultureInformation(string name, string locale)
               {
                   Thread.CurrentThread.CurrentUICulture = new CultureInfo(name);
                   Thread.CurrentThread.CurrentCulture = new CultureInfo(locale);
                   Session["UICulture"] = Thread.CurrentThread.CurrentUICulture;
                   Session["Culture"] = Thread.CurrentThread.CurrentCulture;
               }
```

Configuring Localization in an Application

To avoid changing the application source code each time you add support for a new culture to your application, you can use loose coupling by setting the culture name in the web.config file. This ensures that the application's culture settings are configurable. This information is then read by the application at runtime.

The <appSettings> element of the web.config file can be used to specify the culture name. Here are two examples:

Listing 6-27
```
<appSettings>
    <add key = "Culture" value = "fr-FR">
    </add>
</appSettings>
```

Listing 6-28
```
<appSettings>
    <add key = "Culture" value = "en-GB">
    </add>
</appSettings>
```

The culture type specified in the web.config file can be read by using System .ConfigurationSettings.AppSettings in your application. Note that System.Configuration .ConfigurationSettings.AppSettings is a class in the System.Configuration namespace in the system.dll assembly.

The source code follows.

Listing 6-29
```
string culture =
  System.Configuration.ConfigurationSettings.
AppSettings["Culture"].ToString();
ResourceManager resourceManager = new
  ResourceManager(typeof(TestForm).Namespace.ToString()+"."+culture,
  Assembly.GetExecutingAssembly());
CultureInfo cultureInfo = new CultureInfo(culture);
string message = resourceManager.GetString("ID",cultureInfo);
Response.Write(message);
```

In the preceding code, I created an instance of the ResourceManager class by passing the resource and the assembly in which the resource is embedded as parameters. The ResourceManager class provides access to the resources for a particular culture.

Next, I created an object of the CultureInfo class, and passed the culture name to the parameterized constructor of the class. Then, I called the GetString method on the ResourceManager instance and passed the ID string as key and the instance of the CultureInfo class as parameters.

The resource value is returned as a string, and it can be used as needed in the application. For the sake of simplicity, I displayed the message using the Response. Write method. This concept can be used to set the text of a particular control in a specific language by reading the locale-specific text from the resource. The current locale is specified in the web.config file.

For example, the following example sets the copyright on a label control in the web.

Listing 6-30
```
lblCopyright.Text = resourceManager.GetString("Copyright",culture);
```

Here the copyright message would be displayed in the label control based on the current culture that is set in the web.config file. Either the satellite assembly or the application's assembly should have the resources for all the cultures supported by the application.

Using Script Globalization and Localization

You can use the ScriptManager control to globalize and localize client script files. The following code snippet illustrates how you can use Sys.UI.DomEvent to globalize a date using a client side script:

Listing 6-31
```
<head runat="server">
    <title>Illustrating Script Globalization</title>
</head>
<body>
    <form id="Form1" runat="server">
        <asp:ScriptManager ID="ScriptManager1"
 runat="server"
EnableScriptGlobalization="true"/>
        <asp:UpdatePanel ID="UpdatePanel1"
 runat="server"
ChildrenAsTriggers="False"
                            UpdateMode="Conditional">
            <ContentTemplate>
                    <asp:Button ID="btnClick"
runat="server"
Text="Display System Date" />
                    <asp:Label ID="lblDate" runat="server"></asp:Label>
            </ContentTemplate>
        </asp:UpdatePanel>
    </form>
</body>
</html>
<script type="text/javascript">
    Sys.UI.DomEvent.addHandler($get("btnClick"), "click", displayDate);
    function displayDate() {
      var dt = new Date();
      try {
        $get('lblDate').innerHTML =
dt.localeFormat("dddd, dd MMMM yyyy HH:mm:ss");
      }
```

```
      catch(e) {
        alert(e.message);
      }
    }
</script>
```

Note that you should set globalization to "auto" in your application's web.config file, as shown here:

Listing 6-32 `<globalization culture="auto" />`

Then, you can set your default culture before you execute the application, as follows:

Listing 6-33 `<globalization culture="en-GB" />`

CHAPTER 7

The ASP.NET Security Model

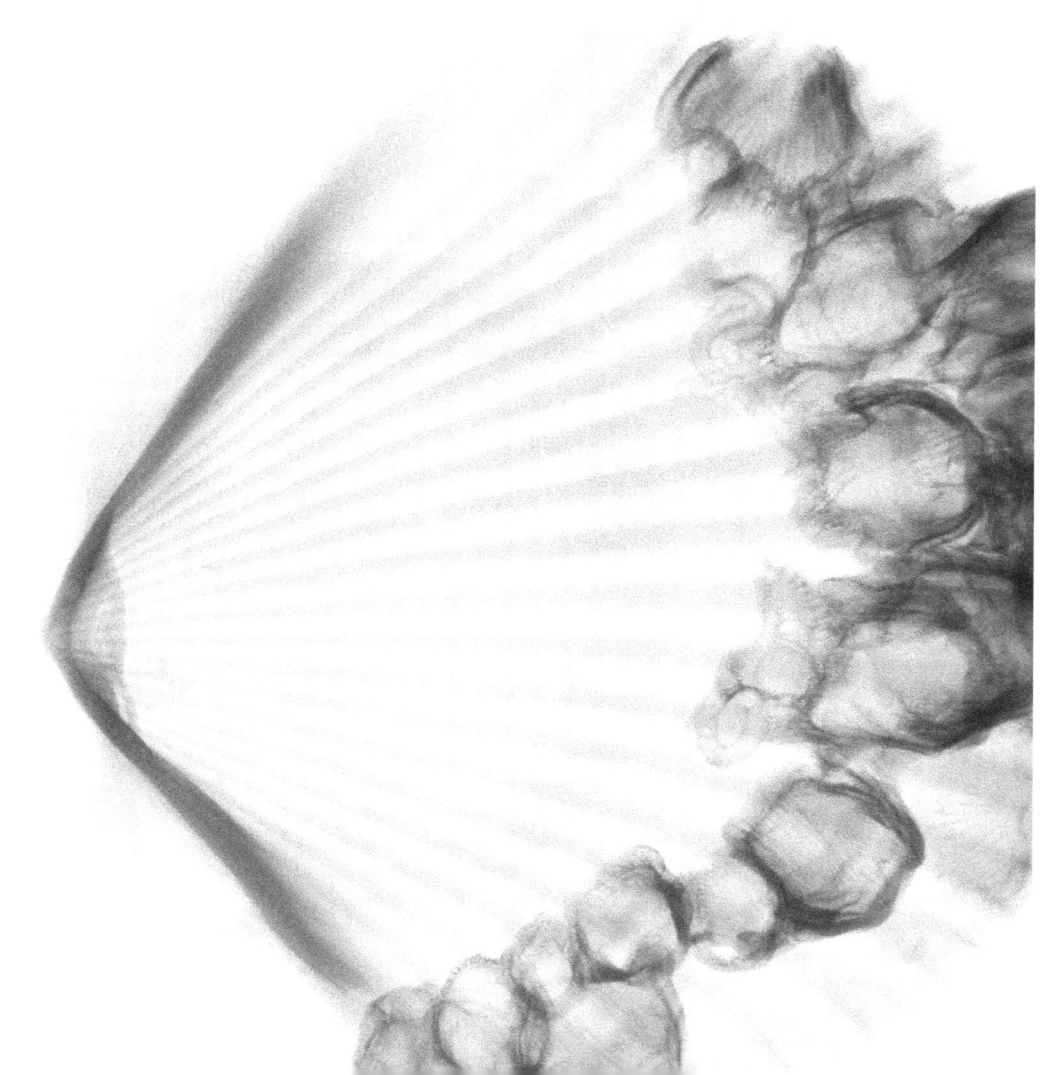

ecurity of web applications is an important issue when designing efficient and robust applications. ASP.NET provides excellent support for application security.

Three of the most important concepts related to ASP.NET security are authentication, authorization, and impersonation. You use *authentication* to validate the user's credentials. *Authorization* is the process that restricts access to resources to authenticated users. *Impersonation* allows ASP.NET to execute code in the context of an authenticated and authorized client.

Authentication

Authentication is the process used to identify that users are who they say they are. In other words, it is used to validate the credentials of the user. Note that a user can only be authorized for access to resources of the application if the user has already been authenticated for the application. So, we may say that only authenticated users can be authorized for access to the resources of an application. The default authentication mode is anonymous authentication.

The application's web.config file contains all of the configuration settings for an ASP.NET application. It is the job of the authentication provider to verify the user's credentials and decide whether a particular request should be considered authenticated or not. An authentication provider is used to prove the identity of the users on a system.

ASP.NET provides these ways to authenticate a user:

- Forms authentication
- Windows authentication
- Passport authentication

Accordingly, there are three authentication providers in ASP.NET to support the preceding authentication modes. Here is the general syntax for specifying authentication in the application's web.config file:

Listing 7-1
```
<configuration>
  <system.web>
    <authentication  mode = " [ Windows | Forms | Passport | None ] ">
    </authentication>
  </system.web>
</configuration>
```

NOTE *There is also another authentication mode—the anonymous authentication mode. In the anonymous authentication mode, IIS doesn't check the validity of a user. It allows any user to access the web site.*

Forms Authentication

Forms authentication is based on browser cookies. Typically, the user will enter their username and password and click a login button; the form then validates this information against values in a persistent store, usually a text file or database.

Once a user is authenticated, the user's credentials are stored in a cookie for use in that session. Forms authentication supports both session and persistent cookies. When a user has not logged in and requests any page in the application, he or she is redirected to the login page of the application.

You can specify the authentication mode in the application's web.config file as shown in the following code listing:

Listing 7-2
```
<configuration>
  <system.web>
   <authentication mode="[Windows/Forms/Passport/None]">
   </authentication>
  </system.web>
</configuration>
```

The following needs to be specified in the application's web.config file to use Forms authentication in ASP.NET:

Listing 7-3
```
configuration>
<system.web>
<authentication mode="Forms"/>
<forms name="Login" loginUrl="Login.aspx" />
<authorization>
<deny users="?"/>
</authorization>
</system.web>
</configuration>
```

The <deny users="?"> statement specifies that permissions are granted only to authenticated users. Users who are not authenticated are not granted any permissions. Note that the question mark (?) indicates all non-authenticated and anonymous users.

The following code snippet shows how Forms authentication validates user information. This is shown in the following code snippet:

Listing 7-4
```
String username = txtUserName.Text;
String password = txtPassword.Text;
bool isUserValid = false;
//Code to validate the user name and password
isUserValid = ValidateUserCredentials
(txtUserName.Text, txtPassword.Text);
if(isUserValid)
{
FormsAuthentication.RedirectFromLoginPage(txtUserName.Text, False);
```

```
else // User is not valid
lblMessage.Text = "Invalid login credentials...";
}
private bool ValidateUserCredentials(String userName, String password)
{
// Write code here to connect to the
//database where the user credentials are
// stored and then verify whether the
//user's credentials those are passed as
//parameters to this method are correct.
//The method would return true if success,
//false otherwise.
}
```

The ValidateUserCredentials method accepts a username and password, connects to the database where the user's credentials are stored, and verifies whether the credentials are correct.

The RedirectFromLoginPage static method creates an authentication ticket and is used to redirect an authenticated user back to the originally requested URL or the default URL. The authentication ticket creates a persistent cookie that becomes a part of the HttpResponse object. Later, when the user tries to access a page in a restricted folder, the ASP.NET framework uses the cookie to retrieve the ticket and determine whether the user has access to that particular resource. The first parameter to this method identifies the user, and the second specifies whether the user's authentication cookie needs to be persisted across multiple site visits.

The user's credentials can be also be specified in the web.config file, as illustrated in the following listing:

Listing 7-5
```
<configuration>
<system.web>
<authentication mode="Forms">
<forms loginUrl="LoginForm.aspx">
<credentialspasswordFormat="Clear">
<user name="Joydip"
password="Joydip1@3" />
</credentials>
</forms>
</authentication>
<authorization>
</system.web>
</configuration>
```

If you want the authentication ticket to time out after 30 minutes, you can use sliding expiration in the authentication element in your application's web.config file, as shown below:

Listing 7-6
```
<authentication mode="Forms">
    <forms
        slidingExpiration="true"
```

```
            timeout="30"
      />
</authentication>
```

You can also set the requireSSL property to true in your application's web.config file to restrict the authentication tickets to HTTPS connections only. Here is an example:

Listing 7-7
```
<forms loginUrl="Login.aspx"
        requireSSL="true" ... />
```

Note that the default login page is named Login.aspx. If you want a different login page, you can specify one in the login URL, as follows:

Listing 7-8
```
<forms loginUrl="MyLogin.aspx"
        requireSSL="true" ... />
```

Also, you can use the machineKey element to encrypt and validate authentication tickets:

Listing 7-9
```
<configuration>
    <machineKey>
        decryption="AES"
        validation="SHA1"
      decryptionKey="1513F567EE75F7FB5AC0AC4
          D79E1D9F25430E3E2F1BCDD3370BCFC4EFC97A541"
      validationKey="32CBA563F26041EE5B5
          FE9581076C40618DCC1218F5F447634EDE8624508A129"
    <machineKey/>
      </system.web>
</configuration>
```

Windows Authentication

Windows authentication is the default authentication mode in ASP.NET. With this mode, a user is authenticated based on his or her Windows account. Windows authentication can be used only in an intranet environment where the administrator has full control over the users in the network.

The following code listing illustrates how you can set up Windows authentication in your application's web.config file.

Listing 7-10
```
<authentication mode="Windows"/>
<authorization>
<allow users ="*" />
</authorization>
```

NOTE *The asterisk symbol (*) indicates all users, including authenticated and anonymous users. Hence, the* <allow users = "*"> *statement in Listing 7-10 grants all permissions to both anonymous and authenticated users.*

Types of Windows Authentication

Windows authentication in ASP.NET can be one of the following types:

- **Basic authentication**   Users of the application must provide a Windows username and password to log in and access the application. This authentication mode is not at all secure.

- **Anonymous authentication**   The IIS web server will let any user access the application without any authentication checking.

- **Digest authentication**   This is similar to Basic authentication, but the password is hashed before it is sent across the network. This offers improved security.

- **Integrated Windows authentication**   This authentication mode uses network authentication protocols—passwords are not sent over the network.

Configuring Windows Authentication in IIS

To set up Windows authentication in IIS, follow these steps:

1. Open IIS Manager on your system.
2. Right-click on the web site for which Windows authentication is to be enabled, and select Properties.
3. Switch to the Directory Security tab.
4. In the Anonymous Access and Authentication Control section, click the Edit button.
5. Make sure that the Anonymous Access option is not selected, and select the Integrated Windows Authentication check box.
6. Click OK to save the settings.

Passport Authentication

Passport authentication is an authentication strategy that makes use of Microsoft's Passport service to authenticate the users of an application. It allows users to create a single sign-in (SSI) name and password that they can use to access any site that has implemented the Passport SSI service.

Passport authentication is quite secure because it is built on cryptography and eliminates credentials-management hassles in the application. Internally, .NET Passport uses SSL, HTTP redirects, and cookies; the security is provided mainly by using a strong and secure symmetric key encryption algorithm. You can use this authentication technique in conjunction with role-based authorization to provide robust security.

Implementing Passport Authentication

In this section we'll discuss how you can implement Passport authentication in your applications.

Downloading and Installing the Passport SDK   To get started with Passport authentication, you first need to download and install the Passport SDK from http://download .microsoft.com.

Once done, you'll need to register your application with the Microsoft Passport Server. The next section discusses how you can enable Passport authentication mode for your application in the web.config file.

Enabling Passport Authentication in IIS   To enable Microsoft .NET Passport authentication on a particular web site, follow these steps:

1. Open IIS Manager on your system.
2. Right-click on the web site for which .NET Passport authentication is to be enabled, and click on Properties.
3. Switch to the Directory Security tab.
4. In the Anonymous Access and Authentication Control section, click the Edit button.
5. Select the .NET Passport Authentication check box.
6. Click OK to save the settings.

The following code snippet illustrates how you can enable Passport authentication in ASP.NET.

Listing 7-11
```
<configuration>
<system.web>
<authenticationmode="Passport">
<passportredirectUrl="LoginForm.aspx" />
</authentication>
<authorization>
<deny users="?" />
</authorization>
</system.web>
</configuration>
```

You can also use the location tag to specify the pages that require login, as shown in the following code snippet:

Listing 7-12
```
<configuration>
    <system.web>
        <authentication mode="Passport">
         <passport redirectUrl="/LoginForm.aspx" />
        </authentication>
        <authorization>
          <allow users="*" />
        </authorization>
    </system.web>
    <location path="MainMenu.aspx">
```

```
        <system.web>
            <authorization>
             <deny users="?" />
            </authorization>
        </system.web>
    </location>
</configuration>
```

You can then access the Passport Manager methods in your application, as follows:

Listing 7-13
```
void Page_Load(Object sender, EventArgs e)
{
PassportIdentity passportIdentity =
(PassportIdentity) Page.User.Identity;
Response.Write("Please sign-in to
access the website" + passportIdentity.LogoTag2());
}
```

ASP.NET also supports custom authentication. In such a case, the authentication mode has to be specified as none in the web.config file:

Listing 7-14
```
<authentication mode="none">
```

Then you need to write your own custom authentication provider.

Authorization

Authorization is a process by virtue of which an authenticated user can have access to the resources of an application. As stated previously, only an authenticated user can be authorized. In other words, authorization is a process that provides access only to the resources of an application's authenticated users.

The syntax for specifying authorization in ASP.NET is as follows:

Listing 7-15
```
<authorization>
< [ allow | deny ] [ users ] [ roles ] [ verbs ] />
</authorization>
```

There can be two types of authorization in ASP.NET: File authorization and URL authorization.

File Authorization

File authorization is only active if the application is configured to use Windows authentication. File authorization is performed using the FileAuthorizationModule, which checks the file's access control list (ACL) to determine whether a particular user should have access to the file.

URL Authorization

URL authorization can be used to allow or deny access to specific parts of an application. It is implemented using the URLAuthorizationModule, which maps users and roles to URLs in ASP.NET applications.

This is the complete syntax for using URL authorization in ASP.NET:

Listing 7-13
```
<configuration>
    <system.web>
        <authentication mode="Windows" />
         <authorization>
             <allow users="domain\user1, domain\user2, domain\user3 />
             <deny users="domain\user4, domain\user5, domain\user6 />
         </authorization>
     </system.web>
</configuration>
```

The following code snippet illustrates how you can set up authorization in your web.config file to allow access to Jini and deny everyone else.

Listing 7-17
```
<authorization>
    <allow users = "Jini" />
    <deny users = "*" />
</authorization>
```

The following specification in the web.config file allows or grants access to the user Joydip but denies the same to Jini and all anonymous users.

Listing 7-18
```
<authorization>
    <allow users="Joydip"/>
    <deny users="Jini"/>
    <deny users="?"/>
</authorization>
```

The following example shows how you can grant access to Banhisikha and all members of the Admin role while denying access to Joydip and all anonymous users.

Listing 7-19
```
<authorization>
    <allow users = "Banhisikha" />
    <allow roles = "Admin" />
    <deny users = "Joydip" />
    <deny users = "?" />
</authorization>
```

Refer to Listing 7-19 above. Note how the <allow> and <deny> elements have been ordered. It should be noted that the first one that matches the request is used. Hence, if you were to add a <deny users="*" /> to the top of the list, it would always deny everyone, regardless of any <allow /> elements that followed it.

It is also possible to specify the location path where the authorization settings are applicable using the `<location>` directive. The following code snippet illustrates this:

Listing 7-20
```
<configuration>
<location path = "Test.aspx">
<system.web>
<authorization>
<allow users = "?"/>
</authorization>
</system.web>
</location>
</configuration>
```

You can also restrict or grant the ability to perform a GET or POST to one or more users of the ASP.NET application. The following code snippet illustrates how we can allow the user Jini to do a POST, while the other users can do only a GET.

Listing 7-21
```
<authorization>
<allow verb = "GET" users = "*" />
<allow verb = "POST" users = "Jini" />
<deny verb = "POST" users = "*" />
</authorization>
```

It is also possible to use the location element to provide access to one or more files and directories. In essence, you can specify the authorization settings for particular files and directories using the location element. The following example enables access to the Login.aspx page to an anonymous user.

Listing 7-22
```
<configuration>
    <location path = "Login.aspx">
        <system.web>
            <authorization>
                <allow users = "?" />
            </authorization>
        </system.web>
    </location>
</configuration>
```

NOTE *You can specify the target framework in your application's web.config file using the compilation debug attribute as shown below:*

```
<compilation debug="true" targetFrameworkMoniker="
.NETFramework,Version=v4.0">
```

How Do Authentication and Authorization Work?

When a request is sent to the web server, the server first checks the validity of the incoming request. If the authentication mode is anonymous (which is the IIS default), the request is authenticated automatically. If the authentication mode has been overridden in the application's web.config file settings, IIS performs the specified authentication check before the request is passed on to ASP.NET.

ASP.NET then checks whether impersonation is enabled or not. If impersonation is enabled, ASP.NET executes the request with the identity of the entity on behalf of which it is performing the task; otherwise, the application executes with the identity of the IIS local machine and the privileges of the ASP.NET user account.

Finally, the ASP.NET engine performs an authorization check on the resources requested by the authenticated user, and if the user is authorized, it returns the request through the IIS pipeline.

Impersonation

Impersonation is a technique that gives a user access to a resource in an application as though he or she were someone else; it allows the ASP.NET process to act as another specified user. Impersonation is disabled by default. The IIS Web Server impersonates the users using its own IUSR account.

Impersonation in ASP.NET is used to decide whether or not a particular request from a user should be executed using the account of the requested user or that of the local system-process account. ASP.NET uses the local system-process account for all anonymous requests. Note that impersonation is not enabled by default, so ASP.NET executes all code using the same account as the ASP.NET process.

What Happens if Impersonation Is Enabled?

If impersonation is enabled, a check is made to see whether anonymous access is enabled in IIS:

- If anonymous access is enabled, the request is served using the IUSR_machinename account.
- If anonymous access is disabled, the request is served using the account of the authenticated user.

What Happens if Impersonation Is Disabled?

If impersonation is disabled, a check is made to see whether anonymous access is enabled in IIS.

- If anonymous access is enabled, the request is served using the system-level process account.
- If anonymous access is disabled, the request is served using the account of the authenticated user.

In any of these cases, permissions for the account are checked in the Windows ACL for the resources.

Setting Up Impersonation

Impersonation is disabled by default and can be specified in the web.config file by using one of the two lines in the following code snippet.

Listing 7-23
```
<identity impersonate="true"/>

<identity impersonate="false"/>
```

It is also possible to use a particular identity for all authenticated requests by specifying the following in the application's web.config file:

Listing 7-24
```
<identity impersonate="true" username="username" password="password"/>
```

To enable impersonation for a specific identity, you can use the following syntax in the application's web.config file:

Listing 7-25
```
<identity impersonate="true"
userName="domain\user"
password="password" />
```

So, you can impersonate a specific user (Jini, for example) for all requests on all the web pages of the application by using the <identity> tag in your application's web.config file as shown in the following code snippet:

Listing 7-26
```
<identity impersonate="true" userName="Jini" password="Bulti" />
```

Note that impersonation should be used with utmost care. Impersonation can drastically affect the application's performance and scalability.

The ASP.NET Provider Model

The ASP.NET provider model provides a pluggable architecture. The ASP.NET provider model can also be used to design and develop your custom providers seamlessly. There are two providers in the ASP.NET: the role provider and the membership provider. The ASP.NET Provider Model includes the following built-in providers:

- Membership Providers
- Role Management Providers
- Profile Providers
- Site Map Providers

- Session State Providers
- Web Event Providers
- Web Parts Personalization Providers
- Protected Configuration Providers

The ProviderBase Abstract Class

The ProviderBase abstract class is the base of all classes in the ASP.NET provider model. The MembershipProvider and RoleProvider abstract classes are inherited from the ProviderBase class. You can also extend these classes to implement your own custom providers.

Here is what the ProviderBase class looks like:

Listing 7-2
```
public class ProviderBase
{
  public virtual string Name
  {
    get;
  }
  public virtual string Description
  {
    get;
  }
  public virtual void Initialize
(string name, NameValueCollection config);
}
```

Role-Based Security

Role-based security allows you to provide access to one or more application resources based on the "role" of the user. The following code snippet illustrates how you can check roles for particular users and restrict access to the resources accordingly.

Listing 7-28
```
if ( User.IsInRole("Administrator"))
{
    Response.Write("You are an Administrator");
}
else if (User.IsInRole("Managers"))
{
    Response.Write("You are a Manager");
}
else if (User.IsInRole("Developers"))
{
    Response.Write("You are a Developer");
}
else if (User.IsInRole("Users"))
```

```
{
   Response.Write("You are a User");
}
else if (User.IsInRole("Testers"))
{
   Response.Write("You are a Tester");
}
else
{
   Response.Write("The User is not valid");
}
```

For example, you could provide access to the Admin section of the menu to users who are administrators:

Listing 7-29
```
if (User.IsInRole("Administrator"))
   AdminTab.Visible = true;
```

You can also assign roles to authenticated users by using the OnAuthenticate event of the authentication module. To do this, you need to create an instance of System .Security.Principal.GenericPrincipal and assign it to the current user, as shown in the following code snippet:

Listing 7-30
```
public void Application_AuthenticateRequest(Object s, EventArgs e)
{
   if (HttpContext.Current.User != null)
   {
      if (HttpContext.Current.User.Identity.
         AuthenticationType.Equals("Forms"))
      {
         System.Web.Security.FormsIdentity identity =
            HttpContext.Current.User.Identity;
         String[] roles = new String[5];
         roles[0]= "Architects";
         roles[1]= "Testers";
         roles[2]= "Developers";
         roles[3]= "Technical Writers";
         HttpContext.Current.User =
            new System.Security.Principal.GenericPrincipal
            (identity,roles);
      }
   }
}
```

Membership-Based Security

The membership provider allows you to validate and store user credentials in an ASP.NET application. It works with Active Directory and SQL Server and Access databases by default. However, you can extend this API to work with other databases as well. There are two membership providers in ASP.NET: SqlMembership and AccessMembership. Here is what the default membership provider settings look like in the machine.config file:

Listing 7-31

```
<membership>
  <providers>
    <add name="AspNetSqlMembershipProvider"
type="System.Web.Security.SqlMembershipProvider,
System.Web, Version=2.0.0.0, Culture=neutral,
 PublicKeyToken=b03f5f7f11d50a3a"
connectionStringName="LocalSqlServer"
    enablePasswordRetrieval="false"
    enablePasswordReset="true"
    requiresQuestionAndAnswer="true"
    applicationName="/"
    requiresUniqueEmail="false"
    passwordFormat="Hashed"
    maxInvalidPasswordAttempts="5"
    minRequiredPasswordLength="7"
    minRequiredNonalphanumericCharacters="1"
    passwordAttemptWindow="10"
    passwordStrengthRegularExpression="" />
  </providers>
</membership>
```

CHAPTER 8

Tracing and Debugging in ASP.NET

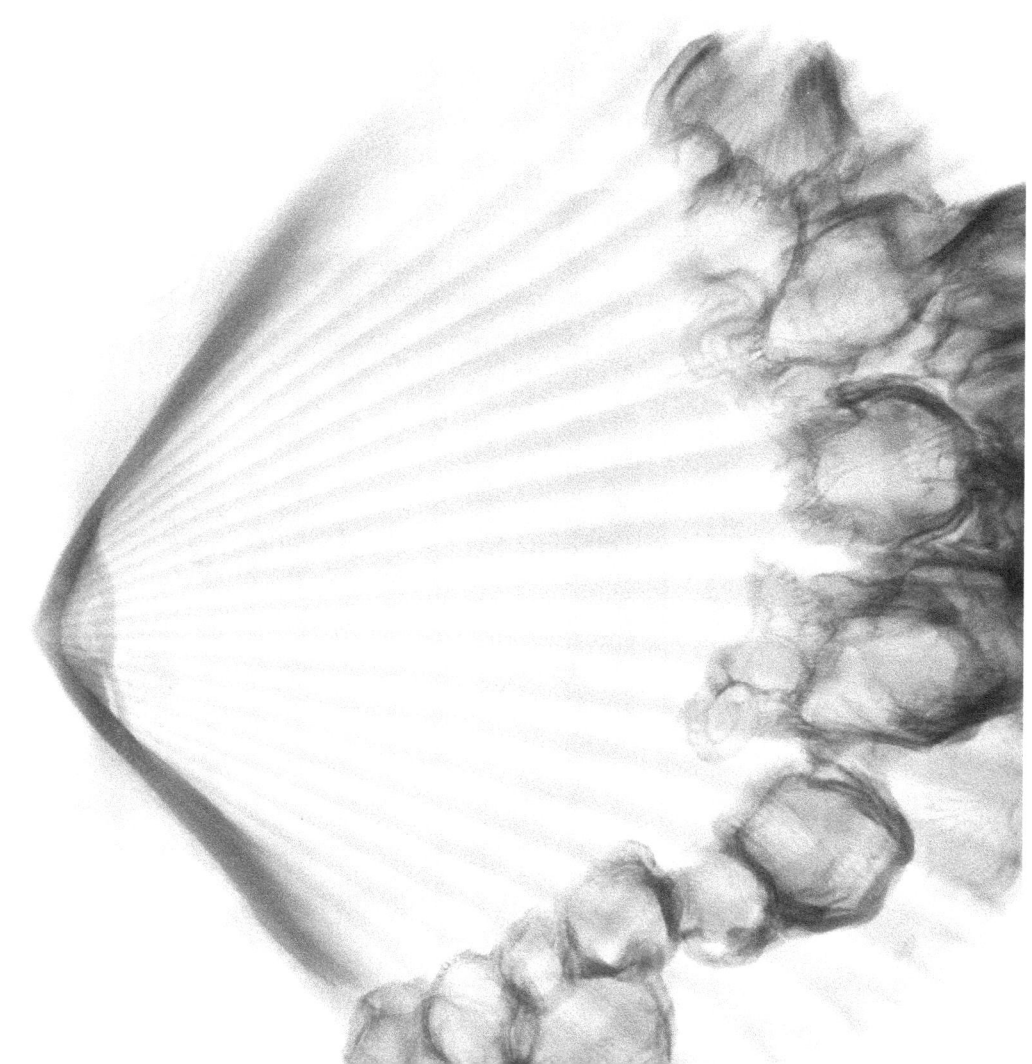

D ebugging and tracing are two of the best techniques for efficiently detecting and tracking bugs at execution time or after deploying your application. In ASP .NET, you can directly write trace and debug statements in your application's code, and you need not remove those statements prior to deploying your application.

To debug your code at runtime, you can set a breakpoint and step into the code to search for potential errors. You can use tracing to view the diagnostic information of the web pages of your application at execution time. This chapter presents how you can use debugging and tracing efficiently in ASP.NET applications.

The System.Diagnostics Namespace

The System.Diagnostics namespace contains classes that can be used for tracing and debugging applications. You can use the classes in this namespace to handle tracing programmatically in your applications.

The major classes in this namespace include the following:

- **System.Diagonostics.ConditionalAttribute**   This class is used to implement conditional methods defined in the Trace and Debug classes.
- **System.Diagonostics.BooleanSwitch**   This class provides a Boolean switch that can be used to turn on and off the debugging and tracing output.
- **System.Diagostics.Debug**   This is a sealed class that contains a set of methods and properties for debugging your application's code.
- **System.Diagnostics.StackTrace**   This class represents a stack trace—a collection of one or more stack frames.
- **System.Diagnostics.StackFrame**   This class is used to provide information about a StackFrame. (A StackFrame represents a method call on the call stack on the currently executing thread.)

Tracing

Tracing in ASP.NET can be used to retrieve diagnostic information about a web page at execution time. When tracing is enabled for a page, ASP.NET appends diagnostic information in the page's output to the requesting browser. Tracing information includes details of the request, the trace information, the headers collection, the forms collection, the cookies collection, the server variables, and also the control tree.

You can view the trace log details for a specific request by navigating to the root of your application and then using the trace viewer application called trace.xsd to view the trace details.

The complete syntax for specifying tracing is as follows:

Listing 8-1
```
<trace enabled="[true|false]"
       localOnly="[true|false]"
       pageOutput="[true|false]"
       requestLimit="[request limit as integer]"
       traceMode="[SortByTime|SortByCategory]" />
```

In the sections that follow, we will look at how to enable or disable tracing at the page or application level, and see how tracing and debugging can be handled by using declarative code as well as programmatically.

Enabling Trace Information at the Page Level

To enable tracing at the page level, you can use the Trace attribute in the @Page directive, as shown here:

Listing 8-2
```
<%@ Page Trace="true" %>
```

You can optionally set the TraceMode property to sort the trace output either by time or by category. Here is how you can do this:

Listing 3-3
```
<%@ Page Language="C#" Trace="True" TraceMode="SortByCategory" %>
```

Enabling Trace Information at the Application Level

You can also enable display of trace information for all the pages of your application. When you enable trace information for your entire application like this, the ASP.NET runtime will collect trace information limited by the maximum number of requests you specify.

Here is how you can enable trace information in your application's web.config file:

Listing 8-4
```
<configuration>
  <system.web>
    <trace enabled="true" requestLimit="30"/>
  </system.web>
</configuration>
```

The preceding listing limits the trace information to a maximum of 30 requests at any point in time.

The following listing illustrates how you can enable trace information for browsers on computers other than the server of origin. Notice that the requestLimit attribute is set to 40, so you can have a maximum of 40 requests for which trace information will be captured by the ASP.NET at runtime.

Listing 8-5
```
<configuration>
  <system.web>
    <trace enabled="true"
requestLimit="40"
localOnly="false" />
  </system.web>
</configuration>
```

The following table describes the trace configuration attributes that you can set in the web.config file.

Attribute	Description
Enabled	This attribute is used to specify whether or not tracing is enabled for the application.
PageOutput	This is used to specify whether the trace information should be displayed on all pages of the application and also in the trace.xsd tool. If the value is true, the trace information is displayed both on the web pages and also in the trace.xsd trace viewer utility. The default value of this attribute is false.
RequestLimit	This attribute is used to specify the number of trace requests to store on the web server. The default value of this attribute is 10.
LocalOnly	If the value of this attribute is set to "true", it indicates that the trace.xsd trace-viewer utility is available only on the host web server where the application is in execution. The default value of this attribute is false.
TraceMode	This attribute is used to specify whether the trace information should be displayed based on a sorted order by time or by category. Note that the default sort order is time.

The Trace Class

In the previous sections, we looked at how to handle tracing in ASP.NET applications using declarative code. In this section, we will discuss how to handle tracing programmatically.

The Trace class in the System.Diagnostics namespace can be used to display trace information. The following piece of code illustrates how you can specify tracing this way.

Listing 8-6
```
using System;
using System.Diagnostics;
class MyTrace
{
    static void Main()
    {
        Trace.Listeners.Add(new TextWriterTraceListener(Console.Out));
        Trace.AutoFlush = true;
        Trace.Indent();
        Trace.WriteLine("Start Trace Output");
        Console.WriteLine("Demonstrating Tracing");
        Trace.WriteLine("End Trace Output");
        Trace.Unindent();
    }
}
```

The TraceContext Class

The TraceContext class can be used to capture and display the execution details of a web request in ASP.NET applications. The following table describes the members of the TraceContext class.

Member	Description
IsEnabled	This indicates whether or not tracing is enabled. A value of "true" implies that tracing is enabled; a value of "false" implies that tracing is disabled. The default value is "false".
Write(message)	This method is used to write a particular message to the trace output.
Write(category, message)	This method is used to write a particular message and also the information to the trace output.
Warn(message)	This method is used to write a particular message to the trace output in red type to signify a warning.
Warn(category, message)	This method is used to write a particular message and also the message category to the trace output in red type to signify a warning.

Writing Custom Trace Messages

You can write trace messages in the trace output using either the Trace.Write or the Trace.Warn method. In the latter case, the messages appear in red type. You can optionally specify the trace category while using either of these methods.

Note that the trace messages are written to trace output only if tracing is enabled for a particular page. You can determine whether tracing is enabled for a page by using the IsEnabled property. Here is an example:

Listing 8-7
```
if (Trace.IsEnabled)
    Trace.Write("Test", "Tracing is enabled.");
```

The following example illustrates how you can write custom trace messages using Trace.Write and Trace.Warn.

Listing 8-8
```
SqlConnection sqlConnection = new SqlConnection();
    SqlCommand sqlCommand = new SqlCommand();
    sqlConnection.ConnectionString =
"Data Source=.;Initial Catalog=Employee;
User ID=sa;Password=sa;
providerName=System.Data.SqlClient";
        try
        {
        if(Trace.IsEnabled)
        Trace.Write("Information", "Connecting to the database");
        sqlConnection.Open();
        if (Trace.IsEnabled)
        Trace.Write("Information", "Connected...");
        sqlCommand.CommandText = "Select EmployeeID,
            EmployeeName from Employee";
        sqlCommand.Connection = sqlConnection;
        if (Trace.IsEnabled)
        Trace.Write("Information", "Executing Query...");
        SqlDataReader sqlDataReader = sqlCommand.ExecuteReader();
        if (Trace.IsEnabled)
```

```
      Trace.Write("Information", "Executed Query Successfully...");
   }
   catch (Exception ex)
   {
       if (Trace.IsEnabled)
       Trace.Warn("Error", ex.Message, ex);
   }
   finally
   {
     if (Trace.IsEnabled)
     Trace.Write("Information", "Closing Connection...");
     sqlConnection.Close();
     if (Trace.IsEnabled)
     Trace.Write("Information", "Connection Closed...");
   }
```

Trace Listeners

Trace listeners are used to respond to trace information and then delegate it to the proper destination. Here is how you can configure a trace listener in the application's web.config:

Listing 8-9
```
<configuration>
<system.diagnostics>
  <trace>
    <listeners>
      <add name="TestListener"
          type="System.Diagnostics.TextWriterTraceListener,System"
          initializeData="C:\TestTraceListener.log" />
      <remove type="System.Diagnostics.DefaultTraceListener,System"/>
    </listeners>
  </trace>
</system.diagnostics>
</configuration>
```

You can have the following types of trace listeners in .NET:

- DefaultTraceListener
- EventLogTraceListener
- TextWriterTraceListener

All of these trace listeners are derived from the TraceListener abstract base class.

Implementing a Custom Trace Listener

To implement your own custom listener class, you need to create a subclass from the TraceListener abstract base class. You should then implement your own versions of the Fail, Flush, Write, and WriteLine methods in the custom trace listener.

Note that both the Trace and Debug classes contain a TraceListenersCollection type property called Listeners—you can use this to add or remove listeners.

The following is a complete implementation of a custom trace listener:

Listing 8-10
```
using System;
using System.Collections.Generic;
using System.Configuration;
using System.Web;
using System.Diagnostics;
namespace Tracing
{
    public class CustomTraceListener : TextWriterTraceListener
    {
        private static readonly object lockObj = new Object();
        private static readonly String separator = " <==> ";
        public CustomTraceListener(string fileName)
            : base(fileName)
        {
        }
        public CustomTraceListener(string fileName, string listenerName)
            : base(fileName, listenerName)
        {
        }
        public override void Write(string message)
        {
            lock (lockObj)
            {
                base.Write(DateTime.Now.ToShortDateString() +
                separator + message);
            }
        }
        public override void WriteLine(string message)
        {
            lock (lockObj)
            {
                base.WriteLine(DateTime.Now.ToShortDateString() +
                separator + message);
            }
        }
        public override void Write(string message, string category)
        {
            lock (lockObj)
            {
                base.Write(DateTime.Now.ToShortDateString() +
                separator + message + separator + category);
            }
        }
    }
```

```
        public override void WriteLine(string message, string category)
        {
            lock (lockObj)
            {
                base.WriteLine(DateTime.Now.ToShortDateString() +
                separator + message + separator + category);
            }
        }
    }
}
    public class CustomTraceLogger
    {
        private static CustomTraceListener customTraceListener = null;
        private static readonly String fileName = "C:\\Test.log";
        static CustomTraceLogger()
        {
            customTraceListener = new CustomTraceListener(fileName);
            Trace.Listeners.Add(customTraceListener);
        }
        public static CustomTraceListener TraceListenerInstance
        {
            get
            {
                return customTraceListener;
            }
        }
    }
}
```

The following code snippet illustrates how you can remove the default trace listener and then add the custom trace listener in your application's configuration file:

Listing 8-11
```
<configuration>
  <system.diagnostics>
   <trace autoflush="true" indentsize="2">
    <listeners>
     <remove name="Default"/>
     <add name="CustomTraceListener"
      type="Tracing.CustomTraceListener,Tracing"/>
    </listeners>
   </trace>
  </system.diagnostics>
</configuration>
```

The TraceSwitch Class

The TraceSwitch class can accept one of the following trace levels:

Level	Value
Off	0
Error	1
Warning	2
Info	3
Verbose	4

These levels can be set either through the application's configuration file or by using code. It is advisable, however, to specify the values for this class through the application's configuration file for better flexibility.

You can specify the switch in your application's configuration file as shown here:

Listing 8-12
```
<configuration>
    <system.diagnostics>
    <switches>
        <add name="Test" value="3" />
    </switches>
    </system.diagnostics>
</configuration>
```

You can then create an instance of the TraceSwitch class and use it to write trace output as shown here:

Listing 8-13
```
private static TraceSwitch traceSwitch =
new TraceSwitch("Test", "Trace Demo");
    private void WriteTraceMessages()
        {
            if (traceSwitch.TraceVerbose)
            {
                Trace.Write("Trace Message - Verbose");
            }
            else if (traceSwitch.TraceError)
            {
                Trace.Write("Trace Message - Error");
            }
            else if (traceSwitch.TraceInfo)
            {
                Trace.Write("Trace Message - Information");
            }
            else if (traceSwitch.TraceWarning)
            {
                Trace.Write("Trace Message - Warning");
            }
        }
```

The BooleanSwitch Class

Conditional attributes are fine as long as your application is in the development stage. But how do you turn debugging on or off in the production environment?

The System.Diagnostics.BooleanSwitch class comes to the rescue. You can set your debug switch in the application's configuration file and then read it in your application code. The BooleanSwitch class, unlike the TraceSwitch class, can accept either on or off as its value. In either case, the constructor of the TraceSwitch or the BooleanSwitch classes reads the information from the configuration file and sets the value of the switch appropriately.

You can specify a switch in your application's configuration file as shown in the following code snippet:

Listing 8-14
```
<system.diagnostics>
<switches>
<add name="_Debug" value="1" />
</switches>
</system.diagnostics>
```

You can then use the BooleanSwitch class to retrieve the switch value and perform the needed operations, like this:

Listing 8-15
```
private static BooleanSwitch debug =
new BooleanSwitch("_Debug", "Debug Test");
if(debug.Enabled)
{
   //Write your custom debugging code here
}
```

The StackTrace Class

A StackTrace instance contains a collection of StackFrame instances, each of which contains trace information for a particular call. The following method illustrates how you can display trace information for the currently executing file, line number, and method using the StackTrace class.

Listing 8-16
```
private void PrintTraceInformation(bool needFileInfo)
{
    StackTrace stackTrace = new System.Diagnostics.
        StackTrace(needFileInfo);
    for (int i = 0; i < stackTrace.FrameCount; i++)
    {
        StackFrame stackFrame = stackTrace.GetFrame(i);
        Debug.WriteLine(" File Name: " + stackFrame.GetFileName() +
        " Line Number: " + stackFrame.GetFileLineNumber() +
        " Method Name: " + stackFrame.GetMethod());
    }
}
```

Debugging

Debugging is the process of searching for potential errors in your source code while the application is executing. You can turn debugging on in your application's web.config file as shown here:

Listing 8-17
```
<configuration>
  <system.web>
    <compilation debug="true">
    </compilation>
  </system.web>
<configuration>
```

Note that if the debug attribute for your application is not set and the application is executed in Debug mode, you will be prompted to set debugging on. When you click the OK button, the application's web.config file will be updated with the debugging support.

Conditional Compilation

Conditional compilation is one of the most important features in .NET. To use conditional compilation, you need to specify the Conditional attribute to your methods and attribute classes.

The following method can be used to write debug statements while the application is executing in Debug mode:

Listing 8-18
```
[Conditional("DEBUG")]
        private static void WriteDebugMessages(String message)
        {
            Debug.WriteLine(message);
        }
```

The Conditional attribute provides a clean way of writing debug statements in your code. Optionally, you can also use a switch in your configuration to control debugging output, as shown in the following code snippet:

Listing 8-19
```
Debug.WriteIf(debug.Enabled, "This is a test message");
```

When you execute the application in Debug mode and this method is called from within your application's code, the message will be written to the Debug console. If you execute the same application in Release mode, the message will not be displayed. You need not change any portion of your application's code—just execute it in Release mode and the debug statements will not be executed at all. So, there isn't any performance penalty to including debugging statements.

Debugging Support in Visual Studio

To debug your applications in the Visual Studio IDE, simply press the F5 key to start your program.

Also, you can optionally attach the Visual Studio debugger when your application is executing. To do this, select the Attach to Process option in the Debug menu of the Visual Studio IDE, and specify the instance of the browser that you want the debugger to be attached to.

Tracing and Debugging ASP.NET Ajax Applications

You can use the Debug class belonging to the Sys namespace in ASP.NET Ajax to display trace information for your ASP.NET Ajax applications.

If you use the Sys.Debug class, you should set the Debug attribute of the compilation section in your application's web.config file to true, and the ScriptMode attribute of the ScriptManager control to Debug mode.

The Sys.Debug class contains the following methods:

- Sys.Debug.trace(message)
- Sys.Debug.clearTrace()
- Sys.Debug.fail(message)
- Sys.Debug.assert(condition,message,displaycaller)
- Sys.Debug.traceDump(object,name)

The following example illustrates how you can use Sys.Debug to debug your Ajax-enabled ASP.NET applications:

Listing 8-20
```
<html xmlns="http://www.w3.org/1999/xhtml" >
<head>
<script language="javascript" type="text/javascript">
function ShowTraceInformation()
{
    Sys.Debug.trace(Form1.txtName.value);
}
function ClearTraceInformation()
{
    Sys.Debug.clearTrace();
}
</script>
</head>
<body>
    <form id="Form1" runat="server">
        <asp:ScriptManager ID="ScriptManager1" runat="server" />
            <asp:Label ID="lblName"
                runat="server" Text="Enter your name:">
            </asp:Label>
            <input id="txtName" maxlength="70" type="text" />
            <table>
            <tr>
            <td>
```

```
            <input id="btnShowTrace" type="button"
                value="Show Trace" style="width: 80px"
                onclick="ShowTraceInformation();" /><br />
            </td>
            <td>
            <input id="btnClearTrace" type="button"
                value="Clear Trace" style="width: 80px"
                onclick="ClearTraceInformation();" /><br />
            </td>
            </tr>
            </table>
            <br />
        <textarea id='txtAreaTraceConsole'
            rows="25" cols="50" title="Trace Console">
        </textarea>
    </form>
</body>
</html>
```

Notice the use of the Sys.Debug.trace() and Sys.Debug.clearTrace() methods. While the former is used to display the trace information, the latter clears the trace information from the txtAreaTraceConsole TextArea control.

NOTE *Prior to deploying your Ajax-enabled ASP.NET applications, you should set the mode to Release and the Debug attribute to false. You should also set the ScriptMode property of the ScriptManager control in your Ajax-enabled pages to Release mode before you deploy your application.*

CHAPTER 9

Dynamic Data

A SP.NET Dynamic Data is a framework that enables you to quickly build data-driven applications based on LINQ to SQL or Entity Framework. The Dynamic Data framework lets you customize the look and feel of your web pages seamlessly, and also specify attributes on the data classes for performing validation that include: required fields, range checking, type checking, pattern matching using regular expressions, and custom validation. This chapter takes a look at the Dynamic Data framework in ASP.NET and discusses how you can use it in your applications.

The ASP.NET Dynamic Data Framework

The Dynamic Data framework provides a pluggable data model API to support additional LINQ-compliant providers, such as ADO.NET Data Services. The ASP.NET Dynamic Data framework takes care of routine CRUD operations, data relations, and displaying the user interface using display templates. This allows you to concentrate on developing the business logic, user-interface code, validation logic, and application modeling. The Dynamic Data framework uses database metadata to discover the database tables, and it exposes them using ASP.NET Web Service URIs. Another striking feature of Dynamic Data is its ability to perform automated validation based on the constraints defined in the data model, and its ability to change the markup for the GridView and DetailsView controls dynamically. The following code snippet illustrates the markup code of a GridView control that can leverage Dynamic Data features in a web page:

Listing 9-1
```
<asp:GridView ID="GridView1" runat="server"
AutoGenerateColumns="True" DataKeyNames="EmployeeID"
DataSourceID="LinqDataSource1">
</asp:GridView>
<asp:LinqDataSource ID="LinqDataSource1" runat="server"
ContextTypeName="MyDataContext" EnableDelete="True"
EnableInsert="True" EnableUpdate="True" TableName="Employee">
</asp:LinqDataSource>
```

Features at a Glance

Here are the exciting features provided by the ASP.NET Dynamic Data framework at a glance:

- **Support for Field templates**   Field templates enable you to customize data controls seamlessly.
- **Support for Validation**   The Dynamic Data framework enables you to use attribute-driven validation on the data classes.

The DynamicControl in ASP.NET

The ASP.NET Dynamic Data framework also introduces a new web control called DynamicControl that can be used in FormView or ListView controls to provide a dynamic user interface based on the database schema of the underlying database. This control can be used by template-bound data controls of ASP.NET, like FormView or ListView. You can also use this control in the TemplateField field of a GridView or a DetailsView control. The section on "Entity Templates" later in this chapter shows how you can use DynamicControl in your applications to leverage the features of the ASP.NET Dynamic Data framework.

Dynamic Data Templates

In ASP.NET Dynamic Data, you can have two types of templates: page level and field level. The former uses a routing mechanism to map the URL to the data model at runtime, and the latter relates to the user controls that map the data types in your logical, or data, model. Note that this model is also known as the relational model. A Dynamic Data web site can leverage the page templates and controls and also the power and flexibility of the LinqDataSource or EntityDataSource controls. You also can use custom design templates to control how data is displayed.

Creating a Dynamic Data Web Site

In this section we will discuss how we can create dynamic data web sites, i.e., web sites that can leverage the features of the ASP.NET Dynamic Data framework.

Creating the Dynamic Data Web Site in Visual Studio

To create a Dynamic Data web site, first select File | New | Web Site from the menus, and then select one of the two web site templates, Dynamic Data Linq to SQL Web Site or Dynamic Data Entities Web Site, as shown in Figure 9-1. Select the former if you use LINQ to SQL as your data access source; choose the second option if you want to use the ADO.NET Entity Framework as your data access source.

Registering the Data Model

Next, you need to use the Global.asax file to set the RegisterRoutes parameters for the application, and also the name of the ObjectContext type and scaffolding information. Look at the Global.asax file to see how the RegisterRoutes method is called and how you can register a data model there. Here is an example of registering a data model in that method:

Listing 9-2
```
var context = new ContextConfiguration(){ScaffoldAllTables = true};
model.RegisterContext(typeof(AdventureWorksEntities), context);
```

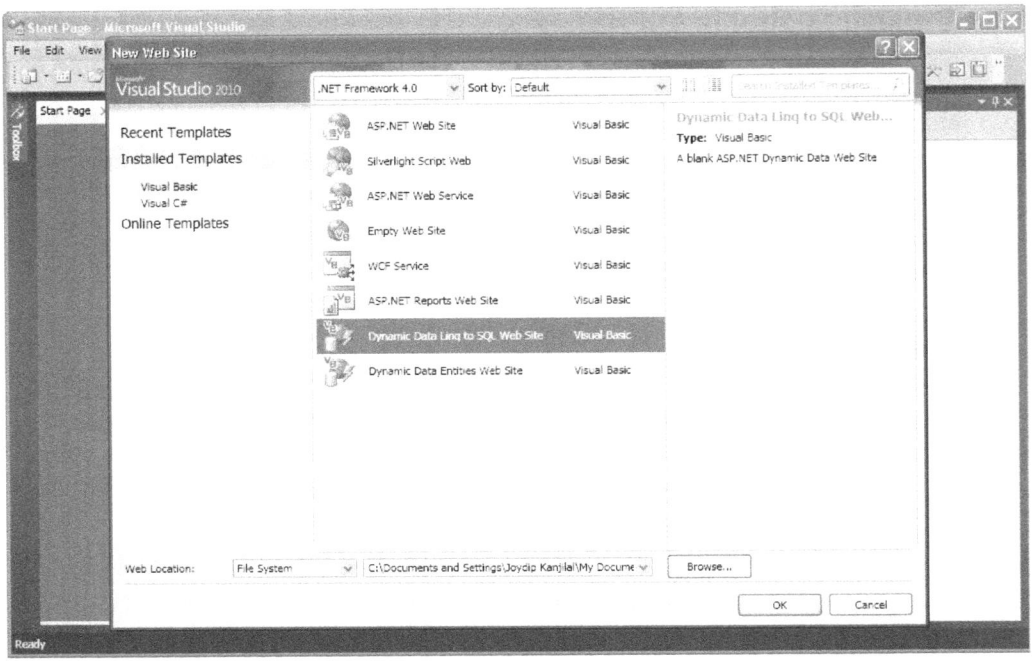

FIGURE 9-1   Creating a Dynamic Data web site

This is what the Global.asax file initially looks like:

Listing 9-3
```
<%@ Application Language="C#" %>
<%@ Import Namespace="System.Web.Routing" %>
<%@ Import Namespace="System.Web.DynamicData" %>
<script RunAt="server">
    public static void RegisterRoutes(RouteCollection routes) {
        MetaModel model = new MetaModel();
        //                    IMPORTANT: DATA MODEL REGISTRATION
        // Uncomment this line to register LINQ
// to SQL classes or an ADO.NET Entity Data
        // model for ASP.NET Dynamic Data.
//Set ScaffoldAllTables = true only if you are sure
        // that you want all tables in the data model
// to support a scaffold (i.e. templates)
        // view. To control scaffolding for individual
// tables, create a partial class for
        // the table and apply the [Scaffold(true)]
 //attribute to the partial class.
        // Note: Make sure that you change "YourDataContextType"
```

```
// to the name of the data context
        // class in your application.
        //model.RegisterContext(
//typeof(YourDataContextType),
//new ContextConfiguration() { ScaffoldAllTables = false });
        // The following statement supports
//separate-page mode, where the List, Detail, Insert, and
        // Update tasks are performed by using
//separate pages. To enable this mode,
//uncomment the following
 // route definition, and comment
//out the route definitions in the combined-page
// mode section that follows.
        routes.Add(new DynamicDataRoute("{table}/{action}.aspx") {
            Constraints = new RouteValueDictionary
(new { action = "List|Details|Edit|Insert" }),
            Model = model
        });
        // The following statements support
//combined-page mode,
//where the List, Detail, Insert, and
        // Update tasks are performed by
//using the same page. To enable this mode,
//uncomment the
        // following routes and comment out
//the route definition in the
//separate-page mode section above.
        //routes.Add(new DynamicDataRoute
//("{table}/ListDetails.aspx") {
        //      Action = PageAction.List,
        //      ViewName = "ListDetails",
        //      Model = model
        //});
        //routes.Add(new DynamicDataRoute
//("{table}/ListDetails.aspx") {
        //      Action = PageAction.Details,
        //      ViewName = "ListDetails",
        //      Model = model
        //});
    }
    void Application_Start
(object sender, EventArgs e) {
        RegisterRoutes(RouteTable.Routes);
    }
</script>
```

Creating the DataContext and the Data Classes

You now need to create a LINQ data context. We will use the AdventureWorks database in this example.

The first step is to register LINQ to SQL classes or an ADO.NET Entity Data model for your ASP.NET Dynamic Data web site. To do this, you need to uncomment the following line in the Global.asax file and specify the data context you just created.

Listing 9-4
```
model.RegisterContext(typeof(YourDataContextType),
 new ContextConfiguration()
{ ScaffoldAllTables = false });
```

This is what the Global.asax file will look like with the commented lines removed:

Listing 9-5
```
<%@ Application Language="C#" %>
<%@ Import Namespace="System.Web.Routing" %>
<%@ Import Namespace="System.Web.DynamicData" %>
<script RunAt="server">
    public static void RegisterRoutes(RouteCollection routes) {
        MetaModel model = new MetaModel();
        model.RegisterContext(typeof
(DataClassesDataContext), new ContextConfiguration()
 { ScaffoldAllTables = true });
routes.Add(new DynamicDataRoute("{table}/{action}.aspx") {
            Constraints = new RouteValueDictionary
(new { action = "List|Details|Edit|Insert" }),
            Model = model
        });
    }
    void Application_Start(object sender, EventArgs e) {
        RegisterRoutes(RouteTable.Routes);
    }
</script>
```

Executing the Application

If you execute the application now, you will see the output as shown in Figure 9-2.

Apart from displaying the records, you can also insert, edit, and delete records. If you click on the Employees link on the web page (shown in Figure 9-2), you can see the individual Employee records. The ASP.NET Dynamic Data framework generates code automatically to create dynamic web forms using a standard set of page templates, including List.aspx, Insert.aspx, Edit.aspx, and Details.aspx. As you can see in Figure 9-3, you can create a data-driven web site easily—no coding is required.

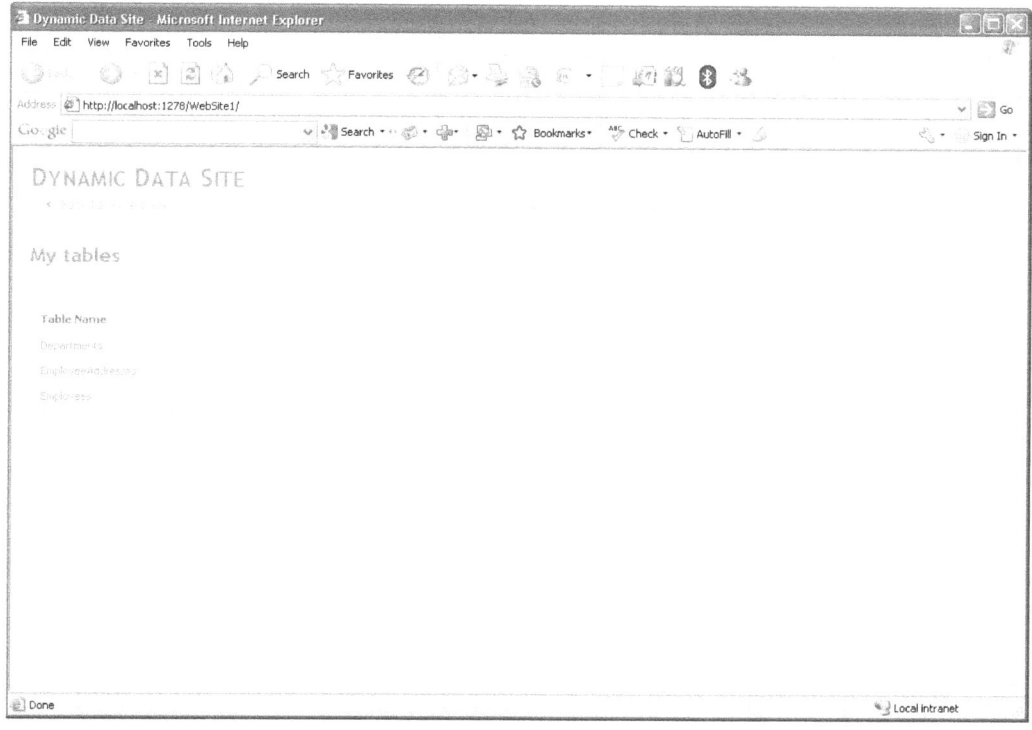

FIGURE 9-2   The ASP.NET Dynamic Data web site in action

Customizing the Display

You can also customize what the display will look like. To do this, add a partial class that has the same name as your entity class in the data model. Then apply the DisplayName and ScaffoldColumn attributes, as shown here:

Listing 9-6
```
using System;
using System.Collections.Generic;
using System.Linq;
using System.Web;
using System.ComponentModel;
using System.ComponentModel.DataAnnotations;
using System.Web.DynamicData;
[TableName("Department")]
public partial class Department
{
    [DisplayName("Department Name")]
    public object Name { get; set; }
    [DisplayName("Group Name")]
    public object GroupName { get; set; }
```

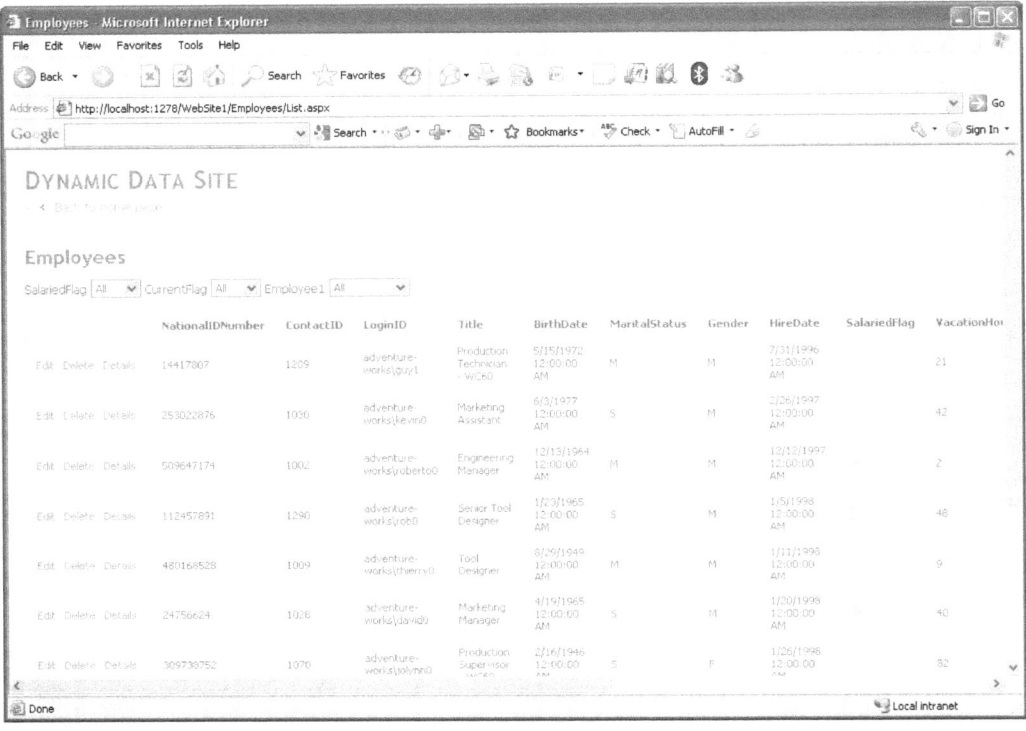

Figure 9-3 Displaying the employee records

```
[ScaffoldColumn(false)]
public object DepartmentID { get; set; }
[ScaffoldColumn(false)]
public object ModifiedDate { get; set; }
}
```

The DisplayName attribute allows you to set the display name for the column, and the ScaffoldColumn attribute allows you to either hide or unhide the column.

Using Routes

There are three different ways you can specify URL routing:

- **Table-specific**   Use this to specify routing that is based on a table, whatever the action.

- **Action-specific**   Use this type for routing based on actions like List, Insert, and Edit when the routing is not dependent on the table name.

- **Table- and action-specific**   Use this type of routing when the routing is based on both the table name and the action.

For example, if the table is Employee and the action is List, Details, Edit, or Insert, you can specify the route so that Employee.aspx is invoked as follows:

Listing 9-7
```
routes.Add(new DynamicDataRoute("{table}/{action}Employee.aspx")
{
Constraints = new RouteValueDictionary
(new {action = "List|Details|Edit|Insert"}),
Model = model,
Table = "Employee",
});
```

The next example shows an action-specific route where the control is routed to a specific web page based on an action, regardless of the table:

Listing 9-8
```
routes.Add(new DynamicDataRoute("{table}/{action}Display.aspx")
{
Constraints = new RouteValueDictionary(new {action = "List"}),
Model = model,
});
```

Lastly, here is how you can specify a route that is based on both the table and action:

Listing 9-9
```
routes.Add(new DynamicDataRoute("pages/{action}Display.aspx")
{
Constraints = new RouteValueDictionary(new {action = "List "}),
Model = model,
Table = "Employee",
});
```

Performing Validations

You can validate user input by using custom validation techniques. The ASP.NET Dynamic Data framework allows you to perform input validation using attributes or a DynamicValidator control. To apply input validation on user input, you need to create a partial class whose name coincides with one of the entity classes and then apply the MetadataType attribute to it.

There are various attributes that you can use to validate input data, including the following:

- RangeAttribute
- RequiredAttribute
- RegexAttribute

Here is a typical example:

Listing 9-10
```
[Range("Salary",1000,150000,
ErrorMessage="Error in Salary
the valid input range should be
between 1000 and 150000")]
public partial class Payroll
{
}
```

You can also perform validation using the LINQ to SQL OnPropertyChanging partial methods. Here is an example:

Listing 9-11
```
public partial class Payroll
{
  partial void OnSalaryChanging(double? value)
  {
    if (value >= 1000 && value <= 150000)
      return;
    else
      throw new
        ValidationException
("Error in Salary the valid input range should be
between 1000 and 150000");
  }
}
```

Here is a complete example that illustrates how you can validate a Department entity:

Listing 9-12
```
using System.Web;
using System.ComponentModel;
using System.ComponentModel.DataAnnotations;
using System.Web.DynamicData;
[TableName("Department")]
[MetadataType(typeof (DepartmentMetadata))]
public partial class Department
{
}
public partial class DepartmentMetadata
{
    [Required]
    [StringLength(50, ErrorMessage =
"Department Name should not exceed 50 characters")]
    public object Name { get; set; }
    [Required]
    [StringLength(25, ErrorMessage =
"Group Name should not exceed 25 characters")]
    public object GroupName { get; set; }
}
```

Handling Exceptions

Exceptions are errors that occur at runtime and interrupt the normal flow of program operation. You can handle exceptions in the ASP.NET Dynamic Data framework by using the DataContext. The DataContext is the gateway to the LINQ to SQL framework. The DataContext tracks the changes made to the entities in LINQ to SQL.

Here is an example:

Listing 9-13
```
public override void SubmitChanges
(System.Data.Linq.ConflictMode conflictMode) {
    try {
        base.SubmitChanges(conflictMode);
    }
    catch (Exception ex) {
        throw new ValidationException(null, ex);
    }
}
```

You can also do the same at the method level, as follows:

Listing 9-14
```
partial void DeleteDepartment(Department instance) {
    try
    {
        ExecuteDynamicDelete(instance);
    }
    catch (Exception ex) {
        throw new ValidationException(null, ex);
    }
}
```

If you are using the ADO.NET Entity Framework, you can also handle exceptions globally by creating a custom class that extends the DynamicValidator class, like this:

Listing 9-15
```
public class McGrawHillValidator : DynamicValidator
{
    protected override void ValidateException
(Exception exceptionInstance)
    {
        if (!(exceptionInstance is
IDynamicValidatorException) &&
!(exceptionInstance is ValidationException))
        {
            while (exceptionInstance.InnerException != null)
            {
                exceptionInstance = exceptionInstance.InnerException;
            }
            exceptionInstance =
```

```
new ValidationException
(null, exceptionInstance);
        }
        base.ValidateException(exceptionInstance);
    }
}
```

If you look at one of the pages inside the Templates folder in the Solution Explorer, you will see the use of LinqDataSource:

Listing 9-16
```
<asp:LinqDataSource ID="DetailsDataSource"
 runat="server" EnableDelete="true">
                <WhereParameters>
                    <asp:DynamicQueryStringParameter />
                </WhereParameters>
</asp:LinqDataSource>
```

On the other hand, if you use the Entity Framework as your data source, it uses an EntityDataSource control, as shown here:

Listing 9-17
```
<asp:EntityDataSource ID="DetailsDataSource"
 runat="server" EnableDelete="true">
                <WhereParameters>
                    <asp:DynamicQueryStringParameter />
                </WhereParameters>
</asp:EntityDataSource>
```

You should also specify the mapping information inside the <pages> element of your application's web.config file, as shown here:

Listing 9-18
```
<pages>
   <tagMapping>
     <add tagType="System.Web.DynamicData.
DynamicValidator" mappedTagType=
"McGrawHillValidator"/>
   </tagMapping>
</pages>
```

Working with Dynamic Data Entity Applications

A Dynamic Data Entity application uses the ADO.NET Entity Framework as its data source. The Entity Framework is an extended object-relational mapping (ORM) technology from Microsoft that you can use to model and query data. It allows you to use the Entity SQL (ESQL) query language and LINQ, and it provides support for entity inheritance, entity composition, and change tracking. The primary objective of the Entity Framework is to objectify your application's data by adding a level of abstraction on top of the relational model. Chapter 3 discusses the ADO.NET Entity Framework in more detail.

You can create a Dynamic Data entity application much the same way we created a Dynamic Data web application in the earlier "Working with Dynamic Data Web Sites" section. To do this, select Dynamic Data Entities Web Site (instead of Dynamic Data LINQ to SQL Web Site) from the list of the templates displayed in Figure 9-1. Then create an Entity Data Model (EDM) using the Entity Data Model Designer in Visual Studio. Lastly, specify the name of your data model in the Global.asax file, as shown here:

Listing 9-19
```
<%@ Application Language="C#" %>
<%@ Import Namespace="System.Web.Routing" %>
<%@ Import Namespace="System.Web.DynamicData" %>
<script RunAt="server">
    public static void RegisterRoutes(RouteCollection routes) {
        MetaModel model = new MetaModel();
        model.RegisterContext(typeof(
AdventureWorksModel.AdventureWorksEntities),
 new ContextConfiguration() { ScaffoldAllTables = true });
        routes.Add(new DynamicDataRoute("{table}/{action}.aspx") {
            Constraints = new RouteValueDictionary
(new { action = "List|Details|Edit|Insert" }),
            Model = model
        });
    }
    void Application_Start(object sender, EventArgs e) {
        RegisterRoutes(RouteTable.Routes);
    }
</script>
```

Note that you can set the ContextType property explicitly in your code and then use the RegisterControl method of the DynamicDataManager class to register a control. Here's an example of doing that:

Listing 9-20
```
protected void Page_Init(object sender, EventArgs e)
{
    EntityDataSource1.ContextType =
        typeof(AdventureWorksModel.AdventureWorksEntities);
    DynamicDataManager1.RegisterControl(GridView1);
}
```

Converting an Existing Web Site to a Dynamic Data Web Site

You can add Dynamic Data features to an existing web site. To do this, you need to copy the DynamicData folder to the root of the target web site. Next, create an App_Code folder in the target web site and copy the content of the Dynamic Data web site's App_Code folder into this folder. Then update the Global.asax file to provide support for Dynamic Data in the target web site—you should have the RegisterRoutes properly called in the Application_Start event handler. Also, the target web site's web.config file needs to be updated so that the following assemblies are referenced:

- System.Web.Abstractions
- System.Web.Routing
- System.ComponentModel.DataAnnotations
- System.Web.DynamicData
- System.Data.Linq

Here is what the assemblies section in the target web site's web.config file should look like:

Listing 9-21
```
<system.web>
  <compilation>
    <assemblies>
      <add assembly="System.Web.Abstractions,
 Version=3.5.0.0, Culture=neutral,
PublicKeyToken=31BF3856AD364E35"/>
      <add assembly="System.Web.Routing,
Version=3.5.0.0, Culture=neutral,
PublicKeyToken=31BF3856AD364E35"/>
       <add assembly="System.ComponentModel.DataAnnotations,
 Version=3.5.0.0, Culture=neutral,
PublicKeyToken=31BF3856AD364E35"/>
        <add assembly="System.Web.DynamicData,
Version=3.5.0.0, Culture=neutral,
PublicKeyToken=31BF3856AD364E35"/>
        <add assembly="System.Data.Linq,
Version=3.5.0.0, Culture=neutral,
PublicKeyToken=B77A5C561934E089"/>
    </assemblies>
  </compilation>
<system.web>
```

Next, you should register the necessary modules in your application's web.config file, as shown below:

Listing 9-22
```
<validation validateIntegratedModeConfiguration="false"/>
<modules runAllManagedModulesForAllRequests="true">
  <remove name="ScriptModule"/>
  <remove name="UrlRoutingModule"/>
  <add
    name="ScriptModule"
    preCondition="managedHandler"
    type="System.Web.Handlers.ScriptModule, System.Web.Extensions,
      Version=3.5.0.0, Culture=neutral,
```

```
              PublicKeyToken=31BF3856AD364E35"/>
      <add name="UrlRoutingModule"
        type="System.Web.Routing.UrlRoutingModule, System.Web.Routing,
            Version=3.5.0.0, Culture=neutral,
              PublicKeyToken=31BF3856AD364E35"/>
    </modules>
```

Finally, you should register the necessary handlers in your web.config file:

Listing 9-23
```
<handlers>
  <add
    name="UrlRoutingHandler"
    preCondition="integratedMode"
    verb="*" path="UrlRouting.axd"
    type="System.Web.HttpForbiddenHandler, System.Web,
        Version=2.0.0.0, Culture=neutral,
          PublicKeyToken=b03f5f7f11d50a3a"/>
</handlers>
```

The DynamicDataManager Control

The DynamicDataManager control should be included in your web page so that you can enable Dynamic Data support for your data controls.

In ASP.NET 4.0, the DynamicDataManager control has been enhanced—you can now configure it declaratively much like other ASP.NET controls. Here is an example:

Listing 9-24
```
<asp:DynamicDataManager ID="MyDynamicDataManagerControl"
  runat="server"
    AutoLoadForeignKeys="true">
  <DataControls>
    <asp:DataControlReference
ControlID="MyGridViewControl" />
  </DataControls>
</asp:DynamicDataManager>
<asp:GridView id="MyGridViewControl"
 runat="server"
</asp:GridView>
```

As an example, here is the complete markup code for using a DynamicDataManager control to provide Dynamic Data support on controls in a web page.

Listing 9-25
```
<body>
    <form id="form1" runat="server">
    <asp:DynamicDataManager
ID="DynamicDataManager1"
runat="server" AutoLoadForeignKeys="true" />
    <asp:GridView ID="GridView1"
runat="server"
```

```
    DataSourceID="LinqDataSource1"
AllowPaging="True"
        AllowSorting="True"
AutoGenerateColumns="False"
 DataKeyNames="EmployeeID">
        <Columns>
            <asp:DynamicField DataField="EmployeeID" />
            <asp:DynamicField DataField="FirstName" />
            <asp:DynamicField DataField="LastName" />
            <asp:DynamicField DataField="Address" />
            <asp:DynamicField DataField="Phone" />
        </Columns>
    </asp:GridView>
    <asp:LinqDataSource ID="LinqDataSource1"
 runat="server" ContextTypeName="MGHDataContext"
        TableName="Employee">
    </asp:LinqDataSource>
    </form>
</body>
```

The GridView control in the preceding example should also be registered with the DynamicDataManager control as shown here:

Listing 9-26
```
protected void Page_Init(object sender, EventArgs e)
    {
        DynamicDataManager1.RegisterControl(GridView1);
    }
```

The DynamicHyperLink Control

The DynamicHyperLink control is used to create links that can display related data or perform actions defined in the Global.asax file. Here is the complete syntax of the DynamicHyperLink control:

Listing 9-27
```
<asp:DynamicHyperlink
    ID="string"
    Action="Details|Edit|Insert|List"
    ContextTypeName="string"
    DataField="string"
    TableName="string"
    OnDataBinding="DataBinding event handler"
    OnPreRender="PreRender event handler"/>
```

You can use the DynamicHyperLink control to create links of three types:

1. Links to MetaTable objects
2. Table-row data-bound links
3. Unbound links

The DynamicHyperLink control enables you to build links to web pages of a Dynamic Data web site seamlessly. Here is an example:

Listing 9-28
```
<asp:DynamicHyperLink ID="DynamicHyperLink1" runat="server"
    Action="List" TableName="Employee"> Display Employee Records
</asp:DynamicHyperLink>
```

The preceding markup code creates a link to the List page for the Employee table based on routes that have been defined in the Global.asax file.

Here is another example that shows how you can use the DynamicHyperLink control inside a GridView control for editing data:

Listing 9-29
```
<asp:GridView ID="MyGridView1" runat="server"
            AllowPaging="true" PageSize="10"
            DataSourceID="MyLinqDataSource1">
            <Columns>
                <asp:TemplateField>
                    <ItemTemplate>
                        <asp:DynamicHyperLink ID="DynamicHyperLink1"
                            runat="server" Action="Edit"
                            Text="Edit Data" />
                    </ItemTemplate>
                </asp:TemplateField>
            </Columns>
        </asp:GridView>
        <aspX:MyLinqDataSource ID="LinqDataSource1"
 runat="server"
            ContextTypeName="AdventureWorksDataContext"
            TableName="Employee"/>
```

Entity Templates

Entity templates enable you to customize the layout of data in a Dynamic Data web site without having to create a custom page. Here is an example of an entity template:

Listing 9-30
```
<asp:EntityTemplate runat="server"
ID="EntityTemplateContainer1">
  <ItemTemplate>
    <tr
      <td>
        <asp:Label ID="lblName"
runat="server"
 OnInit="lblName_Init" />
      </td>
      <td>
        <asp:DynamicControl runat="server"
 OnInit="DynamicControl_Init" />
      </td>
    </tr>
```

```
    </ItemTemplate>
</asp:EntityTemplate>
```

Note that ASP.NET 4.0 introduces two new built-in field templates called EmailAddress.ascx and Url.ascx for using email addresses or URLs with the DataType attributes. Here is an example:

Listing 9-31

```
[DataType(DataType.EmailAddress)]
public object Email { get; set; }
[DataType(DataType.Url)]
public object Blog { get; set; }
```

CHAPTER 10

Silverlight

Silverlight is a technology that you can use to create rich, secure, scalable web applications that can run on any platform. It is typically meant for developing and distributing Internet applications or rich Internet applications (RIAs) that use animations, graphics, and video within the context of Microsoft's .NET managed environment.

Silverlight integrates seamlessly with HTML and supports the Common Language Runtime (CLR)—this allows you to create rich, cross-browser, cross-platform Internet applications within the context of the .NET Framework, and, at the same time, integrate animations and graphics into those applications. Silverlight applications can be hosted in IIS or Apache web servers and are downloaded by the web browser in the form of XAP files that contain the assembly manifest file and a collection of one or more assemblies.

What Is Silverlight and Why Is It Useful?

Silverlight is a cross-browser, cross-platform technology that promotes a collaborative application development environment where developers and designers can work together to provide visually stunning experiences in web applications. Microsoft's official Silverlight web site states, "Silverlight is a cross-browser, cross-platform and cross-device browser plug-in that helps companies design, develop and deliver applications and experiences on the Web. A free download that installs in seconds, Silverlight enables a new class of rich, secure and scalable cross-platform experiences." (http://www.microsoft.com/silverlight/overview/default.aspx)

Silverlight (http://silverlight.net) is the new name of Windows Presentation Foundation/Everywhere (WPF/E). It is fast and integrates with HTML easily. Moreover, it is based on the managed environment of CLR. In essence, Silverlight contains a cut-down version of the CLR that can be run within the context of the web browser as a plug-in. So, what you get is amazing graphics coupled with the awesome power and capabilities of Microsoft's .NET managed platform-independent environment. Silverlight applications can distribute full-screen multimedia with support for partial High Definition (HD) video at 720p resolution. With the help of Microsoft's new Dynamic Language Runtime (DLR), Silverlight also supports other languages like JavaScript, Python, and Ruby within the context of the .NET Framework.

XAML Browser Applications (XBAP) and Silverlight

XAML browser applications (also called XBAPs) are rich Internet applications and can be deployed in a web server. Such applications can be executed within the context of a web browser.

Although both XBAPs and Silverlight applications can be rich Internet applications, there are distinct differences between the two. Silverlight is a browser component and is rendered in your web browser as a browser plug-in. It doesn't need the .NET Framework to be installed in the target system for it to work. In contrast, XBAPs can be executed in any system that has the .NET Framework installed. Also, XBAPs can only be executed in Internet Explorer and Firefox browsers, but Silverlight applications can be executed in any browser.

The Prerequisites

In order to work with Silverlight, you need to install Silverlight 3 SDK and Silverlight 3 Tools for Visual Studio 2008 SP1, which can be downloaded from http://silverlight.net/GetStarted/. Alternatively, install Expression Blend along with the relevant service pack so that user interfaces for Silverlight applications can be designed graphically. You also need to have Visual Studio 2010 installed. Note that Visual Studio 2008 SP1 is included in Visual Studio 2010.

> **NOTE** *Silverlight does not require the Microsoft .NET Framework to be installed on the system for it to run; rather, the Silverlight setup downloads everything it requires on the system at runtime.*

Getting Started with Silverlight

To get started using Silverlight, create a new Silverlight project using Visual Studio 2010 by selecting the Silverlight Project template. When prompted about whether you want to use an ASP.NET web project to host Silverlight or to automatically generate a test page to host Silverlight at build time, choose the latter.

You will see two XAML files created in the Solution Explorer: App.xaml and Page.xaml. The Page.xaml file will typically contain the user interface of your application. The App.xaml file contains the application's startup code and the necessary checks to see if Silverlight is running properly on your system.

The code-behind file for App.xaml—App.xaml.cs—looks like the following:

Listing 10-1
```
public partial class App : Application
    {
        public App()
        {
            this.Startup += this.Application_Startup;
            this.Exit += this.Application_Exit;
            this.UnhandledException +=
            this.Application_UnhandledException;
            InitializeComponent();
        }
        private void Application_Startup
        (object sender, StartupEventArgs e)
```

```
        {
            this.RootVisual = new Page();
        }
        private void Application_Exit(object sender, EventArgs e)
        {
        }
        private void Application_UnhandledException
        (object sender,
        ApplicationUnhandledExceptionEventArgs e)
        {
            if (!System.Diagnostics.Debugger.IsAttached)
            {
                e.Handled = true;
                Deployment.Current.Dispatcher.
                BeginInvoke(delegate { ReportErrorToDOM(e); });
            }
        }
        private void ReportErrorToDOM
        (ApplicationUnhandledExceptionEventArgs e)
        {
            try
            {
                string errorMsg = e.ExceptionObject.Message +
                e.ExceptionObject.StackTrace;
                errorMsg = errorMsg.Replace
                ('"', '\'').Replace("\r\n", @"\n");
                System.Windows.Browser.HtmlPage.
                Window.Eval("throw new Error
                (\"Unhandled Error in Silverlight 2 Application "
                + errorMsg + "\");");
            }
            catch (Exception)
            {

                //Usual exception handling code
            }
        }
    }
```

Now place the following code in the Page.xaml file:

Listing 10-2
```
<UserControl xmlns:basics="clr-namespace:
System.Windows.Controls;assembly=
System.Windows.Controls"
xmlns:data="clr-namespace:System.Windows.Controls;
assembly=System.Windows.Controls.Data"
  x:Class="SilverlightApplication1.Page"
    xmlns="http://schemas.microsoft.com/winfx/2006/xaml/presentation"
```

```
        xmlns:x="http://schemas.microsoft.com/winfx/2006/xaml"
        Width="400" Height="300" Background="AliceBlue">
        <Grid x:Name="LayoutRoot" Background="DarkKhaki">
        <basics:Calendar></basics:Calendar>
        </Grid>
</UserControl>
```

Notice the use of the Calendar control inside the Grid control and the styles set for the Grid. When you execute this application, you will see a Calendar control displayed in your browser.

Understanding the Silverlight Controls

Silverlight controls can be divided into these basic categories:

- **Layout controls**   These controls are used to position the elements used in your Silverlight application; typical examples include Canvas, StackPanel, and Grid.

- **Input controls**   These controls are used to accept user input; typical examples include TextBox, TextBlock, Button, CheckBox, RadioButton, and ListBox.

- **Navigation controls**   These controls are used to navigate around your application; typical examples include Scrollbar, ScrollViewer, and HyperlinkButton.

- **Media controls**   These controls are used to provide a rich visual experience in your Silverlight application; examples include MediaElement and Image.

Here are a few code snippets that illustrate how you can work with these controls:

Listing 10-3
```
<Canvas>
        <TextBlock Text="This is a TextBlock"
            Canvas.Top="30" Canvas.Left="30"
            FontFamily="Verdana" FontSize="18"/>
</Canvas>

<Grid x:Name="gridSample" Background="Yellow">
        <Grid.ColumnDefinitions>
            <ColumnDefinition Width="200"></ColumnDefinition>
        </Grid.ColumnDefinitions>
        <Grid.RowDefinitions>
            <RowDefinition Height="200"></RowDefinition>
        </Grid.RowDefinitions>
</Grid>

<ListBox Width="200" Height="100">
        <ListBoxItem Content="Yellow" />
        <ListBoxItem Content="White" />
        <ListBoxItem Content="Black" />
```

```
    <ListBoxItem Content="Blue" />
    <ListBoxItem Content="Green" />
    <ListBoxItem Content="Brown" />
</ListBox>

<ScrollViewer Width="250" Height="150"
    VerticalScrollBarVisibility="Visible">
    <ScrollViewer.Content>
        <TextBlock TextWrapping="Wrap"
            Text="Sample Text" />
    </ScrollViewer.Content>
</ScrollViewer>

<Image x:Name="imageControl" Stretch="None"
Source="images/Sunset.jpg"></Image>
```

Data Binding in Silverlight

Data binding refers to binding data to data controls. Controls bound with data are called data controls. The Data Binding framework in Silverlight enables you to bind data to the data controls either declaratively or programmatically.

This is how you can bind the Address property of an object to the Text property of the corresponding control:

Listing 10-4
```
<TextBox x:Name="txtAddress" Text="{Binding Address}" />
```

You can use the following code to do the same thing:

Listing 10-5
```
<TextBox x:Name="txtAddress">
    <TextBox.Text>
        <Binding Path="Address" />
    </TextBox.Text>
</TextBox>
```

You can also set data-binding modes, like OneTime, OneWay, or TwoWay. OneWay binding is the default. Here are a few examples:

Listing 10-6
```
<TextBox x:Name="txtAddress"
    Text="{Binding Employee.Address, Mode=OneTime}"  />
<TextBox x:Name="txtAddress"
    Text="{Binding Employee.Address, Mode=OneWay}"  />
<TextBox x:Name="txtAddress"
    Text="{Binding Employee.Address, Mode=TwoWay}"  />
```

Working with Data

We would now use a data control that will display tabular data to the user. We will use a DataGrid control in this example.

Here is the XAML code for the DataGrid:

Listing 10-7

```xaml
<UserControl xmlns:data="clr-namespace:
System.Windows.Controls;
assembly=System.Windows.Controls.Data"
  x:Class="McGrawHill.Page"
    xmlns="http://schemas.microsoft.com/winfx/2006/xaml/presentation"
    xmlns:x="http://schemas.microsoft.com/winfx/2006/xaml"
    xmlns:local="clr-namespace:McGrawHill"
    Width="400" Height="300">
    <UserControl.Resources>
        <local:RowIndexConverter x:Key="RowIndexConverter"/>
    </UserControl.Resources>
    <Grid x:Name="LayoutRoot" Background="AliceBlue" >
        <data:DataGrid Name="dataGrid"
            AutoGenerateColumns="False"
            IsReadOnly="False" RowBackground="Lavender"
            AlternatingRowBackground="Cyan">
            <data:DataGrid.Columns>
                <data:DataGridTextColumn Header="First Name"
                    CanUserSort="False"
                    Binding="{Binding Converter={StaticResource
                    RowIndexConverter},
                    ConverterParameter=FirstName}"/>
                <data:DataGridTextColumn Header="Last Name"
                    CanUserSort="False"
                    Binding="{Binding Converter={StaticResource
                    RowIndexConverter},
                    ConverterParameter=LastName}"/>
                <data:DataGridTextColumn Header="Address"
                    CanUserSort="False"
                    Binding="{Binding Converter={StaticResource
                    RowIndexConverter},
                    ConverterParameter=Address}"/>
                <data:DataGridTextColumn
                    Header="Phone"
                    CanUserSort="False"
                    Binding="{Binding Converter={StaticResource
                    RowIndexConverter},
                    ConverterParameter=Phone}"/>
            </data:DataGrid.Columns>
        </data:DataGrid>
    </Grid>
</UserControl>
```

The preceding code listing shows how you can specify binding information declaratively, using markup code in XAML. You can also specify the binding information programmatically using the code shown in the following snippet:

Listing 10-8
```
this.dataGrid.Columns.Add(
            new DataGridTextColumn
            {
                Header = "First Name",
                Binding = new Binding("FirstName")
            });
this.dataGrid.Columns.Add(
            new DataGridTextColumn
            {
                Header = "Last Name",
                Binding = new Binding("LastName")
            });
this.dataGrid.Columns.Add(
            new DataGridTextColumn
            {
                Header = "Address",
                Binding = new Binding("Address")
            });
this.dataGrid.Columns.Add(
            new DataGridTextColumn
            {
                Header = "Phone",
                Binding = new Binding("Phone")
            });
```

The RowIndexConverter class implements the IValueConverter interface, which contains the following methods:

Listing 10-9
```
Object IValueConverter.Convert(object value,
Type targetType, object parameter,
 CultureInfo culture)
        {
            throw new NotImplementedException();
        }
Object IValueConverter.ConvertBack(object value,
 Type targetType, object parameter,
 CultureInfo culture)
        {
            throw new NotImplementedException();
        }
```

Here is the complete source code for the RowIndexConverter class:

Listing 10-10
```
public class RowIndexConverter : IValueConverter
    {
        #region IValueConverter Members
        object IValueConverter.Convert
(object value,
 Type targetType, object parameter,
 System.Globalization.CultureInfo
 culture)
        {
            GridRow record = (GridRow)value;
            return record[(String)parameter];
        }
        object IValueConverter.ConvertBack
(object value, Type targetType,
object parameter,
System.Globalization.CultureInfo
 culture)
        {
            throw new NotImplementedException();
        }
        #endregion
    }
```

The GridRow class contains a Dictionary instance that holds the data to be bound to each of the rows of the DataGrid. Here is the code for the GridRow class:

Listing 10-1
```
public class GridRow
    {
        private Dictionary<String, Object>
 _data = new Dictionary<String, Object>();
        public Object this [String index]
        {
            get
            {
                return _data[index];
            }
            set
            {
                _data[index] = value;
            }
        }
    }
```

And lastly, here is the complete code of the Page class—the user interface.

Listing 10-12
```
public partial class Page : UserControl
{
    public Page()
    {
        InitializeComponent();
        dataGrid.ItemsSource = PopulateData();
    }
    private List<GridRow> PopulateData()
    {
        List<GridRow> lstRow = new List<GridRow>();
        GridRow row = new GridRow();
        row["FirstName"] = "Joydip";
        row["LastName"] = "Kanjilal";
        row["Address"] = "Kolkata";
        row["Phone"] = "11111111";
        lstRow.Add(row);
        row = new GridRow();
        row["FirstName"] = "Jamal";
        row["LastName"] = "Dudekula";
        row["Address"] = "Hyderabad";
        row["Phone"] = "22222222";
        lstRow.Add(row);
        row = new GridRow();
        row["FirstName"] = "Tilak";
        row["LastName"] = "Tarafder";
        row["Address"] = "Hyderabad";
        row["Phone"] = "33333333";
        lstRow.Add(row);
        row = new GridRow();
        row["FirstName"] = "Vilail";
        row["LastName"] = "Shaji Kumar";
        row["Address"] = "Cochin";
        row["Phone"] = "44444444";
        lstRow.Add(row);
        row = new GridRow();
        row["FirstName"] = "Vinod";
        row["LastName"] = "Kumar Naidu";
        row["Address"] = "Hyderabad";
        row["Phone"] = "55555555";
        lstRow.Add(row);
        row = new GridRow();
        row["FirstName"] = "Sanjit";
        row["LastName"] = "Sil";
        row["Address"] = "Kolkata";
        row["Phone"] = "66666666";
        lstRow.Add(row);
        row = new GridRow();
        row["FirstName"] = "Sudhakar";
```

```
        row["LastName"] = "Kayyam";
        row["Address"] = "Hyderabad";
        row["Phone"] = "77777777";
        lstRow.Add(row);
        row = new GridRow();
        row["FirstName"] = "Ranjan";
        row["LastName"] = "Bhuyan";
        row["Address"] = "Cuttack";
        row["Phone"] = "88888888";
        lstRow.Add(row);
        row = new GridRow();
        row["FirstName"] = "Oindrilla";
        row["LastName"] = "Roy Chowdhury";
        row["Address"] = "Kolkata";
        row["Phone"] = "99999999";
        lstRow.Add(row);
        return lstRow;
    }
}
```

When you execute the application, the DataGrid will be displayed in the browser as shown in Figure 10-1.

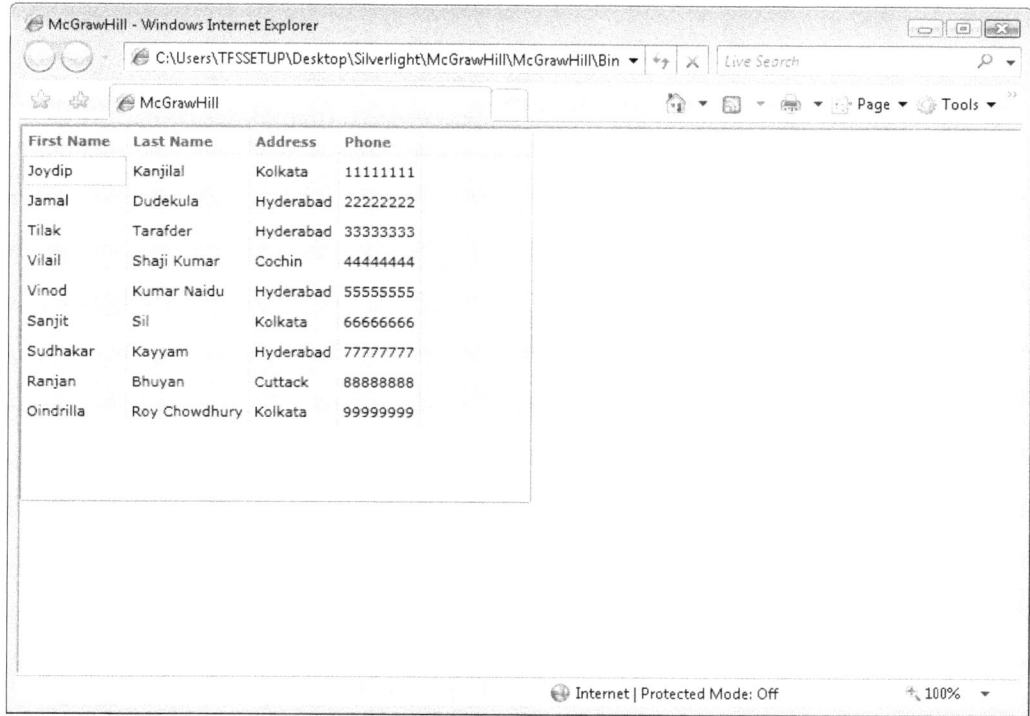

FIGURE 10-1   The Silverlight DataGrid control in action

Sorting Data

You can also use SortDescriptions in your DataGrid so that the data is sorted just before it is loaded into the DataGrid. You can do this in XAML or by using code.

Here is how you can specify SortDescriptions using XAML:

Listing 10-13
```
<UserControl xmlns:data=
"clr-namespace:System.Windows.Controls;
assembly=System.Windows.Controls.Data"
  x:Class="McGrawHill.Page"
    xmlns="http://schemas.microsoft.com/winfx/2006/xaml/presentation"
    xmlns:x="http://schemas.microsoft.com/winfx/2006/xaml"
    xmlns:local="clr-namespace:McGrawHill"
    Width="400" Height="300">
    <UserControl.Resources>
        <local:RowIndexConverter x:Key="RowIndexConverter"/>
    </UserControl.Resources>
    <Grid x:Name="LayoutRoot" Background="AliceBlue" >
        <data:DataGrid Name="dataGrid"
            AutoGenerateColumns="False"
            IsReadOnly="False" RowBackground="Lavender"
            AlternatingRowBackground="Cyan">
            <data:DataGrid.Columns>
                <data:DataGridTextColumn Header="First Name"
                    CanUserSort="False" Binding="{Binding
                    Converter={StaticResource RowIndexConverter},
                    ConverterParameter=FirstName}"/>
                <data:DataGridTextColumn Header="Last Name"
                    CanUserSort="False" Binding="{Binding
                    Converter={StaticResource RowIndexConverter},
                    ConverterParameter=LastName}"/>
                <data:DataGridTextColumn Header="Address"
                    CanUserSort="False" Binding="{Binding
                    Converter={StaticResource RowIndexConverter},
                    ConverterParameter=Address}"/>
                <data:DataGridTextColumn Header="Phone"
                    CanUserSort="False" Binding="{Binding
                    Converter={StaticResource RowIndexConverter},
                    ConverterParameter=Phone}"/>
            </data:DataGrid.Columns>
        <data:DataGrid.SortDescriptions>
            <scm:SortDescription
                PropertyName="FirstName" Direction="Ascending" />
            <scm:SortDescription
                PropertyName="LastName"
                Direction="Ascending" />
            <scm:SortDescription
                PropertyName="Phone"
                Direction="Descending" />
```

```
                </data:DataGrid.SortDescriptions>
            </data:DataGrid>
            </data:DataGrid>
        </Grid>
</UserControl>
```

You can do the same thing using code too, as follows:

Listing 10-14
```
dataGrid.ItemsSource = PopulateData();
dataGrid.SortDescriptions.Add(
new SortDescription("FirstName",
 ListSortDirection.Ascending));
dataGrid.SortDescriptions.Add(
new SortDescription("LastName",
 ListSortDirection.Ascending));
dataGrid.SortDescriptions.Add(
new SortDescription("Phone",
ListSortDirection.Descending));
```

Deploying Silverlight Applications

Deploying a Silverlight application is quite simple: just copy your application's assembly into the production environment. To do this, you first need to create a folder in IIS and configure it as a virtual directory. Then copy the compiled assembly from the ClientBin folder to that new folder.

An XAP file is basically a zipped version of your Silverlight solution. It is generated automatically when you compile your Silverlight application and contains the assembly manifest and one or more assemblies. The web browser downloads these XAP files at runtime.

The Silverlight XAP file resides in a subfolder called ClientBin (in the development system). You should also ensure that the additional dependent resources are placed in the same location. Also, you should add the MIME type for XAP files in your IIS web server so that those files are streamed seamlessly.

Once your folder has been created and configured as a virtual directory, you will need an HTML page to invoke your Silverlight application. It could look something like this:

Listing 10-15
```
<!DOCTYPE html PUBLIC "-//W3C//DTD XHTML 1.0 Transitional//EN"
"http://www.w3.org/TR/xhtml1/DTD/xhtml1-transitional.dtd">
<html xmlns="http://www.w3.org/1999/xhtml" >
<head>
    <title>Deploying a Silverlight Application</title>
        <script type="text/javascript" src="Silverlight.js"></script>
    <script type="text/javascript" src="Page.xaml.js"></script>
    <style type="text/css">
        .silverlightHost { width: 640px; height: 480px; }
    </style>
</head>
```

```
<body>
    <div id="SilverlightControlHost" class="silverlightHost" >
        <script type="text/javascript">
            createSilverlight();
        </script>
    </div>
</body>
</html>
```

As you can see, the preceding file references two .js files: Silverlight.js and Page.xaml.js. The location of the generated assembly is specified in the markup code of the Page.xaml file, as shown in the following listing:

Listing 10-16
```
<Canvas xmlns="http://schemas.microsoft.com/client/2007"
        xmlns:x="http://schemas.microsoft.com/winfx/2006/xaml"
        x:Name="testCanvas" Loaded="Page_Loaded"
        x:Class="McGrawHillProject.Page;
        assembly=ClientBin/McGrawHillProject.dll"
        Width="640" Height="480" Background="White"/>
```

The XAP file can also be referred to directly from within your HTML as shown here:

Listing 10-17
```
<div id="silverlightControlHost">
    <object data="data:application/x-silverlight-2,
    " type="application/x-silverlight-2"
    width="100%" height="100%">
        <param name="source" value="McGrawHill.xap"/>
        <param name="onerror" value="onSilverlightError" />
        <param name="background" value="white" />
        <param name="minRuntimeVersion" value="3.0.40307.0" />
        <param name="autoUpgrade" value="true" />
        <a href=http://go.microsoft.com/fwlink/?LinkID=141205
        style="text-decoration: none;">
            <img src=http://go.microsoft.com/fwlink/?LinkId=108181
            alt="Get Microsoft Silverlight"
            style="border-style: none"/>
        </a>
    </object>
    <iframe style='visibility:hidden;height:0;
    width:0;border:0px'>
    </iframe>
</div>
```

CHAPTER 11

Web Parts

W eb Parts are an integrated set of controls used to create web sites that can enable their users to modify the content, appearance, and behavior of those web pages seamlessly. In essence, Web Parts enables you to easily build customizable and dynamic user interfaces in web applications. You can easily move, hide, maximize, or display Web Parts controls in ASP.NET.

ASP.NET provides you with a number of Web Parts controls you can integrate into your applications. You can also build and deploy custom Web Parts controls using the ASP.NET Web Parts infrastructure. This chapter takes a look at Web Parts and how they can be implemented in ASP.NET applications.

What Are Web Parts Controls?

A Web Parts control is an ASP.NET server control that end users can add to a Web Parts page at runtime, allowing them to change the content, appearance, and behavior of the web page. Web Parts helps you divide your page into one or more manageable sections.

A Web Parts control is a modular unit of information with a specific purpose, and it forms the basic building block of a Web Parts page. Web Parts assemblies can contain one or more Web Parts controls. The System.Web.UI.WebControls.WebParts namespace contains a list of classes, interfaces, and enumerations that are collectively known as the Web Parts control set. These classes can be used to create web pages whose content, behavior, and appearance can be changed or personalized at runtime.

NOTE *Web Parts are nothing new. They were first introduced in 2001 in Microsoft SharePoint Services—an offering from Microsoft that facilitates collaboration, document management, content management, workflows, and reporting.*

Here is an example of a Web Parts control:

Listing 11-1
```
<title>Demonstrating Web Parts in ASP.NET</title>
</head>
<body>
    <form id="Form1" runat="server">
    <asp:WebPartManager ID="WebPartManager1" runat="server"/>
        <asp:WebPartZone ID="WebPartZone1" runat="server">
            <ZoneTemplate>
                <cc1:SampleWebPart ID="swPart1" runat="server"/>
            </ZoneTemplate>
        </asp:WebPartZone>
    </form>
</body>
```

Web Parts supports personalization, export and import of data, role-based access, and communicability.

Understanding the Web Parts Controls

The most important point you need to know is that, when using Web Parts, a web page is divided into one or more regions called *zones*. These zones enable you to control the layout of the Web Parts controls.

There are a number of controls you can choose from to develop your Web Parts. Web Parts controls can be divided into two main categories:

- Web Part Managers
- Web Part Zones

Figure 11-1 illustrates the Web Parts controls available.
You can have the following types of Web Part Zones:

- Catalog Zone
- Editor Zone
- Connection Zone

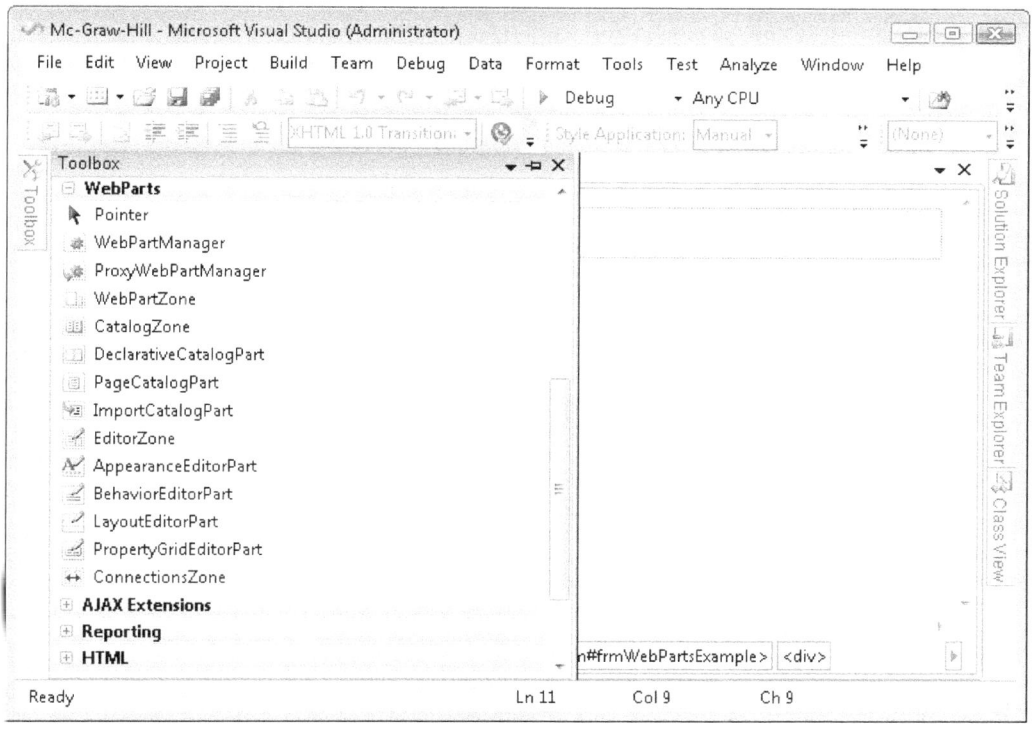

FIGURE 11-1   The Web Parts controls in the toolbox

Web Part Manager

The Web Part Manager is an invisible control that should be included in every web page that uses a Web Parts control. It manages the page's personalization state and ensures smooth communication amongst the controls and zones in a web page. Here is what the syntax for this control looks like:

Listing 11-2
```
<asp:WebPartManager ID="WebPartManagerID" runat="server">
</asp:WebPartManager>
```

Web Part Zone

The Web Part Zone is the next control in the hierarchy. A WebPartZone is used to host your Web Parts controls. Here is the syntax for creating this control:

Listing 11-3
```
<asp:WebPartZone ID="WebPartZoneName" runat="server"
HeaderText="Sample WebPartZone"></asp:WebPartZone>
```

Catalog Zone

The Catalog Zone is the main control used to host ASP.NET Catalog Part server controls in your web pages. A catalog is a list of Web Parts controls or other server controls that are visible when a web page has been set in Catalog display mode.

A Catalog Zone control can contain one or more Catalog Parts. These are the Catalog Part controls available:

- DeclarativeCatalogPart
- PageCatalogPart
- ImportCatalogPart

Here is how you can use this control:

Listing 11-4
```
<asp:CatalogZone ID="CatalogZone1" runat="server">
  <ZoneTemplate>
    <asp:PageCatalogPart ID="PageCatalogPart1" runat="server" />
  </ZoneTemplate>
</asp:CatalogZone>
```

Notice the use of the <ZoneTemplate> tag. You can use it to place your PageCatalogPart controls inside the CatalogZone.

Editor Zone

The Editor Zone control is used to modify the behavior, appearance, and layout of a Web Parts control in your web page. The Editor Zone control should have one or more <ZoneTemplate> tags inside it.

Here is how you can use this control:

Listing 11-5
```
<asp:EditorZone ID="EditorZone1" runat="server">
<ZoneTemplate>
    <asp:AppearanceEditorPart
ID="AppearanceEditorPart1"
 runat="server" />
    <asp:BehaviorEditorPart ID="BehaviorEditorPart1" runat="server" />
    <asp:LayoutEditorPart ID="LayoutEditorPart1" runat="server" />
</ZoneTemplate>
</asp:EditorZone>
```

As you can see, the <BehaviorEditorPart>, <LayoutEditorPart>, and <AppearanceEditorPart> tags are used to modify the behavior, layout, and appearance of the Web Parts control.

Connection Zone

The Connection Zone control lets you to set the properties of a connection and enable or disable the connection as required. The <asp:ConnectionsZone> control can be used to connect the properties of Web Parts controls in the same web page.

The following is the markup code of a Web Parts control with two zones—left and right. The left zone contains a calendar control and the right zone contains a login control.

Listing 11-6
```
<head runat="server">
    <title>Demonstrating Web Part Zones</title>
</head>
<form id="form1" runat="server">
        <div>
            <asp:WebPartManager ID="WebPartManager1" runat="server">
            </asp:WebPartManager>
        </div>
        <table>
            <tr>
                <td valign="top">
                    <asp:WebPartZone ID="LeftZone" runat="server">
                        <ZoneTemplate>
                            <asp:Calendar ID="Calendar1"
                            runat="server"></asp:Calendar>
                        </ZoneTemplate>
                    </asp:WebPartZone>
                </td>
                <td valign="top">
                    <asp:WebPartZone ID="RightZone" runat="server">
                        <ZoneTemplate>
                            <asp:Login ID="Login1"
```

```
                        TextBoxStyle-BackColor="AliceBlue"
                        runat="server">
                    </asp:Login>
                </ZoneTemplate>
            </asp:WebPartZone>
        </td>
    </tr>
    </table>
</form>
```

Web Parts Modes

Web Parts modes enable you to edit, delete, or personalize a Web Parts control. You can set any of the following Web Parts modes for your Web Parts control:

- Catalog
- Design
- Normal
- Edit

Developing Custom Web Parts Controls

To implement a custom Web Parts control in ASP.NET, you should derive your custom Web Parts class from the WebParts base class belonging to the System.Web.UI.WebControls .WebParts namespace. Here is an example of a custom Web Parts control:

Listing 11-7
```
using System.Web.UI;
using System.Web.UI.WebControls;
using System.Web.UI.WebControls.WebParts;
public class CustomWebPart : WebPart
{
    public CustomWebPart()
    {
        this.Title = "This Is a Custom Web Parts Control";
    }
    protected override void RenderContents(HtmlTextWriter writer)
    {
        writer.Write(
        "This is the content area of the custom Web Parts control");
    }
}
```

As you can see in the preceding code snippet, the RenderContents method should be overridden in your custom WebParts class to write the HTML content in the page.

Display Modes

There are many display modes associated with Web Parts controls. BrowseDisplayMode is set by default, and the other modes are described in the following table:

Display Mode	Description
BrowseDisplayMode	This is the standard view mode where no personalization or editing can be done.
DesignDisplayMode	This mode permits drag-and-drop layout personalization and customization.
EditDisplayMode	This mode permits personalization and customization of Web Parts properties to change appearance and behavior. You can also delete Web Parts controls using this mode.
ConnectDisplayMode	This mode permits users to connect Web Parts controls together at runtime.
CatalogDisplayMode	This mode permits users to add Web Parts controls into Web Part Zones at runtime.

The following method illustrates how you can set the display mode of the WebPartManager control in your web page based on the display mode passed to the method as a string argument:

Listing 11-3
```
private SetDisplayMode(String displayMode)
{
    switch(displayMode)
    {
    case "Connect":
    WebPartManager1.DisplayMode = WebPartManager.ConnectDisplayMode;
    break;
    case "Design":
    WebPartManager1.DisplayMode = WebPartManager.DesignDisplayMode;
    break;
    case "Browse":
    WebPartManager1.DisplayMode = WebPartManager.BrowseDisplayMode;
    break;
    case "Catalog":
    WebPartManager1.DisplayMode = WebPartManager.CatalogDisplayMode;
    break;
    case "Edit":
    WebPartManager1.DisplayMode = WebPartManager.EditDisplayMode;
    break;
}
```

Implementing Web Parts Controls Using User Controls

One way of implementing Web Parts controls is by using user controls and adding them to your Web Parts controls at design time. You can design the content of the user control and also attach events if you wish. Using user controls in Web Parts controls gives you complete designer support and the ability to use event handling with ease.

The following user control contains two TextBox controls, a Button control, and a Label control:

Listing 11-9
```
<%@ Control Language="C#" AutoEventWireup="true"
CodeBehind="WebUserControl1.ascx.cs"
Inherits="Web_Parts.WebUserControl1" %>
<table>
    <tr>
        <td>Enter First Name: </td>
        <td><asp:TextBox ID="txtFirstName"
        runat="server"></asp:TextBox></td>
    </tr>
    <tr>
        <td>Enter Last Name:</td>
        <td><asp:TextBox ID="txtLastName"
        runat="server"></asp:TextBox></td>
    </tr>
        <tr>
        <td>Enter Address:</td>
        <td><asp:TextBox ID="txtAddress"
        runat="server"></asp:TextBox></td>
    </tr>
    <tr>
        <td> </td>
        <td><asp:Button ID="btnDisplay"
        runat="server" OnClick = "btnDisplay_Click"
        Text="Display Message" />
            <br />
            <asp:Label ID="lblMessage" runat="server"></asp:Label></td>
    </tr>
</table>
```

Here is the source code of the btnDisplay event handler in the code-behind for the preceding user control:

Listing 11-10
```
protected void btnDisplay_Click(object sender, EventArgs e)
        {
            if (Validate())
            {
                lblMessage.ForeColor = Color.Green;
                lblMessage.Text = "Name: " + txtFirstName.Text +
                " " + txtLastName.Text + "<BR>" +
                "Address: " + txtAddress.Text;
            }
```

```
        else
        {
            lblMessage.ForeColor = Color.Red;
            lblMessage.Text = "Invalid input...";
        }
    }
```

The Validate method returns true or false depending on whether or not any of the TextBox controls are blank. Here is the code for that method:

Listing 11-11
```
private bool Validate()
{
    if ((txtFirstName.Text.Trim().Length == 0)
  || (txtLastName.Text.Trim().Length == 0)
  || (txtAddress.Text.Trim().Length == 0))
        return false;
    return true;
}
```

And here is the complete source code of the user control:

Listing 11-12
```
using System;
using System.Drawing;
namespace Web_Parts
{
    public partial class WebUserControl1 : System.Web.UI.UserControl
    {
        protected void Page_Load(object sender, EventArgs e)
        {
        }
        protected void btnDisplay_Click(object sender, EventArgs e)
        {
            if (Validate())
            {
                lblMessage.ForeColor = Color.Green;
                lblMessage.Text = "Name: " +
                txtFirstName.Text + " " +
                txtLastName.Text + "<BR>" + "Address: " +
                txtAddress.Text;
            }
            else
            {
                lblMessage.ForeColor = Color.Red;
                lblMessage.Text = "Invalid input...";
            }
        }
```

```
        private bool Validate()
        {
            if ((txtFirstName.Text.Trim().Length == 0) ||
            (txtLastName.Text.Trim().Length == 0) ||
            (txtAddress.Text.Trim().Length == 0))
                return false;
            return true;
        }
    }
}
```

We will now use this user control in the Web Parts control. You need to register the user control in your web form so that you can use it. Here is how you would do that:

Listing 11-13
```
<%@ register tagprefix="UserControl" tagname="WebUserControl1"  Src="~/
WebUserControl1.ascx"%>
```

The complete source code of the Web Parts control in Design View mode is as follows:

Listing 11-14
```
<%@ Page Language="C#"
AutoEventWireup="true"
CodeBehind="Default.aspx.cs"
Inherits="Web_Parts._Default" %>
<%@ register tagprefix="UserControl"
    tagname="WebUserControl1"
    Src="~/WebUserControl1.ascx"%>
<!DOCTYPE html PUBLIC "-//W3C//DTD XHTML 1.0 Transitional//EN" "http://
www.w3.org/TR/xhtml1/DTD/xhtml1-transitional.dtd">
<html xmlns="http://www.w3.org/1999/xhtml" >
<head id="Head1" runat="server">
    <title>Demonstrating a Custom Web Parts Control</title>
</head>
<body>
    <form id="form1" runat="server">
        <div>
            <asp:WebPartManager ID="WebPartManager1" runat="server">
            </asp:WebPartManager>
        </div>
        <table>
            <tr>
                <td valign="top">
                    <asp:WebPartZone ID="LeftZone" runat="server">
                        <ZoneTemplate>
                            <asp:Calendar ID="Calendar1"
                            runat="server"></asp:Calendar>
                        </ZoneTemplate>
                    </asp:WebPartZone>
                </td>
```

```
        <td valign="top">
            <asp:WebPartZone ID="RightZone" runat="server">
                <ZoneTemplate>
                    <UserControl:WebUserControl1
                    ID="MyControl1" runat="server" />
                </ZoneTemplate>
            </asp:WebPartZone>
        </td>
      </tr>
    </table>
  </form>
</body>
</html>
```

Figure 11-2 shows what the Web Parts control looks like in Design View mode.

When you execute the application, you can see the control in action. The Web Parts control will have two zones, with a Calendar control in one and the user control in the other. Figure 11-3 shows the output in the web browser when the application is executed.

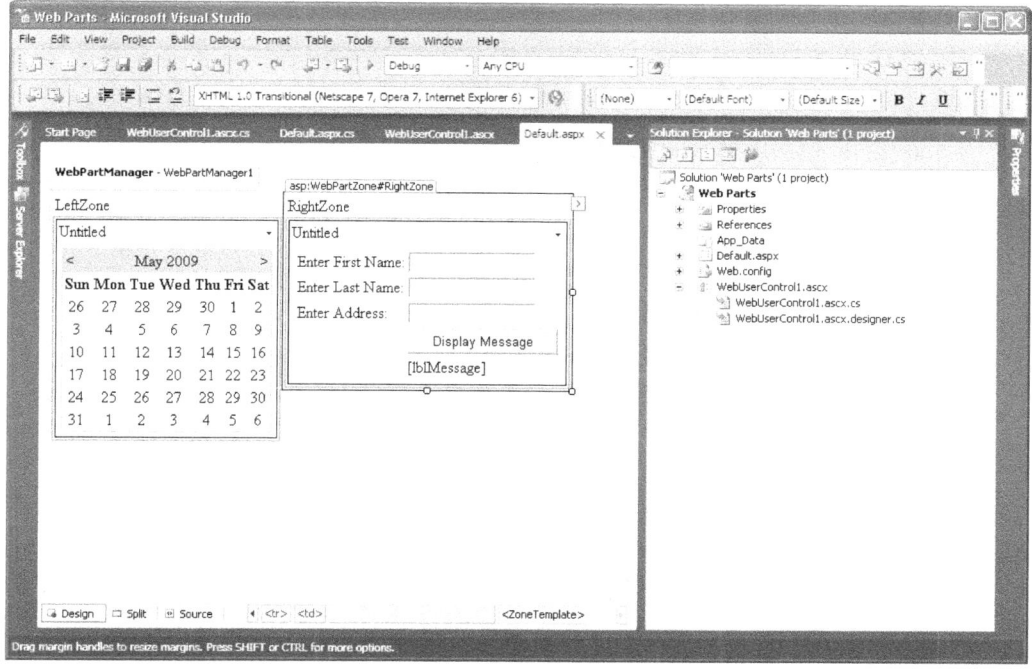

FIGURE 11-2   The custom Web Parts control in Design View mode

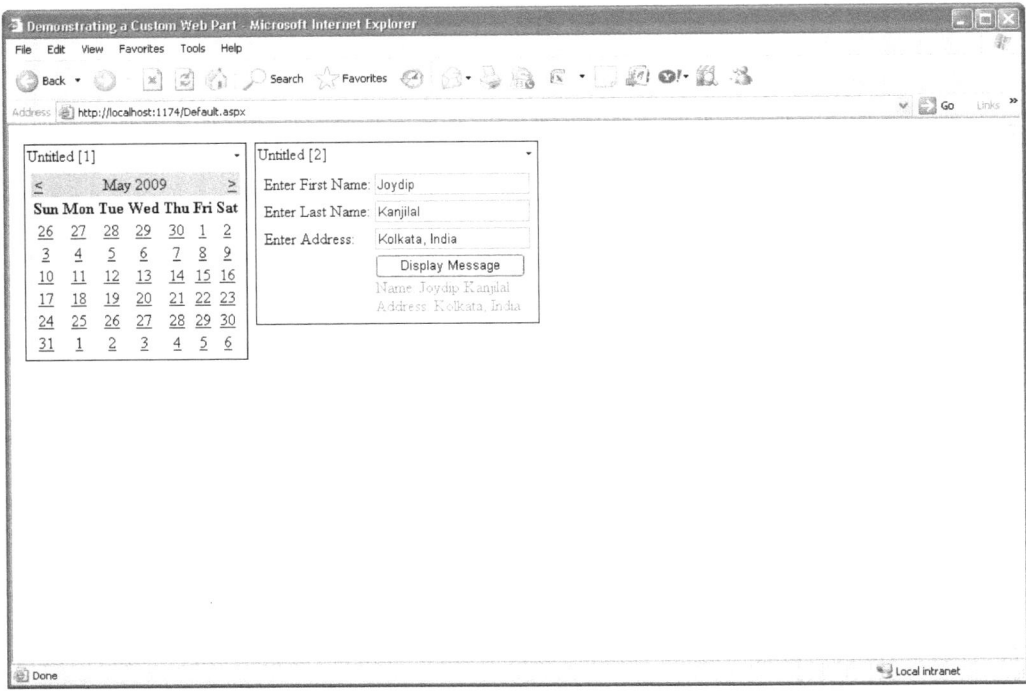

FIGURE 11-3   The custom Web Parts control in action

Ajax and Web Parts

Ajax was primarily designed and developed to provide a fast and responsive user interface, and it can give a great boost to an application's performance. You can use it to cut down on network load and bandwidth usage and retrieve only the data required—this will give you faster and richer user interfaces, as well as better response times.

You can implement Ajax in your Web Parts controls in two ways, by using either client-side callbacks or the UpdatePanel control. In this section we will discuss how the later can be used.

Using the UpdatePanel Control

To Ajax-enable a Web Parts web page, simply take a ScriptManager control and place the custom control inside an UpdatePanel control. Here is an example:

Listing 11-15
```
<head id="Head1" runat="server">
    <title>An Ajax-Enabled Custom Web Part</title>
</head>
<body>
    <form id="form1" runat="server">
```

```
        <div>
            <asp:WebPartManager ID="WebPartManager1" runat="server">
            </asp:WebPartManager>
            <asp:ScriptManager ID="ScriptManager1" runat="server">
            </asp:ScriptManager>
        </div>
        <table>
            <tr>
                <td valign="top">
                    <asp:WebPartZone ID="LeftZone" runat="server">
                        <ZoneTemplate>
                            <asp:UpdatePanel ID="UpdatePanel1"
                            runat="server">
                            <ContentTemplate>
                             <asp:Calendar ID="Calendar1"
                             runat="server"></asp:Calendar>
                            </ContentTemplate>
                            </asp:UpdatePanel>
                        </ZoneTemplate>
                    </asp:WebPartZone>
                </td>
                <td valign="top">
                    <asp:WebPartZone ID="RightZone" runat="server">
                        <ZoneTemplate>
                        <asp:UpdatePanel ID="UpdatePanel2"
                        runat="server">
                            <ContentTemplate>
                            <UserControl:WebUserControl1
                            ID="MyControl1" runat="server" />
                            </ContentTemplate>
                            </asp:UpdatePanel>
                        </ZoneTemplate>
                    </asp:WebPartZone>
                </td>
            </tr>
        </table>
    </form>
</body>
```

In the preceding code listing, there are two zones, a left zone and a right zone. The Calendar control is placed inside the <ContentTemplate> tag of the UpdatePanel control in the left zone. The WebUserControl1 user control is placed inside the <ContentTemplate> tag of another UpdatePanel control in the right zone. Any control that is placed inside the UpdatePanel control will participate in the partial page-rendering process. It should be noted that you can have multiple UpdatePanel controls in your web page, but only one ScriptManager control.

CHAPTER 12

Language Integrated Query (LINQ)

L anguage Integrated Query (LINQ) is a query translation pipeline integrated into Microsoft's .NET Framework to provide querying capabilities using languages that run on top of the .NET Framework. You can use LINQ to express your queries using any languages that targets the .NET Framework. In essence, LINQ acts as a layer between your application and your data store, and enables you to represent data as objects and query that data in your object model.

Why LINQ?

Why should we use LINQ? How does it help you? LINQ queries are compiled at compile time and are strongly typed. This is unlike T-SQL queries, which are checked only at runtime. The LINQ approach reduces complexity and allows you to design and debug your queries seamlessly.

LINQ also provides a unified model for accessing data in various data sources, including relational databases, XML files, objects, and entities, using a syntax that resembles SQL. In essence, LINQ is designed to provide a unified programming model for accessing any data source directly.

LINQ addresses the impedance mismatch that exists between programming languages and data stores. Using LINQ also reduces complexity for developers who need to query data from in-memory objects in collections.

Here is a LINQ query you can use to retrieve the names of the customers who live in India:

Listing 12-1
```
var query = from c in Customers
where c.Country == "India" select c.CustomerName;
```

Operators in LINQ

LINQ offers various kinds of operators for performing query operations over collections or object arrays. The System.Query assembly contains a static class named System .Query.Sequence that contains methods called *standard query operators*. Standard query operators are operators used in LINQ queries.

There are two groups of standard query operators:

- Standard query operators for IEnumerable(T)
- Standard query operators for IQueryable(T)

The first type operates on objects that implement the IEnumerable(T) interface. This type can be used while working with LINQ to Objects. The other type operates on objects that implement the IQueryable(T) interface. This type can be used while working with LINQ to SQL, LINQ to DataSets, or LINQ to Entities. Table 12-1 lists the various operators in LINQ along with their types.

Operator Type	Operators
Aggregation	Aggregate Average Count LongCount Max Min Sum
Conversion	Cast OfType ToArray ToDictionary ToList ToLookup ToSequence
Element	DefaultIfEmpty ElementAt ElementAtOrDefault First FirstOrDefault Last LastOrDefault Single SingleOrDefault
Equality	EqualAll
Generation	Empty Range Repeat
Grouping	GroupBy
Joining	GroupJoin Join
Ordering	OrderBy ThenBy OrderByDescending ThenByDescending Reverse
Partitioning	Skip SkipWhile Take TakeWhile
Quantifying	All Any Contains
Restriction	Where
Selection	Select SelectMany
Set	Concat Distinct Except Intersect Union

TABLE 12-1   LINQ Operators

We will now explore how we can make use of the LINQ operators in applications. Consider the following Contact class that comprises a list of properties:

Listing 12-2
```
public class Contact
{
    public int ContactID { get; set; }
    public String FirstName { get; set; }
    public String LastName { get; set; }
    public String Phone { get; set; }
    public String City { get; set; }
    public String State { get; set; }
    public String Zip { get; set; }
    public String Country { get; set; }
}
```

You can populate a list of the Contact class as follows:

Listing 12-3
```
List<Contact> contacts = new List<Contact>
{
  new Contact { FirstName="Joydip",
LastName="Kanjilal", Phone="11111111",
City="Hyderabad", State="AP",
Zip="500001",Country="India"},
  new Contact { FirstName="Oindrilla",
 LastName="Roy Chowdhury", Phone="21111111",
City="Kolkata", State="WB", Zip="700002",
Country="India"},
  new Contact { FirstName="Soma",
 LastName="Roy Chowdhury", Phone="31111111",
 City="Kolkata", State="WB",
Zip="700002",Country="India"}
};
```

You can then use the selection operator to retrieve the details of all contacts that reside in Kolkata, as shown in the following code snippet:

Listing 12-4
```
var query = from c in contacts where c.City.Equals("Kolkata") select c;
```

You can also group the data to be retrieved:

Listing 12-5
```
var query = from c in contacts group c
  by c.City into g
select new {Count = g.Count()};
```

LINQ Implementations

Microsoft has categorized LINQ into these distinct areas:

- **LINQ to Objects** Used to query in-memory objects or collections of in-memory objects
- **LINQ to XML** Used to query data retrieved from XML data sources
- **LINQ to ADO.NET** Used to query relational databases
  - **LINQ to SQL** Used to query SQL Server databases only
  - **LINQ to DataSet** Used to query DataSet and DataTable instances
  - **LINQ to Entities** Used to query data retrieved through the ADO.NET Entity Framework

LINQ to Objects

LINQ to Objects is used to query in-memory objects or collections of objects. It is compliant with T:System.Collections.IEnumerable or T:System.Collections.Generic in-memory objects or collections of in-memory objects.

The following code listing illustrates how you can use LINQ to iterate through a collection of custom business entities.

Listing 12-6
```csharp
using System;
using System.Collections.Generic;
using System.Linq;
using System.Text;
namespace LinqSampleProject
{
    public class Customer
    {
        public int CustomerID { get; set; }
        public string FirstName { get; set; }
        public string LastName { get; set; }
        public string Address { get; set; }
    }
    class Program
    {
        static void Main(string[] args)
        {
            List<Customer> customers = new List<Customer> {
            new Customer { CustomerID=1,
FirstName="Joydip", LastName="Kanjilal",
Address="Kolkata"},
            new Customer { CustomerID=2,
 FirstName="Jamal", LastName="Dudekula",
```

```
Address="Hyderabad"},
        new Customer { CustomerID=3,
FirstName="Ranjan", LastName="Bhuyan",
Address="Cuttack"},
        new Customer { CustomerID=4,
FirstName="Vilail", LastName="Shaji",
Address="Coimbatore"},
        new Customer { CustomerID=5,
FirstName="Sudhakar", LastName="Kayyam",
Address="Hyderabad"}};
        var customerList = from c in customers
                           where c.Address.Equals("Hyderabad")
                           orderby c.FirstName
                           select c;
        foreach (var cust in customerList)
        {
            Console.WriteLine(cust.FirstName);
        }
        Console.Read();
    }
  }
}
```

LINQ to XML

LINQ to XML is used to map LINQ queries or LINQ statements to their corresponding XML data sources. In essence, you can use LINQ to XML and apply standard query operators to retrieve data from XML data sources.

Consider the following XML file called Customers.xml.

Listing 12-7
```
<?xml version="1.0" encoding="utf-8" ?>
<Customers>
  <Customer>
    <CustomerID>1</CustomerID>
    <FirstName>Joydip</FirstName>
    <LastName>Kanjilal</LastName>
    <Address>Kolkata</Address>
  </Customer>
  <Customer>
    <CustomerID>2</CustomerID>
    <FirstName>Jamal</FirstName>
    <LastName>Dudekula</LastName>
    <Address>Hyderabad</Address>
  </Customer>
  <Customer>
    <CustomerID>3</CustomerID>
    <FirstName>Ranjan</FirstName>
    <LastName>Bhuyan</LastName>
```

```
    <Address>Cuttack</Address>
    </Customer>
    <Customer>
      <CustomerID>4</CustomerID>
      <FirstName>Vilail</FirstName>
      <LastName>Shaji</LastName>
      <Address>Coimbatore</Address>
    </Customer>
    <Customer>
      <CustomerID>5</CustomerID>
      <FirstName>Sudhakar</FirstName>
      <LastName>Kayyam</LastName>
      <Address>Hyderabad</Address>
    </Customer>
</Customers>
```

The following class can be used to create a list of new customers or retrieve customers from the XML file:

Listing 12-8

```
public class CustomerData
    {
        public static IEnumerable<Customer> CreateNewCustomers()
        {
            return new List<Customer>
            {
            new Customer { CustomerID=1,
FirstName="Joydip", LastName="Kanjilal",
 Address="Kolkata"},
            new Customer { CustomerID=2,
 FirstName="Jamal", LastName="Dudekula",
 Address="Hyderabad"},
            new Customer { CustomerID=3,
 FirstName="Ranjan", LastName="Bhuyan",
Address="Cuttack"},
            new Customer { CustomerID=4,
 FirstName="Vilail", LastName="Shaji",
Address="Coimbatore"},
            new Customer { CustomerID=5,
FirstName="Sudhakar", LastName="Kayyam",
Address="Hyderabad"}};
        }
        public static List<Customer> GetCustomers()
        {
            XDocument xDocument = XDocument.Load(@"C:\Customers.xml");
            var customerList = from customer in
xDocument.Descendants("Customer")
                        select new Customer
```

```
                                {
                                    CustomerID =
int.Parse(customer.Element("CustomerID").Value),
 FirstName = customer.Element("FirstName").Value,
LastName = customer.Element("LastName").Value,
Address = customer.Element("Address").Value
                                };
            return customerList.ToList();
        }
        public static List<Customer>
GetCustomerByName(String firstName, String lastName)
        {
            XDocument xDocument = XDocument.Load(@"C:\Customers.xml");
            var customerList = from customer
in xDocument.Descendants("Customer")
                                where
customer.Element("FirstName").Value.Equals(firstName) &&
customer.Element("LastName").Value.Equals(lastName)
                                select new Customer
                                {
                                    CustomerID =
int.Parse(customer.Element("CustomerID").Value),
                                    FirstName =
customer.Element("FirstName").Value,
 LastName = customer.Element("LastName").Value,
Address = customer.Element("Address").Value
                                };
            return customerList.ToList();
        }
        public static List<Customer> GetCustomerByID(int customerID)
        {
            XDocument xDocument = XDocument.Load(@"C:\Customers.xml");
            var customerList = from customer in
xDocument.Descendants("Customer")
where customerID == int.Parse(customer.Element("CustomerID").Value)

                                select new Customer
                                {
                                    CustomerID =
int.Parse(customer.Element("CustomerID").Value),
                                    FirstName =
customer.Element("FirstName").Value,
LastName = customer.Element("LastName").Value,
Address = customer.Element("Address").Value
                                };
            return customerList.ToList();
        }
    }
```

Here is how you can use the CustomerData class to retrieve data from the XML file:

Listing 12-9
```
List<Customer> customersList = CustomerData.GetCustomers();
var customerList = from c in customersList
                   where c.Address.Equals("Hyderabad")
                   orderby c.FirstName
                   select c;

foreach (var cust in customerList)
{
    Console.WriteLine(cust.FirstName);
}
```

LINQ to ADO.NET

LINQ to ADO.NET makes use of ADO.NET to connect to and work with data from relational databases.

LINQ to DataSet

The ability to explicitly cache data in a disconnected mode of operation is one of the most striking features in ADO.NET. The DataSet is a disconnected representation of the database, and LINQ to DataSet allows you to query data from DataSet or DataTable instances.

The following code listing illustrates how LINQ to DataSet can be used to query data in a DataTable instance.

Listing 12-10
```
DataTable dtCustomer = new DataTable();
dtCustomer.Columns.Add("CustomerID", typeof(Int32));
dtCustomer.Columns.Add("FirstName", typeof(String));
dtCustomer.Columns.Add("LastName", typeof(String));
dtCustomer.Columns.Add("Address", typeof(String));
dtCustomer.Rows.Add(1, "Joydip", "Kanjilal", "Kolkata");
dtCustomer.Rows.Add(2, "Jamal", "Dudekula", "Hyderabad");
dtCustomer.Rows.Add(3, "Ranjan", "Bhuyan", "Cuttack");
dtCustomer.Rows.Add(4, "Vilail", "Shaji", "Coimbatore");
dtCustomer.Rows.Add(5, "Sudhakar", "Kayyam", "Hyderabad");
var result = from row in dtCustomer.AsEnumerable()
             select row;
foreach (var customer in result)
    Console.WriteLine(customer["CustomerID"] +
 "\t" + customer["FirstName"]);
```

LINQ to SQL

LINQ to SQL was previously known by the name of DLINQ. It is an ORM tool that can be used to query SQL Server databases. When a LINQ to SQL query is executed, the LINQ to SQL component actually traverses the expression tree and converts the LINQ query to an equivalent SQL statement that the underlying database can understand.

When you use LINQ to SQL, you will need to create a DataContext. The basic purpose of a DataContext is translating the LINQ to SQL queries to corresponding vendor-specific T-SQL statements.

Here is an example of a typical LINQ to SQL query:

Listing 12-11
```
var result = from p in Products
    WHERE where p.Price > 35000 && p.Category == "Laptops"
    select new { p.ProductID, p.Price};
```

This query would at runtime be converted to the following equivalent SQL statement:

Listing 12-12
```
SELECT ProductID, Price From Products
WHERE Price > 35000 AND Category = 'Laptops'
```

Implementing a Sample Application Using LINQ to SQL

You can use the built-in LINQ to SQL designer in Visual Studio 2010 to create your LINQ to SQL classes. To do so, follow these steps:

1. Create a new Web Application in Visual Studio 2010, give it a name, and save it.

2. Right-click on the Solution Explorer and select Add | New Item.

3. Select LINQ to SQL Classes from the list of templates (as shown in Figure 12-1), give it a name, and save it.

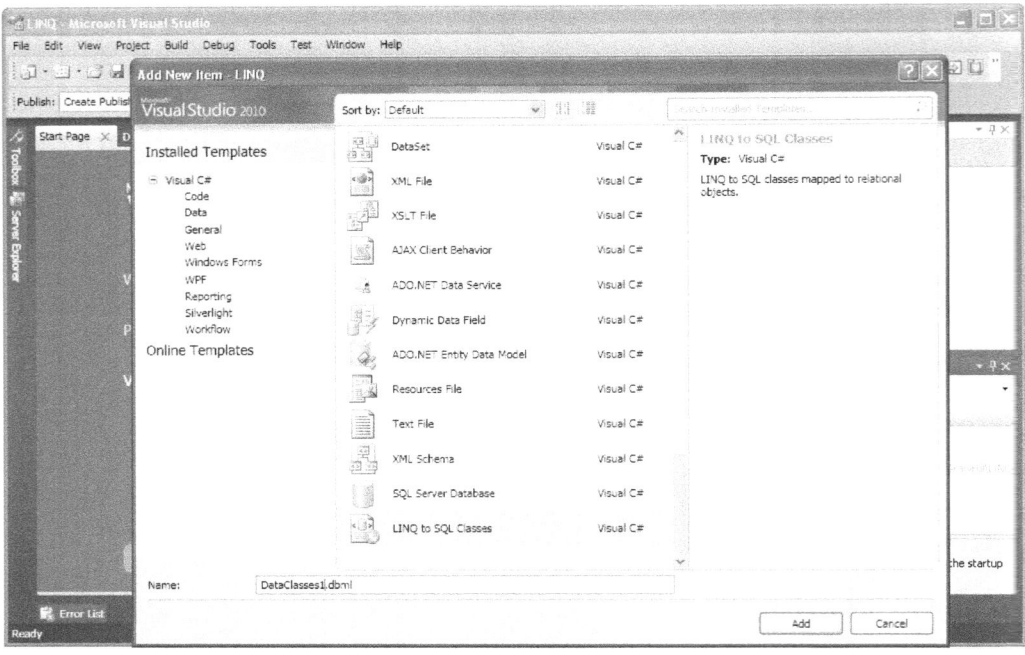

FIGURE 12-1   Creating a LINQ to SQL class

4. In the Server Explorer, connect to the AdventureWorks database.

5. Drag and drop the Department table onto the .dbml file you just created. The .dbml file should look like the one shown in Figure 12-2.

6. Drag and drop a LinqDataSource control onto your web form and configure it to use the data context you just created. The markup code of the LinqDataSource control will look like this:

Listing 12-13

```
<asp:LinqDataSource ID="LinqDataSource1" runat="server"
        ContextTypeName=
"LINQ.DataClasses1DataContext"
EnableDelete="True"
        TableName="Departments">
    </asp:LinqDataSource>
```

7. Take a GridView control in the web form and assign the DataSourceID property of the control to the LinqDataSource you just created.

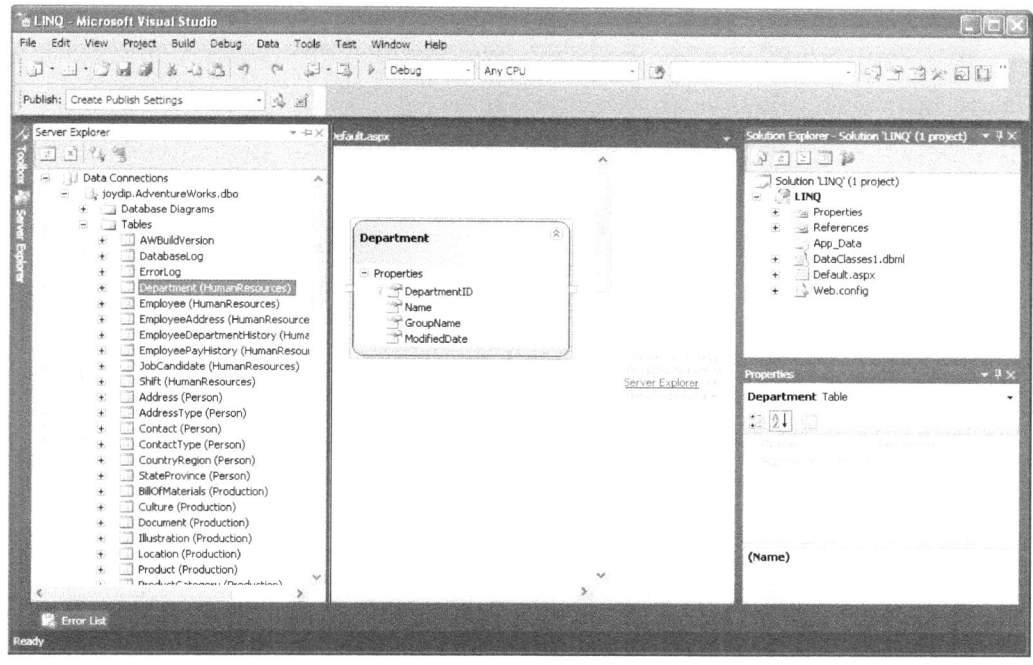

FIGURE 12-2   The LINQ to SQL class in Design View mode

You are done! Here is what the markup code of the GridView control will look like:

Listing 12-14
```
<asp:GridView ID="GridView1" runat="server" AllowPaging="True"
            AllowSorting="True" AutoGenerateColumns="False"
DataKeyNames="DepartmentID"
            DataSourceID="LinqDataSource1">
            <Columns>
                <asp:BoundField DataField="DepartmentID"
 HeaderText="Department ID"
                        InsertVisible="False"
ReadOnly="True"
SortExpression="DepartmentID" />
                <asp:BoundField DataField="Name"
 HeaderText="Department Name"
                        SortExpression="Name" />
                <asp:BoundField DataField="GroupName"
 HeaderText="Group Name"
                        SortExpression="GroupName" />
            </Columns>
        </asp:GridView>
```

The complete markup code for the web form is as follows:

Listing 12-15
```
<html xmlns="http://www.w3.org/1999/xhtml" >
<head runat="server">
    <title>Working with LINQ</title>
</head>
<body>
    <form id="form1" runat="server">
    <div>
        <asp:GridView ID="GridView1" runat="server" AllowPaging="True"
            AllowSorting="True"
AutoGenerateColumns="False"
DataKeyNames="DepartmentID"
            DataSourceID="LinqDataSource1">
            <Columns>
                <asp:BoundField
DataField="DepartmentID"
 HeaderText="Department ID"
                        InsertVisible="False"
 ReadOnly="True" SortExpression=
"DepartmentID" />
                <asp:BoundField
DataField="Name"
HeaderText="Department Name"
                        SortExpression="Name" />
                <asp:BoundField
```

```
DataField="GroupName"
 HeaderText="Group Name"
                   SortExpression="GroupName" />
            </Columns>
        </asp:GridView>
    </div>
    </form>
    <asp:LinqDataSource ID="LinqDataSource1" runat="server"
        ContextTypeName=
"LINQ.DataClasses1DataContext"
 EnableDelete="True"
        TableName="Departments">
    </asp:LinqDataSource>
</body>
</html>
```

When you execute the application, the records of the Department table will be displayed in a GridView control in the web browser, as shown in Figure 12-3.

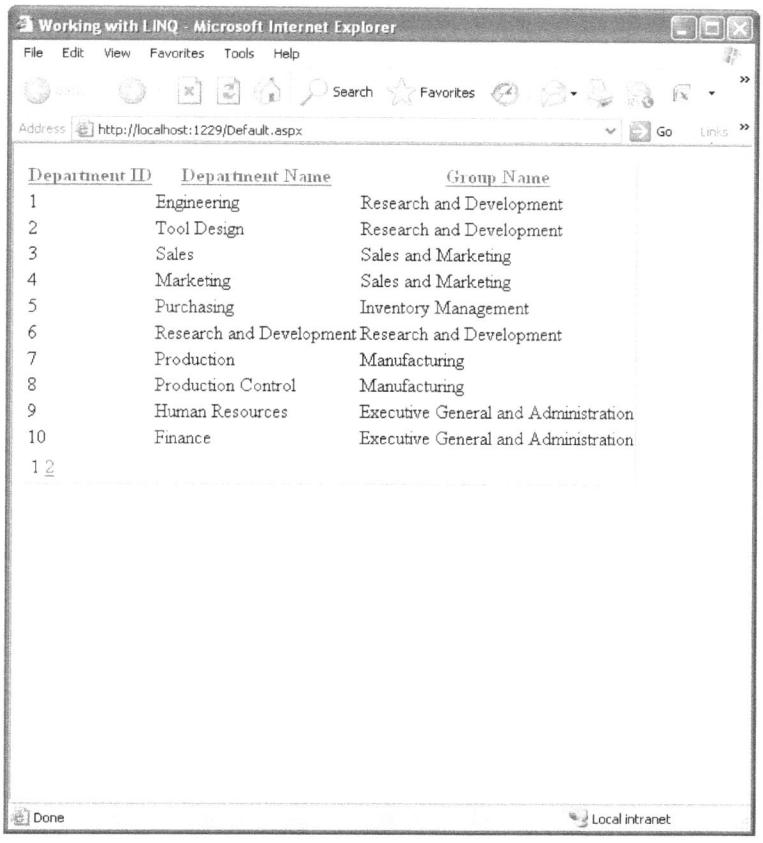

FIGURE 12-3 The LINQ to SQL application in execution

Tips for Improving LINQ to SQL Performance

There are a lot of ways to boost your application's performance when using LINQ. We will look at a few in this section:

- Turning off the ObjectTrackingEnabled property
- Using multiple data contexts
- Turning off optimistic concurrency
- Selectively retrieving and filtering data
- Using compiled queries

Turning off the ObjectTrackingEnabled Property   Turn off the ObjectTrackingEnabled property for the DataContext if it is not required. This boosts the application's performance if you need not use object tracking and want to only read data and not modify it. Turning it off will also ensure that the unnecessary identity management of the objects is turned off—the DataContext need not store this information because no change statements need to be generated.

To turn off object tracking, you can use the following code:

Listing 12-16
```
using (AdventureWorksDataContext context =
new AdventureWorksDataContext())
{
  context.ObjectTrackingEnabled = false;
}
```

Using Multiple Data Contexts   The DataContext in LINQ represents a single unit of work. Rather than having one DataContext for all database objects you have in your application, you should use one DataContext per unit of work to eliminate the overhead cost of identity management and change tracking and hence improve the application's overall data access performance.

You can also monitor and analyze the queries generated by the DataContext by using the DataContext's Log property. Here is an example:

Listing 12-17
```
using (AdventureWorksDataContext context =
 new AdventureWorksDataContext())
{
  context.Log = Console.Out;
}
```

Turning off Optimistic Concurrency   Unless there is a specific reason to use optimistic concurrency, turn it off.

The following example illustrates how you can turn off optimistic concurrency using the UpdateCheck.Never enumeration in your generated LINQ to SQL classes:

Listing 12-18
```
[Column(Storage="_Address", DbType="NText",
           UpdateCheck=UpdateCheck.Never)]
public string Address
```

```
    get
    {
      return this._Address;
    }
    set
    {
      if ((this._Address != value))
      {
        this.OnAddressChanging(value);
        this.SendPropertyChanging();
        this._Address = value;
        this.SendPropertyChanged("Description");
        this.OnAddressChanged();
      }
    }
  }
}
```

Selectively Retrieving and Filtering Data   Ensure that your LINQ to SQL queries retrieve only the data you need. The following code snippet illustrates how you can use the Take and Skip methods to retrieve selected data.

Listing 12-19
```
private IList<Customer> GetCustomers
(int startingPageIndex, int pageSize)
{
  using (AdventureWorksDataContext context =
  new AdventureWorksDataContext())
  {
    return context.Customers
            .Take<Customer>(pageSize)
            .Skip<Customer>(startingPageIndex * pageSize)
            .ToList<Customer>();
  }
}
```

You can also filter data in several ways in LINQ queries. This will also reduce the amount of the data you retrieve and hence boost performance. Here is an example:

Listing 12-20
```
using (AdventureWorksDataContext context =
new AdventureWorksDataContext())

  DataLoadOptions options = new DataLoadOptions();
  options.AssociateWith<Employee>
emp=> emp.Employees.Where<Employee>
employee => !employee.Retired));
  context.LoadOptions = options;
```

Using Compiled Queries   When you are using the same query again and again, you can use compiled queries for faster data retrieval.

For example, you could compose a compiled query to retrieve the details of all continuing products and store it in a static class called MyCompiledQueries as follows:

Listing 12-21
```
public static class MyCompiledQueries
{
  public static Func<AdventureWorksDataContext, IEnumerable<Category>>
    GetProducts
    {
      get
      {
        Func<AdventureWorksDataContext, IEnumerable<Product>> func =
          CompiledQuery.Compile
<AdventureWorksDataContext, IEnumerable<Product>>
            ((AdventureWorksDataContext context) => context.Products.
              Where<Product>(p => !p.Discontinued));
        return func;
      }
    }
}
```

You could then use this compiled query in your code like this:

Listing 12-22
```
using (AdventureWorksDataContext context =
 new AdventureWorksDataContext())
{
  MyCompiledQueries.GetProducts(context);
}
```

LINQ to Entities

LINQ to Entities is another flavor of LINQ that is used to query data from the ADO .NET Entity Data Model (EDM) in a strongly typed manner. You can use it to create, compose, and express strongly typed queries and retrieve business objects or collections of business objects from the ADO.NET EDM.

Internally, LINQ to Entities uses the Object Services layer to query data from the EDM. The EDM provides a mapping between the conceptual and relational models. A relational model is also known as the logical model. A conceptual model defines the relationships between the entities used in an application.

Here is an example of a typical LINQ to Entities query that returns all customer names from the Customer table of the AdventureWorks database:

Listing 12-23
```
AdventureWorksModel.AdventureWorksEntities
context = new AdventureWorksModel.
AdventureWorksEntities);
var query = from cust in context.Customer
select cust;
foreach (var c in query)
Console.WriteLine(c.CustomerName);
```

Choosing Between LINQ to Entities and LINQ to SQL

LINQ to Entities is actually a superset of LINQ to SQL. It is an extended object-relational mapping (ORM) tool that can be used to retrieve data exposed using the EDM. Using LINQ to Entities, you can define a model for your application and use it to persist data in the database.

Note that you can use LINQ to SQL only for communicating with SQL Server databases. In contrast, you can use LINQ to Entities to communicate with any database. The other areas where LINQ to Entities scores over LINQ to SQL are entity inheritance and entity composition.

You should use LINQ to Entities when you want your data model to be connected to any database and leverage the benefits that LINQ to Entities provide, like entity inheritance, entity composition, change tracking, etc. You can use LINQ to SQL if you are sure that your database will be SQL Server and you need not have such features in your application.

Either way, you can use LINQ to query data in your object model.

CHAPTER 13

ASP.NET Ajax

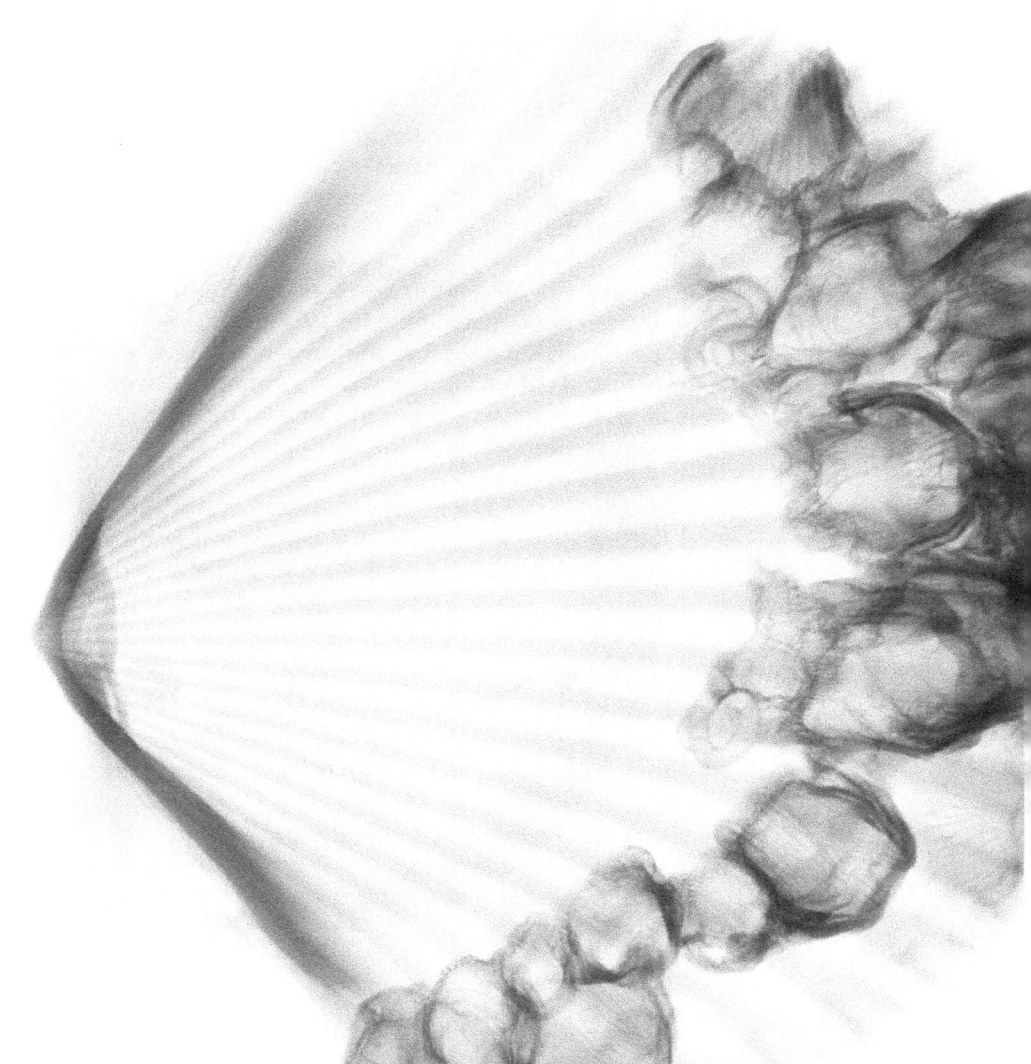

The biggest challenge web application developers face is creating a fast and responsive user interface, and Ajax was developed with that goal in mind. Ajax (short for Asynchronous JavaScript and XML) is a cross-platform combination of technologies that can be used to make your web pages fast, rich, and responsive. By using Ajax, you can cut down on network load and bandwidth usage and retrieve only the data you require. This allows you to produce faster interfaces with better response times.

Since its introduction, Ajax has produced radical changes in how web applications are developed. And with Microsoft taking Ajax to new heights and regularly coming up with new releases, Ajax is set to become the technology of choice for building web applications in the years to come.

Introducing Ajax

Ajax is a mix of a number of technologies. The technologies that make up Ajax are not new. Such technologies have been around for a long time. To cite an example, Netscape's LiveScript (eventually called JavaScript) allowed for asynchronous processing. Netscape also came up with support for Dynamic XML and Microsoft with the XMLHttpRequest object within the browser that could be used to retrieve data from the server asynchronously. The XMLHttpRequest object later paved the way for the birth of Ajax. It was this concept (usage of the XMLHttpRequest object to perform asynchronous operations) that was named Ajax by Jesse James Garrett of Adaptive Path in early 2005.

Ajax made its presence felt within development communities worldwide in late 2005, and since then, it has become popular as one of the best technologies to use for designing applications that have a fast and responsive user interface. It was Google who first led the drive to make Ajax known to the communities worldwide by announcing the first public implementation of Ajax in Google Suggest. Since then, there have been quite a few more such implementations, like Google Maps, Google Suggest, Gmail, Live.com, etc.

Microsoft initially introduced support for Ajax in ASP.NET in the form of a separate add-on called ASP.NET 2.0 Ajax Extensions. This was an extension of ASP.NET that was totally integrated with server-based services and allowed developers to design and implement Ajax-enabled web applications using ASP.NET technology.

Advantages of Ajax

Usage of Ajax has many benefits, the most important being a reduction in the consumption of server resources—reduced server hits, network loads, round trips, etc. Ajax-enabled applications—applications that can leverage the features and benefits of Ajax—can provide a fast and responsive user interface with support for partial page updates.

Partial page updates let you update only specific parts of a page instead of the entire web page during postbacks to the web server. This reduces the consumption of the server's resources (because the memory and processor load is reduced) and it boosts the application's performance.

Drawbacks of Using Ajax

Although Ajax is a powerful technology for improving the response times of web pages in your application, it has certain drawbacks: most significantly, its use of and dependency on JavaScript.

JavaScript is implemented differently in various browsers, such as Internet Explorer, Firefox, and so on. This is a major constraint when you need to make your Ajax-enabled application work on multiple browsers. Also, mobile browsers do not support JavaScript, which implies that Ajax may not be well suited for designing mobile applications.

Using Ajax also makes web pages difficult to debug, it increases the code size of your web pages, and it makes your web pages prone to security threats.

How Does Ajax Work?

Ajax is a mix of JavaScript, HTML, CSS, XML, DOM, and the XMLHttpRequest object. Unlike normal ASP.NET applications, the runtime of an Ajax-enabled ASP.NET web application initially loads the Ajax engine instead of loading a web page. The basic purpose of this engine is to render data for the application's user interface and also communicate with the web server in order to transport data between the web server and web browser. The Ajax engine runs within the context of the web browser and makes use of JavaScript (for data validation, changes to data, etc.) and DOM technologies.

The XMLHttpRequest is one of the major components of the Ajax framework. You can use it in any of today's browsers to implement asynchronous GET or POST requests.

Asynchronous Modes of Execution

Synchronous execution means that until and unless a request is complete in all respects, another cannot start. In other words, requests have to be executed one after the other. Asynchronous execution is a mode in which multiple requests can be executed simultaneously.

The Ajax engine runs within the context of the web browser using JavaScript and DOM technologies. In Ajax, the JavaScript that is loaded when the web page loads is responsible for handling the basic tasks of validating data, changing data, etc., while the data transfer between the user interface and the database happens independently in the background. This is asynchronous execution.

Some Popular ASP.NET Ajax Frameworks

There are plenty of Ajax frameworks available. The most common ones compliant with ASP.NET are Atlas, AJAX.NET Professional, MagicAjax.NET, and Anthem.NET. ASP.NET Ajax is also a popular one, and we'll discuss it separately.

The Atlas Framework

The Atlas framework (http://www.microsoft.com/downloads/details.aspx?FamilyIc =5CC5CE52-45B7-4C64-992C-4F0FBC8C8221&displaylang=en) is an extension to ASF .NET that provides support for asynchronous operations in ASP.NET. It consists of a client-side script library and a collection of server controls.

To work with Atlas, you should add the Microsoft.AtlasControlExtender.dll and AtlasControlToolkit.dll assemblies as references to your project. You also need to specify the following in your application's web.config file:

Listing 13-1
```
<pages>
<controls>
<add namespace="Microsoft.Web.UI"
assembly="Microsoft.Web.Atlas"
tagPrefix="atlas"/>
<addnamespace="Microsoft.Web.UI.Controls"
assembly="Microsoft.Web.Atlas"
tagPrefix="atlas"/>
</controls>
</pages>
```

Here is a snippet of markup code that illustrates how you can use the Atlas UpdatePanel control in your application:

Listing 13-2
```
<atlas:UpdatePanel ID="UpdatePanel1" runat="server">
 <ContentTemplate>
   <asp:GridView ID="GridView1" runat="server" />
     <Columns>
        //Your GridView columns
     </Columns>
   </asp:GridView>
 </ContentTemplate>
</atlas:UpdatePanel>
```

The following code snippet illustrates how the Atlas ScriptManager control can be used:

Listing 13-3
```
<atlas:ScriptManager
EnableScriptComponents="false"
 ID="ScriptManager1" runat="server">
   <Services>
     <atlas:ServiceReference
GenerateProxy="true"
 Path="EmployeeService.asmx" />
   </Services>
   <Scripts>
     <atlas:ScriptReference Path="EmployeeScripts.js" />
   </Scripts>
 </atlas:ScriptManager>
```

The AJAX.NET Professional Framework

AJAX.NET Professional (http://www.ajaxpro.info/) is a popular open source Ajax library for use with ASP.NET. It can be used for designing and implementing Ajax-enabled web applications, and it works with all versions of ASP.NET.

The MagicAjax.NET Framework

MagicAjax.NET (http://sourceforge.net/projects/magicajax), a freely available and flexible Ajax framework, was started as an article at CodeProject by Argiris Kirtzidis. It has been improved a lot since then and is available as a free download.

You can use MagicAjax.NET to Ajax-enable your applications as shown in the following code listing:

Listing 13-4
```
<magicAjax:AjaxPanel runat="server" ID="MyMagicAjaxPanel">
    <asp:ListBox runat="server"
ID="MyListBox"
 DataSourceID="SqlDataSource1"
    DataTextField="EmployeeName" DataValueField="EmployeeID"
    EnableViewState="False" AutoPostBack="True"
    OnSelectedIndexChanged="MyListBox_SelectedIndexChanged">
    </asp:ListBox>
</magicAjax:AjaxPanel>
```

The Anthem.NET Framework

Anthem.NET (http://sourceforge.net/projects/anthem-dot-net) is a free, easy-to-use, cross-browser, open source Ajax toolkit written by Jason Diamond. It is compliant with all ASP.NET versions. The Anthem.NET framework consists of a rich set of controls that you can use to Ajax-enable web applications developed using Microsoft's ASP.NET technology.

Here is an example that illustrates how you can use this framework to Ajax-enable your application:

Listing 13-5
```
<anthem:ListBox runat="server"
ID="MyListBox"
 DataSourceID="SqlDataSource1"
    DataTextField="EmployeeName"
DataValueField="EmployeeID"
    EnableViewState="False"
 AutoCallBack="True"
    OnSelectedIndexChanged=
"MyListBox_SelectedIndexChanged">
</anthem:ListBox>
<anthem:Panel AutoUpdateAfterCallBack="true"
 runat="server">
    <div id="EmployeeRecords"
runat="server">
    </div>
</anthem:Panel>
```

ASP.NET Ajax

ASP.NET Ajax (http://www.asp.net/ajax/) is a free framework from Microsoft that can be used to design and implement cross-browser web applications with rich and responsive user interfaces. ASP.NET 2.0 included support for Ajax using a separate add-on named ASP.NET 2.0 Ajax Extensions. Later, this became a part of the ASP.NET release.

Although Ajax is essentially a client-side technique, most of its real-world deployments call for server-side processing. The ASP.NET Ajax architecture has a framework developed for both client and server ends.

To achieve partial page updates in your ASP.NET web pages through ASP.NET Ajax, you can use the UpdatePanel control. Here is an example:

Listing 13-6
```
<form id="Form1" runat="server">
<asp:ScriptManager ID="ScriptManager1"
runat="server"
EnablePartialRendering="true"/>
   <asp:UpdatePanel ID="UpdatePanel1" runat="server">
   <ContentTemplate>
     //Place other controls/updatable content here
   </ContentTemplate>
 </asp:UpdatePanel>
  </form>
```

The ASP.NET Ajax Client Library

The Microsoft ASP.NET Ajax Client Library is written entirely using the JavaScript scripting language and contains a collection of object-oriented JavaScript classes and their members in the form of .js files, wrapped inside the System.Web.Extensions.dll assembly. The library consists of the Sys.Global, Sys, Sys.Net, Sys.Serialization, Sys.Services, Sys.UI, and Sys.WebForms namespaces.

The following scripts are included in Microsoft ASP.NET Ajax library:

- MicrosoftAjaxCore.js
- MicrosoftAjaxComponentModel.js
- MicrosoftAjaxSerialization.js
- MicrosoftAjaxGlobalization.js
- MicrosoftAjaxHistory.js
- MicrosoftAjaxNetwork.js
- MicrosoftAjaxWebServices.js
- MicrosoftAjaxApplicationServices.js
- MicrosoftAjaxTemplates.js (included in ASP.NET Ajax 4.0)
- MicrosoftAjaxAdoNet.js (included in ASP.NET Ajax 4.0)

The ASP.NET Ajax Server Extensions Framework

This is a framework that comprises a collection of server controls and services that extend the core ASP.NET framework to provide Ajax support. The services provided by this framework include:

- Support for Localization and Globalization
- Support for Authentication
- Support for Debugging and Tracing
- Support for Web services and Application services

The ASP.NET Ajax Architectural Components

The Ajax architecture is composed primarily of two frameworks: the server framework and the client framework.

The Server Framework

The server framework consists of a collection of server controls and services that extend the ASP.NET framework. These are also known as server extensions, and they include support for localization, globalization, debugging, tracing, web services, and application services. The major components of the ASP.NET Ajax server extensions framework include ASP.NET Ajax server controls, the application services bridge, and the web services bridge.

The ASP.NET Ajax Server Controls   The ASP.NET Ajax server controls can be categorized into two distinct groups:

- **Script-management group**   This includes the ScriptManager and ScriptManagerProxy controls. The ScriptManager is the most important control for an Ajax-enabled web page. It facilitates partial page rendering of web pages using the UpdatePanel; it provides access to web services; and it also enables you to register scripts. The other control in this group, the ScriptManagerProxy, acts as a proxy to the ScriptManager control instance.

- **Partial update group**   This group includes the UpdatePanel, UpdateProgress, and Timer controls. The UpdatePanel acts as a container for controls that you can use to specify the portion of your web page where you need partial page rendering. This is the control that works with the ScriptManager control to provide you with an asynchronous callback feature (that is, an asynchronous mode of operation that requires less network and server load). The UpdateProgress controls work together with the UpdatePanel control and are displayed automatically whenever an asynchronous update operation is started.

The Application Services Bridge   The application services bridge is an API that enables different application services, like authentication and profile management, to be invoked from a client-side script.

The Web Services Bridge   The web services bridge is an API that provides access to external web services from client-side scripts. There are JavaScript proxies available to access these web services. Both of these bridges are responsible for asynchronous communication support.

The ASP.NET Ajax Client Framework

The ASP.NET Ajax client framework essentially consists of a set of JavaScript files that form part of a library commonly called the Microsoft Ajax Library. The major components included in this library are the core component layer, the core services layer, and the browser compatibility layer.

The Core Component Layer   The core component layer consists of a set of nonvisual components that provide support for asynchronous communication, networking, localization, XML and JSON serialization, ASP.NET application services, and so on.

The Core Services Layer   The core services layer contains the ASP.NET Ajax Base Class Library and its extensions, which facilitate object-oriented programming, and extensions to the existing JavaScript types.

The Browser Compatibility Layer   The browser compatibility layer is responsible for providing cross-browser support for Ajax-enabled web pages, supporting browsers such as Internet Explorer, Firefox, and so on.

The XMLHttpRequest Object

The XMLHttpRequest object is an API that can be used to transfer data between the web server and client over the HTTP protocol. It uses JavaScript to make requests to the server and process the response, minimizing the postback delays. The XMLHttpRequest object is capable of providing asynchronous execution support in applications.

You can use the XMLHttpRequest object to transfer not only XML, but any type of data between a server and client, including plain text, HTML, or JavaScript Object Notation (JSON). The XMLHttpRequest object forms the heart of Ajax applications and has a good programming model for handling requests and responses effectively. It has improved the performance of dynamic content loading considerably. However, the implementation of the XMLHttpRequest object differs from browser to browser.

Here is how you can create an instance of the XMLHttpRequest object in Internet Explorer:

Listing 13-7 `var xmlHttp = new ActiveXObject("Microsoft.XMLHTTP");`

If you are using the Firefox or Safari browsers, you can just make a call to the constructor of the XMLHttpRequest class without any arguments:

Listing 13-8 `var xmlHttp = new XmlHttpRequest();`

Implementing a Generic XMLHttpRequest Object

The following code listing illustrates how you can implement a method that can be used to retrieve the XMLHttpRequest object for any browser:

Listing 13-9

```
var xmlHttp = false;
function RetrieveXmlHttpRequestObject() {
// check for native XMLHttpRequest object
if(window.XMLHttpRequest && !(window.ActiveXObject)) {
try {
xmlHttp = new XMLHttpRequest();
}
catch(e) {
xmlHttp = false;
.
:
:
.
// check for IE/Windows ActiveX version
else if(window.ActiveXObject) {
try {
xmlHttp = new ActiveXObject("Msxml2.XMLHTTP");
}
catch(e) {
try {
xmlHttp = new ActiveXObject("Microsoft.XMLHTTP");
}
catch(e) {
xmlHttp = false;
.
:
:
:
}
}
```

The preceding method encapsulates the functionality of instantiating the XMLHttpRequest object for different browsers. Before performing any request using this object, it simply checks the status of the xmlHttp variable. If it validates to false, the object has not been instantiated; otherwise, you get an instance of the XMLHttpRequest in this variable for use.

Partial Page Rendering

The default behavior of a web page is to postback to itself when a particular action is performed on an ASP.NET server control. The web server renders all the controls into a page in the response, including controls that have not been changed between postbacks. *Partial page rendering* is when only a portion of a web page is rendered, to avoid complete page refreshes and page flickering. It also enables client-server communication without writing client scripts, and eliminates the need to write browser-compatible code.

This can be done with Microsoft ASP.NET Ajax through the interaction of server controls with the Microsoft Ajax Client Library. The partial page updates are taken care of automatically by the client code injected into the server controls. Partial page rendering can be implemented in ASP.NET Ajax using the UpdatePanel control. Actually any control that is contained inside an UpdatePanel control can participate in partial page rendering.

NOTE *When you are using partial page rendering, you can handle errors by using the AllowCustomErrorsRedirect and AsynPostBackMessage properties. You can also use the AsynPostBackError event of the ScriptManager control, which is raised when there is a page error during an asynchronous postback operation.*

The ScriptManager Control

The ScriptManager is an invisible control, and it's the heart of an Ajax-enabled web page. This control allows for partial page rendering in an Ajax-enabled web page by using the UpdatePanel control. It also provides access to web services and enables you to load and register scripts.

There can be one and only one ScriptManager control in an Ajax-enabled web page. You can place the ScriptManager control in the master pages of your application and inherit all context pages from it.

The ScriptManager control provides access to web services using JavaScript proxy classes and error-handling mechanisms during the processing of asynchronous requests. Here is what the markup code of a ScriptManager control looks like:

Listing 13-10
```
<asp:ScriptManager ID="ScriptManager1" runat="server" />
```

To implement partial page rendering, you need to have a ScriptManager control and at least one UpdatePanel control. You also need to ensure that the SupportsPartialPageRendering and EnablePartialPageRendering properties of the control are set to true. Both of these properties are set to true by default. Here is some sample code that illustrates the ScriptManager control at work:

Listing 13-11
```
<form id="form1" runat="server">
<asp:ScriptManager ID="ScriptManager1" runat="server" />
<div>
<asp:UpdatePanel ID="UpdatePanel1" runat="server">
</asp:UpdatePanel>
</div>
</form>
```

The UpdatePanel Control

The UpdatePanel control is a new server control shipped with the ASP.NET Ajax server extensions framework. This control is responsible for enabling partial page rendering in a web page, thus enhancing the richness of the user interface and improving the application's performance and responsiveness.

You can have only one ScriptManager but multiple UpdatePanel controls in your web page. Here is an example that illustrates how you can use the UpdatePanel control:

Listing 13-12
```
<body>
<form id="form1" runat="server">
<div>
<asp:ScriptManager ID="ScriptManager1" runat="server">
</asp:ScriptManager>
<asp:UpdatePanel ID="UpdatePanel1" runat="server">
<ContentTemplate>
<asp:Label ID="Label1" runat="server" Text="Label"></asp:Label>
<asp:Button ID="Button1" runat="server" OnClick="Button1_Click"
Text="Button" />
</ContentTemplate>
</asp:UpdatePanel>
</div>
</form>
</body>
```

Any postback control (a server control with its AutoPostBack property set to true) inside an UpdatePanel control will cause the latter's content to be refreshed. You can also specify UpdatePanel control triggers to indicate which postback control and event will initiate a refresh of the UpdatePanel control's content. Here is an example that illustrates how you can use the AsyncPostBackTrigger to define a trigger for your UpdatePanel control:

Listing 13-13
```
<asp:Button ID="btnRefresh"
            Text="Refresh"
            runat="server" />
<asp:ScriptManager ID="ScriptManager1"
                   runat="server" />
<asp:UpdatePanel ID="UpdatePanel1"
                 UpdateMode="Conditional"
                 runat="server">
                 <Triggers>
                   <asp:AsyncPostBackTrigger ControlID="btnRefresh" />
                 </Triggers>
                 <ContentTemplate>
                 <fieldset>
                 <%=DateTime.Now.ToString() %>
                 </fieldset>
                 </ContentTemplate>
</asp:UpdatePanel>
```

The ASP.NET Ajax Client-Side Event Model

The client lifecycle events in ASP.NET Ajax are triggered by the Application and PageRequestManager classes.

The Sys.Application object represents the Application object. The Application class belongs to the Sys namespace and contains the init, load, and unload events. Here is a quick glance at the events of the Sys.Application class:

- **init**   This is the initialization event used to initialize client components, controls, etc.

- **load**   This is the load event used to allocate memory and resources and start client-side scripts.

- **unload**   This is the unload event used to deallocate or release resources used by the application.

Note that the constructor of the Sys.Application class contains the following code to attach the load and unload event handlers to the event-handling chain:

Listing 13-14
```
Sys.UI.DomEvent.addHandler
(window, "load", this._loadHandlerDelegate);
Sys.UI.DomEvent.addHandler
(window, "unload",
this._unloadHandlerDelegate);
```

The PageRequestManager class belongs to the Sys.WebForms namespace and is responsible for administering the sequence of events for an asynchronous postback. It contains the initializeRequest, beginRequest, pageLoading, pageLoaded, and endRequest events. Of all these events, only the pageLoaded event is fired for a synchronous postback.

Here is a quick glance at the events of the Sys.WebForms.PageRequestManager class:

- **initializeRequest**   This event is fired during the initialization stage of an asynchronous postback operation.

- **beginRequest**   This event is fired just before the processing of an asynchronous postback operation.

- **pageLoading**   This event is fired after a response to an asynchronous postback is received from the web server, but before any content on the client-side web browser has been updated.

- **pageLoaded**   This event is fired after all content on the web page is refreshed as the result of either a synchronous or asynchronous postback operation.

- **endRequest**   This event is fired after an asynchronous postback operation is complete in its entirety.

The sequence in the preceding list can also vary. If there are multiple postbacks, the events of the most recent postback are fired. If an asynchronous postback is stopped prematurely, some of its events are not fired. For cancelled postbacks, only the initializeRequest event is triggered. For a synchronous postback, when the page is first loaded, or if you refresh the web browser, only the pageLoaded event will be fired.

The two major events in the processing of a web page for a synchronous postback are the window.load and window.unload DOM events. Both of these events belong to the Window object. These events are not fired during an asynchronous postback operation.

To work with the event handlers of the Sys.WebForms.PageRequestManager class, you need to initialize them in the pageLoad event. Here is how you can do this:

Listing 13-15

```
function pageLoad(sender, args)
        {
Sys.WebForms.PageRequestManager.getInstance().
add_initializeRequest(intializeRequestHandler);
Sys.WebForms.PageRequestManager.getInstance().
add_beginRequest(beginRequestHandler);
Sys.WebForms.PageRequestManager.getInstance().
add_pageLoading(pageLoadingHandler);
Sys.WebForms.PageRequestManager.getInstance().
add_pageLoaded(pageLoadedHandler);
        }
        function intializeRequestHandler(sender, args)
        {
            alert("The intializeRequestHandler method has been called");
        }
        function beginRequestHandler(sender, args) {
            alert("The beginRequestHandler method has been called");
        }
        function pageLoadingHandler(sender, args) {
            alert("The pageLoadingHandler method has been called");
        }
        function pageLoadedHandler(sender, args) {
            alert("The pageLoadedHandler method has been called");
        }
```

Improved Ajax Features in ASP.NET 4.0

ASP.NET 4.0 includes a lot of new and improved features that allow the data in JSON format to be rendered and managed perfectly. One of these features is the ability to activate elements declaratively from within the ScriptManager control. Here is an example:

Listing 13-16

```
<asp:ScriptManager ID="ScriptManager1" runat="server"
        ClientElementsToActivate="firstPanel,secondPanel">
    <Scripts>
        <asp:ScriptReference Name="MicrosoftAjaxTemplates.js" />
        <asp:ScriptReference Name="MicrosoftAjaxAdoNet.js" />
    </Scripts>
</asp:ScriptManager>
```

As you can see in the preceding code listing, the two panel controls, firstPanel and secondPanel, are activated. The script files MicrosoftAjaxTemplates.js and MicrosoftAjaxAdoNet.js should be included because they contain most of the new Ajax features in ASP.NET 4.0.

Another great new feature is the ability to select a subset of the Microsoft ASP.NET Ajax framework by using only selective portions of the framework, rather than the framework as a whole. To do this, you need to use the MicrosoftAjaxMode property of the ScriptManager control.

The following code snippet illustrates how you can specify the MicrosoftAjaxMode property to explicitly load the required scripts:

Listing 13-17

```
<asp:ScriptManager ID="ScriptManager1"
    EnablePartialRendering="false"
    MicrosoftAjaxMode="Explicit"
    EnableHistory="true"
    runat="server">
  <CompositeScript>
    <Scripts>
      <asp:ScriptReference Name="MicrosoftAjaxCore.js" />
      <asp:ScriptReference Name="MicrosoftAjaxComponentModel.js" />
      <asp:ScriptReference Name="MicrosoftAjaxSerialization.js" />
      <asp:ScriptReference Name="MicrosoftAjaxHistory.js" />
    </Scripts>
  </CompositeScript>
</asp:ScriptManager>
```

Note that the MicrosoftAjaxMode property can have one of the following three values:

- **Enabled**   This is the default mode. When selected, all Microsoft ASP.NET Ajax scripts are included.

- **Disabled**   This disables all Microsoft ASP.NET Ajax scripts. If this is selected, none of the scripts will be referenced by the ScriptManager control being used.

- **Explicit**   You can select this option to explicitly choose the scripts you would like to be included.

CHAPTER 14

Programming ASP.NET Ajax

A jax, an acronym for Asynchronous JavaScript and XML, is a technology that can be used to make your web pages fast, rich and responsive. Ajax can be used to cut down on the network load and the bandwidth usage by retrieving only the data that is required, resulting in better response times. In the previous chapter we gave an overview of what Ajax is and why it is useful. In this chapter we will take a look at how you can implement an application that can leverage the benefits of Ajax.

Consuming Web Services

One of the most powerful features of Ajax is its ability to consume web services. In this section we will discuss how Ajax can be used to consume a web service. Let's look at an example using the following class that would be used to populate data and return the same data through a web service:

Listing 14-1

```
public class Employee
{
    public int EmployeeID{get;set;}
    public string FirstName{get;set;}
    public string LastName { get; set; }
    public string Address { get; set; }
    public Employee[] GetEmployees()
    {
        List<Employee> empList = new List<Employee>();
        Employee employee    = new Employee();
        employee.EmployeeID = 1;
        employee.FirstName = "Joydip";
        employee.LastName = "Kanjilal";
        employee.Address = "Hyderabad";
        empList.Add(employee);
        employee = new Employee();
        employee.EmployeeID = 2;
        employee.FirstName = "Oindrilla";
        employee.LastName = "Roy Chowdhury";
        employee.Address = "Kolkata";
        empList.Add(employee);
        employee = new Employee();
        employee.EmployeeID = 3;
        employee.FirstName = "Soma";
        employee.LastName = "Roy Chowdhury";
        employee.Address = "Kolkata";
        empList.Add(employee);
        employee = new Employee();
        employee.EmployeeID = 4;
        employee.FirstName = "Rama";
```

```
        employee.LastName = "Kanjilal";
        employee.Address = "Kolkata";
        empList.Add(employee);
        employee = new Employee();
        employee.EmployeeID = 5;
        employee.FirstName = "Amal";
        employee.LastName = "Kanjilal";
        employee.Address = "Kolkata";
        empList.Add(employee);
        return empList.ToArray();
    }
  }
```

We will implement a web service called SampleService that would return an array of instances of the Employee class shown in listing 14-1 above.

Before we take a look at how the web service called SampleService would be implemented, let's understand how you need to call the web service from Ajax. Any Ajax-enabled web page should have the ScriptManager control in it. Listing 14-2 shows how you can take the help of the ScriptManager control in the web page and add a ServiceReference element inside it to register a web service so that it can be used in the web form:

Listing 14-2
```
<asp:ScriptManager ID="ScriptManager1" runat="server" >
    <Services>
      <asp:ServiceReference Path="SampleService.asmx" />
    </Services>
</asp:ScriptManager>
```

We can then call this web service in the web form as follows:

Listing 14-3
```
<script language="javascript" type="text/javascript">
    function pageLoad()
    {
        Samples.GetEmployees(onSuccess);
    }
    function onSuccess(result)
    {
        var output = document.getElementById("Results");
        output.innerHTML = result;
    }
    function onFailure(result)
    {
        context.innerText = "Error Occurred in the Web Service...";
    }
</script>
```

The output text will be displayed in a span control. Here is the markup code:

Listing 14-4
```
<form id="Form1" runat="server">
        <asp:ScriptManager runat="server" ID="scriptManager">
            <Services>
                <asp:ServiceReference path="ServerTime.asmx" />
            </Services>
        </asp:ScriptManager>
<body>
        <form id="Form1" runat="server">
         <asp:ScriptManager runat="server" ID="scriptManager1">
                <Services>
                    <asp:ServiceReference path="SampleService.asmx" />
                </Services>
            </asp:ScriptManager>
        </form>
        <hr/>
        <div>
            <span id="Results"></span>
        </div>
</body>
```

The SampleService web service would contain a web method called GetEmployees()
that would return an array of Employee instances. Here is what the web method would
look like:

Listing 14-5
```
[WebMethod]
        public Employee[] GetEmployees()
        {
            return new Employee().GetEmployees();
        }
```

Here is the complete code of the SampleService web method:

Listing 14-6
```
using System;
using System.Collections.Generic;
using System.Linq;
using System.Web;
using System.Web.Services;
namespace Samples
{
    public class Employee
    {
        public int EmployeeID{get;set;}
        public string FirstName{get;set;}
        public string LastName { get; set; }
        public string Address { get; set; }
        public Employee[] GetEmployees()
```

```
        {
            List<Employee> empList = new List<Employee>();
            Employee employee   = new Employee();
            employee.EmployeeID = 1;
            employee.FirstName = "Joydip";
            employee.LastName = "Kanjilal";
            employee.Address = "Hyderabad";
            empList.Add(employee);
            employee = new Employee();
            employee.EmployeeID = 2;
            employee.FirstName = "Oindrilla";
            employee.LastName = "Roy Chowdhury";
            employee.Address = "Kolkata";
            empList.Add(employee);
            employee = new Employee();
            employee.EmployeeID = 3;
            employee.FirstName = "Soma";
            employee.LastName = "Roy Chowdhury";
            employee.Address = "Kolkata";
            empList.Add(employee);
            employee = new Employee();
            employee.EmployeeID = 4;
            employee.FirstName = "Rama";
            employee.LastName = "Kanjilal";
            employee.Address = "Kolkata";
            empList.Add(employee);
            employee = new Employee();
            employee.EmployeeID = 5;
            employee.FirstName = "Amal";
            employee.LastName = "Kanjilal";
            employee.Address = "Kolkata";
            empList.Add(employee);
            return empList.ToArray();
        }
    }
}
[WebService(Namespace = "http://tempuri.org/")]
[WebServiceBinding(ConformsTo = WsiProfiles.BasicProfile1_1)]
[System.ComponentModel.ToolboxItem(false)]
[System.Web.Script.Services.ScriptService]
  public class SampleService : System.Web.Services.WebService
    {
        [WebMethod]
        public Employee[] GetEmployees()
        {
            return new Employee().GetEmployees();
        }
    }
}
```

The Parser Error

When you mix callbacks and postbacks in your Ajax-enabled ASP.NET applications, you might encounter the PageRequestManagerParser. Basically, you will encounter this error when the response object is modified during partial page updates.

In partial page rendering, only a portion of a web page is rendered instead of the entire web page, improving the responsiveness of the application. The response object is modified due to calls to the Response.Write() and Response.Redirect() methods. When you encounter this error the message will read: "Sys.WebForms .PageRequestManagerParserErrorException: The message received from the server could not be parsed." Also, the PageRequestManagerTimeoutException can occur if the response times out—if the response is not sent by the web server within a specific period of time.

This parser error generally occurs when you mix postbacks and callbacks in your code. To replicate this error, follow these steps:

1. Drag and drop a ScriptManager control into your Ajax-enabled web page.

2. Drag and drop an UpdatePanel control and a Button control inside the ContentTemplate tag of the UpdatePanel.

   The markup code in your web form will look like this:

Listing 14-7

```
<form id="form1" runat="server">
<asp:ScriptManager ID="ScriptManager1" runat="server" />
<asp:UpdatePanel ID="MyUpdatePanel" runat="server">
<ContentTemplate>
<asp:Button ID="btnClick" runat="server" Text="Click Me..."
OnClick="Button1_Click" />
</ContentTemplate>
</asp:UpdatePanel>
</form>
```

3. In the code-behind file for this web form, write an event handler for the Button control as follows:

Listing 14-8

```
protected void btnClick_Click(object sender, EventArgs e)
{
 Response.Write("Generating the Parser Error Excepting");
}
```

4. Execute the application and click on the Button control.

The parser error message will be displayed.

Avoiding the Parser Error

To avoid this parser error, you can set the AutoEventWireup, EnableEventValidation, ValidateRequest, and SmartNavigation attributes to false and specify the ScriptModule properly in the application's web.config file. Also, you should avoid using Response .Write() calls in your Ajax-enabled ASP.NET web pages.

NOTE *The following types of exceptions exist in the Sys.WebForms namespace:*
  PageRequestManagerParserErrorException
  PageRequestManagerServerErrorException
  PageRequestManagerTimeoutErrorException

To avoid a parser error in the program we just implemented, replace the call to Response.Write() by using a Literal control in the web form. You can then assign any text to this control without encountering the parser error. Here is what the modified markup code will look like:

Listing 14-9
```
<form id="form1" runat="server">
<asp:ScriptManager ID="ScriptManager1"
runat="server" />
<asp:UpdatePanel ID="MyUpdatePanel"
runat="server">
<ContentTemplate>
<asp:Literal ID="Literal1"
runat="server" Text="" />
<asp:Button ID="btnClick"
runat="server" Text="Click Here..."
OnClick="btnClick_Click" />
</ContentTemplate>
</asp:UpdatePanel>
</form>
```

In the code-behind file, you can assign some text to the Literal control, as follows:

Listing 14-10
```
protected void btnClick_Click(object sender, EventArgs e)
{
Literal1.Text = "ASP.NET 4.0 Programming - McGraw-Hill Publishers");
}
```

Now when you click on the Button control, you won't encounter the parser error.
Note that the PageRequestManager class belongs to the Sys.WebForms namespace, and it contains the initializeRequest, beginRequest, pageLoading, pageLoaded, and endRequest events. As and when a partial page update occurs, the page manager triggers a beginRequest event, so you can trap exactly when the partial update occurs. To do so, you need to use the instance of the PageRequestManager class and register a callback method, like this:

Listing 14-11
```
<asp:UpdatePanel ID="upTest" runat="server">
    <ContentTemplate>
        <asp:Button ID="btnClick" runat="server" Text="Click Me..."
/>
    </ContentTemplate>
</asp:UpdatePanel>
<script language="javascript" type="text/javascript">
pageManager.add_beginRequest(TestRequestCallback);
```

```
function TestRequestCallback()
{
        alert('Begin request event has been called...');
}
</script>
```

Working with Authentication and Profile Services

ASP.NET Ajax provides excellent support for working with authentication and profile services. Both authentication and profile services are part of the ASP.NET Ajax Extensions Library and are available through the Sys.Services.AuthenticationService and Sys.Services.ProfileService classes, respectively.

Working with the Authentication Service

Authentication is the process of identifying and validating a user's credentials to verify the authenticity of a user. Once a user is authenticated, the process called authorization checks to see what resources this authenticated user is permitted access to.

You can access the ASP.NET authentication service from client-side scripts by using the AuthenticationService class. This class contains two methods: login and logout. The former is used to validate the user's credentials, and the latter is used to clear all authentication cookies and enable the user to log out. You can access the AuthenticationService object from any web form that contains a ScriptManager control.

NOTE *For the authentication service to work, you will need to enable cookies in your web browser.*

To use the authentication service, enable it in the application's web.config file as follows:

Listing 14-12
```
<system.web.extensions>
  <scripting>
    <webServices>
      <authenticationService enabled="true" />
    </webServices>
  </scripting>
</system.web.extensions>
```

You should also enable form authentication in your application's web.config file:

Listing 14-13
```
<configuration>
  <system.web>
    <authentication mode="Forms"/>
    <forms name="LoginForm" loginUrl="LoginForm.aspx" />
    <authorization>
        <deny users="?"/>
    </authorization>
  </system.web>
</configuration>
```

To perform authentication asynchronously from a client-side script, you will need to specify the AuthenticationService in your ScriptManager control, as follows:

Listing 14-14
```
<asp:ScriptManager ID="ScriptManager1" runat="server" >
            <AuthenticationService Path="Verify.asmx" />
</asp:ScriptManager>
```

We will next create a web service file called Verify.asmx where you need to write custom code to authenticate the user. You will then have the necessary web methods inside this web service to perform the login and logout actions. Listing 14-15 shows how the user credentials are validated in this web service using the Membership provider.

Listing 14-15
```
[WebMethod]
public bool Login(string userName,
string password, bool createPersistentCookie)
{
    if (Membership.Provider.ValidateUser(userName, password))
    {
        FormsAuthentication.SetAuthCookie
(userName, createPersistentCookie);
        return true;
    }
    else
    return false;
}
[WebMethod]
public void Logout()
{
    FormsAuthentication.SignOut();
}
```

Working with the Profile Service

The Profile object in ASP.NET is used to store user profile information. You can enable the profile service in your Ajax-enabled ASP.NET application by specifying the following in your application's web.config file:

Listing 14-16
```
<system.web.extensions>
  <scripting>
    <webServices>
      <profileService enabled="true" />
    </webServices>
  </scripting>
</system.web.extensions>
```

You can define the profile properties in the profile section, as shown here:

Listing 14-17
```
<profile enabled="true">
            <properties>
                <add name="Author"
defaultValue="Joydip Kanjilal"
type="string"
                            allowAnonymous="true" />
                <add name="Technical Reviewer"
 defaultValue="Anand Narayaswamy"
type="string"
                            allowAnonymous="true" />
            </properties>
</profile>
```

You can also define groups in order to group profile information. Here is an example:

Listing 14-18
```
<profile enabled="true">
<add name=" Backgroundcolor" type="System.String"
    defaultValue="white" />
  <add name=" Foregroundcolor" type="System.String"
    defaultValue="red" />
        <properties>
        <group name="Contact">
          <add name="FirstName" type="string"/>
          <add name="LastName" type="string"/>
          <add name="Address1" type="string"/>
          <add name="Address2" type="string"/>
          <add name="City" type="string"/>
          <add name="State" type="string"/>
          <add name="PinCode" type="string"/>
          <add name="Country" type="string"/>
        </group>
      </properties>
</profile>
```

Debugging and Tracing

Debugging and tracing are two of the most important concepts for tracking code errors and improving the productivity of an application as a whole. You can use the Debug class in the Sys namespace to display debug information.

The Sys.Debug class contains the following methods:

- Sys.Debug.trace(message)
- Sys.Debug.clearTrace()
- Sys.Debug.fail(message)
- Sys.Debug.assert(condition, message, displayCaller)
- Sys.Debug.traceDump(object, name)

If you want to use Sys.Debug in your Ajax-enabled ASP.NET application, set the debug attribute in the compilation section of your application's web.config file to true, and set the ScriptMode property of the ScriptManager control to true. Here is how you can enable debugging support in your application's web.config file:

Listing 14-19
```
<configuration>
  <system.web>
   <compilation debug="true">
   </compilation>
  </system.web>
<configuration>
```

To enable debugging support in Internet Explorer, follow these steps:

1. In the Tools menu of the web browser, click Internet Options.
2. Switch to the Advanced tab, and uncheck the Disable Script Debugging and Disable Script Debugging (Other) check boxes.
3. Click OK.

You can start your application in debug mode from Visual Studio by pressing the F5 key or by opening the Debug menu and selecting the Start Debugging option. You can also attach the Visual Studio debugger when the application is executing. To do this, open the Debug menu of the Visual Studio IDE, select the Attach to Process option, and then select the instance of Internet Explorer that you would like the debugger attached to.

NOTE *For improved performance, it is always a good practice to set the release version of your Ajax-enabled web application to release mode when you deploy it, and also to set the debug attribute to false in the application's web.config file. Also, you should set the ScriptMode property of the ScriptManager control in all Ajax-enabled web pages in your application to release mode. Here is an example:*

Listing 14-20
```
<asp:ScriptManager ID="ScriptManager1"
 runat="server" ScriptMode="Release">
```

You can use the Sys.Debug.trace(message) and Sys.Debug.clearTrace() methods to show and clear trace information in your Ajax-enabled ASP.NET applications. Here is an example:

Listing 14-21
```
function ShowTraceInformation()
    {
        var message = Form1.txtName.value;
        Sys.Debug.trace(message);
    }
    function ClearTraceInformation()
    {
        Sys.Debug.clearTrace();
    }
```

The following is the complete markup code for showing and clearing trace information in your application.

Listing 14-22

```
<html xmlns="http://www.w3.org/1999/xhtml" >
<head><title>Illustrating Tracing in ASP.NET Ajax Applications</title>
<script language="javascript" type="text/javascript">
    function ShowTraceInformation() {
        var message = Form1.txtName.value;
        Sys.Debug.trace(message);
    }
    function ClearTraceInformation()
    {
        Sys.Debug.clearTrace();
    }
</script>
</head>
<body>
    <form id="Form1" runat="server">
        <asp:ScriptManager ID="ScriptManager1" runat="server" />
            <asp:Label ID="lblName"
runat="server" Text="Enter your name:">
</asp:Label>
            <input id="txtName" maxlength="50" type="text" />
            <table>
            <tr>
            <td>
            <input id="btnShowTraceInformation"
 type="button" value="Show Trace"
 style="width: 100px"
onclick="ShowTraceInformation();" />
<br />
            </td>
            <td>
            <input id="btnClearTraceInformation"
type="button" value="Clear Trace"
style="width: 100px"
onclick="ClearTraceInformation();" />
<br />
            </td>
            </tr>
            </table>
            <br />
        <textarea id='TraceConsole'
rows="5" cols="50" title="Trace Console">
</textarea>
    </form>
</body>
</html>
```

As you can see in Listing 14-22, the trace information is displayed in a TextArea control named TraceConsole when the btnShowTraceInformation button control (Show Trace) is clicked. When you click on the other button control, i.e., btnClearTraceInformation (Clear Trace), the trace information displayed is erased or cleared from the TextArea. Note that the trace information displayed is actually the name you would type in the TextBox control named txtName, as shown in Figure 14-1.

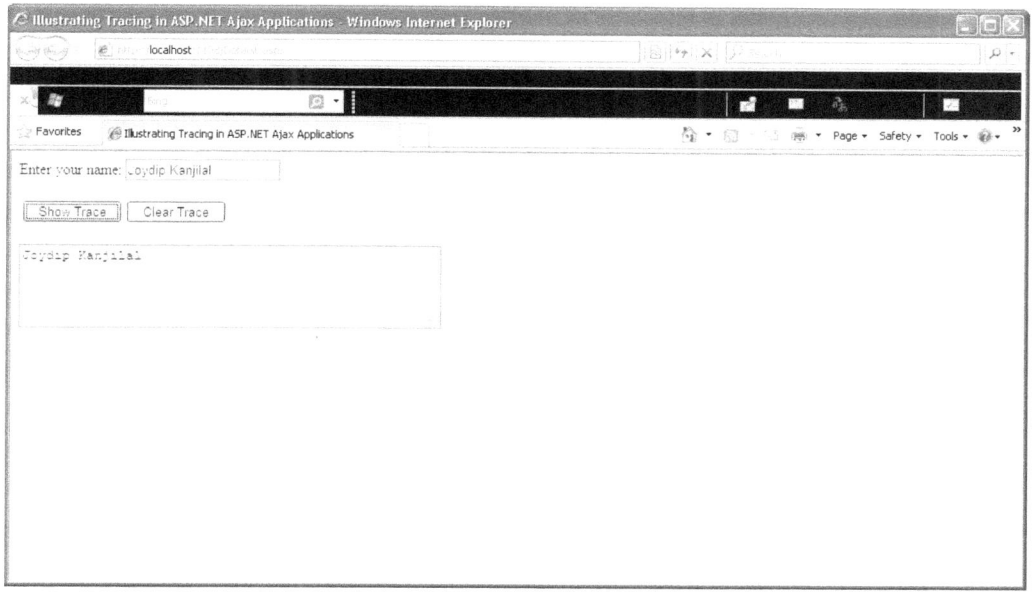

FIGURE 14-1   Displaying trace information

CHAPTER 15

Web Services

W eb services enable programs written in different languages running on different platforms to communicate with each other. Web services are based on the Simple Object Access Protocol (SOAP) and are used to exchange data amongst similar or disparate systems. The W3C group defines a web service as "a software system designed to support interoperable machine-to-machine interaction over a network. It has an interface described in a machine-processable format (specifically WSDL). Other systems interact with the Web service in a manner prescribed by its description using SOAP messages, typically conveyed using HTTP with an XML serialization in conjunction with other Web-related standards." (http:// www.w3.org/TR/ws-arch/)

This chapter takes a look at web services and related concepts, and it explains how you can implement a simple web service in .NET. It also discusses the security aspects of web services.

What Are Web Services?

A Web service is a group of functions packaged together for use in a common framework throughout a network. Essentially, Web services act as interfaces to software components that can be accessed using XML messages over SOAP and HTTP. Interoperability, security, and the ability to publish and expose functionality are the most important reasons why Web services are so popular these days.

SOAP, the Web Services Description Language (WSDL), and Universal Description, Discovery, and Integration (UDDI) are the de facto standards for Web services. XML is used to describe the operations to be performed and the data to be exchanged, and related information about a Web service, such as transport protocols, is stored in a WSDL document. UDDI is a platform-independent open framework that enables dynamic discovery of Web services.

Web Services vs. Microsoft .NET Remoting

Remoting is a technology that enables two processes, a server and a client, running in homogenous environments (the same system, the same network, or across networks) to communicate with each other. Remoting requires you to have the .NET Framework running on both the server and client sides. Both Web services and Remoting present frameworks for developing distributed applications in Microsoft .NET's managed environment, but there are subtle differences between the two.

You can use Web services for cross-platform integration over HTTP using XML and SOAP even through firewalls. On the other hand, you can use Remoting to allow different components to interact across application domains. Note that Remoting can be used over any protocol but it doesn't work smoothly through firewalls. Also, unlike Remoting, Web services are stateless due to the stateless nature of the HTTP protocol.

Web services are used to exchange data in heterogeneous environments. In other words, Web services can be used to exchange data across platforms, irrespective of the environments in which the systems are running. Hence, you can invoke a Web service created in .NET from a Java client. In contrast, Remoting can be used only in homogenous environments.

How Do Web Services Work?

To make Web services work, you need a service provider who provides the service, and a service requester to consume the service. Services are published in a central repository called the service registry, which contains the definitions and Uniform Resource Locators (URLs) of the services.

Service requests and responses are sent in the form of XML and SOAP messages. Hence, the service requester makes SOAP requests and receives SOAP responses back from the service provider. The proxy class on the client side receives the request, serializes the request into a SOAP request, and forwards it to the remote Web service. The remote Web service on the server side deserializes this request, executes the web method, packs the results into a SOAP response packet, and sends this response back to the client.

A Web Service proxy enables you to invoke Web Service methods (commonly known as Web Methods) in any environment that has support for SOAP and Web Service proxies. The command line utility called wsdl.exe can be used to generate proxy classes for a Web Service.

Web Services Description Language

WSDL is an XML-based, platform-independent description language that is used to describe Web services. Specifically, it describes a set of SOAP messages and how these messages are exchanged across networks.

A typical WSDL document includes the type description, message description, port type, service description, and binding specification details. The following listing shows the structure of an empty WSDL document.

Listing 15-1
```
<definitions>
<types>
   definition of the types
</types>
<message>
   definition of the messages
</message>
<portType>
   definition of the ports
</portType>
<binding>
   definition of the bindings
</binding>
</definitions>
```

Universal Discovery, Description, and Integration

UDDI is a platform-independent, open framework that facilitates dynamic discovery of Web services over the Internet.

The UDDI registry is a web-based distributed directory that maintains pointers to published Web services and their information. Once a Web service has been published, it can be looked up and discovered at any time.

Wikipedia states, "Universal Description, Discovery, and Integration (UDDI) is a platform-independent, Extensible Markup Language (XML)-based registry for businesses worldwide to list themselves on the Internet. UDDI is an open industry initiative, sponsored by the Organization for the Advancement of Structured Information Standards (OASIS), enabling businesses to publish service listings and discover each other and define how the services or software applications interact over the Internet." (http://en.wikipedia.org/wiki/Universal_Description_Discovery_and_Integration)

Simple Object Oriented Protocol

SOAP (www.w3.org/TR/SOAP) is an open standard, stateless, text- and XML-based protocol. SOAP is platform-independent and can be used to exchange data between heterogeneous web applications, even through firewalls. Note that SOAP can be used over both HTTP and SMTP protocols. The basic advantages of SOAP over other protocols of its kind are scalability, performance, and activation.

The W3C group has officially defined SOAP as a protocol that "a lightweight protocol for exchange of information in a decentralized, distributed environment. It is an XML based protocol that consists of four parts: an envelope that defines a framework for describing what is in a message and how to process it, a set of encoding rules for expressing instances of application-defined data types, a convention for representing remote procedure calls and responses and a binding convention for exchanging messages using an underlying protocol. SOAP can potentially be used in combination with a variety of other protocols; however, the only bindings defined in this document describe how to use SOAP in combination with HTTP and the experimental HTTP Extension Framework." (http://www.w3.org/TR/2001/WD-soap12-20010709/)

Anatomy of a SOAP Message

The requesting data that a client sends to the server is called a SOAP request. The server receives this request, processes it, and sends a response back to the client. This returning data is known as the SOAP response. The communication back and forth between the client and server takes place through the HTTP protocol.

A typical SOAP message declaration consists of the following:

- A root element called the envelope that recognizes the XML file format:

```
<SOAP: Envelope>
</SOAP: Envelope>
```

- An optional header element:

```
<SOAP: Header>
</SOAP: Header>
```

- The body of the SOAP message, which includes the request and response elements

A typical SOAP message is structured like this:

Listing 15-2
```
<SOAP: Envelope>
  <SOAP: Header>
  </SOAP: Header>
  <SOAP: Body>
  </SOAP: Body>
</SOAP: Envelope>
```

The following is an example of a SOAP header with authentication information in it:

Listing 15-3
```
<?xml version="1.0" encoding="utf-8"?>
<soap:Envelope xmlns:soap="http://schemas.xmlsoap.org/soap/envelope/"
xmlns:soapenc="http://schemas.xmlsoap.org/soap/encoding/"
xmlns:xsi="http://www.w3.org/1999/XMLSchema-instance"
xmlns:xsd="http://www.w3.org/1999/XMLSchema">
 <soap:Header>
  <SampleAuthenticationHeader xmlns="http://tempuri.org/">
<Username>joydip</Username> <Password>joydip1@3</Password>
  </SampleAuthenticationHeader>
 </soap:Header>
 <soap:Body>
  <GetData xmlns="http://tempuri.org/"/>
 </soap:Body>
</soap:Envelope>
```

And this is an example of a SOAP request message:

Listing 15-4
```
<soap:Envelope xmlns:soap="http://schemas.xmlsoap.org/soap/envelope/"
xmlns:soapenc="http://schemas.xmlsoap.org/soap/encoding/"
xmlns:xsi="http://www.w3.org/1999/XMLSchema-instance"
xmlns:xsd="http://www.w3.org/1999/XMLSchema">
    <soap:Body>
      <AddIntegers xmlns="AddIntegersWebServiceNamespace">
        <paramA>100</a>
        <paramB>200</b>
      </AddIntegers>
    </soap:Body>
</soap:Envelope>
```

This is the SOAP response for the preceding SOAP request:

Listing 15-5
```
<soap:Envelope xmlns:soap="http://schemas.xmlsoap.org/soap/envelope/"
xmlns:soapenc="http://schemas.xmlsoap.org/soap/encoding/"
xmlns:xsi="http://www.w3.org/1999/XMLSchema-instance"
xmlns:xsd="http://www.w3.org/1999/XMLSchema">
    <soap:Body>
      <AddIntegersResponse xmlns="AddIntegersWebServiceNamespace">
        <AddIntegersResult>300</AddResult>
      </AddIntegersResponse>
    </soap:Body>
</soap:Envelope>
```

The following is an example of a typical SOAP message with its HTTP headers:

Listing 15-6
```
POST /McGraw-hill/Test.asmx HTTP/1.1
Connection: Keep-Alive
Content-Length: 150
Content-Type: text/xml
Host: localhost
User-Agent: MS Web Services Client Protocol 1.0.2204.19
SOAPAction: "http://tempuri.org/Sample"
<?xml version="1.0"?>
<soap:Envelope xmlns:soap="http://schemas.xmlsoap.org/soap/envelope/"
xmlns:soapenc="http://schemas.xmlsoap.org/soap/encoding/"
xmlns:xsi="http://www.w3.org/1999/XMLSchema-instance"
xmlns:xsd="http://www.w3.org/1999/XMLSchema">
  <soap:Body>
    <Sample xmlns="http://tempuri.org/"/>
  </soap:Body>
</soap:Envelope>
```

Why Use SOAP?

The Distributed Component Object Model (DCOM), Remote Procedure Call (RPC), and Internet Inter-ORB Protocol (IIOP) were all restricted to homogenous environments. SOAP was designed by a group of vendors including Microsoft, IBM, and Lotus to enable methods to be invoked across networks on disparate systems. SOAP is used for business-to-business integration and for distributed applications.

NOTE *Although SOAP is scalable, language- and platform-neutral, and simple to use, it is slower than Common Object Request Broker Architecture (CORBA) or Remote Method Invocation (RMI), and it doesn't have any standardized mechanism for dynamic discovery of services.*

The most common messaging pattern used in SOAP is Remote Procedure Call (RPC). When using RPC, the client sends a request message to the server, and the server in turn sends a response message to the client. SOAP is similar to DCOM and CORBA in the sense that they all provide an RPC mechanism for invoking remote methods. However, SOAP differs from those technologies because it provides the XML open standard for exchanging data between homogenous or heterogeneous distributed applications.

SOAP Transport Protocols

Unless otherwise specified, the transport protocols used in Web services include HTTP/POST, HTTP/GET, and SOAP. The binding information for these protocols is included automatically in the WSDL document that is generated when you create a Web service. However, you can also remove such bindings using the <protocols> element in the application's web.config file as shown here:

Listing 15-
```
<webservices>
  <protocols>
    <remove name="HttpPost" />
    <remove name="HttpGet" />
  </protocols>
</webservices>
```

This example would ensure that the HTTP/POST and HTTP/GET protocols are not included by the WSDL generator when the WSDL document is generated.

Creating and Consuming Web Services in .NET

To implement a Web service, you need the following components:

- A Web service that runs on a web server
- A client application that invokes the Web service
- A WSDL document that describes the Web service and specifies how to discover the Web service

Web services can be implemented in couple of ways. The first is a self-contained service that has a single .asmx page containing both the Web service header and the source code for the Web service. Here is an example:

Listing 15-
```
<%@ WebService Language="C#" Class="TestWebService" %>
using System;
using System.Web;
using System.Web.Services;
public class TestWebService
{
  [WebMethod]
  public string Display()
  {
    return "McGraw Hill Publishers";
  }
}
```

Note the header at the top of the preceding code; it specifies the name of the class and the language to be used.

The second way to implement a Web service is to have the Web service header separate from an external Web service class. Here is an example:

Listing 15-9
```
<%@ WebService Language="c#"
  Codebehind="TestWebService.asmx.cs" Class="TestWebService" %>
```

To access this Web service from a client application, you need to add a reference to this Web service and then call its methods.

Listing 15-10
```
Service s = new Service();
MessageBox.Show(s.Display());
```

Creating the Web Service

In this section we will create a simple Web service using Visual Studio 2010.

To create the Web service, first open Visual Studio 2010 and create a new ASP.NET Web Service Application project, as shown in Figure 15-1.

Next, open the Service1.asmx file created by default. When you open this file in code view, it will look like this:

Listing 15-11
```
using System;
using System.Collections;
using System.ComponentModel;
using System.Data;
using System.Linq;
using System.Web;
using System.Web.Services;
```

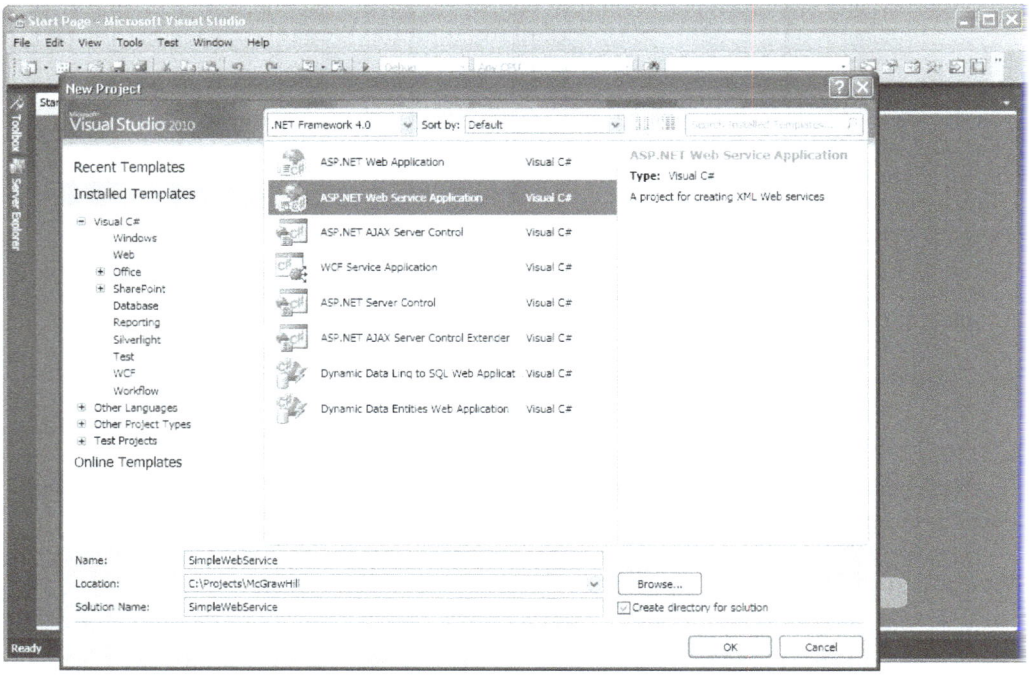

FIGURE 15-1 Creating a new ASP.NET Web Service Application project

```
using System.Web.Services.Protocols;
using System.Xml.Linq;
namespace SimpleWebService
{
  [WebService(Namespace = "http://tempuri.org/")]
  [WebServiceBinding(ConformsTo = WsiProfiles.BasicProfile1_1)]
  [ToolboxItem(false)]
  // To allow this Web service to be
//called from script, using ASP.NET AJAX,
//uncomment the following line.
  // [System.Web.Script.Services.ScriptService]
  public class Service1 : System.Web.Services.WebService
  {
    [WebMethod]
    public string HelloWorld()
    {
      return "Hello World";
    }
  }
}
```

The WebService attribute, which you can see in the preceding code listing, is a member of the System.Web.Services namespace, and it provides clients with a way to locate the Web service. There are three parts to this attribute:

- the description of the Web service
- the namespace
- the name of the Web service

Note that a Web service class is one that extends the System.Web.Services.WebService class and contains one of more web methods. The Service1 class in Listing 15-11 is a Web service class. A web method should have the [WebMethod] attribute over it to imply that it is a web method. The HelloWorld() web method in the preceding code listing is created by default.

Web services expose their functionality using web methods, which can be called over the Web using HTTP. The WebMethod attribute has many associated properties that can be used to change the behavior of the web method:

- **Description** Provides a textual description of the web method
- **MessageName** Specifies a name for the web method (this is particularly useful if you have polymorphic web methods in your class and you want those methods to be uniquely identified using textual names)
- **EnableSession** Enables the session state for a web method; set to false by default

- **CacheDuration**   Denotes the number of seconds for which the response will be stored in the cache memory
- **TransactionOption**   Used when you need transactional operations; set to false by default.
- **BufferResponse**   Facilitates buffering of the output; enabled by default

---

NOTE *The web methods can call transaction-enabled objects, but they themselves cannot be part of a transactional operation due to the stateless nature of the HTTP protocol.*

The following example illustrates how you can use these properties:

Listing 15-12
```
[WebService(Namespace="http://localhost/MGHServices/",
    Description="This is a sample description.")]
public class TestService : System.Web.Services.WebService
{
  [WebMethod(MessageName="Test",
      Description="Write your description for the web method here.")]
  public string Test(string parameter)
  {
    //write your custom code here
  }
[WebMethod(CacheDuration=40)]
  public string Display(string parameter)
  {
    //write your custom code here
  }
}
```

You can replace the default web method with the following method, which will retrieve all vendor details from the AdventureWorks database.

Listing 15-13
```
[WebMethod]
        public List<String> GetVendorNames()
        {
            string strConnectionString =
"Data Source=.;Initial Catalog=
AdventureWorks;Integrated Security=True;";
            DataSet dataSet = new DataSet();
            using (SqlConnection sqlConnection = new
SqlConnection(strConnectionString))
            {
                sqlConnection.Open();
                String sqlString =
"Select Name From Purchasing.Vendor";
```

```
            using (SqlCommand sqlCommand =
new SqlCommand(sqlString, sqlConnection))
            {
                using (SqlDataReader sqlDataReader =
sqlCommand.ExecuteReader())
                {
                    List<String> vendorList = new List<String>();
                    while (sqlDataReader.Read())
                    {
                        vendorList.Add
(sqlDataReader["Name"].ToString());
                    }
                    return vendorList;
                }
            }
        }
    }
```

You can run this Web service directly by pressing the F5 key. The output should look like Figure 15-2.

When you execute the GetVendorNames web method directly, the output will look like Figure 15-3.

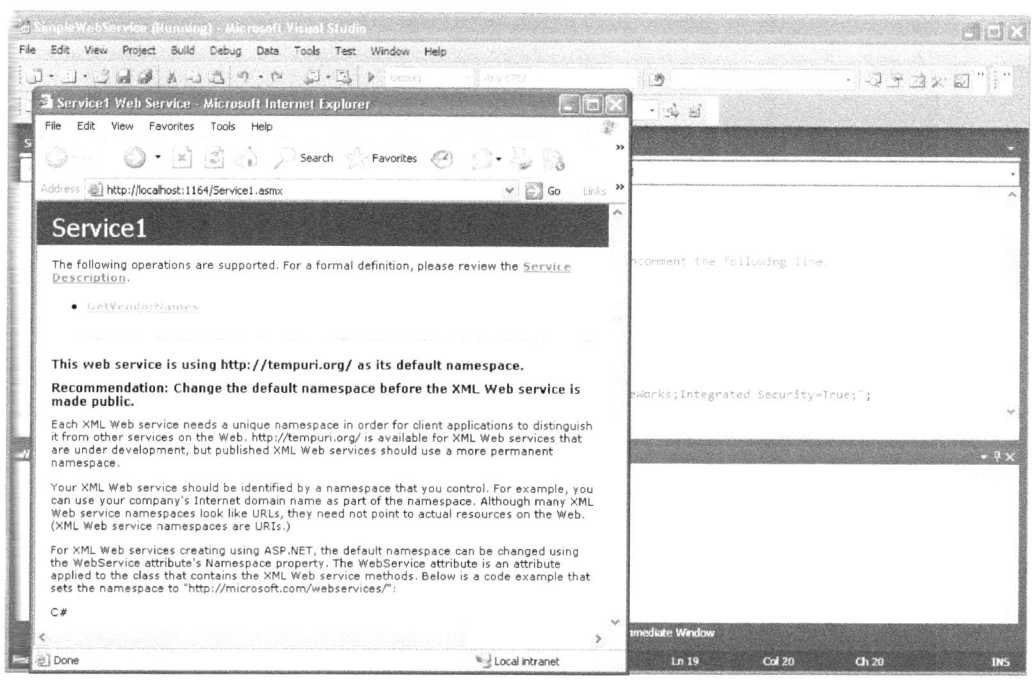

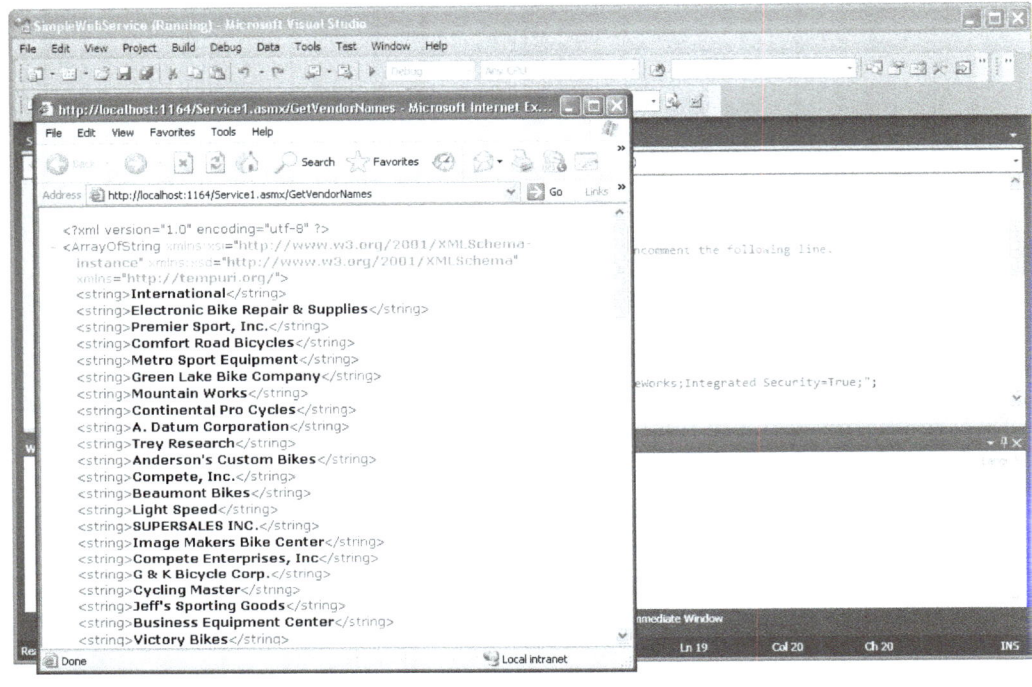

FIGURE 15-3   The GetVendorNames web method as shown in the browser

Consuming the Web Service

You can call a Web service using HTTP/POST, HTTP/GET, and SOAP.

To consume the Web service you have just created, create a web application project and add the Web service as a web reference to it, as shown in Figure 15-4.

NOTE *You can create a proxy class for your Web service by using the wsdl.exe command-line tool or by using the Add Web Reference option in Visual Studio.*

Figure 15-5 shows how the web service files look when viewed in the Solution Explorer.

In the Default.aspx file in the web client project you have created, add a ScriptManager control and use the ServiceReference tag to point to the Web service you created earlier, like this:

Listing 15-14
```
<asp:ScriptManager runat="server" ID="ScriptManager1">
        <Services>
            <asp:ServiceReference Path=
"http://localhost:1035/Service1.asmx" />
        </Services>
    </asp:ScriptManager>
```

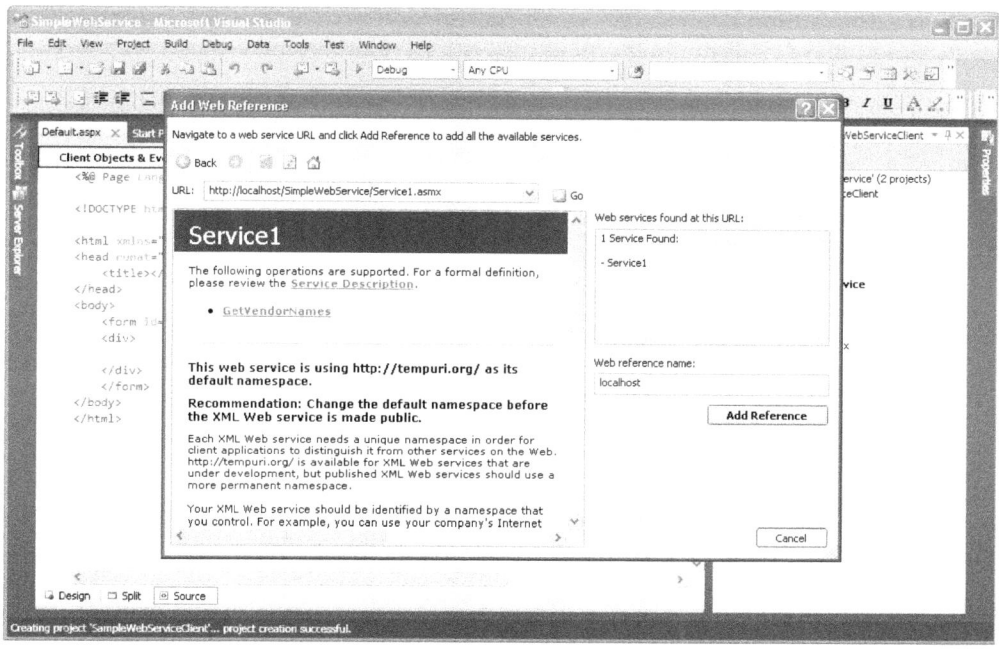

FIGURE 15-4   Adding the web reference

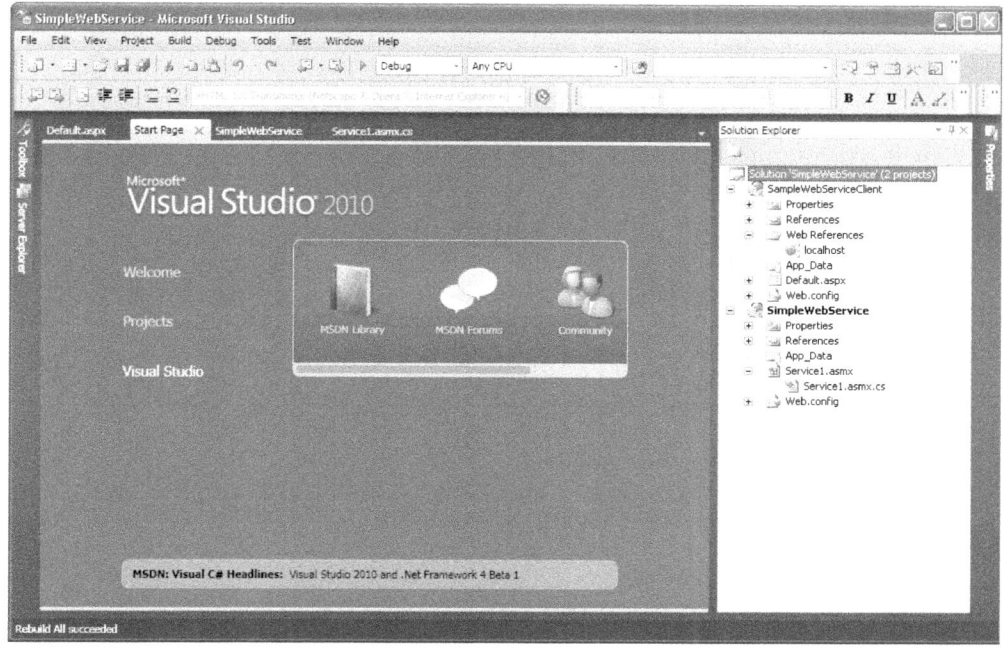

FIGURE 15-5   The Web service files as viewed in the Solution Explorer

Now add a button control that, when clicked, will invoke the GetVendorNames() JavaScript method. This method will in turn call the GetVendorNames() web method.

Listing 15-15
```
<input id="btnFetchData"
type="button" value="Get Vendor Names"
 onclick="GetVendorNames()" />
```

We will display the list of the vendor names in a <span> control.

Listing 15-16
```
<div>
    <span id="spanOutput"></span>
</div>
```

The GetVendorNames() script method calls the GetVendorNames() web method from the client side. Listing 15-17 shows the code of the GetVendorNames() script method.

Listing 15-17
```
function GetVendorNames()
{
    SimpleWebService.Service1.GetVendorNames(OnSuccess, OnError);
}
```

The OnSuccess() and OnError() methods are passed as references. The code listing below shows the OnSuccess() and OnError() methods.

Listing 15-18
```
function OnSuccess(args) {
        var outputElement = document.getElementById("spanOutput");
        outputElement.innerHTML = args;
    }
    function OnError(args) {
        alert("Error calling the Web service method.");
    }
```

Here is the complete markup code that shows how the web service is being called using client side scripts.

Listing 15-19
```
<html xmlns="http://www.w3.org/1999/xhtml">
<head>
    <title>Web service request</title>
    <script language="javascript" type="text/javascript">
        function GetVendorNames() {
            SimpleWebService.Service1.
GetVendorNames(OnSuccess, OnError);
        }
        function OnSuccess(args) {
            var outputElement = document.getElementById("spanOutput");
            outputElement.innerHTML = args;
        }
        function OnError(args) {
            alert("Error calling the Web service method.");
        }
    </script>
</head>
```

```
<body>
    <form id="Form1" runat="server">
    <asp:ScriptManager runat="server" ID="ScriptManager1">
        <Services>
            <asp:ServiceReference Path=
"http://localhost:1035/Service1.asmx" />
        </Services>
    </asp:ScriptManager>
    <div>
        <input id="btnFetchData"
type="button" value="Get Vendor Names"
 onclick="GetVendorNames()" />
    </div>
    </form>
    <hr />
    <div>
        <span id="spanOutput"></span>
    </div>
</body>
</html>
```

When you execute the application and click on the button control, the vendor names are retrieved and displayed in the web browser as shown in Figure 15-6.

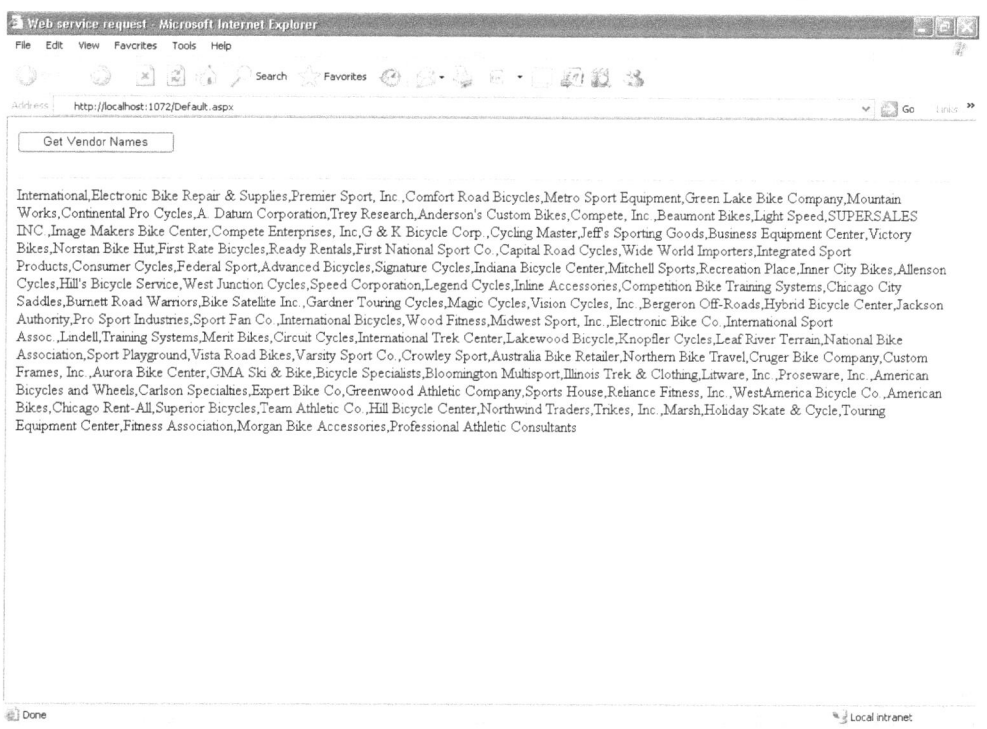

F IGURE 15-6   Executing the GetVendorNames web method

Web Services Security

Security in Web services is a major concern, and there are many ways to ensure that your Web service is secure. Note that an HTTP-based security mechanism is one of the best ways to ensure the safety of your Web service.

To ensure that confidential data sent in HTTP-based SOAP messages is secure, you can run the service over Secure Socket Layer (SSL). Or you can use ASP.NET and IIS security together to implement robust Web services.

You can also restrict access to your Web service by using the web.config file as shown in the following code snippet:

Listing 15-20
```
<configuration>
        <system.web>
                <authorization>
                        <allow users="*" />
                </authorization>
        </system.web>
        <location path="EmployeeDataService.asmx">
                <system.web>
                        <authorization>
                                <deny users="?" />
                        </authorization>
                </system.web>
        </location>
</configuration>
```

You can use the CurrentPrincipal static property of the Thread class to display information about the currently logged on user. The following web method returns the name of the currently logged on user:

Listing 15-21
```
[WebMethod]
public String DisplayUserInformation() {
    return "Running as User : " +
        Thread.CurrentPrincipal.Identity.Name;
}
```

If you are using Windows Authentication, you can use the User property of System .Web.Services.WebService and convert it to a WindowsPrincipal instance to check for authentication. The WindowsPrincipal class contains an Identity property that can be used to determine whether the current user has the necessary permissions for accessing the Web service. It also has a Boolean property called IsInRole that can be used to determine whether the current Windows user has been assigned a group.

Here is an example that illustrates how you can use the WindowsPrincipal class to secure your Web service:

Listing 15-22
```
using System;
using System.Data;
using System.Data.SqlClient;
```

```csharp
using System.Web.Services;
using System.Security.Principal;
public class TestWebServices : WebService
{
    private const String
connectionString =
"server=.;InitialCatalog=TestDB;
UID=joydip;
PWD=joydip1@3";
    private const String SecurityError = "Security Error Occurred";
    private const String DatabaseError = "Database Error Occurred";
    private SqlConnection sqlConnection = null;
    private SqlCommand sqlCommand = null;
    [WebMethod]
    public string GetUserSecurityTokenID(int userID)
    {
        WindowsPrincipal windowsPrincipal =
(WindowsPrincipal)this.User;
        if (!windowsPrincipal.IsInRole("WebService"))
            return SecurityError;
        else
        {
            try
            {
                sqlConnection = new SqlConnection(connectionString);
                sqlConnection.Open();
                sqlCommand = new SqlCommand();
                sqlCommand.Connection = sqlConnection;
                sqlCommand.CommandText =
"SELECT TokenID FROM Users Where UserID='"+
userID.ToString().Trim()+"'";
                sqlCommand.CommandType = CommandType.Text;
                Object userToken = sqlCommand.ExecuteScalar();
                if (userToken == null)
                    return DatabaseError;
                else
                    return userToken.ToString();
            }
            catch (SqlException sqlEx)
            {
                return sqlEx.Message;
            }
            catch (Exception ex)
            {
                return ex.Message;
            }
            finally
            {
```

```
                    if (sqlConnection.State == ConnectionState.Open)
                    {
                        sqlConnection.Close();
                    }
                }
            }
        }
    }
```

Note how the GetUserSecurityTokenID(int userID) method has been used in Listing 15-22—it accepts the userID as a parameter and returns the userToken from the database table as its return value. Necessary try–catch exception blocks have been used to trap runtime errors. If the connection state of the connection instance is open, it is closed in the finally block.

You can also implement Web Services Enhancements 1.0 for Microsoft .NET (WSE), provided with Microsoft .NET, to secure your Web services. You can use it to digitally sign, encrypt, and add security credentials to all SOAP messages. Here is an example that shows how you can do this using the <soapExtensionTypes> element in your application's web.config file:

Listing 15-23

```
<system.web>
    <webServices>
        <soapExtensionTypes>
            <add type="Microsoft.Web.Services.
                WebServicesExtension,
                Microsoft.Web.Services,Version=1.0.0.0,
                Culture=neutral,
                PublicKeyToken=31bf3856ad364e35"
                priority="1" group="0" />
        </soapExtensionTypes>
    </webServices>
</system.web>
```

CHAPTER 16

Windows Communication Foundation

The Windows Communication Foundation (WCF) is a framework that can be used for designing and developing applications that can intercommunicate. WCF was introduced initially as part of .NET Framework 3.0 in 2006. WCF is based on service-oriented architecture (SOA) and enables multiple clients to consume one or more services. SOA is a collection of well-defined loosely coupled services, where each service can be modified independently of the other services intact to address business challenges. WCF actually represents a new paradigm for developing SOA applications using the managed environment of Microsoft .NET. This chapter takes a look at the basics of SOA and WCF, and shows you how to implement a WCF service using Visual Studio 2010.

Service-Oriented Architecture

Service-oriented architecture (SOA) is the best scalable solution for reducing complexity in software. It is one of the most popular architectural paradigms today. It provides seamless integration of loosely coupled distributed applications or services over a network. Web services, J2EE, and CORBA are implementations of SOA.

Building Blocks of SOA

SOA is based on the following components:

- A service
- A service provider who provides the service
- A service consumer who uses the service
- A service registry
- A service contract

The Service

A *service* may be defined as of a stateless, self-contained, independent business function that accepts one or more requests and returns one or more responses using a well-defined, standard interface. It may also be defined as an autonomous system that has the capability to accept one or more requests and return one or more responses through well-defined interfaces.

What are the properties of a service? One of the most important properties of a service is that the interface contract should be platform-independent so that the service can be used on any platform. Also, a service should have the ability to be dynamically located and invoked at runtime.

A service should be independent of the technology on which it was designed and developed; rather, it should focus on the business functions for the application that uses the service. The service consumer and service provider should be loosely coupled.

The Service Provider

The *service provider* is the entity that is responsible for providing the service. It is the network-addressable entity that accepts and executes requests from the service consumers.

The service provider publishes its contract in a database called the service registry, which in turn is used for dynamic access by service consumers at runtime.

The Service Consumer

The *service consumer* is the entity that uses the service. The service consumer is responsible for locating the service, binding to the service, and executing the service methods.

The Service Registry

The *service registry* is a database of published services. The service provider is responsible for registering the services to be published in the service registry. The service registry is a network-based registry that is used by the service consumers to bind to at runtime. In essence, the service registry is a repository where the service providers register their services so that the service consumers can locate them when needed. The service registry provides scalability, decoupling, support for hot updates, and dynamic service lookup facilities.

The Service Contract

A *service contract* specifies how the consumer of a service will interact with the service provider. It is used to specify the format of the service request and the service response.

The Service Proxy

The service provider provides a *service proxy* to the service consumer. The service proxy locates the contract and the reference to the service provider and executes the request by invoking the required method.

The Service Lease

A *service lease* specifies how long the service is valid. The service registry grants the service consumer a service lease. When the lease expires, the service consumer must request a fresh lease from the registry.

Messages

Service producers and consumers communicate through *messages*. These are typically constructed using XML documents that conform to XML schema.

The Service Description

The *service description* consists of the parameters, constraints, and policies that define how to invoke the service.

Advertising and Discovery

The ability of a service to communicate its description to the service consumers is known as *advertising*. Advertising is of two types: pull and push. In the former, service consumers request that the provider send them the service description. In the latter, the service provider automatically sends the service description to the service consumer. Discovery refers to locating the published services at runtime.

Benefits of Service Orientation

The major benefits of a service-oriented approach include platform independence; loose coupling between the service producer and consumer; support for incremental development, deployment, and maintenance; location transparency; lower maintenance costs; and easy integration of the service and its components.

The Windows Communication Foundation

The Windows Communication Foundation (WCF) is centered on these key concepts: services, clients, messages, and intermediaries. WCF supports communication in enterprise applications, and it is interoperable and can be integrated with other technologies seamlessly. According to MSDN, "Windows Communication Foundation (WCF) is Microsoft's unified programming model for building service-oriented applications. It enables developers to build secure, reliable, transacted solutions that integrate across platforms and interoperate with existing investments." (http://msdn.microsoft.com/en-us/library/ms735119.aspx)

In WCF, services communicate with clients by sending and receiving messages. WCF messages can be transmitted using HTTP, TCP, MSMQ, or named pipes. Intermediaries are the programs between a service and its consumer or client.

WCF services are described using WSDL. A WCF service consists of a service class that implements the service, a hosting environment that hosts the service, and one or more endpoints that enable clients to connect to the service. In essence, WCF provides a unified framework for building service-oriented applications rapidly.

WCF integrates other middle-tier technologies like Remoting, MSMQ, Web services, and the like. One of the most important features of a WCF service is its ability to be hosted in IIS, Windows Services, and standalone applications like Windows Forms, WPF Forms, etc. WCF applications are interoperable and configurable and can be easily integrated with other technologies.

WCF Fundamentals

In this section we will explore the fundamental concepts in WCF. A WCF service is based on three principles.

- **Address**   This is used to identify the location of the service.
- **Binding**   This is used to indicate how you can interact with the service.
- **Contract**   This indicates what the service does for you.

Address

The address of a WCF service denotes where the service is located. Here is what the address format of a typical WCF service would look like:

Listing 16-1   `supported transport protocol://machinename[:port]/path`

Note that the machine name denotes the server name where the WCF service has been hosted. A port is a unique unsigned integer that identifies a service provided by a process running over a network. The port you need to mention, as shown in the code snippet above for a WCF service, is the port where the service would listen.

Binding

Binding indicates how the service can communicate with other services and clients. There are some predefined bindings in WCF, but you can also create your own custom bindings. To implement custom binding in WCF, you should make use of the System.ServiceModel.Channels namespace. The built-in bindings in WCF are as follows:

- BasicHttpBinding
- MsmqIntergrationBinding
- NetTcpBinding
- NetNamedPipeBinding
- NetMsmqBinding
- NetPeerTcpBinding
- WSHttpBinding
- WSDualHttpBinding
- WSFederationHttpBinding

Contracts

Contracts in WCF are used to define behavior of the service, i.e., what the service would do for you. There are three types of contracts in WCF:

- **Service contract**   This is just an interface to the service. A service can have multiple service contracts.
- **Data contract**   These are used to define the structure for data that is passed to the methods.
- **Message contract**   These contracts enable you to change the structure of messages.

Messages

Messages are the means of communication in WCF. The WCF service and WCF client communicate through messages using one of the following patterns:

- **Simplex**   This is a one-way communication pattern.
- **Request-Reply**   This is a two-way asynchronous messaging pattern.
- **Duplex**   This is a two-way synchronous messaging pattern.

> **NOTE** *The address of a WCF service denotes the destination of the messages, i.e., where the messages should be delivered. The binding information is used to denote how these messages should be sent and the contract denotes what each message should contain.*

Endpoints

Endpoints are used to associate a service contract and binding with the address so that the service consumers can access the service. In essence, the address, binding, and contract, together are known as the endpoint of the service. Note that a WCF service can expose multiple endpoints, although a particular client must choose which endpoint it is connecting to.

Channels

Essentially, channels are used to create, send, and receive messages. These act as a bridge between a service producer and a service consumer, and they are of the following types:

- Simplex Input
- Simplex Output
- Request-reply
- Duplex

Configuring a WCF Service

To configure a WCF service, you need to use the <serviceModel> attribute in your application's web.config file and specify information pertaining to the WCF service, such as the service name, endpoints, service behavior, and bindings. Here is how a typical WCF service is configured in the web.config file:

Listing 16-2
```
<system.serviceModel>
    <services>
        <service name="McGrawHill.SampleService"
            behaviorConfiguration="metadataSupport">
        <endpoint contract="MGH.IServiceContract"
            binding="basicHttpBinding"/>
        <endpoint contract="IMetadataExchange"
            binding="mexHttpBinding" address="mex">
        </endpoint>
    </service>
</services>
```

Creating a Simple WCF Service

To start implementing a WCF service, create a new WCF Service Library project as shown in Figure 16-1.

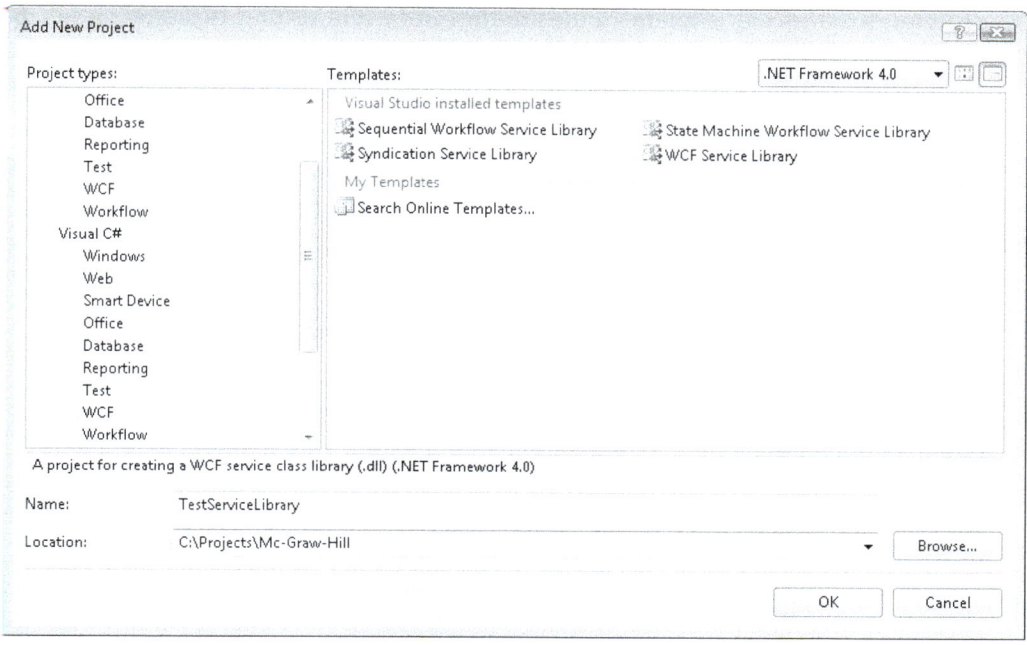

FIGURE 16-1 Creating a WCF Service Library project

The next step is to create an interface as a service contract by using the ServiceContract attribute, as follows:

Listing 16-3
```
[ServiceContract()]
    public interface IDepartment
    {
        [OperationContract]
        List<String> GetDepartments();
    }
```

This interface contains one method called GetDepartments, and it returns a list of department names as Strings. This method is marked using the OperationContract attribute.

NOTE *The OperationContract attribute can be applied on a method to state that the method denotes an operation on a ServiceContract. The ServiceContract attribute on the other hand can be applied on an interface as well as a class.*

The service class will implement the interface shown in Listing 16-4. Here is what the service class would look like:

Listing 16-4
```
public class Department : IDepartment
    {
        String connectionString =
"Data Source=localhost;
Initial Catalog=AdventureWorks;
Integrated Security=True";
        public List<String> GetDepartments()
        {
            List<String> departmentNames = new List<String>();
            using (SqlConnection sqlConnection = new
SqlConnection(connectionString))
            {
                sqlConnection.Open();
                SqlCommand sqlCommand =
new SqlCommand("Select DepartmentID, Name
 from [HumanResources].[Department]");
                SqlDataReader sqlDataReader =
 sqlCommand.ExecuteReader();
                while (sqlDataReader.Read())
                {
                    departmentNames.Add
(sqlDataReader["Name"].ToString());
                }
                sqlDataReader.Close();
            }
            return departmentNames;
        }
    }
```

As you can see, the service class implements the interface declared earlier and defines the GetDepartments method as its only method.

NOTE *To implement applications using the WCF SDK, you should include the System .ServiceModel namespace contained in the System.ServiceModel.dll assembly.*

Here is the complete implementation of the service class and the interface:

Listing 16-5
```
using System;
using System.Collections.Generic;
using System.Text;
using System.ServiceModel;
using System.Runtime.Serialization;
using System.Data.SqlClient;
namespace TestService
```

```
{
    [ServiceContract()]
    public interface IDepartment
    {
        [OperationContract]
        List<String> GetDepartments();
    }
    public class Department : IDepartment
    {
        String connectionString =
"Data Source=localhost;
Initial Catalog=AdventureWorks;
Integrated Security=True";
        public List<String> GetDepartments()
        {
            List<String> departmentNames = new List<String>();
            using (SqlConnection sqlConnection = new
SqlConnection(connectionString))
            {
                sqlConnection.Open();
                SqlCommand sqlCommand =
new SqlCommand("Select DepartmentID, Name
 From [HumanResources].[Department]");
                SqlDataReader sqlDataReader =
 sqlCommand.ExecuteReader();
                while (sqlDataReader.Read())
                {
                    departmentNames.Add
(sqlDataReader["Name"].ToString());
                }
                sqlDataReader.Close();
            }
            return departmentNames;
        }
    }
}
```

The next step is to compile the service. Here is how you can configure the service:

Listing 16-6
```
<?xml version="1.0"?>
<configuration>
  <system.serviceModel>
    <services>
      <service name="TestService.IDepartment"
               behaviorConfiguration="metadataSupport">
        <endpoint contract="TestService.IDepartment"
                  binding="basicHttpBinding"/>
        <endpoint address="mex"
           binding="mexHttpBinding"
```

```
            contract="IMetadataExchange"/>
        </service>
      </services>
      <behaviors>
       <serviceBehaviors>
          <behavior name="metadataSupport">
            <serviceMetadata />
          </behavior>
        </serviceBehaviors>
      </behaviors>
   </system.serviceModel>
</configuration>
```

Next, you need to create a virtual directory in IIS and provide anonymous access to it. Once that's done, create a bin folder and copy the compiled assembly into it.

You can now create a .svc file to define the service. This file will be used to create proxy classes using the SvcUtil command-line tool. Here is what the Service.svc file should look like:

Listing 16-7
```
<%@ServiceHost language="c#"
Debug="true" Service=
"TestService.IDepartment" %>
<%@Assembly Name="DepartmentService" %>
```

You can now generate the proxy code using the SvcUtil.exe command-line utility as follows:

Listing 16-8
```
svcutil http://localhost/TestService/
Service.svc /out:TestServiceProxy.cs
```

When executed, the preceding command will generate two files in the destination path specified: TestServiceProxy.cs and Output.config.

Now that the service has been created and the proxy class generated, you can go ahead and consume your service from a client application. You just need to add a reference to the System.ServiceModel namespace, along with the proxy code and the configuration file generated earlier to the solution. And you're done!

Implementing a Simple Ajax-Enabled WCF Service

In this section we will discuss how we can implement a simple Ajax-enabled WCF service in Visual Studio 2010. To get started with implementing a WCF service, right-click on the Solution Explorer and select the AJAX-Enabled WCF Service template as shown in Figure 16-2.

If you open the service in the XML editor, it will look like this:

Listing 16-9
```
<%@ ServiceHost Language="C#" Debug="true"
Service="Mc_Graw_Hill.Chapter_16.SampleService"
 CodeBehind="SampleService.svc.cs" %>
```

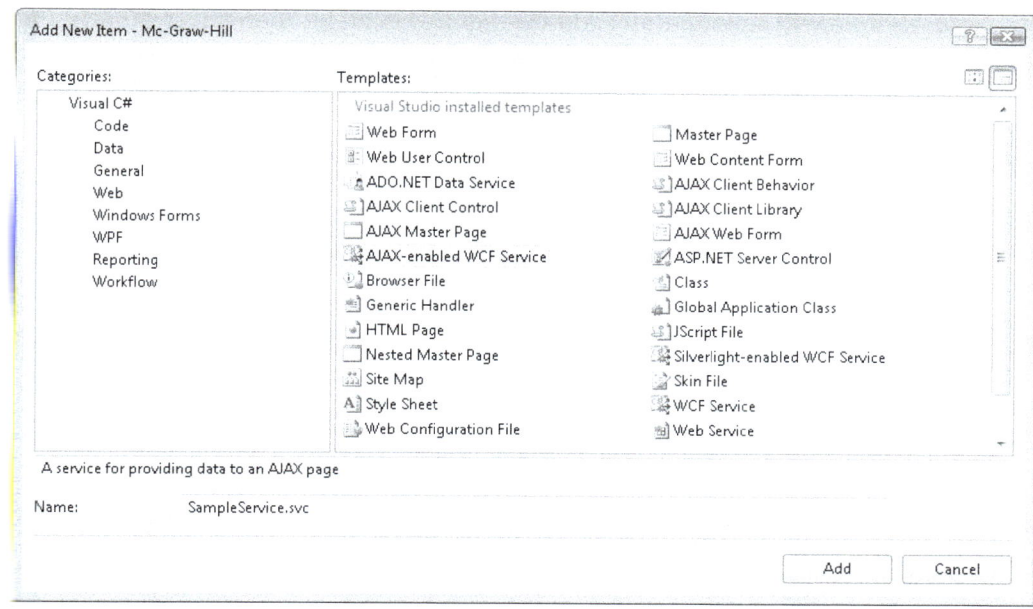

FIGURE 16-2   Creating an Ajax-enabled WCF service

If you open the service class in the code-behind, it will look like this:

Listing 16-10
```
using System;
using System.Linq;
using System.Runtime.Serialization;
using System.ServiceModel;
using System.ServiceModel.Activation;
using System.ServiceModel.Web;
namespace Mc_Graw_Hill.Chapter_16

    [ServiceContract(Namespace = "")]
    [AspNetCompatibilityRequirements
 RequirementsMode =
AspNetCompatibilityRequirementsMode.Allowed)]
    public class SampleService
    {
        // Add [WebGet] attribute to use HTTP GET
        [OperationContract]
        public void DoWork()
        {
            // Add your operation implementation here
            return;
        }
        // Add more operations here and
//mark them with [OperationContract]
    }
}
```

Visual Studio will automatically add the required configuration information in the application's web.config file. It will look like this:

Listing 16-11
```xml
<system.serviceModel>
        <behaviors>
            <endpointBehaviors>
                <behavior name="Mc_Graw_Hill.Chapter_16.
SampleServiceAspNetAjaxBehavior">
                    <enableWebScript />
                </behavior>
            </endpointBehaviors>
        </behaviors>
        <serviceHostingEnvironment aspNetCompatibilityEnabled="true" />
        <services>
            <service name="Mc_Graw_Hill.Chapter_16.SampleService">
                <endpoint address=""
behaviorConfiguration="Mc_Graw_Hill.Chapter_16.
SampleServiceAspNetAjaxBehavior"
binding="webHttpBinding" contract="Mc_Graw_Hill.Chapter_16.
SampleService" />
            </service>
        </services>
</system.serviceModel>
```

Now let's add a method called GetNames in the service class:

Listing 16-12
```csharp
[OperationContract]
        public List<String> GetNames()
        {
            List<String> objList = new List<String>();
            objList.Add("Joydip Kanjilal");
            objList.Add("Tilak Tarafder");
            objList.Add("Oindrilla Roy Chowdhury");
            objList.Add("Soma Roy Chowdhury");
            objList.Add("Amal Kanjilal");
            objList.Add("Rama Kanjilal");
            return objList;
        }
```

Here is the complete source code for the service class:

Listing 16-13
```csharp
using System;
using System.Linq;
using System.Runtime.Serialization;
using System.ServiceModel;
using System.ServiceModel.Activation;
using System.ServiceModel.Web;
using System.Collections.Generic;
namespace Mc_Graw_Hill.Chapter_16
```

```
    {
        [ServiceContract(Namespace = "")]
        [AspNetCompatibilityRequirements
    (RequirementsMode =
    AspNetCompatibilityRequirementsMode.Allowed)]
        public class SampleService
        {
            // Add [WebGet] attribute to use HTTP GET
            [OperationContract]
            public List<String> GetNames()
            {
                List<String> objList = new List<String>();
                objList.Add("Joydip Kanjilal");
                objList.Add("Tilak Tarafder");
                objList.Add("Oindrilla Roy Chowdhury");
                objList.Add("Soma Roy Chowdhury");
                objList.Add("Amal Kanjilal");
                objList.Add("Rama Kanjilal");
                return objList;
            }
            // Add more operations here and
    //  mark them with [OperationContract]
        }
    }
```

To consume the service named, "SampleService" we created earlier, create a web form and drag and drop a ScriptManager control onto it. The ScriptManager control's ServiceReference tag can be used to refer to the service you just created, as follows:

Listing 16-14
```
<asp:ScriptManager ID="ScriptManager1" runat="server">
        <Services>
                <asp:ServiceReference Path=
"~/Chapter 16/SampleService.svc" />
        </Services>
     </asp:ScriptManager>
```

Now you need to create a button control and a span control in the web form. Here is the complete markup code:

Listing 16-15
```
 <form id="form1" runat="server">
<div>
     <script language="javascript" type="text/javascript">
         function GetNames() {
             SampleService.GetNames(OnSuccess, OnError,null);
         }
         function OnSuccess(args) {
             var outputElement = document.getElementById("spanOutput");
             outputElement.innerHTML = args;
         }
```

```
        function OnError(args) {
            alert("Error calling the web service method.");
        }
    </script>
    <asp:ScriptManager ID="ScriptManager1" runat="server">
        <Services>
            <asp:ServiceReference Path=
"~/Chapter 16/SampleService.svc" />
        </Services>
    </asp:ScriptManager>
    <input id="btnGetData" type="button" value="Get Names"
            onclick="GetNames()"; />
</div>
    <div>
        <span id="spanOutput"></span>
    </div>
</form>
```

When you execute the application and click the button on the web form, the output will look like Figure 16-3.

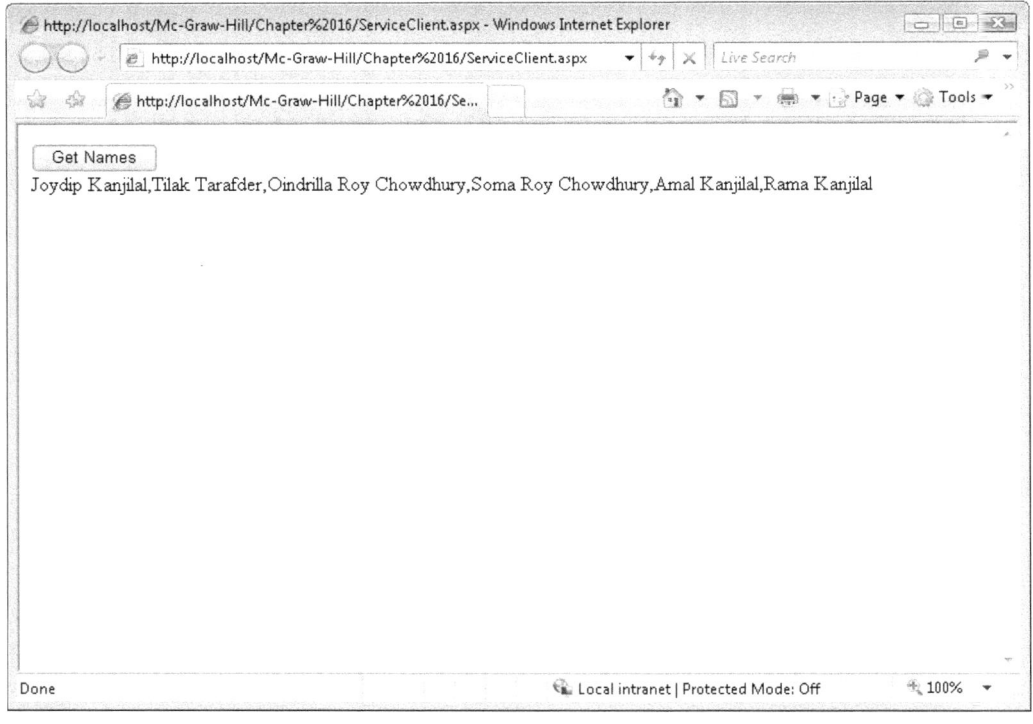

FIGURE 16-3 The Ajax-enabled WCF service at work

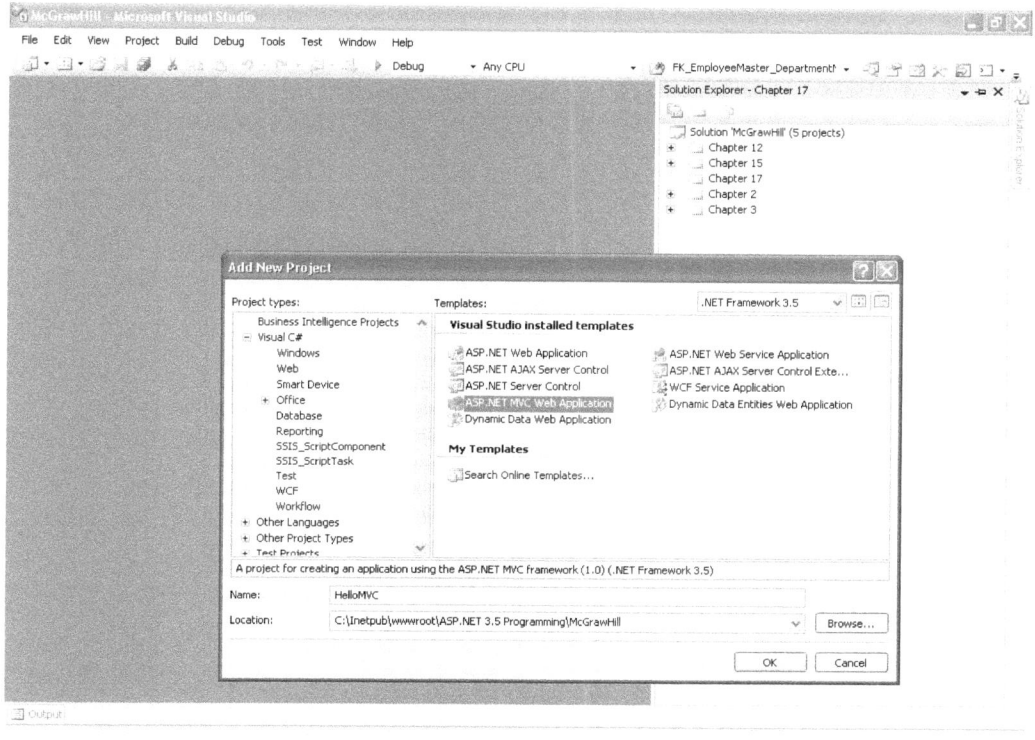

FIGURE 17-1   Selecting the ASP.NET MVC Web Application template

4. When prompted about whether you would like to unit test your project, select Yes, as shown in Figure 17-2.

NOTE *You can add unit testing to your project later, but it is advisable to do it at this point. If you do it now, ASP.NET MVC will add the necessary references and create the unit tests for your project automatically.*

5. Click OK to complete the process.

The ASP.NET MVC Folder Structure

The ASP.NET MVC application will contain a minimum of three top-level directories in its folder structure: /Models, /Views, and /Controllers. These folders will contain files that correspond to the controllers, models, and views you will use in your application. So, the "/Controllers" folder contains all the controller classes, the "/Models" folder contain all the model classes, and the "/Views" folder contain all the view classes that your application makes use of. Additionally, you can have the "/Scripts" folder that stores the script files, the "/Content" folder that stores the css and image files, and also

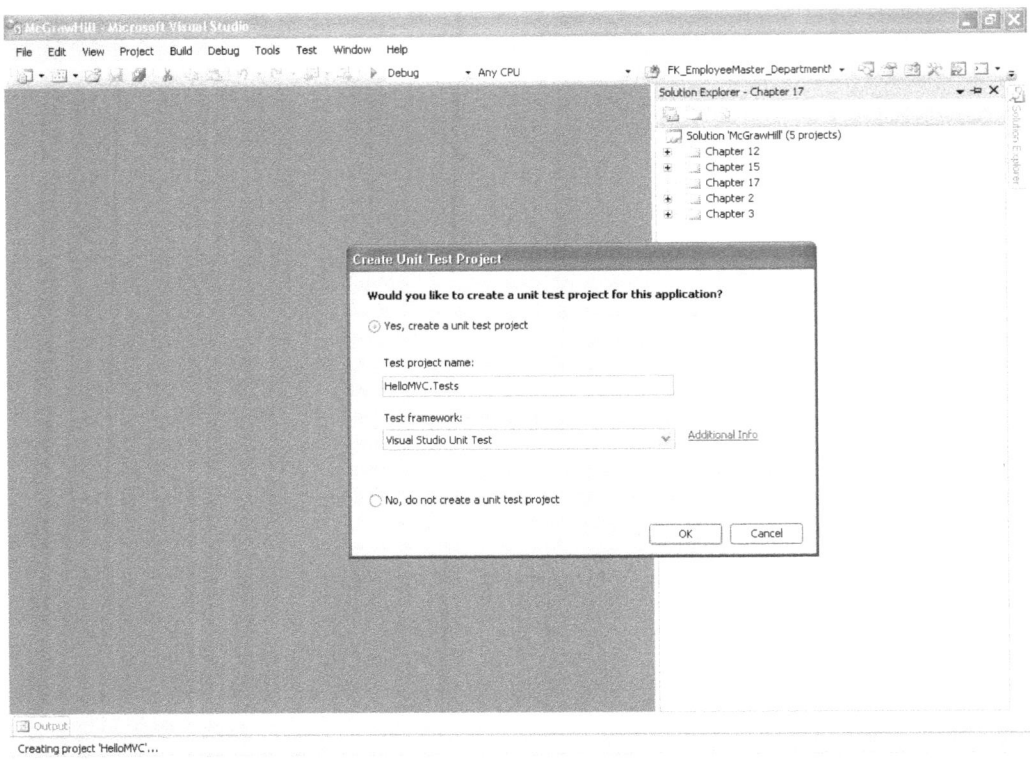

FIGURE 17-2 Creating a unit test project

the "/App_Data" folder that contains the data files that the application uses. Unless there is a specific reason to change it you should use this default structure. Figure 17-3 shows what the folder structure looks like when viewed in the Solution Explorer.

As you can see, two projects have been created: the project, called HelloMVC, and another called HelloMVC.Tests. The latter will be used for unit testing the HelloMVC project.

The Controllers

If you look at the Controllers folder in the Solution Explorer, you'll see two controller class files created, namely, AccountController and HomeController. The latter is the default controller. Here is what the HomeController looks like:

Listing 17-1
```
using System;
using System.Collections.Generic;
using System.Linq;
using System.Web;
using System.Web.Mvc;
namespace HelloMVC.Controllers
```

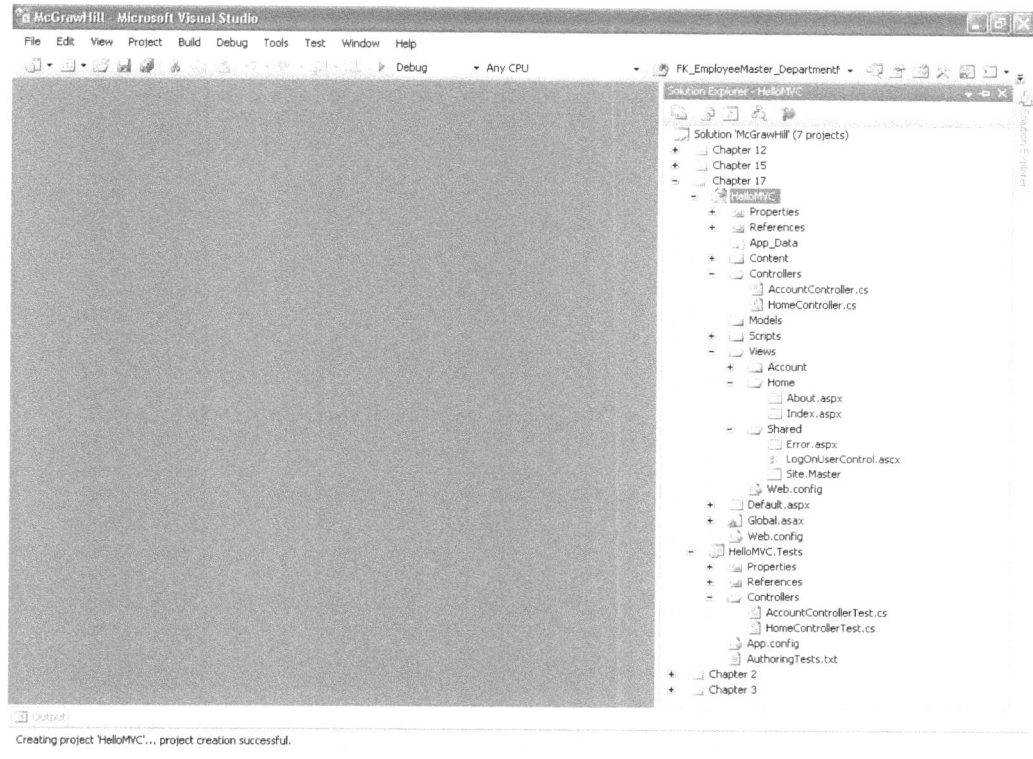

FIGURE 17-3   The HelloMVC folder structure

```
{
    [HandleError]
    public class HomeController : Controller
    {
        public ActionResult Index()
        {
            ViewData["Message"] = "Welcome to ASP.NET MVC!";
            return View();
        }
        public ActionResult About()
        {
            return View();
        }
    }
}
```

Note that the methods that a controller exposes are called as action methods or actions. As you can see in the code listing above, there are two action methods called Index() and View().

The Views

The Views/Home folder contains two views, namely, About and Index. The following code snippet shows what the markup code of the Index.aspx file looks like:

Listing 17-2
```
<%@ Page Language="C#" MasterPageFile="~/Views/Shared/Site.Master"
Inherits="System.Web.Mvc.ViewPage" %>

<asp:Content ID="indexTitle" ContentPlaceHolderID="TitleContent"
runat="server">

    Home Page

</asp:Content>

<asp:Content ID="indexContent" ContentPlaceHolderID="MainContent"
runat="server">

    <h2><%= Html.Encode(ViewData["Message"]) %></h2>

    <p>

        To learn more about ASP.NET MVC visit <a href="http://asp.net/
mvc" title="ASP.NET MVC Website">http://asp.net/mvc</a>.

    </p>

</asp:Content>
```

Here is what the code of the About.aspx file looks like:

Listing 17-3
```
<%@ Page Language="C#" MasterPageFile="~/Views/Shared/Site.Master"
Inherits="System.Web.Mvc.ViewPage" %>

<asp:Content ID="aboutTitle" ContentPlaceHolderID="TitleContent"
runat="server">

    About Us

</asp:Content>

<asp:Content ID="aboutContent" ContentPlaceHolderID="MainContent"
runat="server">

    <h2>About</h2>

    <p>

        Put content here.

    </p>

</asp:Content>
```

Creating Routes

The ASP.NET MVC Framework contains a powerful URL mapping engine to map the incoming URLs to your controller classes. When the application starts, the Application_ Start event handler in the Global.asax file is fired, and a route table is created and registered at that time.

The default route that is created is named Default and is registered in the Global .asax file, but you can create your own routes too. Here is what the Default route looks like:

Listing 17-4
```
using System;
using System.Collections.Generic;
using System.Linq;
using System.Web;
using System.Web.Mvc;
using System.Web.Routing;
namespace HelloMVC
{
    public class MvcApplication :
System.Web.HttpApplication
    {
        public static void RegisterRoutes
(RouteCollection routes)
        {
            routes.IgnoreRoute("{resource}.axd/{*pathInfo}");
            routes.MapRoute(
                "Default", // Route name
                "{controller}/{action}/{id}",// URL with parameters
                new { controller = "Home",
 action = "Index", id = "" }  // Parameter defaults
                );
        }
        protected void Application_Start()
        {
            RegisterRoutes(RouteTable.Routes);
        }
    }
}
```

As you can see in the preceding listing, the RegisterRoutes method is called in the Application_Start() event handler. By default, all incoming URLs will be mapped using this route. You can also map an incoming URL, such as http://localhost/Department/ Marketing, to your own controller using the MapRoute method. Here is an example:

Listing 17-5
```
routes.MapRoute(
    "DisplayDepartment",  // Route name
    "Department/{name}",  // URL with parameters
    new {                 // Parameter defaults
```

```
        controller = "Department",
        action = "Show",
        name = ""
    }
);
```

When you execute the application, the output is similar to what is shown in Figure 17-4.

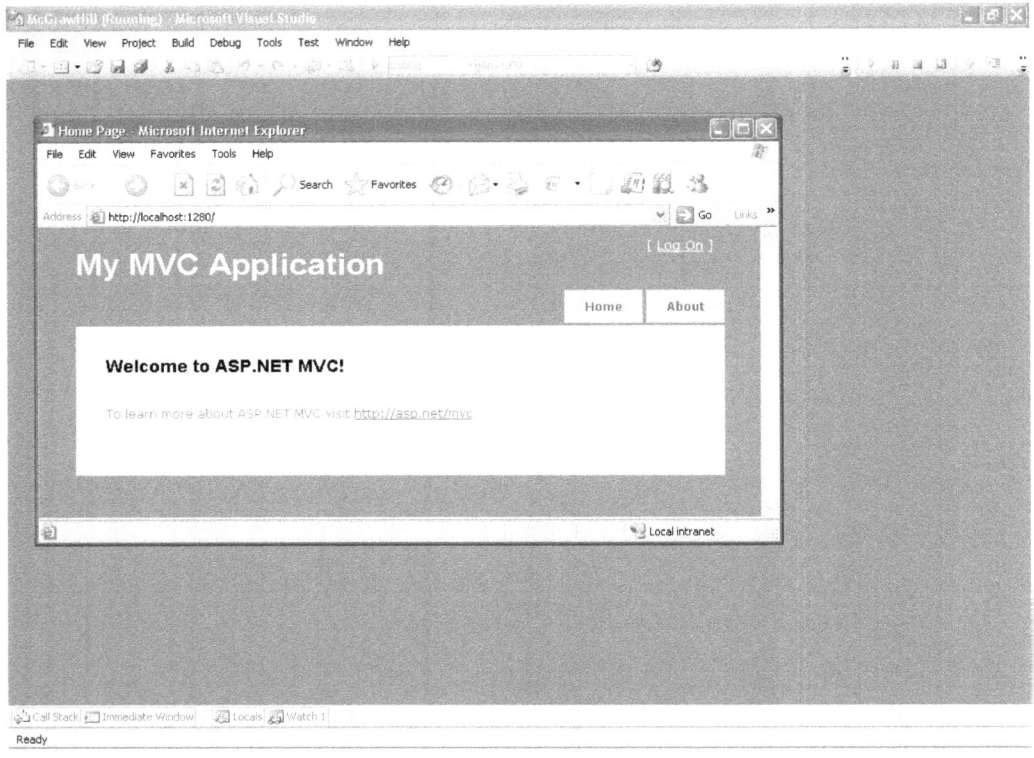

FIGURE 17-4 The HelloMVC application at work!

CHAPTER 18

Program ASP.NET MVC Framework

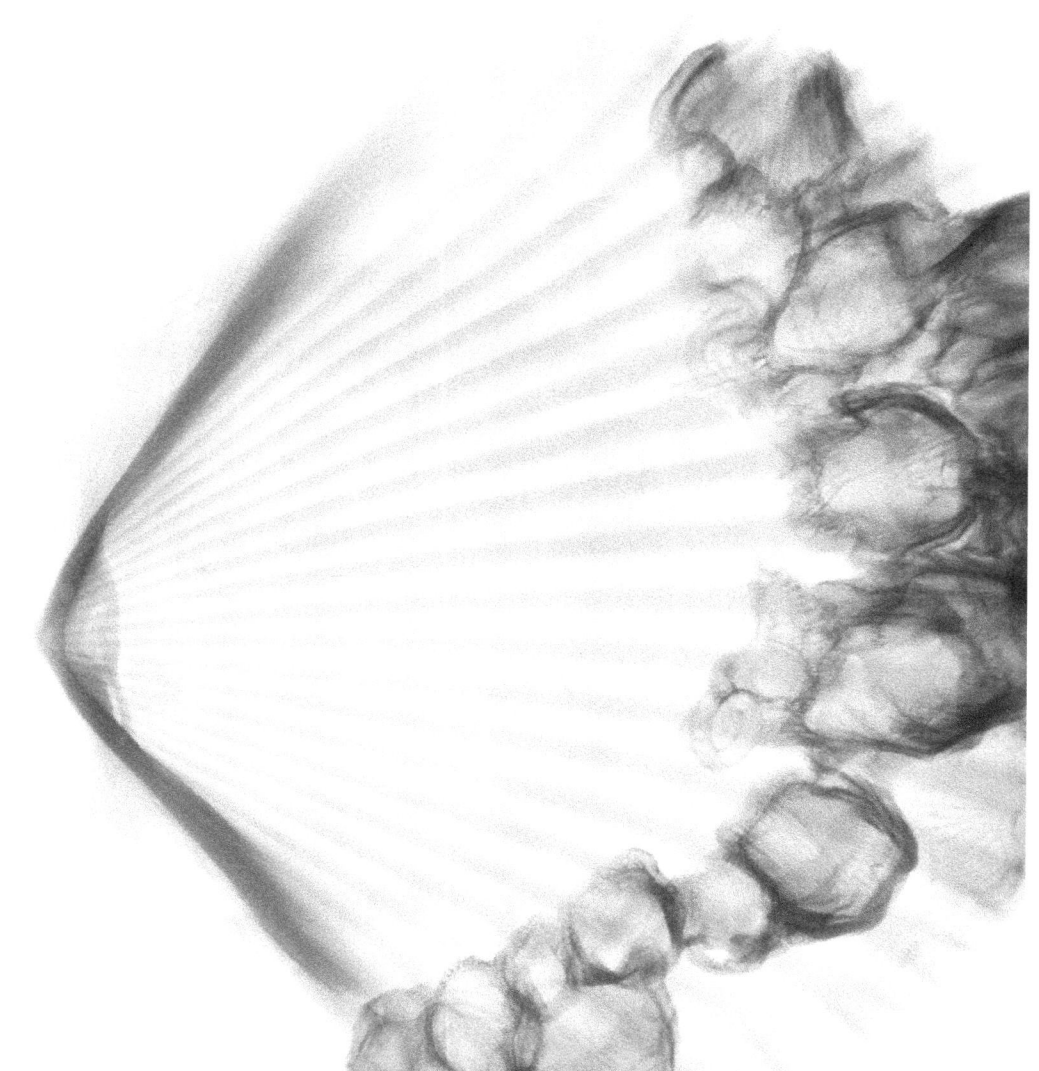

The MVC design pattern facilitates separation of concerns in your application. You can use this design pattern to isolate the business logic and presentation layers of an application. The ASP.NET MVC Framework is based on this design pattern and facilitates a clean separation of concerns and promotes testability, plugability, and maintainability. In the previous chapter we had a look at the ASP.NET MVC Framework and its components. In this chapter we will learn how to program this framework and use its features to unit test applications seamlessly. We will also discuss how we can manage state information in ASP.NET MVC applications.

Implementing CRUD Operations Using ASP.NET MVC

In this section, we will implement an application that can be used to perform create, read, update, and delete (CRUD) operations using the ASP.NET MVC Framework. Follow these steps:

1. Open Visual Studio 2010 and create a new ASP.NET MVC Application.

2. Create a model for the MVC application using ADO.NET Entity Framework Designer. For the sake of simplicity, select the Department table from the AdventureWorks database.

3. Right-click on the Controllers folder in the Solution Explorer and create a new controller.

4. Specify a name for the controller and check the check box under the Controller Name field, as shown in Figure 18-1, to add the action methods for CRUD operations.

5. Open the Site.Master file and specify the link for Department module, as shown in the following listing:

Listing 18-1
```
<li><%= Html.ActionLink("Department", "Index", "Department")%></li>
```

Here is the complete markup code of the Site.Master file:

Listing 18-2
```
<%@ Master Language="C#"
Inherits="System.Web.Mvc.ViewMasterPage" %>
<!DOCTYPE html
PUBLIC "-//W3C//DTD XHTML 1.0 Strict//EN"
 "http://www.w3.org/TR/xhtml1/
DTD/xhtml1-strict.dtd">
<html xmlns="http://www.w3.org/1999/xhtml">
<head runat="server">
   <title><asp:ContentPlaceHolder
ID="TitleContent" runat="server" /></title>
   <link href="../../Content/Site.css"
rel="stylesheet" type="text/css" />
</head>
<body>
```

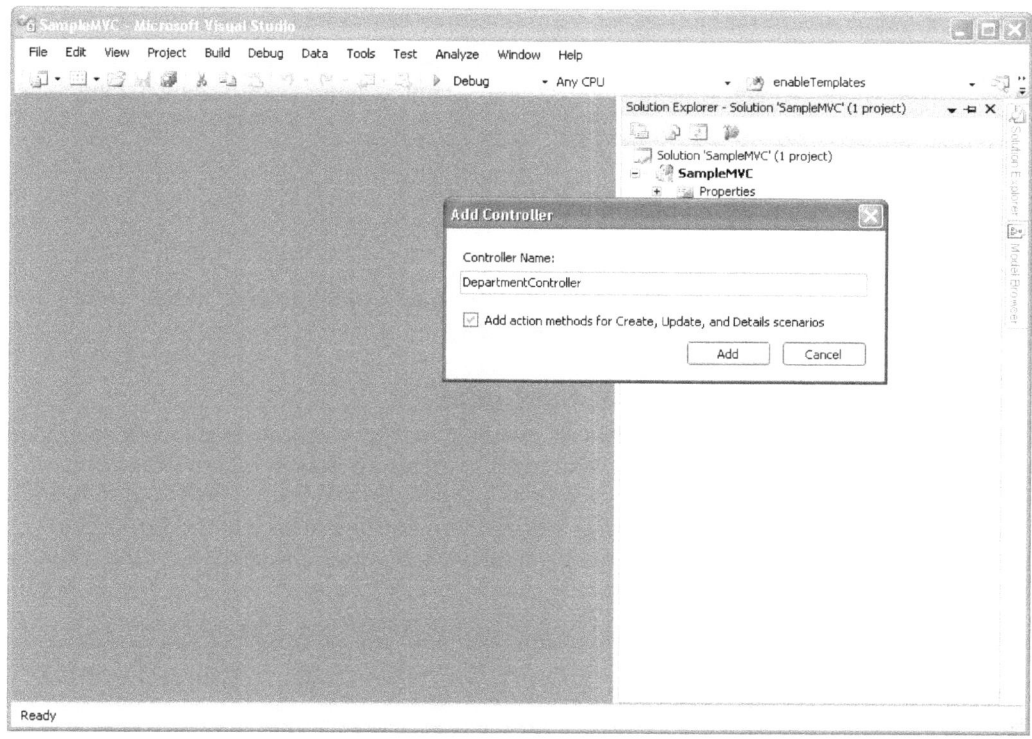

FIGURE 18-1   Creating the Department controller

```
<div class="page">
    <div id="header">
        <div id="title">
            <h1>Using ASP.NET MVC</h1>
        </div>
        <div id="logindisplay">
            <% Html.RenderPartial("LogOnUserControl"); %>
        </div>
        <div id="menucontainer">
            <ul id="menu">
                <li><%= Html.ActionLink
("Home", "Index", "Home")%></li>
                <li><%= Html.ActionLink
("About", "About", "Home")%></li>
                <li><%= Html.ActionLink
("Department", "Index", "Department")%></li>
            </ul>
        </div>
    </div>
```

```
        <div id="main">
            <asp:ContentPlaceHolder ID=
"MainContent" runat="server" />
            <div id="footer">
            </div>
        </div>
    </div>
</body>
</html>
```

When you execute the application, you'll see the Department tab in the home page, as shown in Figure 18-2.

Implementing the Department Controller

You will now need to create the methods for the CRUD operations in the controller class.

To perform the create operation, you need to create an instance of the Department entity, assign the necessary data to each of its properties, and then use the AddObject() method on the DataContext to add the Department entity instance to the DataContext. Finally, you'll need to call the SaveChanges() method to persist the changes to the database.

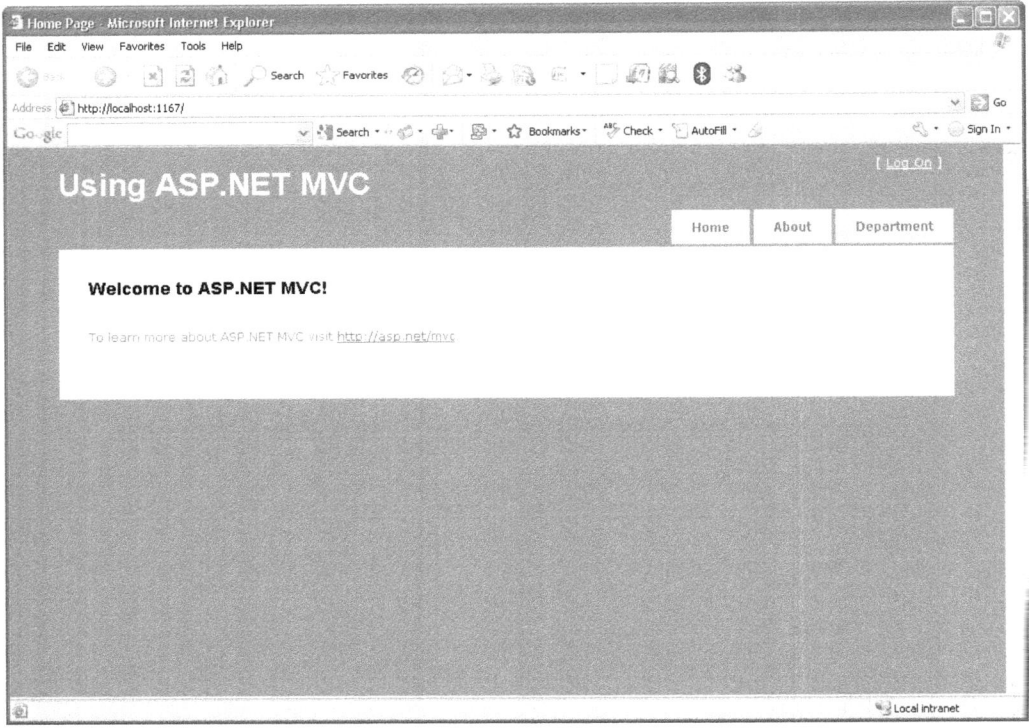

FIGURE 18-2   The sample MVC application home page

Here is the code to do that:

Listing 18-3
```
AcceptVerbs(HttpVerbs.Post)]
        public ActionResult Create(FormCollection collection)
        {
            try
            {
                Department department = new Department();
                department.Name = collection["Name"].ToString();
                department.GroupName = collection["GroupName"].ToString();
                department.ModifiedDate = DateTime.Now;
                dataContext.AddObject("Department",department);
                dataContext.SaveChanges();
                return RedirectToAction("Index");
            }
            catch
            {
                return View();
            }
        }
```

Implementing the Edit method is similar, as shown in the following code snippet:

Listing 18-4
```
[AcceptVerbs(HttpVerbs.Post)]
        public ActionResult Edit(int id, FormCollection collection)
        {
            try
            {
                Department department =
dataContext.Department.First
(dept => dept.DepartmentID == id);
                department.Name = collection["Name"].ToString();
                department.GroupName = collection["GroupName"].ToString();
                department.ModifiedDate = DateTime.Now;
                dataContext.SaveChanges();
                return RedirectToAction("Index");
            }
            catch
            {
                return View();
            }
        }
```

Note that you need not call the AddObject() method while editing the record, because the object is already available in the DataContext. You just need to select the right object based on the DepartmentID.

The Details method is simple—it returns a list of Department records:

Listing 18-5

```
public ActionResult Details(int id)
        {
              Department department =
dataContext.Department.First
(dept => dept.DepartmentID == id);
              return View(department);
        }
```

The complete source code of the DepartmentController class is now as follows:

Listing 18-6

```
using System;
using System.Collections.Generic;
using System.Linq;
using System.Web;
using System.Web.Mvc;
using System.Web.Mvc.Ajax;
using SampleMVC.Models;
namespace SampleMVC.Controllers
{
    public class DepartmentController : Controller
    {
        AdventureWorksEntities dataContext
 = new AdventureWorksEntities();
        public ActionResult Index()
        {
            var query = from d in dataContext.Department
                        select d;
            return View(query);
        }
        public ActionResult Details(int id)
        {
              Department department =
dataContext.Department.First
(dept => dept.DepartmentID == id);
              return View(department);
        }
        public ActionResult Create()
        {
            return View();
        }
        [AcceptVerbs(HttpVerbs.Post)]
        public ActionResult Create
(FormCollection collection)
        {
            try
            {
```

```
            Department department = new Department();
            department.Name = collection["Name"].ToString();
            department.GroupName =
collection["GroupName"].ToString();
            department.ModifiedDate = DateTime.Now;
            dataContext.AddObject("Department",department);
            dataContext.SaveChanges();
            return RedirectToAction("Index");
        }
        catch
        {
            return View();
        }
    }
    public ActionResult Edit(int id)
    {
        Department department =
dataContext.Department.First
(dept => dept.DepartmentID == id);
        return View(department);
    }
    [AcceptVerbs(HttpVerbs.Post)]
    public ActionResult Edit(int id, FormCollection collection)
    {
        try
        {
            Department department =
dataContext.Department.First
(dept => dept.DepartmentID == id);
            department.Name = collection["Name"].ToString();
            department.GroupName =
collection["GroupName"].ToString();
            department.ModifiedDate = DateTime.Now;
            dataContext.SaveChanges();
            return RedirectToAction("Index");
        }
        catch
        {
            return View();
        }
    }
}
}
```

Implementing the Views

Now that you are done implementing the controller class, you need to create the corresponding views. Just right-click while you are on an action method and the corresponding view will be generated.

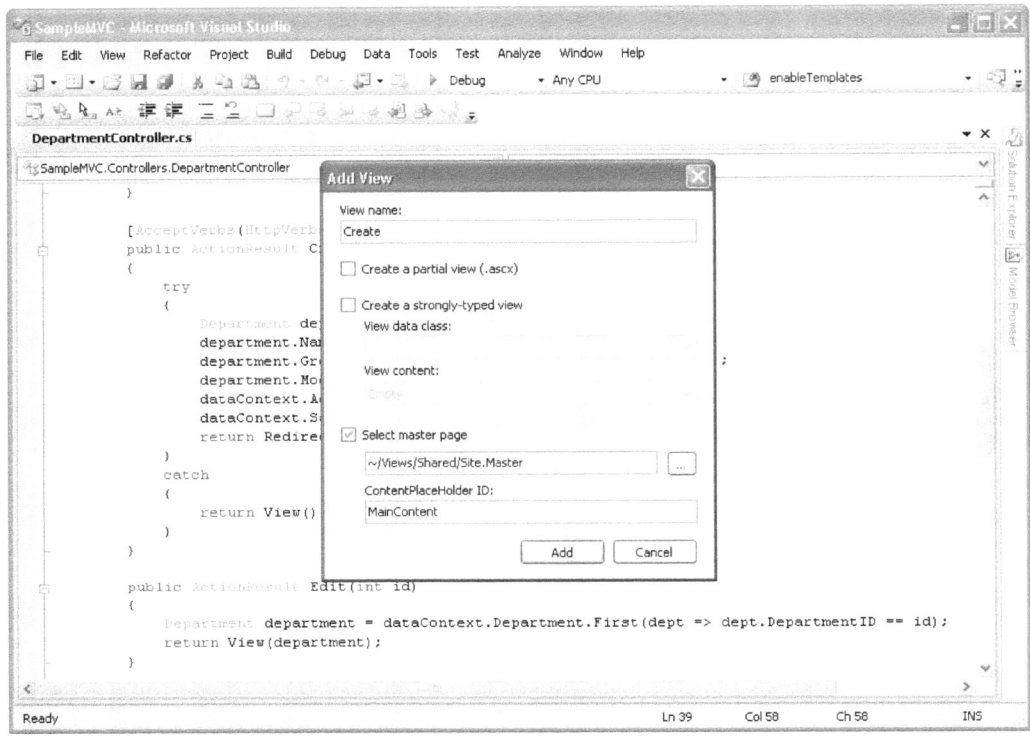

FIGURE 18-3 Creating the view for the Create method

For example, move your cursor to the Create action method in your DepartmentController class, right-click on it, and select the "Add View" option from the context menu that pops up. An Add View dialog will open, as shown in Figure 18-3, and you can create your view for the Create method.

Ensure that you check the Create a strongly-typed view check box and select the appropriate View Data Class and the View Content as shown as in Figure 18-3. When you're done, click Add to create the view. Follow the same steps to create the other views.

Here is what the markup code for Create.aspx (created for the view by following the preceding steps) will look like:

Listing 18-7

```
<%@ Page Title="" Language="C#"
MasterPageFile="~/Views/Shared/Site.Master"
Inherits="System.Web.Mvc.ViewPage
<SampleMVC.Models.Department>" %>
<asp:Content ID="Content1"
ContentPlaceHolderID="TitleContent"
 runat="server">
      Create New Department Record
</asp:Content>
```

```
<asp:Content ID="Content2"
ContentPlaceHolderID="MainContent"
 runat="server">
    <h2>Create</h2>
    <%= Html.ValidationSummary
("Create was unsuccessful.
Please correct the errors and try again.") %>
    <% using (Html.BeginForm()) {%>
        <fieldset>
            <legend>Fields</legend>
            <p>
                <label for="DepartmentID">DepartmentID:</label>
                <%= Html.TextBox("DepartmentID") %>
                <%= Html.ValidationMessage
("DepartmentID", "*") %>
            </p>
            <p>
                <label for="Name">Name:</label>
                <%= Html.TextBox("Name") %>
                <%= Html.ValidationMessage("Name", "*") %>
            </p>
            <p>
                <label for="GroupName">GroupName:</label>
                <%= Html.TextBox("GroupName") %>
                <%= Html.ValidationMessage("GroupName", "*") %>
            </p>
            <p>
                <label for="ModifiedDate">ModifiedDate:</label>
                <%= Html.TextBox("ModifiedDate") %>
                <%= Html.ValidationMessage("ModifiedDate", "*") %>
            </p>
            <p>
                <input type="submit" value="Create" />
            </p>
        </fieldset>
    <% } %>
    <div>
        <%=Html.ActionLink
('Back to List", "Index") %>
    </div>
</asp:Content>
```

The markup code for the Details.aspx file is shown in the following code listing:

Listing 18-8
```
<%@ Page Title="" Language="C#"
MasterPageFile="~/Views/Shared/Site.Master"
Inherits="System.Web.Mvc.ViewPage
<SampleMVC.Models.Department>" %>
<asp:Content ID="Content1"
```

```
    ContentPlaceHolderID="TitleContent"
    runat="server">
     Display Department Details
</asp:Content>
<asp:Content ID="Content2"
 ContentPlaceHolderID="MainContent"
 runat="server">
    <h2>Details</h2>
    <fieldset>
        <legend>Fields</legend>
        <p>
            DepartmentID:
            <%= Html.Encode(Model.DepartmentID) %>
        </p>
        <p>
            Name:
            <%= Html.Encode(Model.Name) %>
        </p>
        <p>
            GroupName:
            <%= Html.Encode(Model.GroupName) %>
        </p>
        <p>
            ModifiedDate:
            <%= Html.Encode(String.Format
("{0:g}", Model.ModifiedDate)) %>
        </p>
    </fieldset>
    <p>
        <%=Html.ActionLink
("Edit", "Edit", new
{ id=Model.DepartmentID }) %> |
        <%=Html.ActionLink
("Back to List", "Index") %>
    </p>
</asp:Content>
```

Here is the markup code for Edit.aspx:

Listing 18-9
```
<%@ Page Title="" Language="C#"
MasterPageFile="~/Views/Shared/Site.Master"
Inherits="System.Web.Mvc.ViewPage
<SampleMVC.Models.Department>" %>
<asp:Content ID="Content1"
 ContentPlaceHolderID="TitleContent"
 runat="server">
    Edit Existing Department Record
</asp:Content>
<asp:Content ID="Content2"
 ContentPlaceHolderID="MainContent"
```

```
    runat="server">
      <h2>Edit</h2>
      <%= Html.ValidationSummary
("Edit was unsuccessful.
Please correct the errors and try again.") %>
      <% using (Html.BeginForm()) {%>
          <fieldset>
              <legend>Fields</legend>
              <p>
                  <label for="DepartmentID">DepartmentID:</label>
                  <%= Html.TextBox("DepartmentID", Model.DepartmentID) %>
                  <%= Html.ValidationMessage("DepartmentID", "*") %>
              </p>
              <p>
                  <label for="Name">Name:</label>
                  <%= Html.TextBox("Name", Model.Name) %>
                  <%= Html.ValidationMessage("Name", "*") %>
              </p>
              <p>
                  <label for="GroupName">GroupName:</label>
                  <%= Html.TextBox("GroupName", Model.GroupName) %>
                  <%= Html.ValidationMessage("GroupName", "*") %>
              </p>
              <p>
                  <label for="ModifiedDate">
ModifiedDate:</label>
                  <%= Html.TextBox("ModifiedDate",
 String.Format("{0:g}", Model.ModifiedDate)) %>
                  <%= Html.ValidationMessage
("ModifiedDate", "*") %>
              </p>
              <p>
                  <input type="submit" value="Save" />
              </p>
          </fieldset>
      <% } %>
      <div>
          <%=Html.ActionLink("Back to List", "Index") %>
      </div>
</asp:Content>
```

Note that the Index.aspx file is stored in the Views | Home folder of your ASP.NET MVC application. Here is the markup code for the Index.aspx: :

Listing 18-10
```
<%@ Page Title="" Language="C#"
MasterPageFile="~/Views/Shared/Site.Master"
Inherits="System.Web.Mvc.ViewPage
<IEnumerable<SampleMVC.Models.Department>>" %>
```

```
<asp:Content ID="Content1"
ContentPlaceHolderID=
"TitleContent" runat="server">
      Index
</asp:Content>
<asp:Content ID="Content2"
ContentPlaceHolderID="MainContent"
 runat="server">
    <h2>Index</h2>
    <table>
        <tr>
            <th></th>
            <th>
                Department ID
            </th>
            <th>
                Name
            </th>
            <th>
                Group Name
            </th>
            <th>
                Modified Date
            </th>
        </tr>
    <% foreach (var item in Model) { %>
            <tr>
            <td>
                <%= Html.ActionLink("Edit",
"Edit", new { id=item.DepartmentID }) %> |
                <%= Html.ActionLink("Details",
 "Details", new { id=item.DepartmentID })%>
            </td>
            <td>
                <%= Html.Encode(item.DepartmentID) %>
            </td>
            <td>
                <%= Html.Encode(item.Name) %>
            </td>
            <td>
                <%= Html.Encode(item.GroupName) %>
            </td>
            <td>
                <%= Html.Encode(String.Format
("{0:g}", item.ModifiedDate)) %>
            </td>
        </tr>
    <% } %>
    </table>
```

```
<p>
    <%= Html.ActionLink
("Create New Department", "Create") %>
    </p>
</asp:Content>
```

Executing the Application

When you execute the application the home page is displayed. You'll need to click on the Department tab to switch to the Department page. Figure 18-4 shows a list of all the department records from the Department table in the AdventureWorks database.

When you click on the Details link for one of the department records, you will see the Details page, shown in Figure 18-5.

You can edit any record from the list of department records by clicking on the Edit link. As you can see in Figure 18-6, you can edit the details and click Save to save the changes.

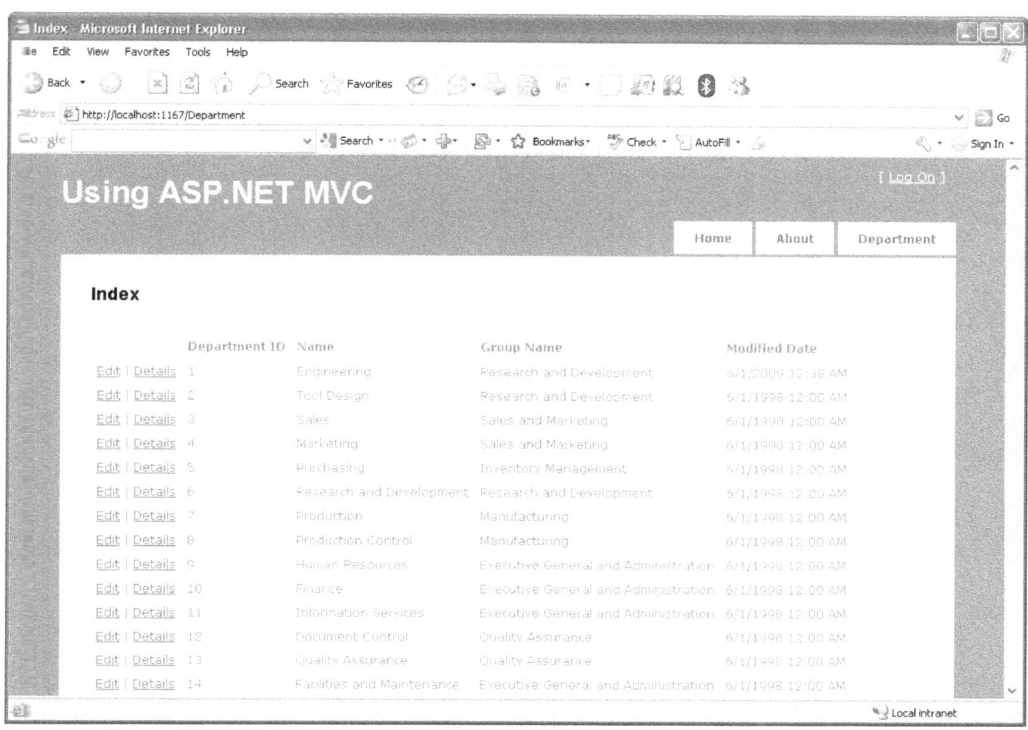

FIGURE 18-4 Displaying the list of all department records

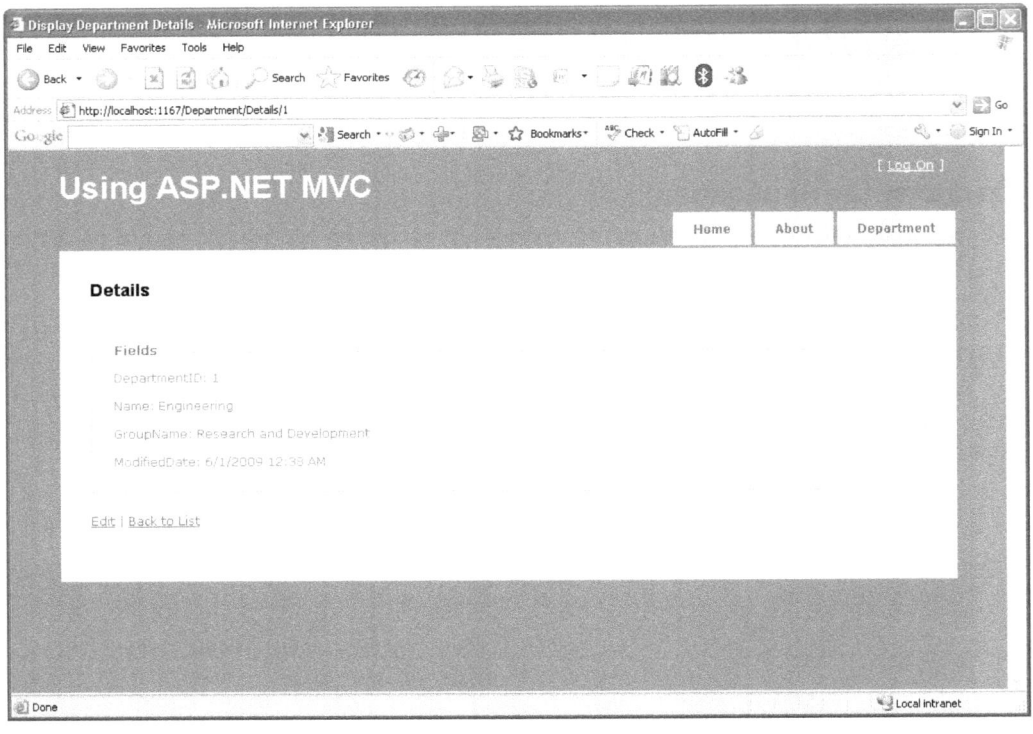

FIGURE 18-5   Displaying the details for a particular department record

Unit Testing with the ASP.NET MVC Framework

Unit testing is a procedure in which you test small units or pieces of your code and make sure that they conform to the expected results. The term "unit" refers to the smallest testable portion of your application's code. The ASP.NET MVC framework provides excellent support for unit testing applications—it allows you to use any unit testing framework, such as NUnit, MBUnit, MSTest, or XUnit.

When you create an ASP.NET MVC project, you can choose to generate a unit test project too. If you do, a new testing project will be created in addition to your ASP.NET MVC project.

NOTE *The Visual Studio unit test framework is only available with Visual Studio 2008/2010 Professional or higher versions. If you are using different versions of Visual Studio, like Visual Studio 2008 Standard Edition or Visual Web Developer 2008 Express, you will have to download and install the NUnit, MBUnit, or XUnit extensions for ASP.NET MVC to work with unit testing. If these are not installed, you will not even be able to see the unit testing dialog.*

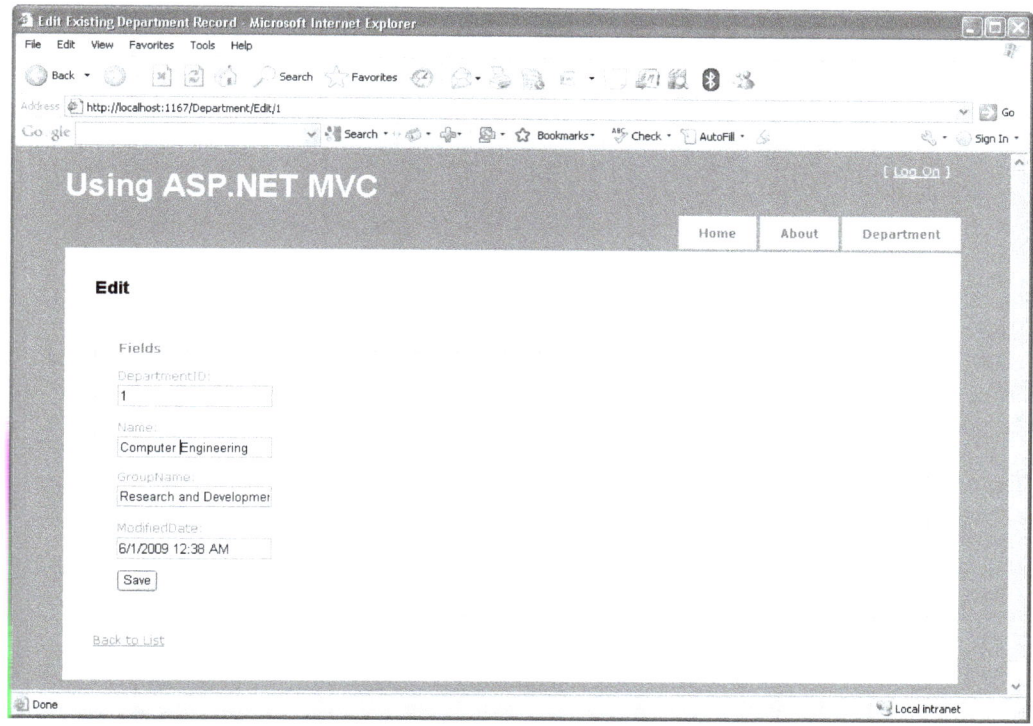

FIGURE 18-6   Editing a department record

The following code listing illustrates how you can execute a unit test on a controller class using the ASP.NET MVC Framework:

Listing 18-11
```
using System.Web.Mvc;
using Microsoft.VisualStudio.TestTools.UnitTesting;
using SampleMVCApp.Controllers;
namespace SampleMVCAppTests.Controllers
{
    [TestClass]
    public class EmployeeControllerTest
    {
        [TestMethod]
        public void DisplayEmployee()
        {
            EmployeeController employeeController =
new EmployeeController();
            ViewResult viewResult =
employeeController.Show("Joydip") as ViewResult;
            ViewDataDictionary viewData =
```

```
viewResult.ViewData as ViewDataDictionary;
            Assert.IsNotNull(viewData.Model);
            Assert.AreEqual("Joydip",
(viewData.Model as
SampleMVCApp.Models.Employee).FirstName);
            Assert.IsNull(viewData["ErrorMessage"]);
        }
    }
}
```

ViewData is a dictionary that is used to pass data from the controller to the view. The controller in an ASP.NET MVC application passes data to the view using this dictionary. The preceding code listing checks whether the data returned is valid using ViewData. The ViewResult.ViewName property returns the name of the view, and you can use it to verify the name of the view.

You can also use the ASP.NET MVC Framework to test the action result returned by the controller. Consider the following code listing showing an EmployeeController.

Listing 18-12
```
using System;
using System.Web.Mvc;
namespace MGH.Controllers
{
 public class EmployeeController : Controller
 {
  public ActionResult Index()
  {
   // Write your custom code for
  // the action logic here.
   throw new NotImplementedException();
  }
  public ActionResult Details(int employeeID)
  {
   if (employeeID < 1)
   return RedirectToAction("Index");
   var employee = new Employee(employeeID, "Joydip");
   return View("Details", employee);
  }
 }
}
```

Here is how you could write a test class for the EmployeeController to test the action method.

Listing 18-13
```
namespace MGH.Controllers
{
[TestClass]
 public class EmployeeControllerTest
```

```
{
[TestMethod]
 public void TestDetailsRedirect()
 {
  var controller = new EmployeeController();
  var result = (RedirectToRouteResult) controller.Details(-1);
  Assert.AreEqual("Index", result.Values["action"]);
 }
}
```

In the preceding code listing, EmployeeControllerTest is the name of the test class. When you call the RedirectToAction() method in the action method of the controller, an instance of RedirectToRouteResult is returned. The TestDetailsRedirect() test method of the EmployeeControllerTest class verifies whether the RedirectToRouteResult should redirect the control to the controller action called Index.

Figure 18-7 illustrates the output when you run the unit tests for a sample ASP.NET MVC project.

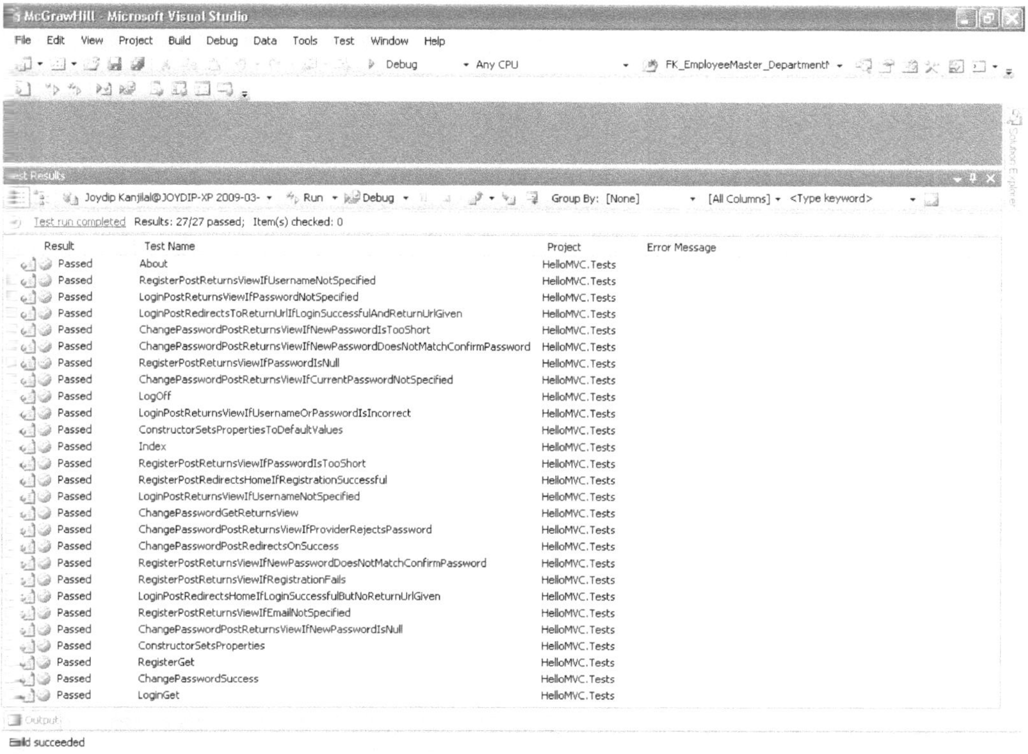

FIGURE 18-7   Running unit tests for an ASP.NET MVC application

State Management Using the ASP.NET MVC Framework

You can use the ASP.NET MVC Framework to store state information across requests. The framework is built on top of the ASP.NET runtime, so you can have access to HttpContext, Request, Response, Session, Cache, Server, and Cookie in your ASP.NET MVC application.

You can configure the session state in the application's web.config file much the same way you can with an ASP.NET application. The following code snippet illustrates how you can use session state in your ASP.NET MVC applications:

Listing 18-14
```
using System.Web.Mvc;
namespace MVCTest.Controllers
{
    public class HomeController : Controller
    {
        public ActionResult Index()
        {
            Session["Test"] =
            "This is a sample text";
            return View();
        }
        public ActionResult ReadData()
        {
            string data = string.Empty;
            if (Session["Test"] != null) {
                data = (string)Session["Test"];
            }
            return View();
        }
    }
}
```

There is also a nice storage mechanism in the ASP.NET MVC framework called TempData that enables you to store state information across requests. Here is how you would use TempData to store and retrieve state information in your ASP.NET MVC applications:

Listing 18-15
```
// To store data
TempData["TestKey"] =
"This is a sample text.";
// To retrieve data
var data = TempData["TestKey"];
```

Output Caching is a feature that enables you to store the output of web pages in cache for later retrieval. This boosts the application's performance, as the subsequent requests for the cached page are served from the cache. You can also enable output caching in your ASP.NET MVC application simply by using the [OutputCache] attribute, as follows:

Listing 18-16
```
[OutputCache(Duration = 60,
VaryByParam="none")]
public ActionResult
DisplayInformation()
{
    ViewData["Title"] =
    "This is the title of the web page.";
    ViewData["Message"] =
    "This is a test message";
    return View();
}
```

In the preceding code listing, output caching has been enabled for the DisplayInformation action method.

ASP.NET MVC 2.0

As of this writing, ASP.NET MVC 2.0 Preview 1 has been released. You can download it from Microsoft's downloads site: http://www.microsoft.com/downloads.

The ASP.NET MVC 2.0 Preview 1 release includes the following new features:

- **Support for templated helpers**   This feature enables you to automatically associate templates with views for editing and displaying values based on a particular data type.

- **Support for areas**   This is a feature that enables you to partition and group functionalities in your ASP.NET MVC application.

- **Support for data annotations**   This is an excellent new feature that enables you to add validation rules to the Model and ViewModel classes within an ASP.NET MVC application. It also provides automatic binding and UI helper validation support in an ASP.NET MVC application.

- **Support for strongly typed UI helpers**   This is a new feature that facilitates better compile-time checking of views and enhanced code Intellisense support for the view templates.

You can get more information on ASP.NET MVC 2.0 from Scott Guthrie's blog: http://weblogs.asp.net/scottgu/archive/2009/07/31/asp-net-mvc-v2-preview-1-released.aspx.

Migrating from ASP.NET MVC version 1.0 to 2.0

Migrating from an existing ASP.NET MVC 1.0 application to ASP.NET MVC 2.0 is easy. Download and install the ASP.NET MVC Framework 2.0 and then copy all views, controllers, and content files from your ASP.NET MVC 1.0 application to the ASP.NET

MVC 2.0 application, and add the necessary assembly references to provide backward compatibility. And that's all you have to do!

Alternatively, you can follow the steps outlined below to migrate your ASP.NET MVC 1.0 application to version 2.0:

1. Replace all occurrences of "System.Web.Mvc, Version=1.0.0.0" with "System.Web .Mvc, Version=2.0.0.0" in your ASP.NET MVC 1.0 application's web.config file.

2. Replace the "System.Web.Mvc 1.0" assembly in the references assemblies of your ASP.NET 1.0 MVC project with "System.Web.Mvc (v2.0.50727)".

3. Unload the ASP.NET MVC 1.0 project and replace "System.Web.Mvc, Version=1.0.0.0" with "System.Web.Mvc, Version=2.0.0.0" in the project file.

4. Add the bindingRedirect element in the ASP.NET MVC 1.0 application's web.config file as shown in the following code listing:

Listing 18-17

```
<runtime>
  <assemblyBinding xmlns=
"urn:schemas-microsoft-com:asm.v1">
    <dependentAssembly>
      <assemblyIdentity name="System.Web.Mvc"
          publicKeyToken="31bf3856ad364e35"/>
      <bindingRedirect oldVersion="1.0.0.0"
newVersion="2.0.0.0"/>
    </dependentAssembly>
  </assemblyBinding>
</runtime>
```

You're done! Your ASP.NET MVC 1.0 application has been migrated to be an ASP.NET MVC 2.0 application.

CHAPTER 19

Working with jQuery in ASP.NET

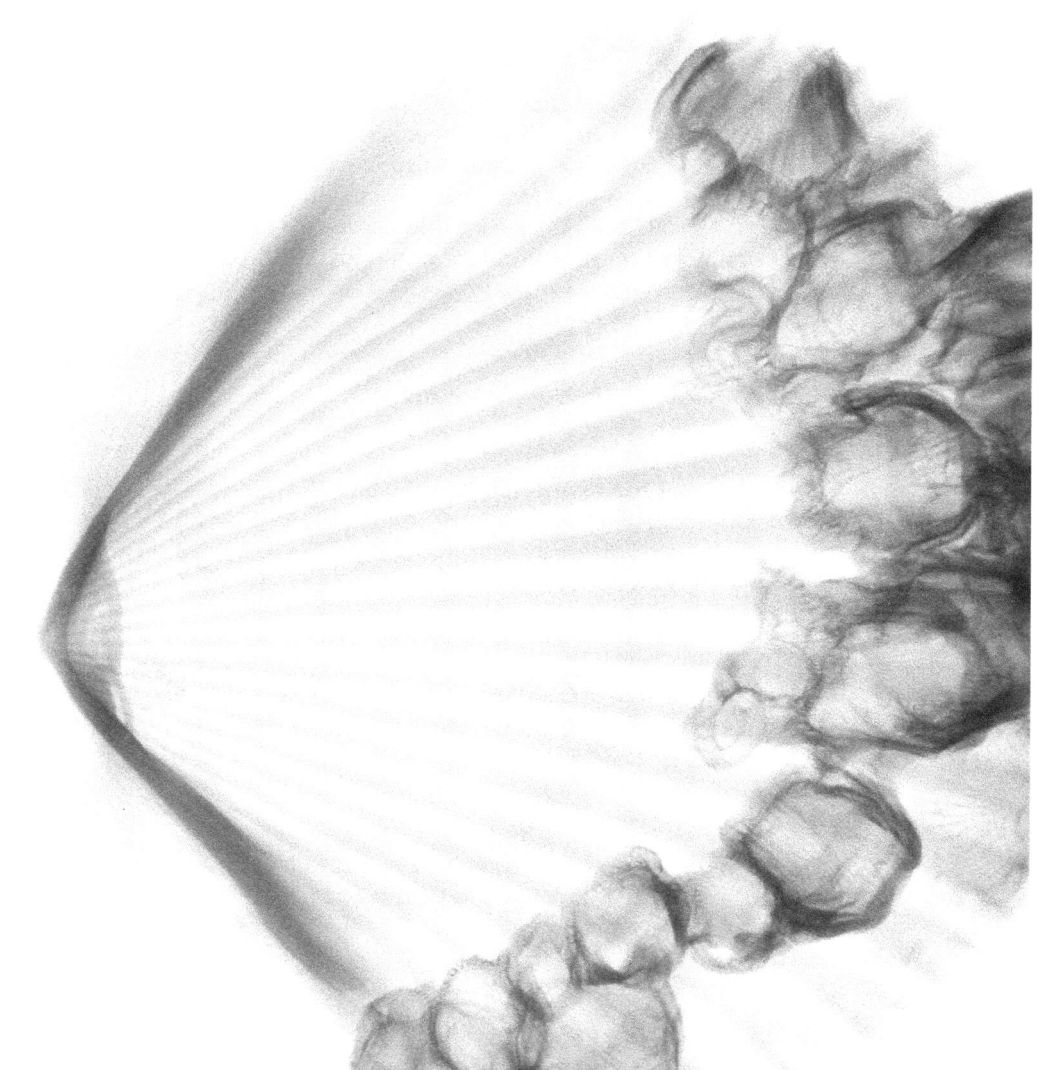

jQuery is an extensible open source JavaScript library that's fast, lightweight, and CSS3 and cross-browser compliant. It simplifies event handling and animations and makes it easier to develop web applications that are responsive. jQuery has become the JavaScript library of choice for building lightning-fast and responsive applications in no time. As the official jQuery web site (http://jquery.com) states, "jQuery is a fast and concise JavaScript Library that simplifies HTML document traversing, event handling, animating, and Ajax interactions for rapid web development. jQuery is designed to change the way that you write JavaScript." (http://jquery.com/)

What Is jQuery?

The jQuery library was first released in 2006 by John Resig, and it became widely popular among web development communities worldwide. With Microsoft integrating jQuery into future releases of Visual Studio .NET, jQuery is well poised to rule the web development community for a long time to come. jQuery will be a part of the Visual Studio 2010 release.

Scott Guthrie explained in his esteemed blog, "A big part of the appeal of jQuery is that it allows you to elegantly (and efficiently) find and manipulate HTML elements with minimum lines of code.... There is a huge ecosystem and community built up around jQuery. The jQuery library also works well on the same page with ASP.NET AJAX and the ASP.NET AJAX Control Toolkit." (http://weblogs.asp.net/scottgu/archive/2008/09/28/jquery-and-microsoft.aspx)

You can use jQuery in combination with ASP.NET Ajax to build truly interactive and highly responsive applications.

Key Features of jQuery

jQuery provides the following features:

- **Browser independence**   jQuery is supported by most modern browsers.
- **Support for a simplified event-handling model**   jQuery provides support for an excellent, easy-to-use, normalized event-handling model with much-reduced code. The jQuery event-handling model is consistent across all browsers. The event object is a cross-browser normalized one, and one event object is always passed as a parameter to an event handler.
- **Seamless extensibility**   jQuery provides support for extensibility through a simple plug-in API that extends the jQuery core library.
- **Structured JavaScript code**   jQuery produces more robust and readable JavaScript code. Its use also reduces the amount of JavaScript code.

Why Use jQuery?

What is so special about jQuery that has caused it to be widely accepted the world over? JavaScript has varying Document Object Model (DOM) and CSS implementations for different browsers, and event management interfaces differ in JavaScript for different browsers. jQuery, on the other hand, provides a common browser API for cross-browser support, and it provides more robust and readable JavaScript code with simplicity of use. jQuery also drastically reduces code. Numerous plug-ins for jQuery are available these days.

Setting up jQuery in ASP.NET

To work with jQuery in ASP.NET, you need the following installed on your system:

- Visual Studio 2010
- The jQuery library (available from http://jquery.com)
- The Visual Studio jQuery plug-in

To use jQuery with ASP.NET, you just need to include the jQuery script library using the JavaScript <script> tag. That's all!

jQuery IntelliSense in Visual Studio

jQuery IntelliSense, a great feature, is now available as a free download, and Microsoft is all set to ship jQuery with future versions of Visual Studio. To use jQuery IntelliSense in Visual Studio, you need to do the following:

- Install the hotfix KB958502 from Microsoft
- Download the jQuery IntelliSense file and place it in the same path as the jQuery library

You can download the hotfix from this link: http://code.msdn.microsoft.com/ KB958502/Release/ProjectReleases.aspx?ReleaseId=1736.

Getting Started with jQuery

There are various ways to include jQuery in your web page:

- Reference a local copy using the <script> tag
- Reference a local copy using the ScriptManager control's ScriptReference property
- Use an embedded script
- Reference a remote copy of the jQuery library

Referencing the jQuery library with the <script> tag is done like this:

Listing 19-1
```
<head runat="server">
    <title>Getting Started with jQuery and ASP.NET</title>
    <script src="../Scripts/jquery-1.2.6.js" type="text/javascript"></script>
</head>
```

You will probably want the jQuery library to be available to all web pages in your application, so you can create a master page and refer to the jQuery library in it. This will ensure that all content pages that inherit this master page have access to the jQuery library and its methods.

In this section, we will implement a sample application that references the jQuery library from the web page by using the <script> tag. Follow these steps:

1. Open Visual Studio 2010 and select File | New | Project.

2. Select .NET Framework 4.0 as the version and the ASP.NET Web Application template from the list of templates displayed.

3. Enter a name for the project and click OK to save it.

4. Create a new folder in the Solution Explorer and name it Scripts.

5. Right-click on this Scripts folder and select Add Existing Item.

6. Browse to the jQuery library and jQuery IntelliSense documentation you have downloaded. Select the two files and click Add to add the files to the Scripts folder.

7. Right-click on the Solution Explorer and create a master page.

8. Drag and drop the jquery-1.2.6.js file from the Solution Explorer onto the Head section of the master page to create a reference, as shown in Figure 19-1.

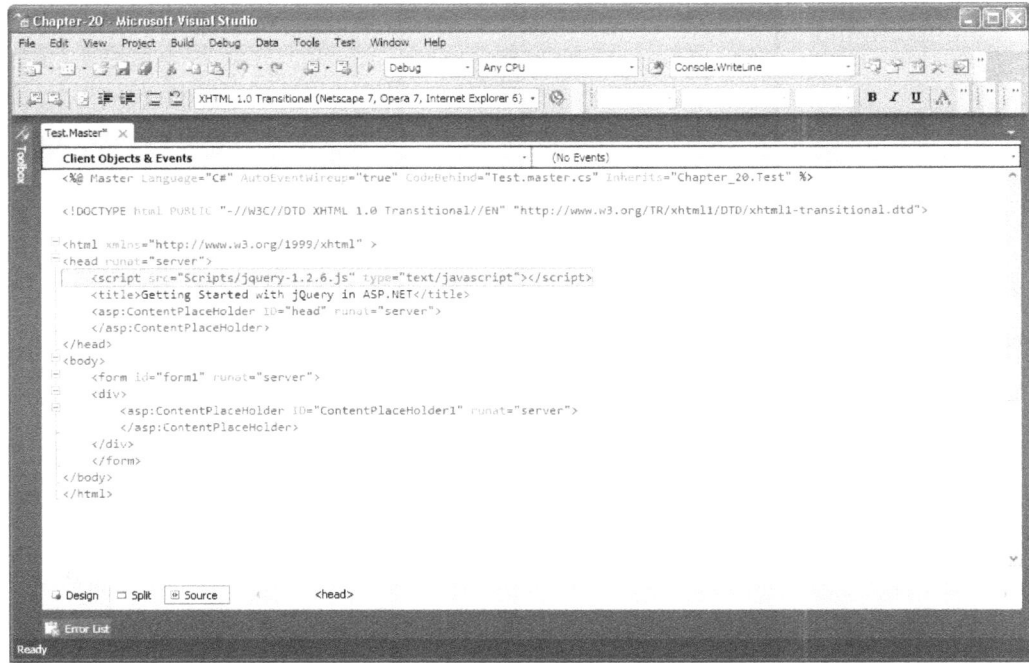

FIGURE 19-1   Creating references for the jQuery library

9. Create a content page that inherits the master page created earlier.

10. Place the following script code in the content page to display an alert message:

Listing 19-2

```
<script type="text/javascript">
        $(document).ready(function()
        {
            alert("Welcome to the World of jQuery!");
        });
</script>
```

The Solution Explorer should now look like Figure 19-2. Notice the script files inside the Scripts folder.

Let's now take a quick look at how the jQuery IntelliSense works in the Visual Studio IDE. Because the hotfix has already been installed, you don't need to add a reference to the jquery-1.2.6-vsdoc.js file in your web form; Visual Studio will automatically search and load the vsdoc file. You just need to ensure that the jQuery runtime library and the vsdoc documentation file are available in the same path.

Here's how MSDN describes IntelliSense: "IntelliSense provides an array of options that make language references easily accessible. When coding, you do not need to leave the Code Editor or the Immediate Mode command window to perform searches on language elements. You can keep your context, find the information you need, insert language elements directly into your code, and even have IntelliSense

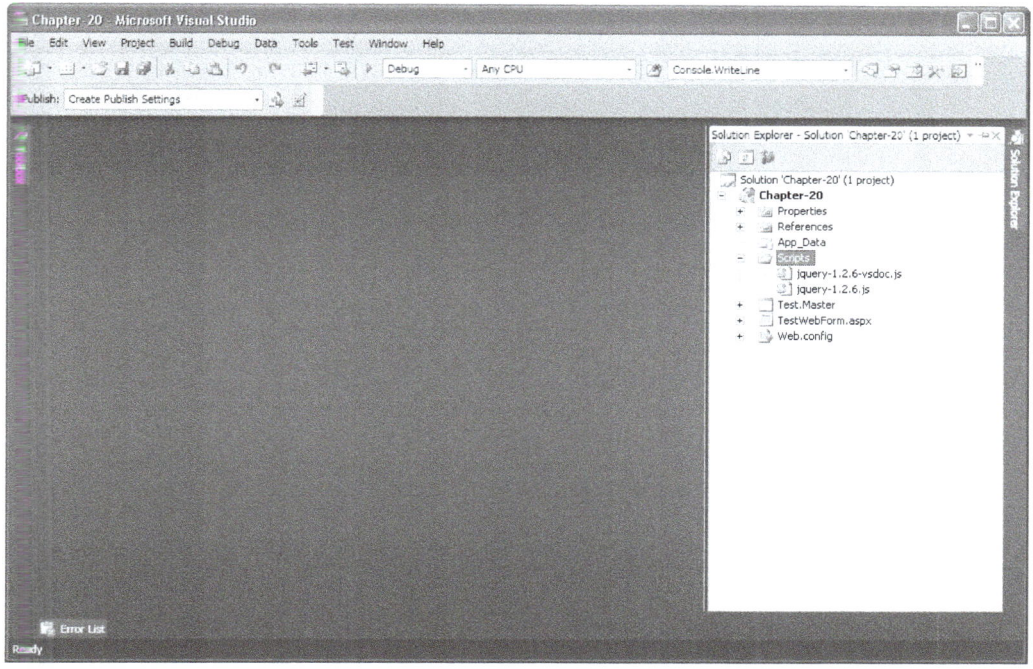

FIGURE 19-2   The Solution Explorer

complete your typing for you." (http://msdn.microsoft.com/en-us/library/
hcw1s69b(VS.71).aspx)

Here is the complete source of the master page you just created:

Listing 19-3
```
<%@ Master Language="C#"
AutoEventWireup="true"
CodeBehind="Test.master.cs"
 Inherits="Chapter_20.Test" %>
<!DOCTYPE html PUBLIC
"-//W3C//DTD XHTML 1.0 Transitional//EN"
 "http://www.w3.org/TR/xhtml1/DTD/
xhtml1-transitional.dtd">
<html xmlns="http://www.w3.org/1999/xhtml" >
<head runat="server">
    <script src="Scripts/jquery-1.2.6.js"
 type="text/javascript">
</script>
    <title>Getting Started with jQuery in ASP.NET</title>
    <asp:ContentPlaceHolder ID="head" runat="server">
    </asp:ContentPlaceHolder>
</head>
<body>
    <form id="form1" runat="server">
    <div>
        <asp:ContentPlaceHolder
ID="ContentPlaceHolder1"
 runat="server">
        </asp:ContentPlaceHolder>
    </div>
    </form>
</body>
</html>
```

This is what the complete markup code in the content page looks like:

Listing 19-4
```
<%@ Page Title="" Language="C#"
MasterPageFile="~/Test.Master"
AutoEventWireup="true"
CodeBehind="TestWebForm.aspx.cs"
 Inherits="Chapter_20.TestWebForm" %>
<asp:Content ID="Content1" ContentPlaceHolderID="head" runat="server">
<script type="text/javascript">
    $(document).ready(function() {
        alert("Welcome to the World of jQuery!");
    });
 </script>
 </asp:Content>
<asp:Content ID="Content2"
ContentPlaceHolderID="ContentPlaceHolder1"
 runat="server">
</asp:Content>
```

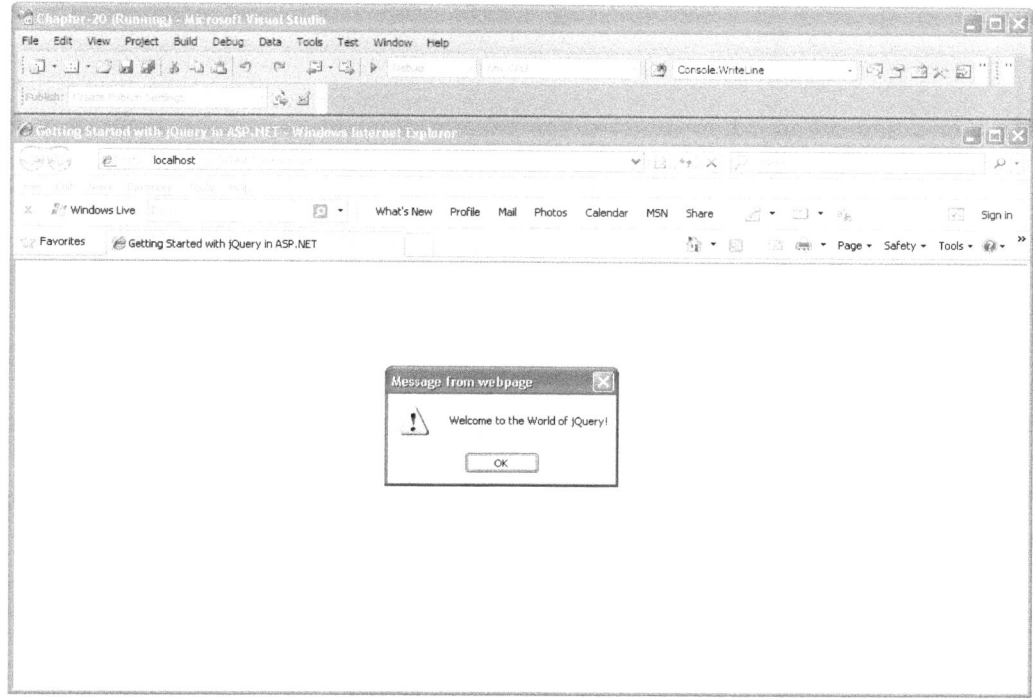

FIGURE 19-3   Your first ASP.NET 4.0 jQuery application at work!

If all is done perfectly, and the application is executed with the content page set as the start page, the output will be similar to what is shown in Figure 19-3.

Client-Side Data Binding Using jQuery

In this section, we will implement a sample application that will illustrate how you can use jQuery to bind data on the client side. In ASP.NET, the term *data binding* implies binding controls to data that is retrieved from a data source, thus providing read or write connectivity between these controls and the data they are bound to. These data sources can be databases, XML files, or even flat files.

Implementing the Sample Application

In this example, we will use jQuery to bind data to a DropDownList control at the client side. This will illustrate how you can return data in JSON format from an HttpHandler that, in turn, would be called using jQuery at the client side.

When it is executed, the application will display two DropDownList controls: one to display department names and the other to display the corresponding employee names. It will look like what is shown in Figure 19-4.

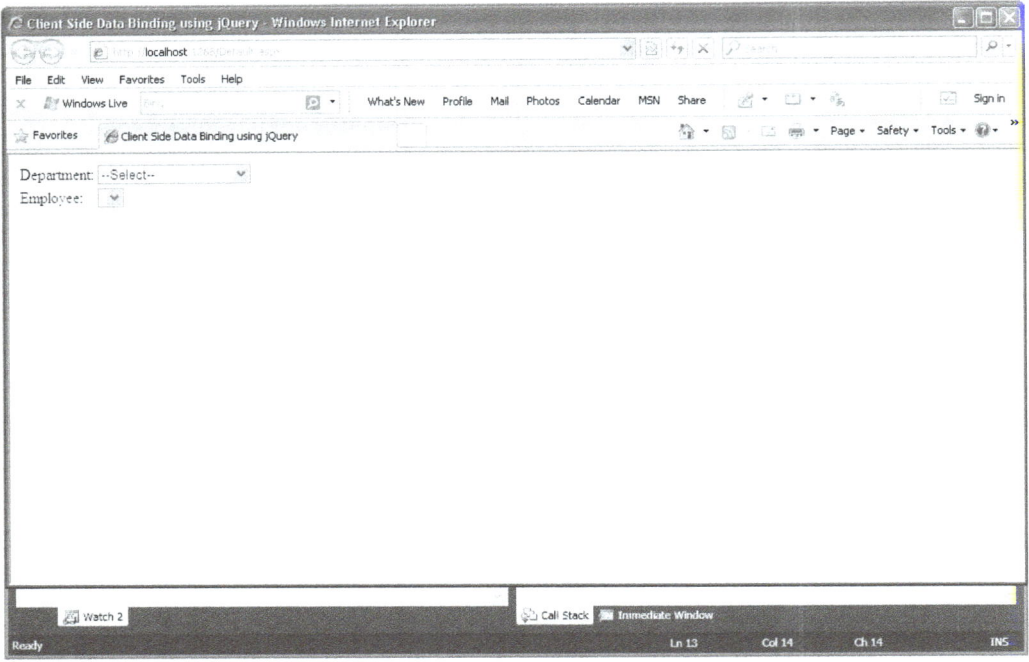

FIGURE 19-4 The ASP.NET jQuery data-binding application at work

If you select a department from the first DropDownList control, you will see the corresponding employee names populated in the second DropDownList control, as shown in Figure 19-5.

To get started creating the application, follow these steps:

1. Open Visual Studio 2010.

2. Select File | New | Project to create a new project.

3. Select ASP.NET Web Application from the list of project templates.

4. Give the project a name and save it.

5. In the Solution Explorer, create a new folder called Scripts.

6. Place the jQuery files inside the Scripts folder.

7. Right-click on the project in the Solution Explorer and select Add New Item.

8. Select Generic Handler from the list displayed, give it a name, and save it.

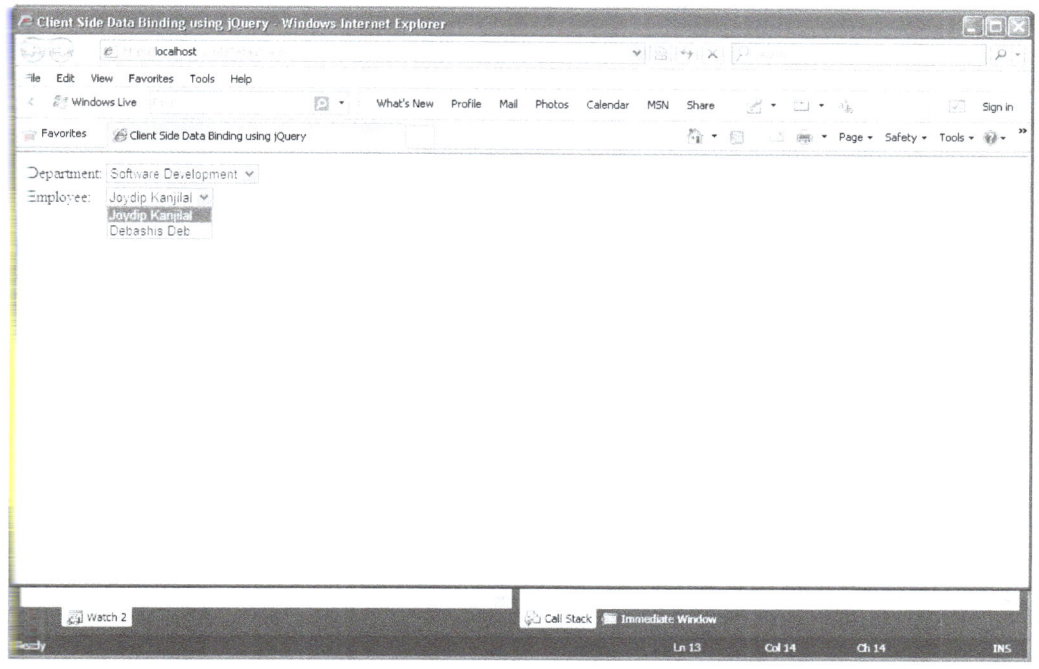

FIGURE 19-5   Listing the employees in the selected department

When you open the handler you just created, it will look like this:

Listing 19-5

```
using System.Web;
namespace DataBinding
{
    public class LoadEmployees : IHttpHandler
    {
        public void ProcessRequest(HttpContext context)
        {
            context.Response.ContentType = "text/plain";
            context.Response.Write("Hello World");
        }
        public bool IsReusable
        {
            get
            {
                return false;
            }
        }
    }
}
```

As you can see, the LoadEmployees HttpHandler contains the ProcessRequest method—you'll need to implement this method now by writing code that returns employee data in JSON format based on the department selected. The following listing shows how you can do this.

Listing 19-6

```
public void ProcessRequest(HttpContext context)
       {
            string DepartmentID =
context.Request.QueryString["DepartmentID"];
            StringBuilder strCities = new StringBuilder();
            if (DepartmentID.Equals("1"))
            {
                strCities.Append("[");
                strCities.Append("{");
                strCities.Append
("\"EmployeeName\":\"Oindrilla Roy Chowdhury\",");
                strCities.Append("\"EmployeeID\":\"1\"");
                strCities.Append("},");
                strCities.Append("{");
                strCities.Append
("\"EmployeeName\":\"Soma Roy Chowdhury\",");
                strCities.Append("\"EmployeeID\":\"2\"");
                strCities.Append("}");
                strCities.Append("]");
            }
            else if (DepartmentID.Equals("2"))
            {
                strCities.Append("[");
                strCities.Append("{");
                strCities.Append
("\"EmployeeName\":\"Joydip Kanjilal\",");
                strCities.Append("\"EmployeeID\":\"3\"");
                strCities.Append("},");
                strCities.Append("{");
                strCities.Append("\"EmployeeName\":\"Debashis Deb\",");
                strCities.Append("\"EmployeeID\":\"4\"");
                strCities.Append("}");
                strCities.Append("]");
            }
            else if (DepartmentID.Equals("3"))
            {
                strCities.Append("[");
                strCities.Append("{");
                strCities.Append
("\"EmployeeName\":\"Tilok Tarafder\",");
                strCities.Append("\"EmployeeID\":\"5\"");
                strCities.Append("},");
                strCities.Append("{");
                strCities.Append
```

```
("\"EmployeeName\":\"Vinod Kumar Naidu\",");
                strCities.Append("\"EmployeeID\":\"6\"");
                strCities.Append("}");
                strCities.Append("]");
            }
            else if (DepartmentID.Equals("4"))
            {
                strCities.Append("[");
                strCities.Append("{");
                strCities.Append("\"EmployeeName\":\"Sanjit Sil\",");
                strCities.Append("\"EmployeeID\":\"7\"");
                strCities.Append("},");
                strCities.Append("{");
                strCities.Append
("\"EmployeeName\":\"Indronil Roy Chowdhury\",");
                strCities.Append("\"EmployeeID\":\"8\"");
                strCities.Append("}");
                strCities.Append("]");
            }
            context.Response.ContentType = "application/json";
            context.Response.ContentEncoding = Encoding.UTF8;
            context.Response.Write(strCities.ToString());
            context.Response.End();
        }
```

As you can see in the preceding code listing, the employee details for the selected department are populated in a StringBuilder instance, and the Response is formed by converting the StringBuilder instance to a String instance.

Now drag and drop the jQuery file from the Solution Explorer onto the Default .aspx web form. This will create the reference to the jQuery library:

Listing 19-
```
<script src="Scripts/jquery-1.2.6.js" type="text/javascript"></script>
```

Next, drag and drop two DropDownList controls onto the Default.aspx web page, and then write the following markup code for the controls:

Listing 19-
```
<table>
        <tr>
         <td>Department:</td>
         <td>
            <asp:DropDownList ID="ddlDepartment" runat="server">
            <asp:ListItem Value="0">--Select--</asp:ListItem>
            <asp:ListItem Value="1">Sales and Marketing</asp:ListItem>
            <asp:ListItem Value="2">Software Development</asp:ListItem>
            <asp:ListItem Value="3">Finance</asp:ListItem>
            <asp:ListItem Value="4">Human Resources</asp:ListItem>
            </asp:DropDownList>
         </td>
        </tr>
```

```
            <tr>
            <td>Employee:</td>
            <td>
                <asp:DropDownList ID="ddlEmployee" runat="server">
                </asp:DropDownList>
            </td>
            </tr>
</table>
```

As you can see in the preceding code listing, the ddlDepartment DropDownList control contains a list of Department names that is statically bound. Data in the other DropDownList control, ddlEmployee, will be bound dynamically at runtime using jQuery.

Now we need to use jQuery to fetch JSON data in the onchange event handler for the ddlDepartment DropDownList control. Here is the code to invoke the HttpHandler:

Listing 19-9

```
<script type ="text/javascript">
        $(document).ready(function()
        {
            $("#ddlDepartment").change(function()
            {
                $("#ddlEmployee").html("");
                var DepartmentID =
$("#ddlDepartment >
option[@selected]").attr("value");
                if (DepartmentID != 0)
                {
                    $.getJSON('LoadEmployees.ashx?
DepartmentID=' + DepartmentID,
function(getEmployees)
                    {
                        $.each(getEmployees, function()
                        {
$("#ddlEmployee").append
($("<option></option>").val
(this['EmployeeID']).html
(this['EmployeeName']));
                        });
                    });
                }
            });
        });
    </script>
```

And you are done! When you execute the application, the output will be similar to what you saw in Figure 19-5 earlier in the chapter.

The Complete Source

Here is what the complete source code for the LoadEmployees HttpHandler looks like:

Listing 19-10

```
using System.Web;
using System.Text;
namespace DataBinding
{
    public class LoadEmployees : IHttpHandler
    {
        public void ProcessRequest(HttpContext context)
        {
            string DepartmentID =
context.Request.QueryString["DepartmentID"];
            StringBuilder strCities = new StringBuilder();
            if (DepartmentID.Equals("1"))
            {
                strCities.Append("[");
                strCities.Append("{");
                strCities.Append
("\"EmployeeName\":\"Oindrilla Roy Chowdhury\",");
                strCities.Append("\"EmployeeID\":\"1\"");
                strCities.Append("},");
                strCities.Append("{");
                strCities.Append
("\"EmployeeName\":\"Soma Roy Chowdhury\",");
                strCities.Append("\"EmployeeID\":\"2\"");
                strCities.Append("}");
                strCities.Append("]");
            }
            else if (DepartmentID.Equals("2"))
            {
                strCities.Append("[");
                strCities.Append("{");
                strCities.Append
("\"EmployeeName\":\"Joydip Kanjilal\",");
                strCities.Append("\"EmployeeID\":\"3\"");
                strCities.Append("},");
                strCities.Append("{");
                strCities.Append("\"EmployeeName\":\"Debashis Deb\",");
                strCities.Append("\"EmployeeID\":\"4\"");
                strCities.Append("}");
                strCities.Append("]");
            }
            else if (DepartmentID.Equals("3"))
            {
                strCities.Append("[");
                strCities.Append("{");
                strCities.Append
```

```
("\"EmployeeName\":\
"Tilok Tarafder\",");
                strCities.Append("\"EmployeeID\":\"5\"");
                strCities.Append("},");
                strCities.Append("{");
                strCities.Append
("\"EmployeeName\":\
"Vinod Kumar Naidu\",");
                strCities.Append("\"EmployeeID\":\"6\"");
                strCities.Append("}");
                strCities.Append("]");
            }
            else if (DepartmentID.Equals("4"))
            {
                strCities.Append("[");
                strCities.Append("{");
                strCities.Append("\"EmployeeName\":\"Sanjit Sil\",");
                strCities.Append("\"EmployeeID\":\"7\"");
                strCities.Append("},");
                strCities.Append("{");
                strCities.Append
("\"EmployeeName\":\
"Indronil Roy Chowdhury\",");
                strCities.Append("\"EmployeeID\":\"8\"");
                strCities.Append("}");
                strCities.Append("]");
            }
            context.Response.ContentType = "application/json";
            context.Response.ContentEncoding = Encoding.UTF8;
            context.Response.Write(strCities.ToString());
            context.Response.End();
        }
        public bool IsReusable
        {
            get
            {
                return false;
            }
        }
    }
}
```

And here's the complete source code of the Default.aspx for your reference:

Listing 19-11
```
<%@ Page Language="C#"
EnableEventValidation="false"
AutoEventWireup="true"
CodeBehind="Default.aspx.cs"
Inherits="DataBinding._Default" %>
```

```
<!DOCTYPE html PUBLIC
"-//W3C//DTD XHTML 1.0 Transitional//EN"
 "http://www.w3.org/TR/xhtml1/DTD/
xhtml1-transitional.dtd">
<html xmlns="http://www.w3.org/1999/xhtml" >
<head runat="server">
    <script src="Scripts/jquery-1.2.6.js"
 type="text/javascript"></script>
    <script type ="text/javascript">
        $(document).ready(function()
        {
            $("#ddlDepartment").change(function()
            {
                $("#ddlEmployee").html("");
                var DepartmentID =
$("#ddlDepartment >
option[@selected]").attr("value");
                if (DepartmentID != 0)
                {
                    $.getJSON('LoadEmployees.ashx?
DepartmentID=' + DepartmentID,
 function(getEmployees)
                    {
                        $.each(getEmployees, function()
                        {
$("#ddlEmployee").append($("<option></option>").val
(this['EmployeeID']).html(this['EmployeeName']));
                        });
                    });
                }
            });
        });
    </script>
    <title>Client-Side Data Binding Using jQuery</title>
</head>
<body>
    <form id="form1" runat="server">
    <div>
    <table>
       <tr>
        <td>Department:</td>
        <td>
            <asp:DropDownList ID="ddlDepartment" runat="server">
            <asp:ListItem Value="0">--Select--</asp:ListItem>
            <asp:ListItem Value="1">Sales and Marketing</asp:ListItem>
            <asp:ListItem Value="2">Software Development</asp:ListItem>
            <asp:ListItem Value="3">Finance</asp:ListItem>
            <asp:ListItem Value="4">Human Resources</asp:ListItem>
```

```
                    </asp:DropDownList>
             </td>
             </tr>
             <tr>
             <td>Employee:</td>
             <td>
                    <asp:DropDownList ID="ddlEmployee" runat="server">
                    </asp:DropDownList>
             </td>
             </tr>
      </table>
          </div>
          </form>
      </body>
      </html>
```

Event Handling in jQuery

jQuery has made event handling much easier by providing a collection of simple event-binding methods and a consistent event context. jQuery provides the .bind() and .unbind() functions to attach and detach event handlers on matched sets. The event handlers accept the function as a parameter; the event object is always passed as a parameter to the event handler; and the "this" pointer refers to the element on which the event has been fired. The normalized event object in jQuery enables you to bridge browser differences—you can run the same event-binding code in almost all web browsers.

You can perform tasks, such as displaying a welcome message or doing some default processing, on loading a web page by using the $(document).ready() event handler. Here is an example that illustrates how you can use this event handler:

Listing 19-12
```
$(document).ready(function()
{
$("span").text("The document ready event handler has been triggered.");
});
```

Even though JavaScript's window.onload seems similar to jQuery's $(document).ready() event handler, there is a striking difference between the two. The former is triggered when the document has been completely downloaded in the web browser. As a result, all the DOM elements can be accessed using JavaScript at this point in time. In contrast, a handler that has been registered with the $(document).ready() event handler is invoked when the DOM for that web page is ready for use. While this indicates that the DOM elements are accessible to your script code, it does not mean that the associated files have all been downloaded. In essence, this event handler enables you to learn when the document is ready to be accessed and the scripts have completed loading. This handler is declared using an anonymous function, which implies that it is inlined inside the .ready() function call.

Method Name	Description
bind	This method is used to associate a method with one or more events for each element contained in a wrapped set.
live	This method is used to bind an event handler to all current and future elements contained in a wrapped set.
One	This method works the same way as the bind method except that it is removed automatically after it has been executed once.
trigger	This method fires the event handler once for each element contained in a wrapped set.
triggerHandler	This method is similar to trigger with the exception that it cancels the default browser activities.
unbind	This method is used to remove the elements previously bound to the wrapped set.

TABLE 19-1   Event-handling methods in jQuery

Table 19-1 summarizes the event-handling methods of the jQuery library. Consider the following markup code:

Listing 19-13
```
<body>
    <form id="form1" runat="server">
    <div>
        <asp:Label ID="Label1"
runat="server"
Text="Click Here">
</asp:Label>
    </div>
    </form>
</body>
```

The following code snippet illustrates how you can trap the mouse-click event to display the coordinates.

Listing 19-14
```
$(document).ready(function() {
        $("#Label1").bind("click", function(e) {
            var str = "X: " + e.pageX + ", Y: " + e.pageY;
            alert("Mouse Clicked at " + str);
        });
```

Table 19-2 lists the events and their purpose in jQuery.

Event Name	Description
beforeunload	This event is fired when the browser window is unloaded or closed explicitly by the user.
blur	This event is fired when a particular element loses focus.
change	This event is fired when a particular element has been changed since it regained focus.
click	This event is fired when the user clicks on a particular element.
dblclick	This event is fired when the user double-clicks on a particular element.
Error	This event is fired when a JavaScript error is detected.
focus	This event is fired when a particular element gains focus.
keydown	This event is fired when a key is pressed.
keypress	This event is fired when a particular key is pressed and then released.
keyup	This event is fired when a particular key is released.
load	This event is fired when a particular element has completed loading.
mousedown	This event is fired when a mouse button is pressed by the user.
mouseenter	This event is fired when the mouse enters an area of a particular element.
mouseleave	This event is fired when the mouse leaves the area occupied by a particular element.
mousemove	This event is fired when the mouse is moved while it is over a particular element.
mouseout	This event is fired when the mouse moves out of the area of a particular element.
mouseover	This event is fired when the mouse enters the area occupied by a particular element. It is also fired when the mouse enters the area occupied by the child elements of a particular element.
mouseup	This event is fired when the user releases the mouse button.
resize	This event is fired when a particular element is resized.
scroll	This event is fired when you scroll a particular element.
select	This event is fired when the user selects text in a text field control.
submit	This event is fired when the form is submitted by the user.
unload	This event is fired when the browser window is unloaded from the memory.

TABLE 19-2 Events in jQuery

You can also trap the mouse-up and mouse-down events and display appropriate messages, as shown in the following code:

Listing 19-15
```
$("div").mouseup(function() {
          $(this).append('<span style="color:Orange;">
Mouse Up.</span>');
          }).mousedown(function() {
          $(this).append('<span style="color:Teal;">
Mouse Down.</span>');
          });
```

You can easily trap the keypress event to validate user input. Here is an example:

Listing 19-16
```
$(document).ready(function() {
          $("#TextBox1").keypress(function(e) {
              if ((e.which >= 65 && e.which <= 90)
|| (e.which >= 97 && e.which <= 122) || e.which == 32)
                  alert("Input is valid");
              else {
                  alert("Input is invalid");
              }
          });
```

Table 19-3 illustrates the members of the jQuery event object.

Plug-Ins in jQuery

One of the greatest benefits of using the jQuery library is that it provides excellent support for extensibility through the use of plug-ins. Plug-ins in jQuery enable you to attach methods and functionality to the jQuery library to facilitate extensibility. There are numerous jQuery plug-ins available—you can develop one yourself!

Member	Description
type	This is used to retrieve the event's name.
target	This is used to retrieve a reference to the DOM element that is the target of the event.
pageX	This is used to retrieve the X mouse coordinate.
pageY	This is used to retrieve the Y mouse coordinate.
preventDefault	This is used to cancel the default browser action for a particular event.
stopPropagation	This is used to stop event bubbling.

TABLE 19-3   Members of the jQuery Event object

You need to wrap a plug-in as shown in the following code snippet:

Listing 19-17   `$.fn.PlugInName = function(){};`

So, if you are implementing a plug-in called CenterImage, you should wrap the plug-in like this:

Listing 19-18   `$.fn.CenterImage = function() {};`

Selectors in jQuery

Selectors are one of the most powerful features in the jQuery library. They enable you to easily access elements or groups of elements in the DOM. jQuery provides you with CSS and XPath selectors to access DOM elements seamlessly; most of jQuery's capabilities revolve around selectors.

Suppose you have an HTML table and you would like to style the table with CSS. If you have a CSS that contains the styles for the header and odd and even rows, you can simply use the following syntax to apply styles to the table:

Listing 19-19
```
<script type="text/javascript">
        $(document).ready(function() {
        $('th').parent().addClass('header');
            $('tr:odd').addClass('odd');
            $('tr:even').addClass('even');
        });
</script>
```

You can select the first td in a table using jQuery's :first filter, like this:

Listing 19-20   `$("td:first").text("This is the first <TD>");`

Or, you can select the last td using :last, as shown in the following code snippet:

Listing 19-21   `$("td:last").text("This is the last <TD>");`

jQuery allows you to concatenate multiple statements in a single statement—a feature known as chainability. In essence, the jQuery wrapper methods return a reference to the jQuery instance, which can in turn be used to create a chain of operations. Here is an example:

Listing 19-22   `$('#td1').addclass('yourCustomStyleClass');`

Here's another example:

Listing 19-23   `$('#btnAddRecord').addclass('yourCustomButtonStyleClass').AddRecord();`

Animations in jQuery

jQuery has great support for animations. You can use the following code snippet to fade out and then fade in a table:

Listing 19-24
```
$(document).ready(function()
    {
        $("#table1").fadeOut(5000); $("#table1").fadeIn(5000);
    }
);
```

The animate function in jQuery can be used to implement custom animations. Here is the complete syntax of the animate function:

Listing 19-25
```
animate( params, [duration], [easing], [callback] )
```

The params parameter denotes a style that you would like to animate. The duration parameter is optional—it's a string that contains one of these values:

- slow
- normal
- fast
- the number of milliseconds the animation should execute

The next parameter, easing, is also an optional parameter, and it can contain one of these two values:

- linear
- swing

The callback parameter is also optional, and it denotes the name of the function that should be executed when the animation is completed. Note that this callback function will be called once for each element on which the animation has been set.

Here is a typical example of how the animate function can be used:

Listing 19-26
```
$("#btnAnimate").click(function(){
        $("#blockToAnimate").animate({
          width: "50%",
          opacity: 0.5,
          marginLeft: "0.8in",
          fontSize: "3em",
          borderWidth: "20px"
        }, 2500 );
    });
```

Let's look at how to implement a simple text animation using the jQuery animate() function. Let's put a span control in a web form with some custom text:

Listing 19-27

```
<span id="animateSpan">Illustrating Animation in jQuery</span>
```

Next, add a button control to the web form—this control will be used to start the animation when it is clicked:

Listing 19-28

```
<input type="button" value="Animate" id="btnAnimate" />
```

Here is how you would call the animate() function in the click event of the button control and use jQuery to animate the text in the span control:

Listing 19-29

```
$("#btnAnimate").click(function() {
        $("#animateSpan").animate({
            width: "50%",
            opacity: 0.56,
            fontSize: "50pt",
            borderWidth: "5px",
            marginLeft: "150px",
            paddingLeft: "250px"
        }, 1500);
    })
```

Consuming a Web Service Using jQuery

Web services enable programs written in different languages running on different platforms to communicate with each other. Web services are based on the Simple Object Access Protocol (SOAP) and are used for exchanging data in heterogeneous environments. You can use jQuery to consume Web services much the same way you can with JavaScript, but more simply.

Consider the following Web service:

Listing 19-30

```
[WebService(Namespace = "http://tempuri.org/")]
[WebServiceBinding(ConformsTo = WsiProfiles.BasicProfile1_1)]
[System.Web.Script.Services.ScriptService]
public class TestWebservice : System.Web.Services.WebService
{
  [WebMethod()]
  public string GetToken()
  {
      return "MGH";
  }
}
```

Here is the syntax you can use to consume the preceding Web service using jQuery:

Listing 19-3
```
$.ajax({
    type: "POST",
    contentType: "application/json; charset=utf-8",
    url: "WebServiceName.asmx/WebMethodName",
    data: "{}",
    dataType: "json"
});
```

Here is the complete markup code that you can use to call the GetToken web method from jQuery in your ASP.NET application:

Listing 19-3
```
<head>
    <title>Calling a Web Service using jQuery in ASP.NET</title>
    <script type="text/javascript" src="jquery-1.2.6.min.js"></script>
<script type="text/javascript">
    $(document).ready(function() {
        $.ajax({
            type: "POST",
            url: "http://TestWebService.asmx/GetToken",
            contentType: "application/json; charset=utf-8",
            data: "{}",
            dataType: "json",
            success: OnSuccess,
            error: OnFailure
        });
    });
    function OnSuccess(result)
    {
        alert("Success!");
    }
    function OnFailure (result)
    {
        alert("The call to the web method failed.");
    }
</script>
</head>
```

Note the use of the OnSuccess and OnFailure functions—they will be called based on whether or not the call to the web method succeeds.

CHAPTER 20

Improving ASP.NET 4.0 Application Performance and Scalability

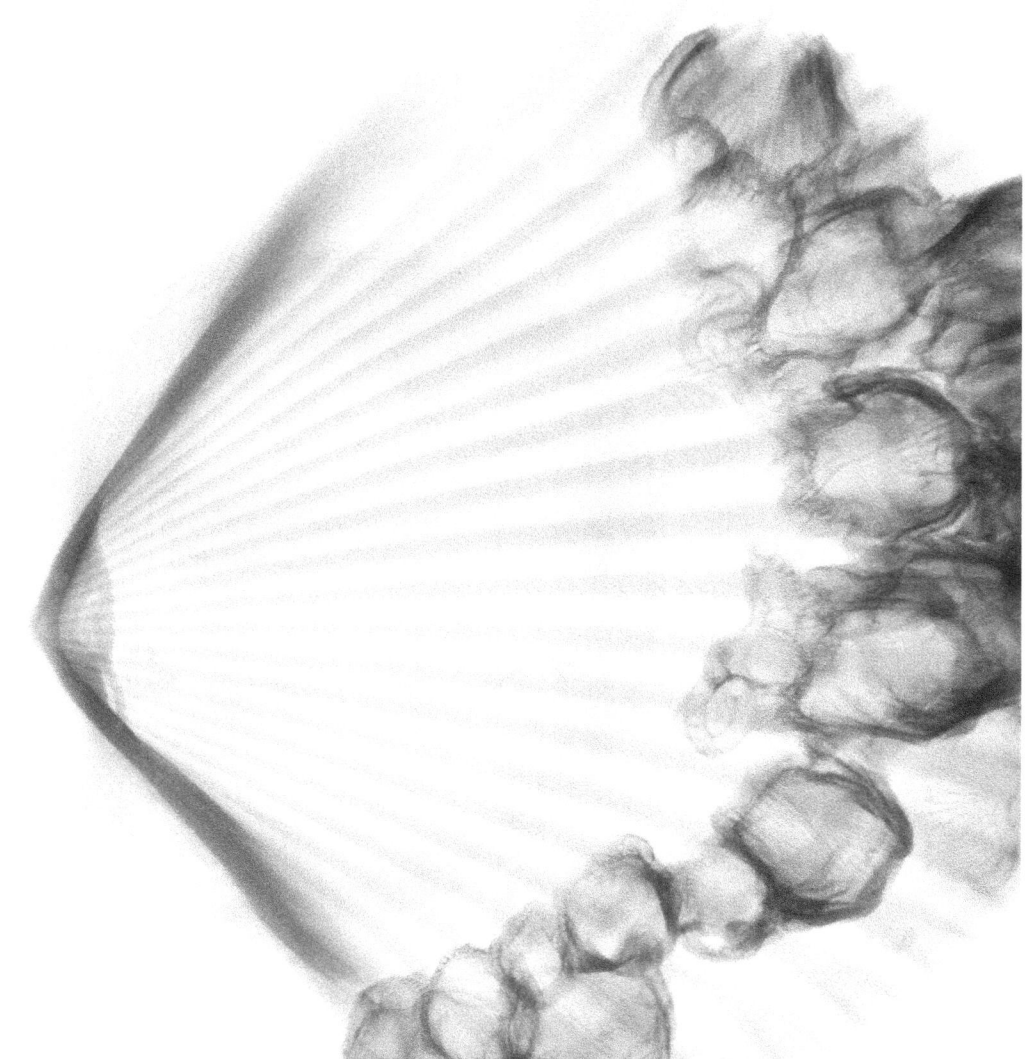

T he most important factors for boosting an application's performance are memory load, processor load, and network bandwidth. This chapter, the last in our journey towards mastering ASP.NET 4.0, will introduce you to the best practices for improving application performance and scalability. Although there is no single methodology that can fit each and every environment, the best practices and guidelines outlined in this chapter can help boost your application's performance to a considerable extent.

Improving Response Times

Response time is the total time it takes for the client to receive a response after sending a request to the web server. Response times of ASP.NET web pages can be improved in various ways, as discussed in the following sections.

Using the Page.IsPostBack Property

You should use the IsPostBack Boolean property of the Page class to reduce network traffic and server processing on a round trip. The following code illustrates how you can make use of Page.IsPostBack to avoid redundant database hits and server processing:

Listing 20-1
```
private void Page_Load(object sender,System.EventArgs e)
  {
     if(!IsPostBack)
       BindDropDownList();
     //Other code
  }
private void BindDropDownList()
  {
     //Code to populate a DataSet instance
     //with data from a database table and then
     //bind it to a DropDownList control
  }
```

As you can see in the preceding code, the BindDropDownList() method is called only the first time the page is loaded. This reduces database hits and unnecessary processing on the server when you are working with relatively constant (or *stale*) data that doesn't change across postbacks. Note that database hits are always costly and should be avoided as much as possible.

Here is a code snippet that illustrates how you can measure the time taken by a web page to render:

Listing 20-2
```
DateTime startTime = DateTime.Now;
protected override void OnPreRender(EventArgs e)
{
 base.OnPreRender(e);
 long timetaken = (DateTime.Now - startTime).TotalMilliseconds;
}
```

Removing Unused HttpModules

You should remove the unused or unnecessary HttpModules from your application's code so as to remove them from the pipeline and improve performance. Here is the list of modules defined in the machine.config file by default:

Listing 20-3
```
<httpModules>
   <add name="OutputCache"
type="System.Web.Caching.OutputCacheModule" />
   <add name="Session"
type="System.Web.SessionState.
SessionStateModule" />
   <add name="WindowsAuthentication"
type="System.Web.Security.
WindowsAuthenticationModule" />
   <add name="FormsAuthentication"
type="System.Web.Security.
FormsAuthenticationModule" />
   <add name="PassportAuthentication"
type="System.Web.Security.
PassportAuthenticationModule" />
   <add name="UrlAuthorization"
type="System.Web.Security.
UrlAuthorizationModule" />
   <add name="FileAuthorization"
type="System.Web.Security.FileAuthorizationModule" />
   <add name="ErrorHandlerModule"
type="System.Web.Mobile.ErrorHandlerModule,
 System.Web.Mobile, Version=1.0.5000.0,
Culture=neutral,
PublicKeyToken=b03f5f7f11d50a3a" />
</httpModules>
```

So, how do you remove the modules you don't need? To remove these modules from the pipeline, you can specify the following in the <httpModules> section of your application's web.config file:

Listing 20-4
```
<httpModules>
   <remove name="Session" />
   <remove name="WindowsAuthentication" />
   <remove name="PassportAuthentication" />
   <remove name="FileAuthorization" />
   <remove name="UrlAuthorization" />
   <remove name="AnonymousIdentification" />
</httpModules>
```

Enabling Page Buffering

A buffer is a region of the main memory that can store temporary data for input and output operations. Buffering improves performance to a great extent as retrieval of data from the main memory is always faster compared to retrieval of data from the disk. You should also set page buffering on unless there is a specific reason to turn it off (page buffering is turned on by default). To use this feature, set Response.Buffer to true, batch all your work on the server, and then call the Response.Flush() method.

You can enable buffering at the page level with the following directive:

Listing 20-5
```
<%@ Page Buffer = "true"... %>
```

You can also set buffering at the application level for all pages in your application by using the <pages> element in the application's web.config file, as follows:

Listing 20-6
```
<pages buffer = "true">
```

Trimming Page Sizes

Reduce page sizes in order to reduce network traffic, such as by removing any unnecessary space and tab characters from the pages.

Also, note that scripts block parallel downloads, so it is always a good practice to ensure that scripts are placed at the bottom of the web page. However, style sheets should be placed at the top for faster rendering. If they are at the bottom, they will disallow progressive rendering of a web page. You can use script includes for static scripts so that they can be cached at the client for subsequent requests.

Here is an example that illustrates how you can use script includes in your web page:

Listing 20-7
```
<script language=javascript src="testscript.js">
```

Another good practice is combining both multiple scripts and style sheets into single files at the time of deployment. This will reduce the number of HTTP requests and improve rendering speed.

For Ajax-enabled web pages, you can set the LoadScriptsBeforeUI attribute to false to ensure that additional script references are added at the end of the <Body> tag. Additionally, you can set the ScriptMode property of the ScriptManager control to false to ensure that the Ajax runtime scripts emitted are optimized. Here is an example:

Listing 20-8
```
<asp:ScriptManager ID ="ScriptManager1"
 runat ="server"
EnablePartialRendering = "true"
 LoadScriptsBeforeUI ="false"
ScriptMode ="Release">
</asp:ScriptManager>
```

Avoid using large images in web pages, and make sure they are optimized for size and display. Also, avoid using nested tables and redundant tags. Finally, you can preload components to take advantage of a browser's idle time. This will boost performance to a noticeable extent.

Using IIS Compression

You can use HTTP compression in IIS to cut down on page sizes. Although there is a slight performance penalty in using HTTP compression, because it requires some extra processing by the web server, it is still recommended. The performance penalty is negligible compared to the huge benefit you get from it; compression can greatly reduce network bandwidth. You can also use compression tools to compress the rendered content.

Using Server.Transfer and Response.Redirect

In this section we will discuss when you should use Server.Transfer and when you should use Response.Redirect methods in your applications. Server.Transfer and Response.Redirect are your choices when you need to redirect from one page to another. Response.Redirect sends a response header to the client that causes the client to send a new request back to the server, so you should use Server.Transfer to redirect to another page within the same application to avoid an unnecessary round trip to the client.

However, you cannot always just replace Response.Redirect calls with Server.Transfer. You need to use Response.Redirect if authentication and authorization checks are required. Further, you can only use Server.Transfer to transfer control to pages within the same application. To transfer to pages in other applications, you must use Response.Redirect.

If using Response.Redirect is a necessity, you can pass a Boolean value false to the overloaded Response.Redirect method to suppress the exception that is raised.

Precompiling

Precompilation is a feature that enables you to precompile your application's code so that the initial load time is minimized. You can precompile web pages in your application to reduce the working set size and minimize the initial load time of your application. You can precompile your application in two ways: in-place precompilation, and precompilation for deployment. While the former enables you to precompile all the web pages of your application and display errors if any, the latter enables you to precompile your application prior to deploying it in the production environment.

Using AutoEventWireUp

You should disable AutoEventWireUp before you deploy your application to the production environment. Note that if the AutoEventWireUp attribute is set to true, the page events get auto-wired.

You can set AutoEventWireUp to false at the page or the application level. Here is how you can set it at the page level:

Listing 20-9
```
<%@ Page Language="C#"
Codebehind="Default.aspx.cs"
 AutoEventWireup="false" %>
```

You can also set the AutoEventWireup attribute to false in the pages section of your application's configuration file:

Listing 20-10
```
<configuration>
   <system.web>
     <pages autoEventWireup="true|false" />
   </system.web>
</configuration>
```

Efficient State-Management Strategies

An efficient state-management strategy plays a major role in boosting an application's performance and scalability as a whole. There are various ways in which an ASP.NET state can be managed efficiently. This section discusses the best strategies as far as state management in ASP.NET is concerned.

Setting Session State

Ensure that you don't store too many objects or large objects in the Session. You should disable Session state if it is not required.

To disable Session state for a specific page, you can use the following markup code:

Listing 20-11
```
<%@ Page EnableSessionState="false" %>
```

To disable Session state for the entire application, use the following code in the web.config file:

Listing 20-12
```
<sessionState mode='Off'/>
```

To disable Session state for all applications that run on the web server, use the following code in the machine.config file:

Listing 20-13
```
<sessionState mode='Off'/>
```

You can also set the Session to read-only for web pages that don't change or don't need to change a value in the Session. Here is how you can achieve this:

Listing 20-14
```
<%@ Page EnableSessionState="ReadOnly"%>
```

To optimize an application's performance, you should also choose the right type of Session storage mode. The correct type depends on a number of factors, such as speed, security, scalability, and reliability. Of the three modes available, InProc is the fastest, though it is not a good choice in a production environment, especially when scalability is important. You can opt for OutProc mode for web sites that have a large amount of traffic and where you need scalability. As far as security is concerned, the SQLServer Storage mode is the best choice.

Reducing Size of ViewState

ViewState is great for storing control state, but it can degrade performance, especially on web sites with large page sizes. Every byte added to a web page by enabling its ViewState causes two bytes of network traffic—one in each direction.

You should reduce the size of ViewState to reduce the page size and hence the network traffic. You can remove the runat="server" form tag completely to reduce page size. If you don't remove this tag, the page passes on about 20 bytes of information to ViewState even when the page's ViewState property is set to false.

ViewState for a web page is turned on by default. To disable ViewState for a single page, set the EnableViewState property to false in the Page directive, as shown here:

Listing 20-15
```
<%@ Page EnableViewState="false" %>
```

To disable ViewState for the entire application, you can specify the following line in the application's web.config file:

Listing 20-16
```
<pages enableViewState="false" />
```

To disable ViewState for all applications, specify the following in the machine.config file:

Listing 20-17
```
<pages enableViewState="false" />
```

Setting Up Caching

Caching improves the performance of web applications to a great extent by storing relatively stale data in memory and serving that data to the application when it is asked for. You have a number of choices for caching data: page output caching, page fragment caching, and data caching. You should cache the right data and choose the right type of caching for your application.

Best Practices in Exception Management

Exceptions are errors that occur at runtime, and improper use of exceptions can drastically reduce the performance of your application. You should try to avoid using exceptions in code unless there is a sufficient reason to do use them. Exceptions take longer to process and hence decrease the application's performance to a considerable extent.

You should not use exceptions to control business logic. Use proper validation techniques to avoid throwing unnecessary exceptions. Here is an example of what you shouldn't do:

Listing 20-18
```
try
{
  ValidateLogin(username, password);
}
catch(Exception e)
{
  ShowMessage();
}
```

The preceding code can be revised to avoid exceptions. Here is an optimized version:

Listing 20-19
```
if(ValidateLogin(username, password))
{
  //Some code
}
else
{
 ShowMessage();
}
```

Avoid rethrowing exceptions because they are expensive—the stack trace is lost and a new stack trace is created. Here is some code that does that:

Listing 20-20
```
try
{
    // Some code that raises an exception
}
catch(Exception ex)
{
    throw ex;
}
```

Here is an optimized version of the preceding code snippet:

Listing 20-21
```
try
{
    // Some code that raises an exception
}
catch(Exception ex)
{
    throw;
}
```

By using the throw statement as shown in Listing 20-21, the stack trace information is not lost. The exception simply gets propagated to the next higher level and the stack trace is preserved.

Efficient Data-Access Strategies

You should optimize your queries for better performance, especially in data-driven applications. You should always choose the right type of data container when storing data in memory.

DataReaders are preferable compared with DataSets for reading data in your application. A DataReader is always faster and consumes much less memory than a DataSet does. DataSets are heavy and consume more memory resources—use them only when you need to. You can use custom business entity classes in lieu of DataSets to pass data from one layer of the application to another, as they are lightweight objects and consume far fewer resources for loading and processing.

Also, ensure that you open database connections as late as possible and release them as early as possible for best utilization of connection pools in your application.

Using Connection Pooling Efficiently

A connection pool is a container of open and reusable connections. Usage of connection pooling boosts the application's performance to a considerable extent. If connection pooling is turned on (as it is by default), a new connection is not created each time the application requests a connection. Rather, a connection from the connection pool is returned to the application. In essence, connection pooling provides you with a pool of ready-to-use idle connections that become live when the need arises. When a connection is closed or disposed of, it is returned to the connection pool. Such connections remain idle until a request for a new connection comes in again.

The data providers in ADO.NET have connection pooling turned on by default. If you need to turn it off, specify Pooling = false in the connection string. Connection pooling, if used efficiently, improves the application's performance to a great extent because the opening and closing of database connections become less resource-intensive.

Using Stored Procedures to Reduce Network Traffic

You should also consider using stored procedures and parameterized queries to reduce the amount of data sent to the server, especially when the application does a lot of data access. Using stored procedures over dynamic queries boosts application performance because it doesn't need to be interpreted, compiled, or even transmitted from the client. As a result, the network traffic and server overhead is reduced.

When a stored procedure is being executed, SQL Server creates an execution plan in memory. Subsequent executions of the procedure are much faster because the plan is already available. In contrast, execution plans for SQL queries are re-created each time the query is executed, resulting in poor performance.

Another point to note here is that when a stored procedure is executed, a message is transmitted from the server to the client that indicates the number of rows that have been affected. You can turn this off to reduce network traffic by including the following statement at the beginning of all the stored procedures you use in your application:

Listing 20-22
```
SET NOCOUNT ON
```

Using Batched Queries

Queries can be executed in a batch to reduce database hits and hence improve performance. Here is an example:

Listing 20-23
```
String connectionString = " … "; // Some connection string
SqlConnection sqlConnection = new SqlConnection();
SqlCommand sqlCommand = new SqlCommand();
sqlConnection.ConnectionString = connectionString;
  try
```

```
{
 sqlConnection.Open();
 sqlCommand.CommandText =
"Select * from Employee; Select * from Department";
 sqlCommand.Connection = sqlConnection;
 SqlDataReader sqlDataReader = sqlCommand.ExecuteReader();
 sqlDataReader.NextResult();
}
catch(Exception e)
{
      //Usual code
}
finally
{
      sqlConnection.Close();
}
```

Efficient Memory and Resource Management Strategies

Efficient memory and resource management in applications goes a long way toward boosting an application's performance as a whole.

Helping Compiler Optimizations

You should write code that helps in compiler optimizations by optimizing assignments, marking classes as sealed if they don't need to be inherited, and so on.

Avoid implementing Finalize unless it is absolutely necessary. This is because if a class has a finalize method implemented inside it, an instance of the class would have to pass through two generations before it is eventually garbage collected. This extra pass increases the overhead involved in cleaning the instance from the memory and hence slows down the application's performance. Also, avoid calling GC.Collect() in your code and always consider using weak references with cached data.

Avoid writing statements such as x = x + 1; it is always preferable to use statements such as x+=1 instead, because in x = x + 1 the JIT evaluates the variable x twice, which is unnecessary.

Also, refrain from using methods that have variable number of parameters. If you have a method with variable number of parameters, code paths would be generated for each possible combination of parameters—this is a potential hindrance to the application's performance. Hence, you should replace such methods with overloaded methods. Classes those need not be inherited should be marked with the "sealed" keyword.

Using Objects Efficiently

You should always avoid promoting objects to higher generations—avoid referring to a short-lived object from a long-lived one. The garbage collector in .NET works in three generations. Generations are actually regions in the managed heap. These generations are: generation 0, generation 1, and generation 2. The short-lived objects are generally placed in lower generations and the longer-lived objects are placed in the higher generations in memory. The garbage collector works much less frequently in the higher generation to clean up objects than it does in the lower generations. Here is an example that illustrates how an object can be unnecessarily promoted to a higher generation:

Listing 20-24
```
class Test
   {
    ArrayList arrList;
     void SomeMethod (ArrayList arrList)
       {
         this.arrList = arrList;
         //Some code
       }
   }
```

Avoid using objects in the class scope unless it is absolutely necessary. It is better to use local objects in lieu of objects in higher scopes so that they remain in memory for less time.

A method call is always an expensive operation. You should consider using inline code for methods that have few statements. Here is an example of a simple method:

Listing 20-25
```
for(int index=0; index< 100;index++)
{
   DisplayMessage();
}
void DisplayMessage()
{
Console.WriteLine("Hello");
}
```

Imagine the number of calls made to the DisplayMessage() method. It is always preferable to inline code in such situations. Here is the optimized code:

Listing 20-26
```
for(int index=0; index< 100;index++)
{
Console.WriteLine("Hello");
}
```

Using Loops

Avoid creating instances inside loops unless there is a specific reason to do so. Here is an example:

Listing 20-27
```
for(int index=0;index<100;index++)
{
   ArrayList arrList = new ArrayList();
   // Some code
}
```

As you can see in the preceding code snippet, each time the loop iterates, a new ArrayList instance is created. Here is the optimized version of the preceding code:

Listing 20-28
```
ArrayList arrList = new ArrayList();
for(int index=0;index<100;index++)
{
   // Now use the ArrayList instance here
}
```

Calling methods or properties inside a loop are also expensive operations. Here is an example that illustrates this:

Listing 20-29
```
ArrayList arrList = new ArrayList();
arrList.Add("Joydip");
arrList.Add("Jini");
arrList.Add("Jane");
arrList.Add("Carly");
for(int i=0; i<arrList.Length;i++)
{
 //Some code
}
```

As you can see in the preceding code, the length property of the ArrayList instance is called every time the loop iterates. For efficiency, the same code can be written as follows:

Listing 20-30
```
ArrayList arrList = new ArrayList();
arrList.Add("Joydip");
arrList.Add("Jini");
arrList.Add("Jane");
arrList.Add("Carly");
for(int i=0, j = arrList.Length; i<j;i++)
{
 //Some code
}
```

Avoiding Finalize and Using Dispose

Avoid implementing Finalize unless there is a specific reason to do so. Also, you should free or dispose of resources that are no longer needed.

Here is an example that illustrates how you can release resources that are no longer in use or are no longer needed in the code:

Listing 20-31
```
//Code that creates a database connection instance
try
{
 con.Open(); //Opens the connection to the database
 //Perform some processing
}
```

```
catch(Exception e)
{
//Write your exception handling code here
}
finally
{
  con.Close(); //Close the database connection here
}
```

Using the Using Block

You can also use the using block as a short form of a try ... finally combination. Note that you can use the using block only for objects that implement the IDisposable interface.

Here is an example that illustrates how you can use the using block in your code:

Listing 20-32
```
using(SqlConnection con = new SqlConnection(connectionString))
{
try
{
 con.Open(); //Opens the connection
 //Perform some processing
}
catch(Exception e)
{
//Write your exception handling code here
}
}
```

Refer to listing 20-31 above. The connection instance has been created and opened inside the scope of the "using" block. In doing this, you need not bother about how the connection instance will be disposed. As soon as the control comes out of the using block, the connection to the database would be closed.

Using Locking and Synchronization

Synchronization is the technique of restricting access to resources when multiple threads need to access them. This is done to avoid conflicts that may arise out of concurrent accesses to a particular resource. You should avoid locking and synchronization unless it is absolutely necessary. You should also always acquire resources as late as possible and release them as early as possible.

When locking objects, ensure that you don't lock on this—the current instance. If you lock on the current object instance (this), all the members of the object are also locked irrespective of whether a lock is required on them. You should also not lock on the type of the object. Rather, you can use a private object to set a lock in your application's code.

Here is an example that illustrates how you can set a lock on an instance efficiently:

Listing 20-33
```
public class Test
{
  private static readonly lockObj = new Object();
  public static Test Singleton
{
  lock(lockObj)
    {
      return new Test();
    }
}
}
}
```

Managing Strings

There are several ways to efficiently manage strings:

- Avoid comparing strings using the == operator.
- Create empty strings using the String.Empty property.
- Test for empty strings using the String.Length property.
- Avoid creating string instances inside a loop.

Here is an example that illustrates how you can use the Length property to test for empty strings:

Listing 20-34
```
String str = "Joydip";
if(str.Length != 0)
Console.WriteLine("The string is not empty");
else
Console.WriteLine("The string is empty");
```

You should also use StringBuilder when you need to concatenate a number of strings. String is immutable, which means that whenever you make any changes to one, you get a whole new String instance. StringBuilder, on the other hand, uses the same buffer to store strings.

Here is an example that repeatedly creates new String instances:

Listing 20-35
```
String str = String.Empty;
for(int index=0; index < 100; index++)
{
    str += index.ToString();
}
```

The following code is the optimized version of the preceding snippet, which will not create any extra String allocations in the heap.

Listing 20-36
```
StringBuilder strBuilder = new StringBuilder();
for(int index=0; index < 100; index++)
{
    strBuilder.Append(index.ToString());
}
```

Avoid Using Late Binding

Binding refers to the act of associating an instance of a class with its member. Binding can be of two types: early binding or late binding.

Late binding adds flexibility, but it is always slow compared to early binding. Late binding is implemented using virtual methods. When a class contains one or more virtual methods, a virtual table is created in memory for that class that contains the mapping information for those virtual methods. The runtime then uses the virtual table to map the virtual methods to the objects on which they are called. As a result, there is additional overhead involved (more processor and memory resource usage) in binding a virtual method to the instance of the class on which the method has been called.

Hence, you should always avoid using late binding in your code. Though it can add flexibility, it would be at the cost of the application's performance.

The following code illustrates how you can implement late binding in C#:

Listing 20-37
```csharp
using System;
namespace Chapter_19
{
    class Base
    {
        public virtual void Display()
        {
            Console.WriteLine("Display method of Base called...");
        }
    }
    class Derived : Base
    {
        public override void Display()
        {
            Console.WriteLine("Display method of Derived called...");
        }
    }
    class Program
    {
        static void Main(string[] args)
        {
            Base b = new Derived();
            b.Display();
            Console.Read();
        }
    }
}
```

Selecting the Right Collections

When using collections, you should choose the right type of collection to avoid the overhead of boxing and unboxing. It is preferable to use strongly typed arrays instead of collections for this reason. However, if using collections is a must, analyze your requirements, select the right collection type, and initialize the collection instances to the appropriate size.

Generic collections are a good choice because they are strongly typed; you can use them to eliminate the boxing and unboxing overhead.

Collection classes in .NET are defined as part of the System.Collections or System .Collections.Generic namespaces. The following code snippet illustrates how you can work with generic lists:

Listing 20-38

```
List<string> list = new List<string>();
list.Add("Joydip");
list.Add("Banhisikha");
list.Add("Oindrilla");
list.Add("Piku");
list.Add("Rama");
list.Add("Amal");
list.Add("Indronil");
```

Efficient Application-Deployment Strategies

This section outlines some of the best strategies that you can adopt before you deploy your application to the production environment.

Tuning the Web.Config and Machine.Config files

You should set the Compilation Debug attribute to false in your application's web.config file. When set to true, your application consumes more memory and processing time, and scripts and images downloaded from the web server do not get cached locally.

You should build your assemblies in Release mode before you deploy the application to the production server. You should also use kernel caching to improve performance (applicable in IIS 6.0 or higher). You can also obfuscate your assemblies before deploying them. Obfuscation reduces the size of the assemblies and improves the application's performance.

It is also good practice to set deployment retail to true in your machine.config file: Doing so will set the debug flag in the application's web.config file to false, disable page output tracing, and force the custom error page to be remote only. Here's how you set that up:

Listing 20-39

```
<configuration>
<system.web>
<deployment retail="true"/>
</system.web>
</configuration>
```

Assembly Versioning and Using Strong Names

Compiled code and/or resources in .NET are called assemblies. An assembly is the smallest unit of versioning, security, deployment, version control, and reusability of code in .NET applications. An assembly contains the assembly identity information (name, version, etc.), manifest and metadata information, the compiled MSIL code, type and security information, and any associated resources that your application makes use of. You should have a good assembly versioning strategy in place.

You can also apply a version stamp to your assembly by using the AssemblyVersion attribute, as shown in the following example:

Listing 20-40
```
[assembly: AssemblyVersion("1.0.1.1")]
```

It is a good policy to have a proper assembly versioning strategy for your application in place. You should also give your assemblies strong names and deploy them in the Global Assembly Cache (GAC) to improve application performance. Assemblies deployed in the GAC load faster because they're verified at install time rather than at runtime.

The sn.exe command-line tool can be used to create strong names. The following command shows how you can use sn.exe to create a strong-named key file called MGH.snk:

Listing 20-41
```
sn -k MGH.snk
```

You can then use the GACUtil tool to place the assembly in the GAC and make it globally accessible:

Listing 20-42
```
GACUtil /i McGrawHillyProject.dll
```

To uninstall the assembly from the GAC, you would use this command:

Listing 20-43
```
GACUtil /u McGrawHillyProject.dll
```

Using Separate Application Pools

Application pools are used to isolate web sites into logical groups. An application pool can contain one or more applications.

It is good practice to create separate application pools for each web application for improved maintainability and to improve the scalability of your web site. Also, disable the default application pool in IIS so that you do not use it for a web site by mistake.

Remember that you can have different applications running in IIS, each having its own recycle time. You can set proper recycle intervals for your application pools in the IIS so that the connectivity to the web server is never lost.

Index